Value-Based Marketing

Value-Based Marketing

Marketing Strategies for Corporate Growth and Shareholder Value

Peter Doyle

WILEY

A John Wiley and Sons, Ltd., Publication

Second edition copyright © 2008 by   John Wiley & Sons, Ltd
                                                The Atrium, Southern Gate
                                                Chichester, West Sussex PO19 8SQ
                                                England

E-mail (for orders and customer service enquiries): cs-books@wiley.co.uk
Visit our Home Page on http://www.wiley.com

Original edition published by John Wiley & Sons Ltd in 2000. This edition updated for John Wiley & Sons Ltd by Laura Mazur with the permission of Sylvia Doyle and with the agreement of an expert Advisory Board.

Other Wiley Editorial Offices

John Wiley & Sons, Inc., 111 River Street, Hoboken, NJ 07030, USA

Jossey-Bass, 989 Market Street, San Francisco, CA 94103-1741, USA

WILEY-VCH Verlag GmbH, Boschstr. 12, D-69469 Weinheim, Germany

John Wiley & Sons Australia Ltd, 42 McDougall Street, Milton, Queensland 4064, Australia

John Wiley & Sons (Asia) Pte Ltd, 2 Clementi Loop #02-01, Jin Xing Distripark, Singapore 129809

John Wiley & Sons (Canada) Ltd, 6045 Freemont Blvd, Mississauga, Ontario M9W 1L1, Canada

Wiley also publishes its books in a variety of electronic formats. Some content that appears in print may not be available in electronic books.

Library of Congress Cataloging-in-Publication Data

Doyle, Peter, 1943 June 23-2003
    Value-based marketing : marketing strategies for corporate growth and shareholder value / Peter Doyle. – 2nd ed.
       p. cm.
    Includes bibliographical references and index.
    ISBN 978-0-470-77314-7 (cloth)
   1. Marketing–Management. 2. Corporations–Valuation. I. Title.
    HF5415.13.D59 2008
    658.8–dc22

                                                                      2008032150

British Library Cataloguing in Publication Data

A catalogue record for this book is available from the British Library

ISBN 978-0-470-77314-7

Typeset in 9.5/13pt Gill Sans Light by Laserwords Private Limited, Chennai, India
Printed and bound in Great Britain by TJ International, Padstow, Cornwall

Contents

PART II
Developing High-Value Strategies

PART III
Implementing High-Value Strategies

Preface

This book is aimed at senior management – marketing, finance, operations managers, and indeed all those with responsibility for the economic performance of their businesses. It is also intended for use on advanced marketing courses on MBA and similar level management programmes.

THE OBJECTIVES

The goals of the book are ambitious – they are no less than to redefine the purpose of marketing and how its contribution should be measured. The result of this redefinition is a concept of marketing that is more practical and more relevant to the objectives of today's top management. Specifically, it is argued that the purpose of marketing is to contribute to maximising shareholder value and that marketing strategies must be evaluated in terms of how much value they create for investors. This concept, which is called *value-based marketing*, does not overthrow the existing body of marketing knowledge. On the contrary, it makes it more relevant and practical by giving it greater clarity and focus.

Many senior managers have noticed a paradox in how firms perceive marketing. On the one hand, every chief executive and mission statement puts marketing at the very top of the agenda. Getting closer to customers and meeting their needs is seen as the cornerstone of building a world-class company. A market orientation is regarded as the essential coordinating focus for all the disciplines and processes of the business. At the same time, marketing professionals, marketing departments and marketing education are not highly regarded. Few chief executives are from a marketing background, most companies do not have a marketing director on the board, and marketing qualifications are often not treated seriously. One leading consulting firm has called marketing departments 'a millstone around an organisation's neck'.

What accounts for this paradox of marketing being paramount but market professionals being disregarded? The main problem is that the marketing discipline has rarely been clear what its objectives are. Most strategy proposals emanating from marketing staff justify investments in advertising or marketing, in terms of increasing consumer awareness, sales volume or market share. But most boards of directors are sceptical that such measures have any clear relation to the firm's long-run profitability. Marketing managers rarely see the necessity of linking marketing spending to the financial value of the business. Given today's enormous pressures on top managers to generate higher returns to shareholders, it is hardly surprising that the voice of marketing gets disregarded. The situation will never be resolved until marketing professionals learn to justify marketing strategies in relevant financial terms.

If managers can show that marketing will increase returns to shareholders, marketing will obtain a much more preeminent role in the board rooms of industry. The discipline itself will also obtain more respect for its greater rigour and direction. The purpose of this book is to demonstrate how marketing creates value for shareholders and to provide managers with the practical tools for developing and evaluating marketing strategies using modern shareholder value analysis.

MARKETING AND SHAREHOLDER VALUE

That the central task of management is to maximise shareholder value has for some time been virtually unanimously accepted by top managers in the USA and the UK, and increasingly in continental Europe and Asia. Shareholder returns grow when a company increases its dividends or when its share price rises. Outside top management, the idea of running a business to maximise shareholder value remains controversial. But today's managers know that unless they do this, their jobs will become vulnerable, the business will be put at risk and new capital will be difficult to obtain. In competitive capital markets, earning returns that shareholders regard as acceptable is a necessity for survival.

Much of the controversy surrounding maximising shareholder returns occurs because the concept is misunderstood. It is most misunderstood among managers. Managers confuse maximising shareholder value with maximising profits. The two are completely different. Maximising profits is about short-term management: cutting costs, reducing investment and downsizing. It is totally antithetical to developing long-term marketing strategies and building world-class businesses. By contrast, shareholder value is a long-term concept; it is about building businesses that last. Despite what managers believe, investors see through short-term tactics that temporarily boost profits. Often share prices actually fall when companies announce cuts in spending on marketing and less ambitious long-term goals.

Value-based marketing is founded on shareholder value analysis – a well-accepted body of financial theory and set of techniques. Shareholder value analysis states that the value of a business is increased when managers make decisions that increase the discounted value of all future cash flows. We show in this book that shareholder value offers enormous opportunities to marketing. First, it enables the purpose of marketing in commercial firms to be clearly defined. Its purpose is to build intangible assets that increase shareholder returns. Second, it explains how marketing strategies need to be evaluated: they are worth pursuing if they increase the net present value of the firm's long-term cash flow. Third, rigorously exploring the effects on shareholder value makes it harder for boards to make arbitrary cuts in marketing budgets and similar measures to boost short-term earnings.

The most important contribution of value-based marketing is to make the shareholder value concept more useful. While more and more chief executives are espousing that their job is to maximise shareholder value, all too often it has become associated with cutting costs and downsizing. In many companies shareholder value has become an accounting tool rather than a general management concept. What many executives have not understood is that shareholder value is more about growth and grasping new market opportunities than reducing expenses. All the companies that have created the greatest value for shareholders in the past decade – Nokia, GE, Cisco and Procter & Gamble – have been market-led, high-growth companies. As we show in the book, creating shareholder value is really about identifying emerging opportunities, putting together marketing strategies that can enable firms to rapidly obtain critical mass, and building lasting relationships with customers. Shareholder value is not built in accounting departments.

THE STRUCTURE OF THE BOOK

The book is in three parts. Part 1 presents the principles of value creation. The first chapter explains the current weaknesses of professional marketing and why its contribution to business performance is disappointing. Chapter 2 presents the theory of shareholder value and shows how these financial principles relate to marketing strategy. Chapter 3 shows why marketing is the principal driver of financial value. Chapter 4 explores why growth is so important to creating shareholder value and how managers can organise to accelerate growth. Part 2 focuses on how to develop strategies that lead to value-creating growth. Chapter 5 explains how to assess the current position of the business and its prospects. Chapter 6 leads on to developing value-based marketing strategies for current and new businesses.

The final part of the book examines how to implement these new high-value strategies. Chapter 7 looks at intangible assets and the role of the brand in building shareholder value. Chapter 8 re-examines pricing from a value perspective and shows how the current theory of pricing often leads to decisions that are too short-term in their orientation. Chapter 9 explores the role of advertising and marketing investments in creating long-term value and how to decide on how much should be spent. The final chapter looks at the implications of the digital age on value-based marketing.

Readers will quickly become aware that this is not a 'one-minute manager' type book. It is a rigorous presentation of some of the most challenging ideas in modern management. It asks the reader to grapple and integrate current work not just from marketing, but also from finance, economics, strategy and information systems. The text is fully referenced with the most influential research and papers. The ideas in this book are so important that it is hoped the reader will feel the challenge is worth taking up. Managers need to be technically accomplished if they are to contribute effectively to the development of their businesses in our rapidly changing world. The aim has been to write this book in a readable style and to include many examples to keep it highly practical and close to the issues in the real world.

This is the second edition of this book. The ideas are still fresh and the analysis still rigorous. The only changes made have been to update case studies where relevant and add new references. It has been done with the guidance of an expert advisory board of acclaimed academics overseeing the editing and updating of the text.

The Advisory Board

Tim Ambler, Senior Fellow, London Business School

Michael J. Baker, Professor Emeritus, Strathclyde Business School

Tony Cram, Programme Director for Business Strategy and Market Innovation, Ashridge Business School

Susan Hart, Dean of Strathclyde Business School

Jean-Claude Larréché, holder of the Alfred H. Heineken Chair at INSEAD

Malcolm McDonald, Emeritus Professor, Cranfield University School of Management and Honorary Professor at Warwick Business School

John Saunders, Professor of Marketing, Aston Business School

Veronica Wong, Professor of Marketing and Director of the Diversity, Knowledge and Innovation Research Programme at Aston Business School

The Editor

Laura Mazur

ACKNOWLEDGEMENTS

Many people have influenced this book. During my fifteen happy years at the University of Warwick I have benefited from the ideas of many of my colleagues including John McGee, Andrew Pettigrew, John Saunders, Howard Thomas and Robin Wensley. At the London Business School I learned from the wisdom of Andrew Ehrenberg and Ken Simmonds. At INSEAD I worked fruitfully with Jean-Claude Larréché and Marcel Corstjens. At Stanford University I was impressed by the work of my colleagues David Montgomery and V. Srinivasan. At Bradford University I worked with Dave Cook, Ian Fenwick, Graham Hooley, Davis Jobber, Jim Lynch and Paul Michelle. My initial interest in marketing models was stimulated during my PhD studies at Carnegie-Mellon University, where I benefited from the supervision of Richard Cyert and the teaching of Nobel laureates Herbert Simon and Robert Lucas.

Most of all, the book reflects what I have learned from my consulting work. In particular, the book is influenced by the cooperation of managers from the following client organisations:

3M	Dixons	Ogilvy
Accenture	Hewlett Packard	Philips
AstraZeneca	IBM	PricewaterhouseCoopers
British Airways	ICI	Saatchi & Saatchi
BMP DDB Omnicom	Johnson & Johnson	Safeway
BP-Amoco	J. Walter Thompson	Shell
British Telecom	KPMG	Tesco
Cabinet Office	Marks & Spencer	Unilever
Cadbury-Schweppes	Mars	Wal-Mart
Coca-Cola	Nestlé	WH Smith
	Novartis	Woolworths

Finally, my deepest thanks are to my wife Sylvia and our sons, Ben and Hugo, who provided me with the support and encouragement to complete this book.

About the author

Peter Doyle was internationally recognised for his teaching and research on marketing and business strategy. He was Professor of Marketing and Strategic Management at the University of Warwick Business School. Previously he held positions at the London Business School, INSEAD, Bradford University and Stanford University.

He was the author of numerous papers which have appeared in most of the world's top journals, including the *Journal of Marketing, Journal of Marketing Research, Management Science* and the *Economic Journal.* His other books include *Marketing Management and Strategy* (Prentice Hall) and *Innovation in Marketing* (Butterworth-Heinemann).

He acted as a consultant to many of the most famous international companies including Coca-Cola, IBM, Nestlé, Cadbury-Schweppes, British Airways, Mars, Johnson & Johnson, Unilever, Shell, BP Amoco, AstraZeneca, Novartis, 3M, Saatchi & Saatchi and Wal-Mart. He also advised such professional bodies as Britain's Cabinet Office, the Institute of Chartered Accountants, the Institute of Directors, the CBI, the Pacific-Asian Management Institute and the Singapore Department of Trade.

Peter Doyle ran executive programmes for senior managers throughout Europe, the United States, South America, Australia and the Far East. He had been voted 'Outstanding Teacher' on numerous university and corporate courses. He had a First Class Honours degree from the University of Manchester and an MBA and PhD from Carnegie-Mellon University, United States. His research twice led him to be awarded the President's Medal of the Operational Research Society and the Best Paper Award of the American Marketing Association.

On reading this book, distinguished international marketing academic Philip Kotler – considered the founding father of marketing – predicted that it was destined to 'spark a revolution in marketing'. This seminal book has indeed persuaded marketers to think differently about the importance of shareholder value and marketing's central role in creating it. Even more importantly, it offers them the tools with which to do it.

Peter Doyle was born on 23 June 1943. His untimely death occurred 30 March 2003. He is sadly missed by family, friends and colleagues. He is survived by his wife Sylvia and his sons Ben and Hugo.

PART I

Principles of Value Creation

Marketing and Shareholder Value

'If you are not willing to own a stock for 10 years don't even think about it for 10 minutes.'

Warren Buffett, Berkshire Hathaway Annual Report

INTRODUCTION AND OBJECTIVES

In recent years creating shareholder value has become the overarching goal for the chief executives of more and more major companies. As we shall see, both theoretically and empirically the case for managers choosing strategies that maximise shareholder value is almost unchallengeable. Those companies which have achieved this suggest that there should be no conflict between marketing and shareholder value.

The illusion of conflict has occurred because many managers have confused maximising shareholder value and maximising *profitability*. The two are completely different. Maximising profitability is short-term and invariably erodes a company's long-term market competitiveness. It is about cutting costs and shedding assets to produce quick improvements in earnings. By neglecting new market opportunities and failing to invest, such strategies destroy rather than create economic value. Strategies aimed at maximising shareholder value are different. They focus on identifying growth opportunities and building competitive advantage. They punish short-term strategies that destroy assets and fail to capitalise on the company's core capabilities.

By the time you have completed this chapter, you will be able to:

- ○   *Describe the new marketing challenges faced by today's managers*

- ○   *Understand the central role of shareholder value*

- ○   *Assess why marketing has too little influence in the board room*

- ○   *Recognise why marketing is the bedrock of shareholder value analysis*

- ○   *Identify how the profession and discipline of marketing need to change to make it more relevant to top management*

The next section discusses the striking new challenges of the information age: global markets, changing industrial structures, the information revolution and rising consumer expectations. It is shown how these changes have far-reaching implications for the strategies and organisations of all businesses. This leads to a discussion of the shareholder value concept and the market-to-book ratio as measures of the success of a business.

A major problem for marketing is that it has not been integrated with the modern concept of financial value creation. This has handicapped the ability of marketing managers to contribute to top management decision-making. Yet marketing-led growth is at the heart of value creation. Without effective marketing, the shareholder value concept becomes little more than another destructive technique gearing management to rationalisation and short-term profits. Value-based marketing is presented as a new approach, which integrates marketing directly into the process of creating value for shareholders and thereby for all stakeholders. Value-based marketing makes the shareholder concept more valuable and marketing more effective.

MANAGING IN THE TWENTY-FIRST CENTURY

The enormous changes in the global market environment explain today's pressures for greater management effectiveness. Competitive capitalism is Darwinian in nature. Businesses succeed when they meet the wants of customers more effectively than their competitors. Corporate profitability depends primarily on the company's ability to offer products and services which customers choose to pay for. But what products and services customers regard as attractive is a function of the market environment. What is an appealing computer, retail store or banking service today will not be tomorrow. Technological change, new competition and changing wants make yesterday's solutions obsolete and create the opportunity for new answers.

The result is that most companies do not usually last very long. De Geus calculated that the average life expectancy of a Western company is well below 20 years.[1] The period over which a successful firm can maintain a profitable competitive advantage is usually even shorter. Normally any innovation in product, services or processes is quickly copied and the surplus profit is competed away. Even where a company endures and grows, its true profitability normally erodes. Studies show that the average company does not maintain a return above its cost of capital for more than seven or eight years.[2]

While the period over which the average business is successful is short, there are companies that do better. There are a few examples of companies that have survived and maintained successful economic performance over a much longer period. Currently examples would include GE, Coca-Cola, Nike and Hewlett-Packard. But quoting examples of excellent companies is a hazardous venture. Great companies have a tendency to go belly-up when the environment changes fundamentally. Few leaders have the perspicacity, courage or capabilities to overturn the strategies, systems and organisation which created their past achievement.

ENVIRONMENTAL CHANGE

Environmental changes affecting the performance of the business can be categorised as macro or micro. *Macroenvironmental* changes are the broad outside forces affecting all markets. These include the major economic, demographic, political, technological and cultural developments taking place today. The *microenvironment* refers to the specific developments affecting the firm's individual industry: its customers, competitors and suppliers. These developments reflect the impacts of the macroenvironmental changes on the specific industry (Figure 1.1).

Today this macroenvironment is experiencing unique historical changes which are fundamentally redrawing the business and social landscape. These changes have been given various names including the 'post-industrial society', the 'global village', the 'third wave' and perhaps most accurately the 'information age'.

Social scientists describe three periods of economic evolution in the Western world: the *agricultural era*, which lasted from around 8000 BC to the mid-eighteenth century; the *industrial era*, which lasted until the late twentieth century;

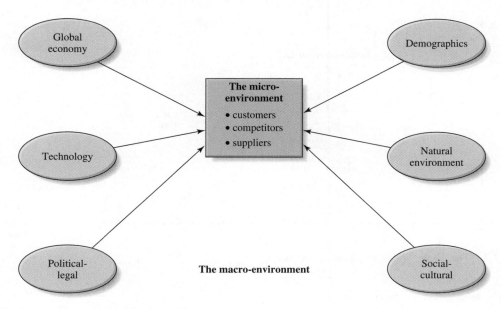

Figure 1.1 The Business Environment

and finally what we will call the *information age*, which began in the 1960s and will last for decades to come.[3] These dates are of course approximate and overlapping. The first era was based on agriculture, with physical labour being the driver of any wealth that was achieved. This eventually gave way to the second era sparked by the industrial revolution, when machinery replaced muscle power, and factories replaced agriculture as the dominant employer, leading to an enormous growth in both agricultural and industrial productivity.

While the agricultural era lasted for over two thousand years, the industrial age lasted only two hundred. The 1960s began to see the end of the industrial era and the beginning of the new information age. Employment in manufacturing began to drop in all the advanced countries and the service sector became the new focus for growth. Blue-collar workers who operated equipment in crowded factories were increasingly replaced by white-collar workers working individually or in small teams using computers and scientific knowledge in office environments. Today, information technology has replaced factories and machine power as the source of productivity growth and competitiveness.

The transitional periods between the three great waves of change have not been smooth. In Figure 1.2 each wave is represented by an 'S' curve that shows an early period of turbulence, followed by a long spell of maturity, and then its eventual demise as new technologies take over. The last decades of the twentieth century witnessed the period of turbulence marking the birth of the information age and the death of the industrial era. The turbulence included record levels of mergers and acquisitions, the collapse of communism in the former USSR and its satellites, and economic crises in South East Asia. All these reflected old second-wave industries and social organisations being pushed aside in the competitive environment of the new information age.

Four aspects in particular of the new information age require fundamental strategic and organisational responses from management:

1.   The globalisation of markets
2.   Changing industrial structures

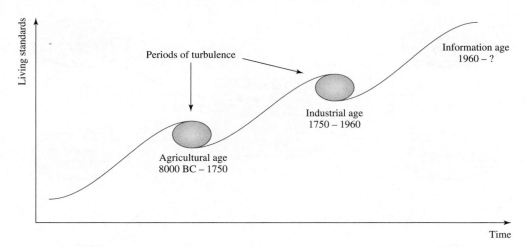

Figure 1.2   The Three Waves of Economic Change

3.   The information revolution
4.   Rising customer expectations

THE GLOBALISATION OF MARKETS

The new information age has seen a dramatic shift to global markets and competition. Across more and more industries, firms that are not building global operations and marketing capabilities are losing out. Recent decades have seen an enormous growth of international trade in goods, services and capital. The General Agreement on Tariffs and Trade (GATT) and its successor organisation the World Trade Organization (WTO) have been the means of nego-tiating a general lowering of barriers to trade between countries and an opening up of markets. The stimulus to this liberalisation of trade has been experience. Governments have seen, often painfully, that protecting home industries and markets from competition does not work. It only leads to higher inflation, lower economic growth and domestic companies lacking the levels of efficiency and entrepreneurial skills ever to be internationally competitive. Other stimuli to the globalisation of markets and competition have been faster and cheaper transportation and a continuing telecommunications revolution that has made global communications cheap, simple and effective. Finally, the barriers to participation in world trade have often come down dramatically. Today any business can open an Internet web site and market to customers from the other side of the world, just as easily as to its customers around the corner.

The result has been the emergence of new transnational companies organised to maximise the opportunities to be gained from the new global market-place and to minimise the costs of serving it. Companies like Microsoft, GE, Intel, Merck, IBM, Starbucks and McDonald's are selling in all the key markets. Their supply chains are equally global, with materials and components sourced from the cheapest locations, assembly and logistics organised from the most effective regional bases, and research and development located where relevant knowledge is most accessible.

In most sectors, small domestically-orientated companies lack the economies of scale to remain competitive over the longer run. The scale economies of the transnational companies lie not so much in manufacturing costs but in information and knowledge. Focused transnationals like Intel, Apple, Dell and Cisco win out because they can afford to spend more on research and development, on building brands, on information technology and on marketing. Once new opportunities are identified they can also marshal the resources that are necessary to capitalise and develop the market.

CHANGING INDUSTRIAL STRUCTURES

The information age is changing the nature of the profit opportunities available to businesses. Many markets that were once at the very heart of the economy have ceased to offer profit opportunities for Western firms. Other new markets are rapidly emerging that offer enormous profit opportunities to companies that can move fast and decisively to capitalise on them.

Manufacturing industries can be divided into two types. One type comprises traditional industries such as textiles, coal mining, heavy chemicals, steel and auto manufacturing, which are relatively labour intensive and make heavy use of raw materials. These industries are relocating rapidly to the developing countries, which have a comparative cost advantage. Such industries also generally suffer the problem of substantial excess manufacturing capacity because these new countries have invested too aggressively in seeking to gain market shares. The result has been falling prices and very poor returns on investment.

The second type of industries are the information- and knowledge-based ones such as pharmaceuticals, communications equipment, electronics and computers, aerospace and biotechnology. Here labour costs are typically less than five per cent of total costs. Most of the costs are information-related: research, design, development, testing, marketing, customer service and support. These are where the profit and growth opportunities occur for information-age companies. Contrary to the popular view, in most Western countries, manufacturing output has not declined in recent decades. What has changed is the switch away from traditional labour-intensive industries to those that are information-based. Second, there has been a sharp decline in manufacturing employment – notably blue-collar work, as these jobs have been automated or moved to the developing countries.

Overall employment has been maintained in information-age countries by the rapid growth of the service sector. Service-sector output has been growing at least twice as fast as manufacturing output in recent decades. In advanced countries services now account for two-thirds of economic output. As living standards continue to rise consumers spend relatively more on services rather than on goods. Health, education, travel, financial services, entertainment and restaurants are all growth markets. Informational technology has also become a massive service industry. Another reason why this will continue is that the output of information-based manufacturing industries is increasingly distributed in service form. For example, pharmaceutical companies or book publishers, rather than exporting drugs or books, will license the rights to produce them. Many items such as music and news are already being downloaded from the Internet rather than bought in the form of a physical product such as a CD.

THE INFORMATION REVOLUTION

Rapid scientific and technological changes continue to radically reshape many industries. But the most dramatic and far-reaching changes of the current era result from the revolution in information technology. Initiated by the development of the mainframe and the personal computer in the 1960s and 1970s, its full implications only really became apparent in the 1990s with the explosion in use of the Internet. By 2001, only a decade after the emergence of the World Wide Web, a fundamental change in business and society had occurred – a critical mass of people, over 200 million, at home and at work, were able to communicate electronically with one another at essentially zero cost, using universal, open standards. By the end of 2007, that number had multiplied exponentially to over 1.3 billion.

The Internet, together with the emergence of broadband cellular radio networks, has created an explosion in connectivity that is revolutionising almost every aspect of business. First, it changes the firm's internal value chain – the way people inside the business organise to design, produce, market, deliver and support its products and services. In the past, businesses had to organise through hierarchies and bureaucracy because information was expensive, difficult and slow to obtain. Today, *intranets*, which instantly and costlessly connect individuals within companies for the exchange of information, make obsolete the need for hierarchical functions. Instead cross-functional teams and informal networking are encouraged, which in turn facilitate flatter, lower-cost organisational structures, faster responses and better customer service.

Second, the information revolution has changed the way the business works with its suppliers. Where partnerships are important, information technology can make them much closer. *Extranets*, which connect companies to each other, can seamlessly integrate buyer and seller into a *virtual business*. A typical example is the jeans maker, Levi. Over the Internet it continuously obtains information on the sizes and styles of its jeans being sold by its major retailers. Levi then electronically orders more fabric for immediate delivery from the Milliken Company, its fabric supplier. Milliken, in turn, relays an order for more fibre to Du Pont, its fibre supplier. In this way the partners take out cost throughout the supply chain, minimise inventory holding and have up-to date information to enable them to respond quickly to changes in consumer demand.

In a similar way, when the bar code of a Procter & Gamble (P&G) product passes across a Wal-Mart scanner, that information is immediately relayed to P&G, which invoices the retailer and makes another, which, in turn, is relayed to the distribution centre. This process has saved Wal-Mart millions of dollars in administration expenses.

On the other hand, where buyers see price as more important than partnerships, the widespread availability of information undermines the suppliers' relationships with customers. For example, component buyers can post their purchasing requirements on Internet bulletin boards and invite bids from anybody inclined to respond. The information revolution has increased the information available to buyers and reduced the cost of switching suppliers. In general, the bargaining power of buyers has been radically increased.

Finally, the information revolution has significantly changed the nature of marketing and the marketing mix (see box, 'Traditional Marketing Meets the Information Revolution'). Traditionally buyers chose suppliers for both the qualities of the products and the information they supplied. For example, retailers like Toys 'R' Us or PC World prospered by offering shoppers a wider selection of merchandise. But such formats are now undermined by search engines on the Internet, which can offer consumers much more choice than any store. This has created many new huge business opportunities for companies able to exploit the informational advantage of the Internet. These include specialist facilitators like Google which assist consumers in their search for information. Others have reconfigured the traditional industry chain to capitalise on electronic communications. Among the most successful in the late 1990s was Amazon.com, which in only four years created the world's biggest book retailing operation, and which had net sales of almost $15 billion by the end of 2007. Its business has broadened significantly beyond books, and includes third parties selling a range of different products and services globally over the Net.

Traditional Marketing Meets the Information Revolution

For two centuries Encyclopaedia Britannica was one of the strongest and best-known brands in the world. Its large sales force successfully encouraged middle-class parents to view purchase of the 32-volume set of encyclopaedias as offering a genuine advantage for their children. Then the home computer and the CD-ROM came along. By the early 1990s Britannica's sales were collapsing.

What went wrong? First the emerging information age changed consumer behaviour. Now parents who wanted to do the right thing for their children bought them a computer rather than printed encyclopaedias. Once Microsoft and others launched CD-ROM versions of encyclopaedias, the game was lost. The cost of producing a CD-ROM was about £1; the cost of producing a printed set of encyclopaedias was around £250. The result was that Microsoft's Encarta could sell at £50 or even be given away free; a set of Encyclopaedia Britannica sold at between £1300 and £2200. Worse, because of its high cost, Britannica needed an expensive direct sales force to sell the product. The cheap CD-ROM versions were almost impulse items, which could be sold through computer shops or marketed to manufacturers for bundling with new computer sales. Finally, children liked computers and CD-ROMS more; a CD-ROM was easier and more fun to use than searching through a formidable set of 32 large books.

When the threat became obvious, Britannica brought out its own CD-ROM, but to avoid undercutting its sales force it charged £755. Not surprisingly, its sales continued to decline. Finally, in 1997 the company recognised the issue, the sales force was disbanded and, under new ownership, the company sought to rebuild the business around the Internet.

The company now offers its extensive information in a variety of formats, including the original print versions, DVD packages, the online site, which also offers daily features, updates and links to news reports, and a mobile version. However, its pre-eminence continues to be challenged by other online encyclopaedias, such as Encarta and Wikipedia – even though the latter might seem to lack the authority of its older rival since it is written collaboratively by volunteers within certain editorial rules.

Britannica's real problem was that its management – like many others – failed to recognise the implications of the information era. The information revolution has made traditional strategies obsolete, destroyed barriers to entry and stimulated new competitors with dramatically lower cost structures and more effective marketing systems. Management recognised too late that its sales force had become an expensive liability and that the computer had become the real competitor. The complacency of Britannica's management is not unique. It is a predicament that a host of major companies have faced in such industries as cars, insurance, travel, financial services and major sectors of retailing and distribution.

Contrast this with Yellow Pages – now called Yell – which didn't make the same mistake as Britannica and was in the forefront of putting its data into electronic formats alongside the more traditional print version. The result is that Yell remains one of the top organisations in its sector.

Sources: Philip B. Evans and Thomas S. Wurster, Strategy and the new economics of information, Harvard Business Review, September/October, 1997, 70–83; The Economist, Encyclopaedias on CD-ROM, 17 February 1996, p. 67; New York Times, Start Writing the Eulogies for Printed Encyclopedias, 23 March 2008.

In many markets, information technology has led to *disintermediation* – the elimination of agents between the supplier and the consumer. Buyers have found that they no longer need retailers, agents or brokers; they can buy at lower cost, and more conveniently, directly from the manufacturer over the telephone or, increasingly, the Internet. Companies like Dell in computers and Direct Line in insurance rapidly grew to market leadership by exploiting this strategic window. When the seller deals directly with end consumers the opportunity is then created to build databases which record *learning* about individual consumer wants and buying behaviour. The seller can then create added value by tailoring messages and even products for individual consumers. The information revolution has thus begun to change marketing from mass communications and standardised brands to one-to-one customised marketing. For the innovators this has offered the opportunity for higher profit margins, greater loyalty and a bigger share of the customer's spending.[4]

RISING CUSTOMER EXPECTATIONS

The information age has brought a marked rise in customer expectations. Buyers have grown to expect higher quality, competitive prices, and better and faster service. The most important causes have been the globalisation of competition and the deregulation of markets. Once markets were opened up to today's aggressive international competitors, companies that lacked a customer orientation or that had inefficient cost structures were soon in trouble. The new wave of Japanese exporters such as Sony, Toyota and Matsushita in the 1960s showed Western companies the new standards of quality required to stay competitive. Concepts like *kaisen* (continuous incremental improvement), Total Quality Management (TQM) and such schemes as the US Baldridge Awards and the European ISO 9000 certification had real effects in raising quality standards. During the 1970s and 1980s major excess capacity became a characteristic of more and more industries – for example, cars, steel, chemicals, electrical goods, agricultural products and banking. This further shifted the priority to gaining customer preference in hypercompetitive markets. Finally, the explosion of information technology gave management new tools for serving customers better: tools to continuously monitor customer needs and to improve the internal processes and supply chains that would enable them to meet, and indeed exceed, customer expectations.

Initially the response to meeting customer needs better was *market segmentation*. Companies brought out an increasing number of product variants to meet the diverse needs of their customers. Nike had 347 types of running shoe, Procter & Gamble had 207 brands and sizes of detergent, United Distillers introduced nine line extensions of its Johnnie Walker brand of scotch whisky, credit card companies offered green, blue, gold and platinum versions, each with minor differences in the service offering, and so on. Media too became more segmented: mass-circulation newspapers and magazines were replaced by a proliferating array of specialists. Digital technology also facilitated an explosive growth in the number of radio and television channels.

The problem with market segmentation was that it was expensive and limited in effectiveness. More variants meant higher manufacturing costs and spiralling inventory levels leading to lower profits and asset turnover. By 2000, the information revolution was beginning to offer a better alternative – *mass customisation*. Media and products could be tailored to the individual customer and made to order, using modern high technology communications and manufacturing systems. Information technology allows companies to record all the information they obtain from consumers through their personal, written, telephone or Internet communications with the company. Creating a database allows companies to learn about the buying behaviour and preferences of customers and to communicate individually and directly with them. Direct marketing creates the opportunity for a dialogue, allowing a precise specification of the customer's wants.

Dell Computer Corporation was one of the pioneers in showing how direct marketing could be allied to a fast response supply chain to produce customised products delivered to the customer's door 48 hours after the order.[5] For the customer one-to-one marketing offers a precise fit to his or her individual requirements. For the supplier it means higher margins and lower investment requirements.

STRATEGIC AND ORGANISATIONAL IMPLICATIONS

Companies survive only if they can adapt to this rapidly changing environment (Figure 1.3). This changing environment determines what products and services customers will find attractive. It also determines the technologies that will be available for companies to produce and market these products and services. By *strategy* we mean the business's

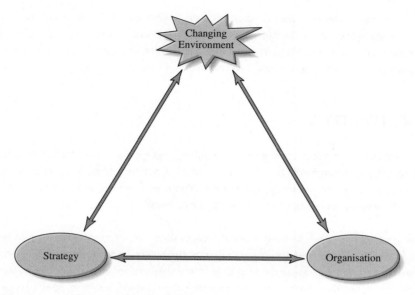

Figure 1.3   Adapting to a Changing Environment

overall plan for deploying resources to create a competitive advantage in its markets. *Organisation* refers to the capabilities the firm possesses and how its staff are led, coordinated and motivated to implement the strategy.

Today the changes in the marketing environment are so momentous that they require radical strategic and organisational change from virtually all companies. Gone are the days when managers could stick to tried and tested formulas to provide continuous growth and profitability. Globalisation, new industrial structures, rapidly changing technologies and new customer expectations are quickly eroding yesterday's markets, while creating phenomenal new opportunities for those that can move fast and decisively to capitalise on the changing environment.

Today five main issues stand out for management:

1.   Participation strategy
2.   Marketing strategy
3.   Operations strategy
4.   Global strategy
5.   Organisational imperatives

PARTICIPATION STRATEGY

As the environment changes, the opportunities to achieve profitable growth change too. Some markets cease to have potential and should be exited; others offer great opportunities and require high investment, innovative strategies and new organisations. Managers have to decide which markets to participate in. To do this they have to objectively assess, first, the future *attractiveness* of the markets in which they operate. Because they differ in intensity of competition and price pressures from customers, some markets will become much more profitable than others. In general, the greatest opportunities are occurring in services, such as entertainment, education, software and mobile telecommunications. Other markets are extremely unlikely to generate returns for shareholders. Many of the old labour- and raw-material intensive industries such as textiles, steel and heavy chemicals fall into this category. Second, managers need to assess their *competitive potential*. With today's fierce global competition, unless a business can create a differential advantage, in terms of either low total cost or a superior product or service that can command a price premium from customers, it will not earn an adequate return.

MARKETING STRATEGY

The information revolution is making obsolete the marketing strategies of many traditional industry leaders. It destroys barriers to entry and transforms the structure of many industries. What is the role of a branch network when customers can bank more conveniently on the web? Who needs retailers and distributors when you can sell direct to consumers? Every aspect of marketing comes up for renewal.

The customer and product mix needs to be strategically reappraised. The information revolution has increased the need for firms to focus. Many firms have too many low-value customers who do not want long-term relationships. They also often have too many products bundled together by the classic informational logic of one-stop shopping. But one-stop shopping loses its premium for customers once information is readily available. Specialists can then generally offer lower prices or superior service by focusing their operations around a single product or customer group.

Pricing strategies also need reviewing. The globalisation of markets, the euro currency and information technology have all made prices more transparent and comparable. Businesses not offering value to customers are seeing their market shares eroding at accelerating rates. The information revolution is having its most dramatic impacts on promotion and distribution strategies. The company's web site is increasingly becoming both the first port of call for customers looking for information and a crucial source of knowledge about customers for the company. More fundamentally, the Internet offers more and more companies of all sizes the opportunity to eliminate intermediaries and deal with consumers directly.

OPERATIONS STRATEGY

To implement a new marketing strategy requires the firm to create an operations strategy capable of delivering it. Companies need to construct a supply chain that can produce the right goods and services, at the right price, in the right place, at the right time. With today's global competition and rising customer expectations, this right strategy usually means low prices, rapid delivery, reliable quality and up-to-date technology.

To meet these demanding expectations a new business model has emerged among today's leading-edge companies built around coordination and focus. We will call this the *direct business model* (Figure 1.4). This model fundamentally reshapes the firm's downstream and upstream activities. *Downstream* the business model is built around bypassing the dealer, selling direct to the customer and making to order. Generally the communications take place over the telephone or, increasingly, the Internet. Selling direct has the crucial advantage of enabling the firm rather than the intermediary to control the relationship with the customer. Information from customers enables the firm to add value and develop loyalty by customising the offer and the communications to the customer's exact requirements. Information also gives the firm leverage over its suppliers because it owns the brand and the customer relationships. The direct business model also cuts distribution costs, eliminates inventories and reduces risks by enabling better forecasting of consumer demand.

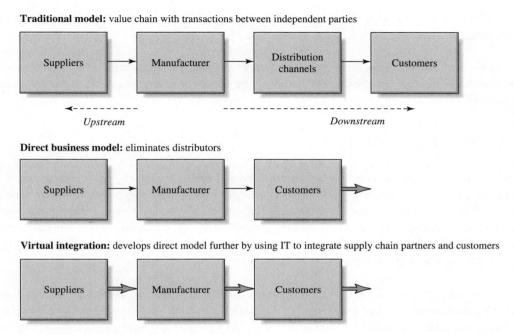

Figure 1.4   The Evolution of a New Business Model

Upstream the model is built around close cooperation with suppliers. Manufacturing and logistics is outsourced to a carefully selected set of partners. These suppliers are linked electronically to the firm and treated like an internal department. Instead of vertical integration – control and coordination through ownership – we have *virtual integration* – control and coordination through information. This reduces the assets required to support rapid growth, minimises financial risk and maximises flexibility. It frees the management to focus on what adds most value today – delivering solutions and systems to customers. The direct business model creates genuine value through customer focus, supplier partnerships, mass customisation and just-in-time manufacturing.

GLOBAL STRATEGY

In today's connected world, every company now needs a global strategy. Industries are globalising at a rush and companies that are not leading, or at least participating, in the new alliances, are becoming non-viable. Manufacturing tended to globalise first but now services are following rapidly. For example, a series of mega-mergers in the 1990s globalised accounting, financial services and most of the advertising industry into a small number of huge global groups. Regional and global groupings have also emerged in telecommunications, banking, contract services and many other areas.

In business-to-business markets – to which most companies belong – the pressure to globalise comes from their customers, which operate across the world. Procter & Gamble and IBM want suppliers and business partners that can interface with their own far-flung geographical operations. The opportunity to spread the costs and lever the investments in research, development and technology also favours global players. Finally, being dependent on a single country market leaves today's local player highly vulnerable. Strategically it is in a weak position to counter-attack against a strong global player moving into its market and being willing to cross-subsidise its entry from profits earned in other markets.

As in most areas of business today, there are big advantages in speed and decisiveness when it comes to global strategy. The longer management prevaricates, the fewer the options are available and the higher the price that has to be paid.

ORGANISATIONAL IMPERATIVES

To implement new strategies requires new organisations. What is different about organisations in the information age? First, employees are different. Blue-collar workers have given way to knowledge professionals. Part-timers and women make up an increasing proportion of the staff. The skills of the new knowledge workers make them less dependent on the company and more mobile. Motivating them requires different work environments and incentives from the past. Second, information and communications technology now permits new and more effective ways for people within the firm to relate to one another and to relate to others in the supply chain.

Finally, the new strategies ushered in by the information age require different responses from staff. A customer orientation becomes more important since more of the staff are now directly involved in providing customer service and customising products and solutions. The priority consumers now give to convenience and speed of response demands much greater empowerment and commitment from staff. The pressure on prices and the need to provide greater shareholder value also drive management to seek higher productivity and better utilisation of assets.

The direction of organisational changes is clear. Delayering has been one major move. Information technology has enabled companies to reduce the number of levels of middle management, providing for greater customer orientation, lower costs and faster response. Second, enhanced connectivity is breaking down functional barriers within firms, permitting a much greater use of cross-functional teams, which again makes for faster response and greater customer focus. The same forces have increased the flow of information between firms, facilitating more effective networks to lever the firm's capabilities with those of its business partners. The final change has been a greater focus on shareholder value. Investors are putting much more pressures on managers either to deliver superior returns or return the cash to shareholders.

The implications of the changing environment for strategy and organisation – and hence for the firm's ability to achieve longer term growth and profitability – can be summarised in five principles:

1. **Strategy must fit the environment.** Companies can remain competitive only when they have products and services which today's customers regard as offering superior value. Perceived value is shaped by the changing macro- and microenvironments within which the firm and its customers operate.

2. **Successful strategies erode.** Winning formulas eventually lose out because the environment changes. Competitors copy successful products and processes. Changing tastes and new technologies make yesterday's successes obsolete.

3. **Effectiveness is more important than efficiency.** Old formulas cannot be preserved by downsizing and cost reduction. Innovative solutions have a way of coming down in costs to offer superior value across all dimensions of value. Success in the information age is about renewal rather than retrenchment.

4. **Speed and decisiveness.** Being first mover when new opportunities occur can carry great advantages. With no direct competition it is much easier to demonstrate a competitive advantage. But being first is not sufficient; the innovator has to create a critical mass in terms of market share. This requires managers decisively shifting resources out of yesterday's businesses into the new opportunities

5. **Organisational adaptation.** Creating these dynamic, customer-orientated businesses that will be required for the new millennium requires leadership and organisational transformation of a high order.

MEASURING SUCCESS: SHAREHOLDER VALUE

The value of a company measures the views of professional investors about the ability of management to master this changing market environment. When a company is seen to be in an attractive market, pursuing a strategy that has a good chance of building a sustainable competitive advantage, then the value of the company rises (see, box 'Shareholder Values Reflect Perceptions of Winning Strategies'). An attractive market and a winning formula should mean that the company will be able to earn a return on its investment above the cost of capital. In this situation management finds it easy to attract outside funds, to make acquisitions and to grow.

Shareholder Values Reflect Perceptions of Winning Strategies

In the late 1990s investors became alert to the potential impact of the Internet on many businesses. Charles Schwab, a leading US stockbroker, also saw the opportunity. In 1998 it launched a global online dealing service to the public. In the following 12 months it was rewarded by a trebling of its market capitalisation. Investors reacted enthusiastically to the potential attractiveness of the market and to the decisiveness of Schwab management. By 2007 it was managing approximately $1.3 trillion for more than seven million individual and institutional clients through the telephone, wireless devices, the Internet and physical offices.

In 1990 nobody had heard of Vodafone, a subsidiary of a British electrical contracting company, Racal. In the following years Vodafone aggressively entered and developed the emerging mobile telephone market, first in the UK then overseas. Its share price soared. By 2007, thanks to a raft of acquisitions around the world, it was the world's largest global operator with a stock market value of almost £100 billion.

The stock market clearly recognises that some markets have much greater prospects for generating corporate earning in the future than others. CMG, a small Dutch start-up specialising in computer services, was floated on the stock market at the end of 1995 with a market capitalisation of £185 million. So impressed were investors by the attractiveness of the industry and CMG's strategy that three years later its market value had soared 16-fold to £2 billion. In 2002 it then merged with the UK's Logica. Logica is a major international force in IT and business services, employing around 40 000 people across 41 countries.

In 2000 Amazon.com, the Internet book retailer, had been going for five years. It had never yet made any profit, but it was valued at $20 billion — more than all the other US booksellers together. Following the dot.com collapse, its value then dropped: in 2004 it was valued at $14 billion, for example. However, by 2008 it had risen again, to $34 billion.

Contrast these examples with conglomerates such as GEC, Hanson and BTR, which, in the 1980s, had emerged through a series of acquisitions to become among Europe's largest companies. All three were characterised by financial and strategic conservatism. Investments had to break even within two years and managers were evaluated against quarterly profitability goals. The result was that none developed significant new products, entered new markets or generated a competitive advantage. A decade later the share values of all three had collapsed, BTR was acquired, and GEC and Hanson were broken up.

When investors perceive a company to be stuck in unattractive markets and to be lacking a competitive advantage, they naturally do not want to invest. The value of the company then declines, making the company difficult to attract resources and making it prone to being acquired.

The value of a company is increased by making the business better. But even if the company performs well, it could still be too small to remain independent. It may be worth more to a larger company with global ambitions than it is as a stand-alone business. Good companies as well as bad companies get bought. The difference is that in the former case shareholders are well rewarded in the higher price that the acquirer has to pay. If managers want to be able to control their own destiny in today's global economy – to remain independent – the company has to get bigger as well as getting better.

The stock market's judgement on the expected financial performance of a company is reflected in its market-to-book ratio.[6] (see box, 'Definition of Shareholder Value'). The main determinant of market value is the ability of management to seize profitable investment opportunities. Company size can be measured by its book value – the accounting value of its equity. The market capitalisation is simply the product of these two components. For example, a market-to-book ratio of 3 and a book value of £10 billion means a market capitalisation of £30 billion.

Definition of Shareholder Value

Shareholder value is created by rising share prices and/or dividends but there are exceptions. If a company buys back its own shares, the individual share price should increase but shareholder wealth is unaffected because the share price times the number of shares stays the same. Likewise, a share price rise may be ephemeral due to rumours or the rise in the market as a whole or otherwise unrelated to the improvement in the underlying business, which is what the shareholder value method of evaluation is trying to track. So in practice we look internally to examine, as a measure of shareholder value increase, the economic value added (EVA) which is defined as the net profit after tax less Weighted Average Cost of Capital (WACC) times capital invested. (EVA is discussed in Chapter 2.)

The implications of this can be seen in Figure 1.5. The management consultants, McKinsey suggest that companies can be mapped into four groups:[7]

1.   **Vulnerable.** Companies like A and B, using relatively small amounts of financial capital and generating relatively low returns, are vulnerable to acquisition. These are often businesses that have been left in mature, unattractive industries and are still focused on the domestic market. They are commonly taken over by larger competitors that can generate higher returns from the same asset base. To have a future, these vulnerable

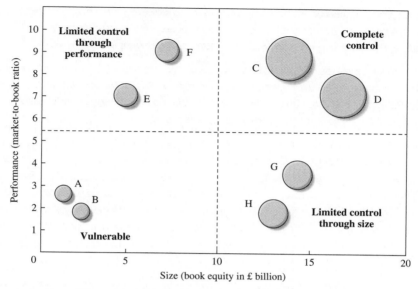

Figure 1.5 Strategic Control as a Function of Performance and Size

companies need either to radically improve the performance of their existing businesses or divest them and reinvest the capital in more attractive industries.

2. **Complete control.** At the opposite extreme are companies like C and D, which are generating high returns from a large capital base. Examples in the late 1990s might be Merck, Intel and GE. Typically these companies are in attractive markets, competing globally and with competitive advantages that give them high market shares. Their high multiples enable them to acquire competitors, and protect them from being acquisition targets themselves. The challenge facing these companies is protecting their positions against the onslaught of new competitors while simultaneously identifying new opportunities to grow sales and profits.

3. **Limited control through performance.** Companies like E and F in the upper left quadrant obtain high returns from relatively small amounts of invested capital. Examples in 2000 might be Cable and Wireless, Reuters and 3Com. They are often specialist niche players in attractive high-tech segments. Their good performance makes them an expensive acquisition. But in the longer run, they are vulnerable to bigger companies that believe they can lever their specialist skills by taking them into global or broader markets. The information technology and service sectors are full of young, successful businesses that fall into this category. To maintain control these companies need to grow aggressively by adding new products and new markets.

4. **Limited control through size.** H and G are large companies producing low returns on capital. Today they include such companies as General Motors, Henkel and Credit Lyonnais. Despite their relatively poor performance they are difficult to acquire because of their sheer size. They are generally older companies, in mature, asset-intensive industries. Their challenge is to improve performance by divesting assets that produce low returns and using the proceeds to capture more attractive opportunities. Should they fail, they are likely eventually to be acquired or merged as part of the cost consolidation process in the industry.

Shareholder value analysis allows management to compare the value of alternative marketing strategies. They can objectively examine which strategy is most likely to increase the market value of the company. They can explore where a particular plan is likely to take them on the strategic vulnerability map (Figure 1.5). Will it move the company towards the area of 'complete control' or towards increased 'vulnerability'?

The key to economic value creation is the company's ability to achieve or maintain competitive advantage in a changing market environment. The inputs into the valuation process are the assumptions about future sales growth, margins and investments that follow from any marketing strategy. For example:

A major European airline believed that deregulation would inevitably lead to greater price competition as new 'no-frills' airlines entered the market. Companies such as Virgin, Ryanair, Easyjet and others had already announced big expansion plans. The airline's review of the industry led it to conclude that its recent market share losses would accelerate unless a new strategy was developed.

Management eventually identified three alternative marketing strategies. The *parity strategy* involved seeking to hold market share by reducing prices towards the level of the new competitors. A major cost reduction exercise would run alongside this plan. The *premium strategy* would refocus the airline around business and first-class passengers. It would include a switch to smaller aeroplanes, with fewer seats for economy passengers. The *dual-brand strategy* envisaged the launch of an entirely new airline codenamed 'Merit'. Merit would be positioned as a no-frills discount airline that would match or even undercut the prices of the new competitors. Here the aim would be to achieve market leadership in both the regular and the discount sectors.

Management made detailed projections of sales, profit margins and investment requirements under the three strategies. On the basis of this analysis they calculated the shareholder value added with each alternative:

Alternative strategy	Shareholder value added
1. Parity strategy	−£40 million
2. Premium strategy	+£70 million
3. Dual-brand strategy	+£185 million

Faced with the analysis, the board of directors had no hesitation in accepting management's radical strategy of dual branding and the new airline was launched ten months later. The parity strategy was demonstrated to be disastrous because, while it stopped the erosion of market share, it led to a huge decline in profitability per passenger. The premium strategy did create value but it was inferior to dual branding because of the effect of the decline in passengers carried.

The board believed that shareholder value analysis had proved its worth. It challenged management to identify and develop new strategies. It encouraged them to think radically, which was necessary with rapid environmental changes increasingly making the status quo a non-viable strategic option. Finally, it provided a criterion for rationally and objectively evaluating strategic choices. All too often in the past, key decisions had been made on the basis of subjective judgements, marketing 'hype' or political wrangling, which had subsequently proved to be wrong.

MARKETING'S LOST INFLUENCE

In today's information age marketing professionals should have become more important in the top councils of business. First, the central issue facing all firms now is understanding and adapting to rapidly changing markets – globalisation, new competition, rising customer expectations and the implications of the information revolution on how companies market. Second, marketing, rather than production, skills have become the key to creating competitive advantage. More and more leading branded goods companies follow the lead of the likes of Coca-Cola, Dell, Nike, Levi's and Armani in outsourcing all their manufacturing to outside suppliers, often in the developing countries. Others, like GE and IBM, see their future not in selling products, but in providing services that offer tailored solutions to the needs of individual customers. Third, marketing performance is the root source of shareholder value. The firm's opportunity to create cash is based first and foremost on its ability to create a competitive advantage that will enable it to attract and retain customers paying satisfactory prices.

But rather than gaining in influence, marketing professionals, whose expertise is in identifying these market opportunities and building customer relationships, appear to have little influence in the board rooms of industry. A survey by the Chartered Institute of Marketing, for example, found that only 17 per cent of the chief executives of Britain's FTSE 100 companies had experience in a marketing job, with 34 per cent coming from finance, 29 per cent rising up the ranks from operations and 19 per cent from general management. Only 14 per cent of those companies had marketing represented on the board.[8] Another study in 2008 of chief executives, financial and marketing directors found a harmful lack of a common understanding of the role of marketing.[9]

Why does the lack of marketing professionalism in the board room matter? It matters because top managers will lack expert guidance on how their customers and competitors' strategies are changing. New market opportunities and threats are unlikely to be recognised speedily and, once recognised, acted upon decisively. If senior management are not focusing on customers and markets, it will mean that other issues fill the agenda. Evidence suggests that managers become preoccupied with short-term budgets, operating rather than strategic issues, and, when difficulties arise, retrenchment rather than renewal. Such myopia is, in the long run, antithetical to genuine value-creating strategies.[10]

Several factors account for this paradox of the growing importance of marketing with the lack of influence of marketing professionals in top management. Of fundamental importance has been the failure of the marketing discipline to incorporate the concept of shareholder value.[11] As a result there is no criteria for judging the success of a marketing strategy or comparing alternatives. This in turn means it is difficult to accept marketing recommendations on product policy, pricing, promotions or, indeed, any element of the marketing mix. All too often marketing managers think a strategy is sensible if it increases sales or market share.[12] But astute top managers know that strategies to maximise market share will very rarely make economic sense. More sophisticated marketing managers will be tempted to use projected profits or return on investment to rationalise their marketing proposals. Unfortunately, this approach has the opposite bias and leads to an under-investment in marketing and a failure to capitalise on opportunities. Modern marketing has not incorporated current strategic valuation techniques and has consequently become marginalised in many board rooms. The marketing discipline lacks the framework for engaging in the strategic debate.

Because the link between marketing strategy and shareholder value has not been made, boards have tended to look at two other more transparent strategies. One has been cost reduction – sometimes disguised by more appealing names such as reengineering, downsizing or right sizing. Unfortunately, in a time of rapid market change, such actions are invariably only palliatives at best. The other common remedy has been acquisition. Acquisitions have broken all records in recent years. They have been seen as a way of generating value by adding top-line growth and by permitting a reduction in average costs. But, again, the evidence is that three out of four acquisitions fail to add value for the acquiring company.[13] Excessive bid premiums, cultural differences between the businesses and a failure to rejuvenate the company's marketing orientation appear to be the major weaknesses.

The failure to place marketing strategy at the centre of the corporate agenda cannot be laid solely at the door of the marketing profession. Financial management has also failed to bridge the marketing–finance interface. Top management still focuses on company accounts that measure only the historical cost of assets and omit internally developed brands and other intangible assets. Yet these marketing assets are now by far the most important sources of shareholder value. The market-to-book ratios for the *Fortune 500* average over 4, implying that over 75 per cent of the value of these companies lies in their brands and other marketing-based intangibles. (Note, however, that if a company has hyped its shares – such as Enron – the share price may not be backed by assets, tangible or intangible.) Companies whose goal is maximising shareholder value need a framework for placing the development and management of marketing assets at the centre of their planning processes. It is these marketing assets – brands, market knowledge and customer and partner relationships – that have become the key generators of long-term profits in today's information age.

MARKETING'S NEW OPPORTUNITY

Shareholder value analysis has become the new standard because of increasing realisation of the defects of conventional accounting. As we shall see, accounting profits encourage an excessively short-term view of business. They also encourage an under-investment in information-based assets – staff, brands, and customer and supplier relationships. In today's information age, the accounting focus only on tangible assets makes little sense now that these intangible assets are the overwhelming source of value creation. Shareholder value analysis (SVA) can avoid both these biases. But to achieve its potential, SVA needs marketing. Similarly, marketing needs SVA if it is to make a real contribution to strategy.

SHAREHOLDER VALUE NEEDS MARKETING

SVA is tautological without a marketing strategy. The shareholder value principle is that a business should be run to maximise the return on the shareholders' investment. SVA provides a tool for calculating the shareholder value added from any given growth, profit and investments projections. But what drives these growth, profit and investment requirements is outside the financial model. SVA does not address how managers can develop strategies that can accelerate growth, increase profit margins and lever investments. These are the objectives of marketing strategy. For example, returning to the earlier airline problem, SVA was able to identify which of the three strategies presented was best, but developing the innovative dual-branding plan came solely from an understanding of the market dynamics and a creative approach to serving different customer segments.

The heart of SVA is that economic value is created only when the business earns a return on investment that exceeds its cost of capital. From economic theory we know that in competitive markets this will only occur when it has a differential advantage in cost or product superiority. Without a unique advantage, competition will drive profits down to the cost of capital. Creating shareholder value is then essentially about building a sustainable competitive advantage – a reason why customers should consistently prefer to buy from one company rather than others. Marketing provides the tools for creating this competitive advantage. These are frameworks for researching and analysing customer needs, techniques for competitive analysis, and systems for measuring and enhancing consumer preference. Effective marketing input allows SVA to be dynamic and growth-orientated. Without it, SVA is static, merely focusing on ways of reducing costs and assets to produce a temporary fillip to cash flow.

The inputs to the SVA model are largely estimates about marketing variables. Key inputs are future sales volumes and prices. The other inputs are costs, investments and the cost of capital. Each of these variables depends on careful analysis and projections of the market. As with all models, the lesson is 'garbage in, garbage out'. Poor judgements about the future behaviour of customers and competitors will make worthless any conclusions from SVA.

SVA only deals with the latter stages of strategic planning. Any decision problem has four steps: (1) perceiving a need to change, (2) identifying alternative courses of action, (3) evaluating the options and (4) making the choice. SVA only provides answers for the last two steps. It does not provide for the continuing analysis of the firm's markets and technologies that is needed to alert management to emerging problems and opportunities. Nor does it suggest alternative strategies – these have to be discovered elsewhere. For example, SVA is not going to alert management to identify great new product or distribution ideas. These are most likely to be generated by staff who are close to customers. Just as marketing needs to be augmented to include developments in finance, so finance needs to be extended and broadened to include developments in marketing.

MARKETING NEEDS SHAREHOLDER VALUE

SVA is a great opportunity for marketing professionals. Traditional accounting, by focusing on short-term profits and ignoring intangible assets, marginalises marketing. In contrast, SVA can bring to the fore the real value drivers in today's globally competitive markets. First, SVA roots marketing in a central role in the board-room process of strategy formulation. The language of the modern board is finance. Actions have to be justified in terms of their ability to increase the financial value of the business. In the past marketing has not been able to measure and communicate to other disciplines the financial value created by marketing activities. This has resulted in marketing professionals being undervalued and sidelined. SVA offers marketing a direct way to show how marketing strategies increase the value of the firm. It provides the framework and language for integrating marketing more effectively with the other functions in the business.

Second, SVA provides marketing with a stronger theoretical base. Traditionally, marketing has tended to see increasing customer loyalty and market share as ends in themselves. But today, top management requires that marketing view its ultimate purpose as contributing to increasing shareholder value. No longer can marketers afford to rely on the untested assumption that increases in customer satisfaction and share will translate automatically into higher financial performance. This dilemma suggests a reformulation of the marketing discipline as about developing and managing intangible assets – customer and channel relationships and brands – to maximise economic value.[14] We call this value-based marketing. This view of marketing is theoretically appealing and also places marketing activities in a pivotal role in the strategy formulation process.

Third, SVA encourages profitable marketing investments. Conventional accounting has treated marketing expenditures as costs rather than investments in intangible assets. Because the long-term profit streams generated by such investments are ignored, marketing in many businesses is underfunded. SVA, however, is future-orientated; it encourages the long-term effects of marketing expenditures to be explicitly estimated. Brand-building investments that would be discouraged under conventional accounting procedures because they reduce current profits are shown as value-creating under SVA.

Finally, SVA penalises arbitrary cuts in marketing budgets. Management have found marketing budgets an easy target when they need to improve short-term profits. For example, cutting brand support will normally boost profitability without significantly affecting sales in the short run. The fact that such policies invariably lead to longer-term erosion in market share and price premiums has been ignored. SVA gives marketing management the tool to demonstrate that these short-term cuts destroy rather than build value. Informed shareholders are likely to react to *ad hoc* cuts in brand support by reducing the market value of the company.

THE SHAREHOLDER VALUE PRINCIPLE

In the past fifteen years or so more and more leading companies have shifted to adopt shareholder value as the criterion for evaluating strategies and the performance of their managers. This criterion asserts that business strategies should be judged by the economic returns they generate for shareholders, as measured by dividends and increases in the company's share price.

Companies that adopt the shareholder value approach accept two assumptions drawn from modern financial theory.[15] The first is that the primary obligation of managers is to maximise the returns for ordinary shareholders of the business. Managers are agents whose task is to act in the interests of the principals – the shareholders with financial ownership rights over the business. The second assumption is about how this is achieved in practice. This states that the stock market value of the company's shares is based on investors' expectations of the cash-generating abilities of the business. This then leads to the definition of the task of management as about developing strategies that maximise the value of these cash flows over time. A company generates cash, i.e. creates value, when its sales exceed its costs (including capital costs).

SVA calculates the total value of a strategy by discounting these cash flows. Discounting reflects that money has a time value. Because cash can earn interest, cash received today is worth more than the same amount received a year or more in the future. Discounting also allows for risk. To take greater risks, investors demand the promise of higher returns. Risk is reflected in the cost of capital used in the discounting formula. The idea of discounting cash flows (DCF) is not new; indeed, it has been the standard for evaluating capital projects for years. But it was not until the 1980s that firms began seriously using DCF for broader strategic planning purposes. It then began to be considered for evaluating marketing strategies.

SVA seeks to identify those strategies that create shareholder value. The stock market's judgement on the expected financial performance of a company is reflected in its market-to-book ratio (see Figure 1.5). If the market value of the shares exceeds the book value of the firm, it has created value. This ratio is a useful insight for measuring how successful management has been in maximising shareholder value.

To evaluate a new strategy proposed by the management team, the future effects of this strategy must be separated from the results of past strategies and investments. The current share price reflects both the values derived from these past decisions as well as shareholders' expectations about what the current management team will do. To judge the current strategy we need to focus on the incremental effect on shareholder value. The essence of the shareholder value approach is that managers create value when their strategy generates a greater economic return than their cost of capital. The cost of capital is what investors would expect to earn if they invested the funds on their own, in businesses with a similar degree of risk.

WHY SHAREHOLDER VALUE?

The spread of value-based management and SVA has been triggered by the changes brought in by the information age. One is the enormous growth of equity markets around the world caused by economic expansion and the declining role of government investment in industry. While government investment is motivated by complex political concerns, the objectives of private equity investors are much simpler and clearer. Private investors expect the pension, insurance and mutual funds that invest their money to maximise their performance. This in turn causes the fund managers to increasingly demand value from the companies they invest in.

The modern shareholder value movement started in the USA and the UK but, with the globalisation of trade and capital flows, it is sweeping into other major countries. Companies are now competing internationally not only for customers but also for capital. The most important criterion for attracting equity capital is its expected economic return. The information revolution is also making markets more efficient. Computers and modelling software make it much quicker to run SVA methodology and test the implications of a company's strategic thinking. The quantity and quality of information available to investors have also increased exponentially in recent years. Finally, the sophistication of modern telecommunications means that money can now travel around the world in seconds. All these trends mean that managers have come under increasing scrutiny from the people whose money they are using.

Companies that do not manage for value find capital more difficult and costly to obtain, handicapping their growth potential. They also become vulnerable more quickly. Non-executive shareholders and fund managers have become notably more proactive in removing top management when they fail to create value for shareholders. The high-profile collapse of once well-regarded companies such as Enron and WorldCom and the dot.com implosion in the early part of the century have made them even more vigilant. Finally, acquisition is a potent threat. When a weak market-to-book ratio indicates a 'value gap', i.e. a difference between the value of the company if it were operated to maximise shareholder value and its current value, an invitation appears for an acquirer to bid for it and replace the existing management.

CHALLENGES TO SHAREHOLDER VALUE

Recall that value-based planning is based on two premises: one is the philosophical assertion that the primary objective of managers is to maximise the returns for shareholders; the other is the technical assumption that the market value of the company is based on investors' expectations of discounted future cash flows. The latter assumption will be explored in Chapter 2, when the more technical aspects of SVA are presented. Here the rationale of the first premise is discussed.

Many writers have pointed out that a company has social and environmental responsibilities and that shareholders are not the only stakeholders in the business.[16] It is argued that in seeking to maximise shareholder value managers ignore these social responsibilities and fail to balance the different stakeholder interests. That these stakeholders may have interests which conflict with those of shareholders is clear. It is also true that they often have longer-term relationships with the company than its shareholders. Today's shareholders are normally financial investors rather than individuals with emotional and long-term personal ties to the business. These other stakeholders fall into the following groups:

❍   **Employees.** *The legitimacy of the claims of employees lies in the long-term commitment many of them make to the firm. In today's information age companies, their special skills also represent intangible assets that are generally more important in creating value than the traditional balance-sheet items. The objectives of employees are normally a combination of employment security, compensation and job satisfaction. Each of these, but particularly security, can conflict sharply with a strategy based on maximising shareholder value. In rapidly changing markets, value-based management will unfortunately often dictate closure or disposals of businesses.*

○ Managers. *The separation of ownership and control in the twentieth century increased the ability of top managers to pursue interests that were not aligned to those of shareholders. Managers have often seen growth and short-term profits as more closely linked to personal rewards in terms of salaries and prestige than shareholder value. Managers too are typically more risk averse in searching for opportunities than shareholders would wish. If the company invests in a risky project, shareholders can always balance the risk by portfolio diversification. Managers, however, have their jobs on the line, and so are hurt more by failure.*

○ Customers. *Without customer value there can be no shareholder value. Even the most focused financial manager understands that the source of a company's long-term cash flow is its satisfied customers. Many managers, especially those with a marketing background, have therefore gone on to argue that maximising customer satisfaction should be the primary goal. The problem is that providing customer satisfaction does not automatically lead to shareholder value. Delighting customers with lower prices than competitors or superior quality and features cannot provide a sustainable advantage if the cost of delivering all this (including the cost of capital) exceeds the price they are paying. The unconstrained maximisation of customer satisfaction certainly conflicts with a shareholder value orientation.*

○ Suppliers. *Today's virtually integrated companies are clearly dependent upon the cooperation and commitment of their network of suppliers. Competition has moved on from competition between individual companies to competition between networks. Suppliers in these networks want long-term security, predictability and satisfactory margins. Again, value management in today's volatile markets will mean that the firm cannot guarantee these relationships. Changing technologies, evolving consumer needs and new sources of supply will bring conflicts between the aspirations of traditional suppliers for stability and the ambitions of shareholders for value.*

○ Community. *The local and national communities where the firm is located will also have interests in the firm's behaviour. Social responsibilities can be divided into those arising from what the firm does to the society, and what it can do for it. The former are the negative impacts – pollution and environmental damage – which arise as by-products of the firm's activities, and which communities increasingly want stopped. The latter are tasks which communities often want businesses to take on, such as preserving employment, helping minorities or improving schooling. Social impacts are caused by, and are the responsibility of, the firm. Social problems, on the other hand, are dysfunctions of society. Accepting responsibility for these social problems can bring sharp conflicts with the goal of maximising shareholder value.*

There are a number of objections to the claims made by advocates of corporate social responsibility and the interests of alternative stakeholders. The most fundamental is that social responsibilities are not the job of business. In a market-based economy that recognises the rights of private property, the only social responsibility of business is to create shareholder value, and to do so legally and with integrity. Managers have neither the expertise nor the political legitimacy to decide what is in the public interest. Such choices in our society are the function of elected governments. If the government is unwilling to ask voters to bear the costs of its social goals, why should a company ask its customers, employees and shareholders to pay through higher prices, lower wages or reduced returns?

Fortunately, there are strong market incentives for value-maximising firms to take into account other stakeholder interests. Crucial is the need to attract, retain and motivate the new 'knowledge workers' whose specialist skills and efforts determine the firm's ultimate competitiveness.[17] Shareholder interest dictates that the firm offers competitive salaries and safe and attractive working conditions. Similarly, it would be suicidal in today's competitive markets not to be dedicated to satisfying customers. Investing in market research, new product development, quality and customer service are central to value management. Sustainability in its broadest sense is also a major concern.

However, when top management eschews shareholder value as the primary goal in favour of 'balancing the interests of stakeholders' the company's strategy loses clarity and focus (see box, 'Getting the Stakeholder Balance Right').

Management can be lured into making investments for reasons of prestige or public relations. They hold on to business units that have no chance of generating economic returns or go on to make ill-considered diversifications. When this occurs a 'value gap' begins to emerge, eventually precipitating a takeover, with all the unpleasant consequences for employees, managers and the community.

Getting the Stakeholder Balance Right

For his book, The Committed Enterprise, *Hugh Davidson carried out in-depth interviews with 125 leaders of high-calibre organisations in for-profit as well as in not-for-profit organisations in Europe and the USA. He found that long-term successful organisations actively aligned their stakeholders. He quotes a typical CEO comment: 'To achieve value for shareholders, you must have very satisfied customers and employees' and notes robust linkages are increasingly being established between customer commitment, employee motivation and shareholder value. To manage what can be conflicting stakeholder needs, however, organisational leaders need to unite then through strong vision and value and recognise how they are changing. He found that the long-term successful organisations were committed from post room to board room to assuring the alignment of stakeholder values and had embedded processes for this purpose.*

Hugh Davidson, The Committed Enterprise, *Butterworth-Heinemann, 2006 (second reprint).*

In the long term, shareholder value is the best strategy for all stakeholders. Ultimately all their claims depend on the firm's ability to generate sufficient cash to meet them. This in turn depends on the firm's competitiveness. The share price reflects the firm's competitiveness. The market value of a company is based on the most informed estimates of its ability to create a competitive advantage and to achieve profitable growth in its markets. Goals which undermine this focus increase costs, misallocate investment and reduce the ability of the firm to compete. While in the short run, employees or managers might be better off, in today's global markets, the non-optimal use of resources is not sustainable, as will become evident in the firm's declining profits and growth performance. All stakeholders are vulnerable when managements fail to create shareholder value.

Many critics of value management forget who shareholders are. Often they are demonised as a small group of wealthy, self-serving individuals set apart from ordinary people. Certainly for the USA and the UK, nothing could be further from the truth. One in three households owns shares directly or through unit trusts in the UK, rather more in the USA. But virtually every household owns shares indirectly through pension funds and other institutional savings. These institutions own 50 per cent of all shares in the USA and 80 per cent in the UK and Japan. Almost everyone now is affected by the market value of shares. Losses, whether due to poor management or incurred in the pursuit of other stakeholder interests, come out of the pockets of employees, pensioners and other individuals with savings. As governments around the world shift pension and social security provision from the public sector to individuals, shareholders become even more 'us' rather than 'them'. Self-interest increasingly pressures business executives and fund managers to maximise shareholder value.

There are two other fundamental and related criticisms of the shareholder value objective. The first is that it does not motivate staff to achieve high performance. The second criticism is that it is not operational – it does not tell employees and managers what to do at a practical level. There are several reasons why maximising shareholder value may not be aspirational. One is that few of the staff will normally be significant shareholders themselves. Another is that they cannot see a direct link between their own specific jobs and the share prices of the company as a whole. Third, share prices often move as a result of macroeconomic factors and market forces unrelated to the performance of management.

Operationally, the problem is that, as noted earlier, while value-based management provides a criterion for strategies to be selected and evaluated, it does not say how these strategies can be constructed. Before a strategy can be put forward for SVA, a method for identifying the need for strategic change must exist. Then there must be a process of constructing strategic options that have prospects of creating competitive advantage and enabling the business to generate cash flows that exceed costs including the cost of capital. If these two prior processes are not well understood SVA can easily become over-focused on downsizing – getting rid of non-performing business units – rather than on exploiting growth opportunities.

To motivate staff and operationalise SVA, managements need a deep understanding of what the value drivers of the business will be in the future. This is why value management should not be thought of as a financial technique: it depends on all the knowledge and skills within the firm. This understanding can be called a *theory of the business*. It is a set of assumptions about what operations will be necessary for the firm to build and sustain a competitive advantage in the industry. These assumptions fall under five headings (Figure 1.6). The first is called the *environmental*

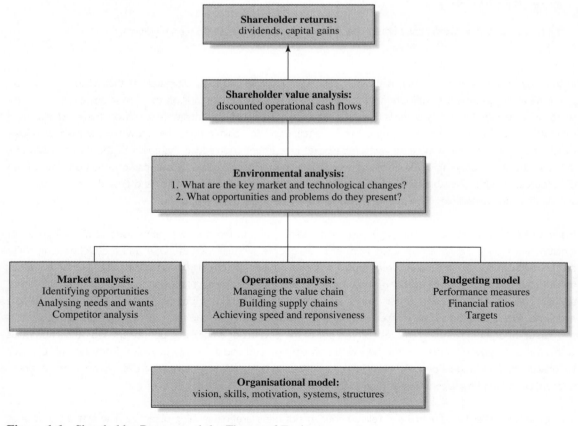

Figure 1.6   Shareholder Returns and the Theory of Business

assessment. It reflects management's analysis of those key developments in the global economy, technology, changing industrial structures and customer expectations that will shape its markets in the future. Changes in this environment should be the triggers that alert managers to the need to reformulate their own business strategy and capability requirements.

The second set of assumptions is contained in the firm's *marketing model.* This contains managers' analysis of which customers the firm can most profitably target and knowledge about what their wants are. It also contains the analysis of the competition: what strategies competitors are likely to follow, what their strengths and weaknesses are, and what capabilities are needed to create a competitive advantage. Next is the *operations model*, which contains the analysis of the best way to structure the firm's value chain to produce and deliver products and service to customers. Then comes the *budgeting model* which contains the key financial ratios management will use to monitor marketing and operations performance. Finally, and of vital importance, is the *organisation model*, which puts together people, leadership, vision and the skills to implement the strategy.

It is only with such a theory of the business that managers can use shareholder value to generate successful growth strategies. And, in an era of low inflation and relatively low overall GNP growth, it is only those companies that can achieve consistent growth that will create substantial increases in shareholder value. A well-grounded understanding of the fundamental value generators also allows managers to overcome the motivational and operational limitations of SVA. It can assign objectives, tasks and resources to measures of marketing, operations and financial performance that automatically lead to increases in shareholder value.

ACCOUNTING-BASED PERFORMANCE MEASURES

PROBLEMS WITH EARNINGS

In spite of the acceptance, in principle, that the task of management is to maximise returns for shareholders, most companies and fund managers still have not adopted value-based management. Accounting earnings rather than cash flows still form the basis for evaluating performance and valuing businesses. The financial press and analysts' reports consistently focus on short-term earnings, earnings per share and price earnings ratios. Despite the clear contrary evidence, the belief still persists that good earnings growth will lead to a parallel growth in the market value of the company's shares. Similarly, managers erroneously believe that if they concentrate on improving return on investment (earnings divided by assets) and return on equity (earnings divided by the book value of shareholder funds), the share price will automatically follow.

There are four reasons why earnings are a poor measure of performance compared to changes in shareholder value. First, unlike cash flow, which underpins SVA, accounting earnings are arbitrary and easily manipulated by management. Different, equally acceptable, accounting methods lead to quite different earnings figures. Prominent examples include alternative ways to compute the cost of goods sold (LIFO versus FIFO), different methods of depreciating assets, and the various choices in accounting for mergers and acquisitions. Different countries have different accounting regulations too, so international companies are frequently quoting different earnings on different stock markets. Not surprisingly, the flexibility of reporting procedures gives management ample opportunity to manipulate reported earnings for their own purposes – opportunities which are commonly taken.[18] But however managers choose to report profits, none of their manipulations or adjustments have any effect on the company's cash flow or economic value. While profits are an opinion, cash is a fact.

The second problem with accounting profits is that, unlike cash flow, they exclude investments. A growing business will invariably have to invest more in working and fixed capital, so that it could easily have positive earnings, but cash could be draining away. On the other hand, depreciation is deducted in the calculation of earnings even though it does not involve any cash outlay. So for a mature business with assets still being depreciated, earnings could well understate cash flows.

Third, earnings ignore the time value of money. This means that even consistent earnings growth can reduce shareholder returns. The economic value of any investment is the discounted value of the anticipated cash flows. The discounting procedure recognises that money has a time value – money today is worth more to investors than a money return tomorrow. Consequently, shareholder value will increase only if the company earns a return on the new investment which exceeds the cost of capital used in the discounting process. Taking a simple example, suppose a company has current earnings (and cash flow) of £20 million and a cost of capital of 10 per cent. It decides to invest £25 million to increase the future levels of earnings by 10 per cent. Unfortunately, while profits and cash flow rise by an agreeable £2 million, the shareholder value of the company falls. This is because when the increased annual cash flow is discounted, it is valued at only £20 million, or £5 million less than the original investment. Shareholders could have done better investing the money themselves elsewhere.

Finally, and perhaps most crucial from a strategic viewpoint, profits produce a short-term managerial focus. Rising earnings can easily disguise a decline in shareholder value because earnings ignore the future implications of current activities. For example, earnings can quickly be boosted by cutting advertising or customer service levels. In the short run this is beneficial, but in the long run it will erode the company's market share, future earnings and shareholder value. Similarly, many activities that lower short-term earnings such as investing in brands and building customer relationships can increase long-term cash flows and shareholder value. The focus on short-term earnings discourages growth-orientated strategies that increase long-term competitiveness and shareholder value. Taking all these problems into account, it is not surprising that there is little or no statistical correlation between earnings per share growth and total shareholder return as measured by dividends and share price appreciation.

PROBLEMS WITH RETURN ON INVESTMENT

Seeking to link earnings to levels of investment, managers routinely measure performance by looking at return on assets (ROA) and return on equity (ROE). The former tends to be used at the business unit level, the latter at the corporate level. Unfortunately, since both use earnings in the numerator, they are subject to all the previous weaknesses, plus some additional ones.

The main new problem is that assets are valued in an equally arbitrary way to earnings. Different, but equally valid, depreciation procedures or capitalisation policies, will lead to different valuations of both assets and equity. With today's information-age companies the implications of the capitalisation problem are striking. The growing importance of knowledge-based companies makes intangible assets far larger than physical assets. But these intangible assets such as brand names, patents, R&D, training and customer loyalty, do not normally appear on the balance sheet. One implication is that it is impossible to use ROA or ROE to evaluate different types of company. For example, pharmaceutical companies and businesses with strong brands would have higher ROAs than traditional manufacturing businesses even if their economic returns were identical, because the assets of the former do not appear in the denominator. As companies gradually invest more in knowledge and less in physical assets, it also makes comparing a company's ROA overtime a dubious indication of performance.

Studies show that ROA generally overstates the true return on investment.[19] The bias is greater for mature companies. Mature companies will often have higher ROAs than growth companies because depreciation policies and inflation will have tended to lower the net book value of their assets. Such figures then often deter management from moving away from declining businesses because they wrongly believe that ROA is correlated with value. Only when SVA is conducted using estimates of future cash flows can it be seen that the growth businesses are often immensely more valuable, and that there is often an inverse correlation between ROA and shareholder value added.

Turning to return on equity, this has all the above problems plus another one. ROE is calculated as ROA factored by gearing – the proportion of assets financed by debt rather than equity. Provided that it earns more than the cost of borrowing, more debt increases the ROE. Even if the amount of debt exceeds the optimal level, further borrowings increase ROE even while the value of the company declines due to increased financial risk.

The Problems with Return on Capital

Many fashionable techniques for judging corporate performance are variations of return on capital. While admirable in theory, all suffer from the weakness that, to calculate a return, one first needs to know the value of a company's assets, and historic book values are often irrelevant. Hence, one sees elaborate adjustments: goodwill write-offs and accumulated depreciation may be added back, the replacement cost of assets can be used or the price originally paid can be adjusted in line with inflation. All the wizardry is fair enough. But it can come at the expense of clear thinking about how to use return on capital in assessing performance ... Such adjustments can simply divert attention from the fact that return on capital employed is not a useful measure for judging operating performance.

Source: The Lex column, Financial Times, 2 January 1997.

Managers and analysts use accounting earnings presumably because they are easy to calculate. But earnings, and all the various valuation measures (P-E ratios, EPS) and performance standards (ROI, ROA, ROE) which utilise them, are subject to fundamental practical, conceptual and empirical weaknesses (see box, 'The Problems with Return on Capital'). Practically their measurement is arbitrary and subjective. Conceptually they are inappropriate because they do not measure changes in value. Earnings are the result of past decisions; value changes are based on future cash flows. Empirically, earnings-based measures do not predict changes in the returns accruing to shareholders. Shareholder value analysis works because it overcomes all three weaknesses. It is fact-based, conceptually robust and highly predictive of actual changes in the market value of businesses. And, unlike accounting numbers, shareholder value calculations are unaffected by the shift from industrial companies to knowledge-based companies built around intangible assets.

THE CHANGING ROLE OF MARKETING

The centrality of marketing in creating growth and shareholder value suggests a new role for marketing both as a discipline and a function (Table 1.1). Traditionally, marketing has been seen as about satisfying the needs of customers more effectively than competitors. The assumption has been that if the company satisfied its customers and won market share, positive financial results would automatically follow. Unfortunately, top management knows

Table 1.1 The Changing Role of Marketing

	Past	Today
Objective of marketing	Create customer value	Create shareholder value
Marketing strategy	Increase market share	Develop and manage marketing assets
Assumptions	Positive market performance leads to positive financial performance	Marketing strategies need to be tested in value terms
Contribution	Knowledge of customers, competitors and channels	Knowledge of how to lever marketing to increase shareholder value
Focus of marketing	Marketing orientation	General management
Skills of marketing	Specialist	Specialist + general
Advocacy	Importance of understanding customers	Marketing's role in creating shareholder value
Concept of assets	Tangible	Intangible
Rationale	Improves profits	Increases shareholder value
Performance measures	Market share, customer satisfaction, return on sales and positive cash flow	Shareholder value: discounted cash flows

that this is not necessarily true. Marketing expenditures, like any other resources, can be wasted, and satisfied customers are not necessarily profitable ones. The concept of marketing that will make it more effective in today's board room is one of contributing to the creation of shareholder value. It can be defined as follows:

Marketing is the management process that seeks to maximise returns to shareholders by developing relationships with valued customers and creating a competitive advantage.

This new concept of marketing shifts it from being a specialist activity to an integral part of the general management process. Where in the past marketing managers were seen as experts on customers, channels and competitors, today they should be seen as experts on how marketing and growth can increase shareholder value. To do this, marketers need to extend their skill base to add expertise in modern financial planning techniques. In the past, marketers have often allowed themselves to be trapped by accounting-orientated management into seeking to justify their marketing strategies in terms of improving immediate earnings. Such a short-term approach is invariably destructive because marketing is primarily about creating and managing assets. Investments in brands and customer relationships – like research and development – rarely pay off in the period in which they occur. They are made to generate and defend cash flows, often for many years ahead. Familiarity with shareholder value analysis has become an essential tool for demonstrating that marketing produces an economic return.

TECHNOLOGY AND THE RESHAPING OF MARKETING

Marketing, like other business disciplines, has to adapt to changing technology. Indeed, the history of marketing can be viewed as a stepwise evolution to a changing technological environment. Over the past century there have been three changes in the orientation of marketing: distribution, selling and brand management. The Internet is consolidating the fourth stage of marketing's evolution: marketing as managing individual relationships with customers.

MARKETING AS DISTRIBUTION

At the beginning of the twentieth century, when marketing began to emerge as a subject of interest, technology was still shaped by the industrial revolution. The companies that succeeded were those that could lever vast amounts of capital to build huge factories that employed mass production techniques turning out standardised products in their millions. Companies that perfected this technology, like Ford, General Motors, Westinghouse and ICI, became the giants of the era. The mass production of standardised products resulted in scale economies that allowed these companies to offer cheap products that small craft-based businesses producing customised products could not match.

In his marketing textbook, Kotler called this business focus the production concept.[20]

The production concept *holds that consumers will favor those products that are widely available and low in cost. Managers of production-oriented organizations concentrate on achieving high production efficiency and wide distribution coverage.*

In this era, the task of marketing was to arrange distribution to enable the products to be shipped to as broad a market as possible. It involved logistics and supply chain management, dealing with suppliers and creating an effective channel to get the goods to the consumer.

MARKETING AS SELLING

In the post-War years the problem began to change. Advances in production technology and the industrialisation of the developing countries began to make mass production too successful. Increasing production capacity led to greater competition and declining prices and profit margins. In addition, rising income levels led to customers wanting more than just basic, standardised products. At this stage the priority of firms began to shift from production to selling. Kotler defined this business focus as the selling concept.

The selling concept *holds that consumers and businesses, if left alone, will ordinarily not buy enough of the organization's products. The organization must, therefore, undertake an aggressive selling and promotions effort.*

In this period, the role of marketing was to organise this aggressive selling effort. Advertising and selling techniques became powerful tools for increasing the appeal of the company's products.

MARKETING AS BRAND MANAGEMENT

During the 1960s, there was an increasing appreciation that a better way of growing the business was not relying on increasingly aggressive and expensive selling and advertising, but instead researching what customers really wanted. The focus began to shift from 'selling what the company produced' to 'producing what the customer wanted'. This led on to the era of branding. Here companies researched the market, grouped customers into market segments sharing similar needs, and designed and positioned brands to these segments. Such companies as Procter & Gamble and Unilever professionalised this brand management concept.

The brand management *concept holds that the key to meeting its organizational goals consists of the company being more effective than competitors in developing brands that create, deliver, and communicate customer value to its chosen target market segments.*

The focus of marketing in this era was on market research, segmentation, positioning and brands. The arrival of computers and the development of databases allowed increasingly sophisticated techniques for tracking and profiling markets. Until well into the 1990s this concept represented the state of the art in marketing. Yet the technology at the time left marketing with one fundamental weakness: most companies had no direct interaction with individual consumers. A Procter & Gamble brand manager knew nothing about an individual consumer even if it was one of the company's most important and loyal users. At most, the manager knew the average needs of a market segment – though this could include several million customers. As a result, brands were a compromised solution, which would meet the needs of some customers and not others. At its core, the brand concept retained a product rather than a customer focus.

MARKETING AS MANAGING INDIVIDUAL CUSTOMER RELATIONSHIPS

In the mid-1990s the Internet brought in technologies which promised to overcome these compromises and usher in a new, more powerful marketing concept. It offered the opportunity to efficiently build relationships with individual consumers that allowed companies to precisely meet their needs with customised products and services. The first breakthrough was the opportunity for individual communication and interaction between company and consumer that the Net offered. This enabled companies to learn about individual needs and to rank customers by importance. Unlike a Procter & Gamble manager, one from Dell or First Direct is armed with detailed information when talking with a customer.

The second breakthrough was the emergence of mass customisation, where companies could make individual rather than standardised products and services. Again, this was facilitated by Internet technology, which fostered a shift from the inflexible vertically integrated company to the flexible network, or hub-and-spoke organisation. Here, the customer's order over the Internet is immediately transferred to the company's component suppliers through its extranet, who begin building the individualised modules. Information technology then coordinates the modules into a customised product that is quickly despatched.

These new 'virtually integrated' companies offer speed, customisation and economies in cost and assets that traditional companies cannot match. The new marketing concept has been called the individual marketing concept.

The individual marketing concept *holds that the key to effective marketing is to use interactive communications to develop individual relationships with consumers based on providing superior value through personalised products and services.*

The new marketing concept treats each consumer as unique and aims to match his or her specific requirements. If the company is doing this job well, the consumer will have very little reason to move. Indeed, moving away from the relationship will be unattractive because of the switching costs resulting from another company having to learn about their needs. Individual marketing also enables the firm to acquire detailed information about the value of each customer. The lifetime value of a customer is defined as the discounted net present value of all future cash flow generated by dealings with the individual. A company has a portfolio of customers. It is the increase in the value of the portfolio that is the best measure of how a company is performing.

Table 1.2 summarises the evolution of marketing to the present concept of building value through individual customer relationships.

Table 1.2   Changing Technologies and the Evolving Marketing Concept

Marketing concept	Distribution	Selling	Brand management	Individual relationships
Products	Single product	Few	Many	Huge, customised
Market size	As big as possible	National to global	Target segments	Individual customer
Competitive tools	Price, costs	Advertising, selling	Positioning, segmentation	Dialogue, customisation
Key technology	Mass production	Television, media	Market research	Internet
Key measures	Production costs, volume	Market share, margins	Brand equity	Customer lifetime value

SUMMARY

1. Companies grow and prosper when they efficiently meet the needs of customers. But efficient products and services are soon made obsolete by rapid environmental changes that create new customer needs, introduce new competition and offer new technologies that provide better answers. Maintaining success requires continual change.

2. In the new millennium four particular changes are reshaping the environment of business: the globalisation of markets, changing industrial structures, the information revolution and rising consumer expectations.

3. Increasing shareholder returns is the best measure of business performance. The market value of a business reflects investors' views of the ability of managers to create long-term profits that exceed its cost of capital.

4. Marketing has too little influence in business because marketing strategies are not effectively linked to shareholder value creation. Growth of sales or market share are not reliable measures of operating performance. The real role of marketing is to create and utilise marketing assets to create future cash flows with a positive net present value.

5. In most companies shareholder value has mistakenly come to be associated with downsizing and rationalisation. Such strategies do not create sustainable increases in cash flow or shareholder value. In today's rapidly changing markets, the greatest increases in value accrue to companies that identify new market opportunities and put in place market-led strategies that promise high future earnings growth.

6. Without effective marketing, shareholder value is a trivial concept. Shareholder value analysis allows management to evaluate alternative strategies, but only marketing insight and investment can create worthwhile strategies in the first place.

7. Marketing, like other business disciplines, has to adapt to changing technology. The history of marketing can be viewed as a stepwise evolution to a changing technological environment. Over the past century there have been three changes in the orientation of marketing: distribution, selling and brand management. The Internet is consolidating the fourth stage of marketing's evolution: marketing as managing individual relationships with customers.

REVIEW QUESTIONS

1.   What are the characteristics of the information age, and how do these affect business?
2.   How does the 'direct business model' contrast with the traditional business model?
3.   What does the market-to-book value ratio indicate?
4.   How does marketing contribute to a more effective shareholder value orientation?
5.   What are the weaknesses of traditional, accounting-based measures of performance?
6.   How can marketing managers use the shareholder value concept?

NOTES ON CHAPTER 1

[1] Arie de Geus, *The Living Company*, Boston, MA: Harvard Business School Press, 1997.

[2] Andrew Black, Philip Wright and John E. Bachman, *In Search of Shareholder Value*, London: Pitman, 1998.

[3] See, for example, Jeremy Hope and Tony Hope, *Competing in the Third Wave*, Boston: Harvard Business School Press, 1997; Peter Drucker, *Managing in a Time of Great Change*, Harmondsworth: Penguin Books, 1995.

[4] Don Peppers and Martha Rogers, *Enterprise One-to-One*, New York: Doubleday, 1997.

[5] Joan Magretta, The power of virtual integration: an interview with Dell Computer's Michael Dell, *Harvard Business Review*, March/April, 1998, 72–85.

[6] The glossary contains a definition of the key financial terms used in the book.

[7] Lowell L. Bryan, Timothy G. Lyons and James Rosenthal, Corporate strategy in a globalizing world: the market capitalization imperative, *McKinsey Quarterly*, no. 3, 1998, 6–19.

[8] Chartered Institute of Marketing, September 2006.

[9] Deloitte, *Marketing in 3D*, January 2008.

[10] For a timely discussion of this, see Tim Ambler, *Marketing and the Bottom Line*, 2nd edn, FT/Prentice Hall, 2003.

[11] See Malcolm McDonald, Brian D. Smith and Keith Ward, *Marketing Due Diligence*, Butterworth-Heinemann, 2007.

[12] See Leslie Butterfield (ed.), *Excellence in Advertising*, Oxford: Butterworth-Heinemann, 1999, pp. 268–271.

[13] David Harding and Sam Rovit, *Mastering the Merger*, Harvard Business School Press, 2004.

[14] Rajendra K. Srivastava, Tasadduq A. Shervani and Liam Fahey, Market-based assets and shareholder value: a framework for analysis, *Journal of Marketing*, **62**, 1998, 2–18.

[15] Richard A. Brearley and Stewart C. Myers, *Principles of Corporate Finance*, 4th edn, New York: McGraw-Hill, 1999.

[16] Whether directors should focus on anything other than shareholders is much debated. For example, see Tim Ambler and Andrea Wilson, The problems of stakeholder theory, *Business Ethics*, **4** (1 January), 1995. Republished in *Business Law: Principles, Cases and Policies*, M. Roszkowski, Harper Collins, 1997.

[17] Peter F. Drucker, *Management Challenges for the 21st Century*, Oxford: Butterworth Heinemann, 1999, pp. 133–160.

[18] Terry Smith, *Accounting for Growth: Stripping the Camouflage from Company Accounts*, 2nd edn, London: Century, 1996.

[19] Alfred Rappaport, *Creating Shareholder Value*, 2nd edn, New York: Free Press, 1998.

[20] Philip Kotler, *Marketing Management*, 10th edn, Englewood Cliffs, NJ: Prentice Hall, 2000, pp. 17–20.)

2 The Shareholder Value Approach

'Of the five business deadly sins, the first and easily the most common is the worship of high profit margins.'

Peter F. Drucker

INTRODUCTION AND OBJECTIVES

Value-based marketing is not primarily about numbers and making complex calculations. It consists of three main elements. First, it is a set of *beliefs* about the objectives of marketing. The basic belief is that the primary task of marketing is to develop strategies that will maximise returns for shareholders. Second, it is a set of *principles* for choosing marketing strategies and making marketing decisions that are consistent with these beliefs. These principles are based on estimating the future cash flow associated with a strategy to calculate the shareholder value added. Finally, it is a set of *processes* that ensure that marketing develops, selects and implements a strategy that is consistent with these beliefs and principles. These processes concern management of the financial, marketing and organisational value drivers of the business. The financial value drivers are those key ratios that have the most significant impact on shareholder value. The marketing drivers are the customer-orientated plans necessary to drive improvement in the financial ratios. The organisational value drivers are the core capabilities, systems and leadership styles needed to create and implement the shareholder value orientation in the business.

Chapter 1 explained the belief in value-based marketing. This chapter explores the principles of value-based marketing. The remaining chapters examine in detail the processes of building a shareholder value approach and the significance of marketing and growth.

By the time you have read this chapter, you will be able to:

- ○   *Describe the principles of shareholder value*
- ○   *Understand how to value different marketing strategies*
- ○   *Identify the financial, marketing and organisational value drivers of the business*
- ○   *Explain how marketing strategies affect shareholder value*
- ○   *Determine whether a growth strategy will increase value*
- ○   *Assess the problems and limitations in operationalising shareholder value analysis*

This chapter contains some challenging technical material. The ideas will be unfamiliar to most marketing managers. But there is nothing here that cannot be mastered by anyone willing to spend time on the material. The techniques described position marketing managers to become much more involved and proactive in developing business strategy. They are the same techniques as boards, consultants, analysts and sophisticated investors use to evaluate business strategies. Without these tools, marketing managers risk being left behind in influencing the big strategic issues facing their businesses. These techniques provide the best framework for evaluating marketing strategy and demonstrating the effectiveness of marketing. In addition, as we show in the following chapters, they lead to a fundamentally different approach to thinking about marketing issues and developing the marketing mix.

The chapter begins by describing the principles of valuation. There are two commonly accepted approaches: the cash flow method and the economic profit (or EVA) approach. Both lead to the same results, but we believe that the cash flow method provides more insights for marketing, and this is our main focus. The key financial drivers of cash flow are identified: sales growth, the operating profit margin and the level of investment. We then show how marketing plays a central role in determining these drivers. Finally, the chapter reviews the organisational basis and core capabilities required to sustain superior marketing and financial performance.

PRINCIPLES OF VALUATION

The basic principle of shareholder value is that a company's share price is determined by the sum of all its anticipated future cash flows, adjusted by an interest rate known as the cost of capital. If the company is expected to generate more cash, perhaps because it develops a new product or has a great advertising campaign, its share price will go up. Conversely, if expected cash flow falls, perhaps because a major new competitor is invading its market, the share price will go down.

The crucial implication of this principle is that the task of management is to maximise the sum of these cash flows. One obvious way to do this is to come up with great marketing strategies that, for example, introduce profitable new products or create strong brands that obtain high market shares.

This basic principle is founded on well-established financial theory. It shows that the amount rational investors will pay for an asset is the future cash flow it generates, discounted by the cost of capital. The cost of capital is the rate of return that investors would expect to receive if they invested elsewhere in assets of similar risk. The sum of these cash flows is called the *present value* (PV) of an asset. It is written as

$$PV = \sum \frac{C_t}{(1+r)^t}$$

This is also called the *discounted cash flow* (or DCF) model. Here Σ refers to the summation of the series of cash flows, C_t, occurring in years 1, 2 ... t and r is the discount rate. For example, suppose a business unit was expected to generate a cash flow of £2 million in each of the next four years, and its cost of capital was 10 per cent, then the present value is:

$$\frac{2}{(1.1)} + \frac{2}{(1.1)^2} + \frac{2}{(1.1)^3} + \frac{2}{(1+1)^4} = £6.4 \text{ million}$$

The *net present value* (NPV) of an asset is the present value plus the initial investment to acquire the asset:

$$NPV = C_0 + \sum \frac{C_t}{(1+r)^t}$$

Note that C_0 is normally negative because the initial investment is a cash payment. For example, if management invested £5 million initially to obtain the above four years of cash flows, then the NPV would be £1.4 million.

The cash flows are discounted for two simple reasons. First, cash today is worth more than cash tomorrow, since money today can be invested to start earning immediately. Second, because risky returns are worth less than safe ones, they are penalised by a higher discount rate. The current rates of return available in the capital market are used to determine how much to discount for time and risk. By calculating the present value of an asset we are in effect estimating the maximum amount people will pay for it, if they have the alternative of investing elsewhere in ventures of comparable risk.

The basic conclusion is that investors should only invest in assets with positive net present values. Otherwise they would have done better to invest elsewhere. To demonstrate the validity of this theory we first look at how this DCF model determines the prices of bonds. The same principles are then applied to show how the prices of shares are determined. Shareholder value analysis simply takes these same ideas and uses them to value businesses and marketing strategies.

VALUING BONDS

A rational and well-understood valuation process that is described exactly by the previous present value formula determines both government and corporate bond prices. Three basic factors determine the value of any bond: (1) the cash flow that investors expect from holding the bond, namely, its annual interest payments and the ultimate return of the principal; (2) the term of the bond, i.e. the number of years to maturity; and (3) the discount rate used by investors to convert the future cash flows into a present value.

As a simplified illustration, suppose that in the year 2000 an investor considers buying a 10 per cent 2005 UK Treasury bond. The bond has an interest rate of 10 per cent and a face value or principal of £1000. This means that each year until 2005 the investor receives an interest payment of £100. The bond matures in 2005 when the Treasury pays the investor the final £100 interest, plus the £1000 principal. To find out how much it is worth paying for this bond, the cash payments need to be discounted to the present value in 2000. To get the discount rate, the investor can look in the *Financial Times* to see the return available on bonds of a similar duration and risk. Medium-term UK government bonds in 2000 were offering a return of about 4.5 per cent. This is what an investor would be giving up to buy the 10 per cent Treasury bond. The present value is then,

$$PV = \sum \frac{C_t}{(1+r)^t}$$

$$= \frac{100}{1.045} + \frac{100}{1.045^2} + \frac{100}{1.045^3} + \frac{100}{1.045^4} + \frac{100}{1.045^5}$$

$$= £1241.45$$

If the actual price is less than this, investors will rush in to take advantage of the positive NPV, causing the price of the bond to rise towards the predicted level. Above this price, investors will not buy, because other similar investments offer a better return. If actual bond prices in practice were compared to those that are predicted by the discounted flow model it would be found that the correlation is virtually perfect. It is now generally accepted that investors value bonds using this DCF formula.[1]

VALUING SHARES

Share prices are determined in essentially the same rational way as bond prices. That the same basic model is employed is hardly surprising since investors normally buy both bonds and shares. As with bonds, investors value shares by discounting expected future cash flows. However, with shares there are three important differences that make estimating the price people should pay more complicated.

First, bonds have a legal obligation to pay a specified amount of cash in the future. Ordinary shares carry no such obligation – the amount they can pay depends on how well the business does. Consequently, the cash flows they offer investors have to be estimated. If the company is not issuing or repurchasing its shares, the cash paid to investors is the dividend. Hence the discounted cash flow model applied to shares is called the *dividend discount model*. Investors' expectations about cash flow will be based on their views of the attractiveness of the company's markets and the effectiveness of the strategies pursued by management. The more optimistic they are about the company's future competitiveness, the higher the anticipated cash flow, and, therefore the higher the valuation of the company's shares. Conversely, the gloomier they are about its markets and the quality of the management, the lower the expected cash flow and the lower will be the share price.

A second important difference is that while bonds normally specify a definite duration over which payments will be made, shares, on the other hand, have no termination date. Consequently share values have to be determined by discounting the forecast cash flows over an infinite period – assuming that there is no reason to expect the business to close its operations. As we shall see, in practice this means investors explicitly forecasting cash flows over some reasonable forecast horizon, say, five to ten years ahead, and then estimating the remaining cash flows over the post-forecast period in the form of a 'continuing' value.

Third, while the discount rate for bonds is directly observable in the market, the cost of capital for discounting company cash flows has to be estimated. It is a function of three factors: the risk-free rate of return (normally taken as the yield on longer term government bonds), the market risk premium (the extra amount to be made on average by investing in equities as compared to risk-free government bonds), and the specific riskiness attached to the company's shares. On average, for both the UK and the USA, the market risk premium has been between 5 and 6 per cent over the past 50 years. So if the yield on 10-year government bonds is 4.5 per cent, this suggests a cost of capital averaging 10 per cent, 1 or 2 points higher for more volatile businesses, and lower for steadier ones.

The return shareholders obtain normally comes in two forms: (1) cash dividends and (2) capital gains or losses on the shares. The value of a share is then the discounted value of forecast dividends plus the discounted value of the share at the end of the forecast period. The general share price formula for estimating the value of a share, P_0 is then:

$$P_0 = \sum_{t=1}^{h} \frac{DIV_t}{(1+r)^t} + \frac{P_h}{(1+r)^h}$$

The first expression is the sum of the discounted dividends from year 1 to year h. The second expression is the share price at some time, h, in the future. Note that the share price, P_h, is valued by a buyer as the sum of the anticipated discounted dividends in the future years after h, plus the share price at some further future period ahead, and so on. Since in principle companies have an infinite life, the ultimate share price can be many decades in the future. This means that the discounted value of the terminal share price will approach zero.[2] For example, a share worth £20 fifty years on is only worth 17 pence today, assuming a discount rate of 10 per cent, i.e. £20 divided by $(1 + 0.1)^{50}$. Consequently, the terminal share price can be ignored and today's share price can be expressed simply as the present value of all future cash dividends,

$$P_0 = \sum_{t=1}^{\infty} \frac{DIV_t}{(1+r)^t}$$

The discounted cash flow formula for the present value of a share is identical to that for any other asset. This is because dividends per share are the same as cash flow per share, i.e. Cash flow = revenue − costs − investments.

By definition, what is not reinvested in the business is paid out as dividends. Therefore another way of valuing shares, which produces an identical figure, is to use forecasts of per share revenues, costs and investment:

$$P_0 = \sum_{t=1}^{\infty} \frac{(\text{cash flow per share})_t}{(1+r)^t}$$

Empirical studies have shown that this discounted cash flow formula is generally a good predictor of actual share prices. Typically the correlation coefficient between predicted and actual share prices is about 0.8.[3]

This is no accident: investment managers and equity analysts have increasingly shifted to cash flow models for estimating share values.[4] The above model calculates a 'warranted' or implied share value. If the actual share price is below the implied value then this discount forms the basis for a 'buy' recommendation. Where the actual share price is at a premium to the implied value then the shares look poor value and are likely to be sold.

The model also demonstrates that the 'City' is not short-term orientated. The value of a share is determined by forecasting dividends over an indefinite time period. Near-term earnings generally explain only a small proportion of the share price. For the major stocks, forecast dividends in the next five years only account for an average of 20 per cent of the market value of the share price.

Still, many marketing managers are not convinced that the stock market takes a long-term view. They point, in particular, to the excessive attention given to quarterly earnings figures. But the attention to current earnings announcements does not contradict the model. Short-term earnings do not themselves have much impact on the share price. However, they may lead investors to reconsider their longer-term forecasts of cash flows. Cash flow consists of earnings less the amount reinvested in the business. Changes in earnings therefore do have a big effect on cash flows. If managers fail to deliver earnings according to expectations in the short term, it may lead investors to question the long-term strategy. To optimise their investment portfolios, investors continually probe for information about the long-term prospects of the companies whose shares they hold. Earnings announcements are an important source of information for investors making and revising long-term forecasts. But shareholder value is not determined by short-term earnings; it is determined by discounting long-term expected cash flow. If marketing can convincingly present strategies that promise long-term growth in cash flow, there is plenty of evidence that this will be rewarded by a rapid rise in the company's market value.

SHAREHOLDER VALUE

Marketing is central to creating shareholder value. The shareholder value approach used to evaluate marketing strategies employs exactly the same model as investors use to value shares. A marketing strategy makes sense if it is likely to enhance the value of the business. The approach starts with the recognition that the economic value of a business, like any other asset, is determined by discounting forecast cash flow by the cost of capital. A marketing strategy then needs to demonstrate that it can increase this discounted cash flow.

The first step in applying the model is to identify the *financial value drivers* that determine cash flow. There are three financial drivers that executives need to manage:

1.   Sales growth

2.   After-tax operating profit margin

3.   Investment requirements

As we shall see, it is not just the *level* of cash flow that is important but also its *timing, duration* and *riskiness*. Cash flow that occurs early is worth more than that occurring later, because money is discounted. Marketing strategies that create enduring cash flows – perhaps by building strong brands – are worth more than strategies that promote only short-term gains. Finally, marketing strategies that are very risky are worth less, because the cash flows they are expected to create are discounted with a higher cost of capital. In other words, to invest in a high-risk marketing strategy, investors will want the expectation of higher cash flow.

These financial value drivers are the *objectives* managers pursue. But to achieve faster sales growth, higher profit margins and to make good investment decisions they need *strategies* (see Figure 2.1). Marketing strategies focus on selecting attractive markets and creating a differential advantage. A marketing advantage is built on the marketing assets the firm has developed: its marketing knowledge, its brands, the loyalty of its customers and its strategic relationships with channel partners. These we term the *marketing value drivers* of the business. Many executives in embracing shareholder value have not understood that strong marketing value drivers are essential to achieve financial performance. Finally, to develop and implement these strategies the firm needs *organisational value drivers*. These are the core capabilities – the skills, systems, motivation and leadership – to be operationally effective.

KEY CONCEPTS

To show how shareholder value is built we need some definitions.[5] The total value of a firm or business unit is called its corporate or *enterprise value*. It consists of the amount belonging to the holders of its debt and equity. The equity portion of the enterprise value is the *shareholder value*. That is:

$$\text{Enterprise value} = \text{Debt} + \text{Shareholder value}$$

Rearranging the equation, we can express shareholder value as:

$$\text{Shareholder value} = \text{Enterprise value} - \text{Debt}$$

So to calculate the shareholder value of a business, its total or enterprise value must be calculated first, and then the value of its debt must be subtracted. It is usual to divide the calculation of enterprise value into two basic components:

1. **Forecast period value.** This is the present value of cash flow from the business's operations during the forecast or planning period – normally the first 5–10 years.

2. **Continuing value.** This is the estimate of the present value of the cash flows that the business generates after the forecast period.

To be more complete and precise, for practical purposes, analysts need to add a third component, *other investments*. Many businesses own securities and other investments that are outside their normal operations. Income from these assets is excluded from the calculation of operational cash flows and their market values are shown separately. Enterprise value can then be written in terms of the three components as:

$$\text{Enterprise value} = \text{Present value of cash flow from operations during forecast period}$$

$$+ \text{ Continuing value}$$

$$+ \text{ Other investments}$$

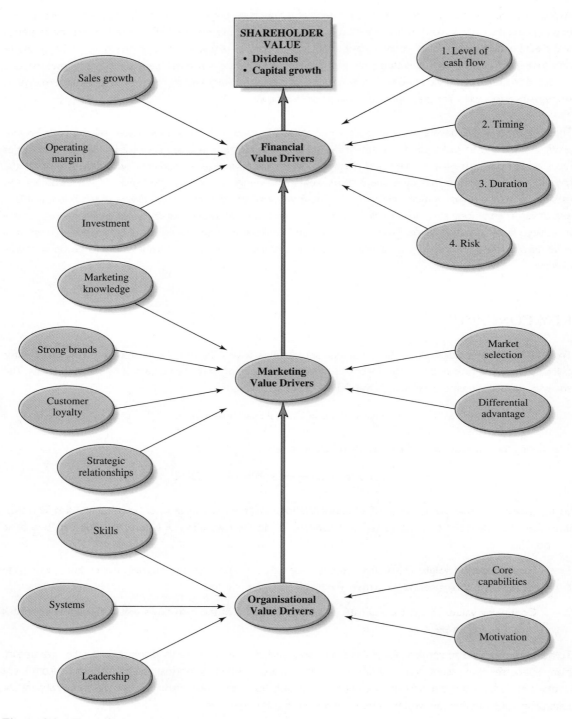

Figure 2.1 The Drivers of Value in a Business

CASH FLOW FROM OPERATIONS

Cash flow is the difference between operating cash inflows and outflows. It is often called *free cash flow*. Cash flow is the source of corporate value because it determines how much is available to pay debtholders and shareholders. Cash flows are estimated for each year of the forecast period and then discounted back to the present using the appropriate cost of capital.

Cash *inflows* are a function of two elements: sales and the operating profit margin. The operating profit margin is the ratio of pre-interest, pre-tax operating profit to sales. Operating profit is sales less the cost of goods, selling and administrative expenses and less depreciation costs. Cash *outflows* are a function of three elements: the cash taxes the company actually pays, and the additional working capital and fixed investment the business will incur in achieving its sales.

To illustrate how these cash flows are calculated consider Alpha Plc with current sales of £100 million, operating profit margin of 10 per cent and a cash tax rate of 30 per cent (Table 2.1). Management introduce a new marketing strategy to accelerate the company's growth. They believe that seven years is the longest period over which it makes sense to attempt detailed forecasts. Over this forecast period sales are predicted to grow at 12 per cent a year in money terms. The operating profit margin and tax rate are forecast to remain the same. The net operating profit after tax is usually called NOPAT.

Growth normally requires additional investment. Management estimates that *incremental net working capital* (debtors, cash and stock, less creditors) will grow at 18 per cent of sales. That is, every additional £100 in sales will require an additional £18 investment of cash in working capital. *Incremental net fixed capital investment* is defined as capital expenditures in excess of depreciation. It is net of depreciation because depreciation was deducted in calculating the operating profit. (An alternative approach that is often used is to add back depreciation to NOPAT and deduct gross investment to calculate free cash flow. This produces the identical result to deducting net investment from NOPAT.) In developing its strategy for the forecast period management will put in its own estimates for capital spending. In the example, incremental capital investment is taken to be 22 per cent of sales. The cash flow that results is shown in the table.

Table 2.1 Alpha Plc: Cash Flow Forecasts (£ million)

Year	Current	1	2	3	4	5	6	7
Sales (£ million)	100.00	112.00	125.44	140.49	157.35	176.23	197.38	221.07
Operating margin (10%)	10.00	11.20	12.54	14.05	15.74	17.62	19.74	22.11
Tax (30%)	3.00	3.36	3.76	4.21	4.72	5.29	5.92	6.63
NOPAT	7.00	7.84	8.78	9.83	11.01	12.34	13.82	15.47
Additional working capital		2.16	2.42	2.71	3.03	3.40	3.81	4.26
Additional fixed capital		2.64	2.96	3.31	3.71	4.15	4.65	5.21
Cash flow		3.04	3.40	3.81	4.27	4.78	5.36	6.00

We can summarise the determinants of cash flow (or free cash flow), then, as:

CASH IN: determined by:

1. Sales growth

2. Operating profit margin

less

CASH OUT: determined by:

3. Cash tax

4. Incremental working capital

5. Incremental fixed investment

COST OF CAPITAL

As noted earlier, it is not just the level of cash flow generated by a marketing strategy that counts but also its timing and the risks involved. To take into account the time value of money and the risks attached to different strategies, future cash flows have to be discounted by the appropriate cost of capital. The central concept of finance is that investments yielding returns greater than the cost of capital will create shareholder value, while those yielding less will decrease it. Calculating the cost of capital has to take into account that capital to finance the business comes from two sources – debt and equity. Each has a different cost so the two have to be weighted.

Calculating the *cost of the debt* component is relatively straightforward. Again, it is based on the cost of new debt not historic debt. It is also the after-tax cost that is calculated since interest on debt is tax deductible. If a company has some publicly quoted debt, for example a corporate bond, the current cost of debt can be obtained directly by looking at market prices and yield quotes. When this information is not directly available it has to be estimated. One way is to look at the yield on debt of companies in a related sector and to use a rating agency such as Moody's or Standard and Poor's to estimate a premium or discount to the published yield figure.

The second component of the cost of capital, the *cost of equity*, is more difficult to estimate. The cost of equity is that expected return which will attract investors to purchase or hold the company's shares instead of those of other companies. This expected return will vary with the specific risk attached to the company's shares. Conceptually, the cost of equity can be divided into two components: a risk-free rate and an equity risk premium. The risk-free rate is usually taken to be the return on long-term government bonds.

The equity risk premium that has to be added to this is in two parts. First, there is the general or *market* risk premium – the amount by which the average return on shares exceeds the risk-free rate. This varies considerably over time, but has averaged around 5–6 per cent. Next, there is the *specific* risk attached to the shares of a particular company. This is called the beta coefficient. If the company's shares are more volatile than the average, the beta coefficient exceeds 1.0. This means the equity risk premium will be above 5 per cent (e.g. a beta of 1.2 would mean an equity premium of 5 × 1.2 = 6 per cent). If it is less volatile, then the coefficient is less than 1.0, leading to a lower premium. Financial service companies regularly calculate these coefficients from data on past share movements and publish them for interested parties.

To illustrate, suppose a company's after-tax cost of debt is 6 per cent and its estimated cost of equity is 11.7 per cent. It plans to raise future capital, 30 per cent by way of debt and 70 per cent by new equity. Then the cost of capital is calculated as:

	Weight (%)	Cost (%)	Weighted cost (%)
Debt (after tax)	30	6.0	1.8
Equity	70	11.7	8.2
Cost of capital			10.0

CONTINUING VALUE

In estimating the value generated by a strategy the calculation is split into two parts. The first part is the value generated in the initial forecast period, and the second is the present value of cash flow after the explicit forecast period, called the continuing, terminal or residual value, i.e.

$$\text{Value} = \frac{\text{Present value of cash flow}}{\textit{during the forecast period}} + \frac{\text{Present value of cash flow}}{\textit{after the forecast period}}$$

$$= \sum_t \frac{CF_t}{(1+r)^t} + \frac{PV_t}{(1+r)^t}$$

There are two reasons for dividing it like this. One is that in the majority of industries, a seven- or eight-year forecast period is the longest period managers feel that they can sensibly put estimates of sales, costs and investments. Beyond that, the implications of changes in economic conditions, competition and technology are too uncertain to forecast, at least with any hope of precision.

The second reason is that seven or eight years is the longest period that any marketing strategy can normally expect to deliver a *differential advantage*. For many strategies the period will be much less. A strategy creates value when it produces returns that exceed the cost of capital and thereby generates positive net present value. A firm's ability to generate these above normal profits depends upon it being able to offer customers something other companies are unable to match. This 'monopolistic advantage' enables it to earn profits above those normally expected by the capital market. The source of this competitive advantage may be innovation which has given the business superior products or processes; it may be brand names which customers trust and value; or it may be the possession of licences, sunk costs or natural monopolies which restrict competitors from entry to the market.[6] But such advantages do not last. High profits attract competitors, substitutes appear, prices fall and above-normal profits fade away. The calculation of the continuing value captures this change. While in the initial forecasting period the business may earn returns above the costs of capital, after this they are assumed to fall to the market average.

The continuing value figure is very important in shareholder value analysis because it is usually larger than the value created in the forecast period. This is illustrated in Figure 2.2, where for a variety of industries, the continuing value figure represents most of the value of the average firm. This is especially the case for growth companies that are likely to generate little or no profit and free cash flow in the early years.

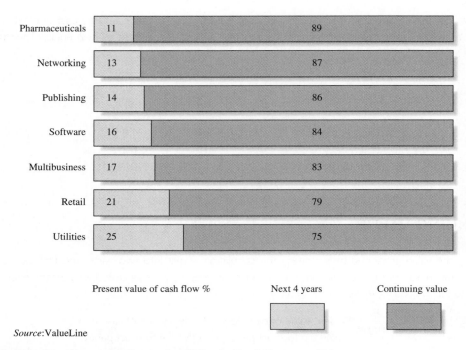

*Source:*ValueLine

Figure 2.2   The Significance of Continuing Value in Total Company Values

The concept of continuing value is very important for marketing. For companies that have identified new market opportunities, it usually makes sense to spend heavily on new product development, developing the brand and opening up new markets. In this way, they pre-empt competition and build a leading strategic position in the industry. While such strategies create value, they absorb rather than generate cash in the formative period. Aggressive marketing strategies may well lead to minimal profits and free cash flow in the early years, but simultaneously be creating enormous value, which is reflected in the high figure for continuing value, and in a rocketing share price. The continuing value reflects shareholders' recognition that in later years, perhaps five or more years ahead, the company will then start generating high free cash flow. Microsoft, Intel and Nokia are examples of companies that have followed exactly this pattern.

In contrast, companies that create high profits and free cash flow in the forecast period tend to be mature businesses or businesses where the management believes it does not have opportunities to invest, perhaps because competition is too strong. In these situations, management will be taking out costs, minimising fixed investment and reducing working capital. Here the continuing value will be small, recognising that the business's competitive position will not be worth much in the future.

Unfortunately, there is no unique method of calculating the continuing value, and different methods often produce sharply different results. The choice of method depends upon a careful judgement of the competitive strength of the business and the value of its brands at the end of the forecast or planning period. The most common method of estimating the continuing value is the *perpetuity method*. This assumes that after the forecast period, competition will drive the return the business earns down to the cost of capital. The effect of this is that further investments, even if they expand the business, do not change its *value*. As a result, future cash flows, after the forecast period, can be treated as what finance managers call a 'perpetuity' or an infinite stream of identical cash flows.

Using the perpetuity method, the present value (at the end of the forecast period) is calculated by dividing the net operating profit after tax by the cost of capital:

$$\text{Perpetuity terminal value} = \frac{\text{NOPAT}}{\text{Cost of capital}}$$

To calculate the present value of the terminal value this figure has to be discounted back over the appropriate number of years. For example, if the net operating profit at the end of a seven-year forecasting period is £8 million and the cost of capital is 10 per cent, then the perpetuity continuing value is £80 million and the present value of this continuing value is £80 million divided by $(1 + 0.1)^7$ or £41 million.

There are a variety of other methods to calculate continuing values.[7] Some companies use the *perpetuity with inflation* method. This adapts the standard perpetuity model by assuming operating profits after the forecast period grows at the rate of inflation. In periods of inflation this will give a higher estimate of the continuing value. The choice of which of the two to use depends upon whether managers believe the firm will have the ability to raise prices in the long term alongside inflation. This will depend upon industry conditions, the business's position in the market and the organisation's ability to maintain its competitiveness over the longer run.

Another common approach to estimating terminal values is the *price/earnings (P/E) ratio* method. Here one looks up the average P/E ratio for mature companies in similar types of industry and uses this to multiply net operating profit in the terminal year. For example, if the net profit was projected as £8 million in the seventh year and the average P/E was 11, the continuing value would be £88 million and its present value £45 million. An alternative is the *market-to-book (M/B) ratio* method. This calculates continuing value by multiplying the projected book value of assets by an average M/B ratio for similar companies. So if the book value of assets in the terminal year is projected to be £60 million and the average M/B ratio is 1.5, the continuing value is estimated at £90 million.

Both these methods can be criticised. Book value nowadays is a poor measure of the real value of a company's assets. Inflation and intangible assets such as patents and brands mean market values are often substantially higher. Inflation and arbitrary accounting choices also often bias earnings. Finally, in choosing ratios, finding a sample of truly similar companies is no simple task. On the other hand, calculating continuing values always depends on judgement. Essentially the purpose of value analysis is to estimate market value – to estimate what investors would pay for a business. When you can observe what they actually pay for similar companies, that is valuable evidence. P/E and M/B ratios can act as common sense checks to test the validity of more scientific methods of valuation.

ILLUSTRATION

Now that the key financial components of shareholder value analysis – cash flow from operations, cost of capital and terminal value – have been reviewed we can demonstrate the complete methodology. Table 2.2 utilises the information about projected cash flows drawn from the sales growth, operating margin, tax and capital requirements summarised in Table 2.1. The discount factor is $1/(1 + r)^t$ where r is the weighted cost of capital (10 per cent) and t is the year in question. Multiplying by this factor discounts future cash flows to their present value. The continuing value is calculated for each year using the perpetuity method. For example, the continuing value at the end of year 1 is computed as follows:

$$\frac{\text{NOPAT}}{\text{Cost of capital}} = \frac{7.84}{0.1} = £78.4 \text{ million}$$

To bring the £78.4 million back to the present value it is multiplied by the appropriate discount factor, 0.909, to obtain £71.27 million.

Table 2.2   Alpha Plc: Calculating Shareholder Value

Year	Cash flow	Discount factor	Present value	Cumulative present value	Present value of continuing value	Cumulative PV + continuing value	Shareholder value added
Base					70.00	70.00	0.00
1	3.04	0.909	2.76	2.76	71.27	74.04	4.04
2	3.40	0.826	2.81	5.58	72.57	78.15	4.11
3	3.81	0.751	2.87	8.44	73.89	82.33	4.18
4	4.27	0.683	2.92	11.36	75.23	86.59	4.26
5	4.78	0.621	2.97	14.33	76.60	90.93	4.34
6	5.36	0.564	3.02	17.35	77.99	95.35	4.42
7	6.00	0.513	3.08	20.43	79.41	99.84	4.50

Other investments	7.00
Enterprise value	106.84
Value of debt	25.00
Shareholder value	81.84

The cumulative present value of cash flows for the entire seven-year forecast period is £20.43 million. When the continuing value at the end of the period of £79.41 million is added, the total value of £99.84 million is obtained. Typically for a growth company, the terminal value is substantially higher than the value created in the forecast period.

To illustrate the distinction between enterprise and shareholder value, it is assumed that Alpha also has other investments of £7 million and debt of £25 million. The other investments are added to the total value to arrive at an enterprise value of £106.84 million. The debt is then deducted to arrive at the £81.84 million figure for shareholder value. Suppose the company has 20 million shares outstanding, and that other investments and debt were planned to remain the same over the forecast period, then the marketing strategy behind Table 2.1 would lead to a predicted rise in the implied share price from £2.60 to £4.09 per share – a pretty satisfactory performance.

Shareholder value added (SVA) in Table 2.2 provides another insight into the success of the strategy in creating value during the forecast period. Where the shareholder value figure shows the absolute economic value predicted over the forecast period, economic value added shows the *change* in value. An increase in value means that management has succeeded in making investments that earn returns above the cost of capital required by the capital market. The value added by this seven-year marketing strategy is £29.8 million. The year-by-year increase in value is calculated by the annual change in 'cumulative PV plus continuing value' totals.

Table 2.3 summarises the expected results from the proposed marketing strategy. The first column summarises the beginning or baseline value of the business – the value of the business before the marketing strategy is introduced. In the base year the business has a NOPAT of £7 million, which would capitalise it, using the perpetuity method, as worth £70 million. Adding other investments and deducting the market value of debt leads to an equity value of £52 million. The new marketing strategy anticipates faster growth and investing at returns that exceed the cost

Table 2.3 Alpha Plc: Shareholder Value Summary

(£ million)	Before strategy	With strategy
Cost of capital (%)	10	10
PV forecast cash flows	0.00	20.43
PV continuing value	70.00	79.41
Total present value	70.00	99.84
Other investments	7.00	7.00
Enterprise value	77.00	106.84
Debt	25.00	25.00
Shareholder value	52.00	81.84
Shareholder value added	0.00	29.84
Shares outstanding (m)	20	20
Implied value per share (£)	2.60	4.09

of capital. Unless there are other strategic options that lead to even higher shareholder value added, the proposed marketing strategy looks attractive to shareholders.

ECONOMIC VALUE ADDED

Currently there are two different approaches to valuation that have found favour with managers and analysts. The first is the one that has been described in the last section and is called the *cash flow* valuation method. The second approach is based on calculating economic profit, or the variant of it that consultants Stern Stewart & Company have trademarked as *Economic Value Added* (EVA®).[8] Both the cash flow and economic profit approaches are built on a common economic foundation and will lead to identical valuations for the business. But while there is no conflict between the two methods they do provide different insights. In particular, the cash flow approach is very effective for valuing different strategic options. This makes it especially useful for exploring how investments in marketing can contribute to building long-term shareholder value. EVA, on the other hand, can be useful for judging ongoing performance and determining whether current policies are creating value. In this book we will focus on the cash flow method, but managers need to be aware of the parallel economic profit approach.

The economic profit model is very intuitive. It starts, like the cash flow model, by recognising that value is created when the return on capital employed exceeds the cost of capital. This is the fundamental principle of valuation:

$$\frac{\text{Return on capital employed}}{\text{Cost of capital}} = \frac{\text{Market value}}{\text{Capital employed}}$$

In other words, investors will push up the market value of a company when it earns a return higher than they can obtain on other investments carrying similar risk, i.e. value is added where

$$ROCE > r$$

where r is the company's weighted average cost of capital. Economic profit or EVA measures the value created in a company in a single period of time. Economic profit differs from accounting profit in that it does not deduct just the interest on debt, but instead deducts a charge for all the capital employed in the business (see box, 'Calculating EVA'). From an economic viewpoint, charging for all the capital resources tied up in the business makes sense. The capital charge is arrived at by applying the company's cost of capital to the amount of capital employed in the business.

Specifically,

$$\text{Economic profit} = \text{NOPAT} - \text{Capital charge}$$

$$= \text{NOPAT} - (\text{Capital employed} \times \text{Cost of capital})$$

An alternative way to define economic profits which brings out the central importance of return on capital employed is

$$\text{Economic profit} = (\text{ROCE} - r) \times \text{Capital employed}$$

The difference between return on capital employed and the cost of capital, i.e. (ROCE–r), is called the *return spread*. Spread times the amount of capital determines economic profit. Only when the spread is positive is management creating economic value. For example, if Alpha had an initial capital of £47 million, a return on capital employed of 15 per cent and a cost of capital of 10 per cent, its economic profit or EVA for the year would be approximately £2.3 million.

Economic profit or EVA is generally used to look at current or past performance. But it can also be used, like the cash flow method, for the crucial job of valuing marketing strategies. The value of a company equals the amount of capital employed, plus a premium or discount equal to the present value of its projected economic profit:

$$\text{Value} = \text{Capital employed} + \text{Present value of projected economic profit}$$

The logic behind this formula is straightforward. If a business earned exactly its cost of capital, r, each period so that the spread was zero, then the discounted value of its projected economic profits would be zero also, and the value would equal the original capital employed. A business is worth more than its initial capital only to the extent that it earns more than its cost of capital. So the premium to capital employed must equal the present value of the company's future economic profit.

It is easy to illustrate that both the cash flow and economic profit valuation approaches give the same results. Looking first at the cash flow method, Alpha has a baseline cash flow before net investment (i.e. NOPAT) of £7 million. Using the perpetuity method, the present value of the business is then £70 million. Using the economic profit or EVA approach, the value of the business is its initial capital employed of £47 million plus the present value of its economic profit of £2.3 million:

$$\text{Present value of economic profit} = \frac{£2.3\text{ m}}{0.1} = £23\text{ m}$$

Alpha's total value then is the identical £70 million.

COMPARING CASH FLOW AND EVA

The major advantage claimed for EVA is that it can link current operating performance to value creation. Calculating economic profit demonstrates whether value has been created for that period. If the return on capital employed has exceeded the cost of capital, i.e. a positive return spread exists, economic value has been added.

By contrast, it is not easy to get a simple measure of performance for a single year from looking at cash flow. Companies can be generating great long-term value and showing declining or even negative cash flow. Many successful entrepreneurial businesses start like this. While profit growth is spectacular, the high return on capital invested encourages a rate of investment that exceeds NOPAT. Issuing new debt or equity finances the deficit cash flow. As long as returns exceed the cost of capital current shareholders will still be better off despite the dilution of their stake. Cash flow is greatly affected by discretionary investments in fixed assets and working capital. Management can easily delay investments simply to inflate cash flow. In a given year, the level of cash flow does not provide information about whether a strategy has created value; economic profit does.

Calculating EVA

Conventional accounting looks at the business from the viewpoint of its lenders rather than its shareholders. For investors, the main concern is not the company's long-run liabilities, but the cash and cash generating assets it has at its disposal.

Thus EVA adds back to the conventional profit figures various non-cash deductions such as deferred tax, goodwill amortisation and bad debt provisions. It also adds back R&D expenditure, which is taken to be not a cost but expenditure on an asset. But the most fundamental change from conventional accounting is the charge to profits of the opportunity cost of all the capital tied up in the business.

The resulting picture can be very different from that presented by traditional accounts. The calculation of EVA is illustrated below for the UK conglomerate Williams Holdings during the mid-1990s. While in conventional terms the company was highly profitable with a return on capital of 7.9 per cent, its EVA worked out as negative. When its cost of capital was taken into account the company was destroying value for shareholders.

Williams Holdings Plc	£m
Operating profit	234
Provision	(12)
Net interest	9
Cash tax	(66)
Other	13
Net return	**178**
Equity	197
Provisions	110
Convertible/Preference	304
Goodwill	1314
Gross debt	338
Capital employed	**2263**
	%
Return on capital	7.9
Cost of capital	9.6
Real return	(1.8)
	£m
EVA	**(41)**

Sources: Natwest Securities; Financial Times, 7 October 1996, p. 12.

The problem with economic profit is the arbitrariness of the calculation of capital employed and consequently of the estimation of the capital charge and the return of capital employed. The cash flow method does not require any estimates of balance sheet values, but the economic profit approach crucially depends upon them. Different companies and consultants use different assumptions in calculating capital. Some use the book value of assets; others seek to adjust to current or replacement values. Distortions arising from accounting conventions are sometimes corrected. These conventions include prudential procedures for bringing forward expected losses, deferred tax provision and other timing adjustments. Some capitalise rather than expense research and development, marketing investments and goodwill. The form of adjustments will vary between different types of business. Companies whose assets are mostly intangibles – brands, patents and contracts – will be particularly tricky. Comparisons of economic profit or EVA across companies need to be treated with considerable caution.

A consequence is that economic profit or EVA can give varying estimates of value added. However, if the focus is on year-to-year *changes* in economic profit rather than on the absolute value then the problem of measuring capital employed disappears. Change in economic profit or EVA is then identical to shareholder value added (SVA).[9] Either can be used as a performance measure.

Finally, it needs to be re-emphasised that *looking at a single year is dangerous.*

Value creation is a long-term phenomenon. High cash flow, high SVA or high economic profit in a single year can easily mask declining long-run competitiveness. It is easy to boost all three in the short-term by cutting back on long-term investment and marketing support. But such actions will result in a decline in the continuing value of the business and eventually in the share price. To determine whether a strategy makes sense, long-term cash flow or economic profits have to be estimated and discounted by the cost of capital to get a true valuation.

FINANCIAL VALUE DRIVERS

We now look at how marketing affects the financial value drivers that determine shareholder value. The NPV formula shows that four operating factors determine shareholder value. Marketing crucially influences each of them:

1. *Anticipated level of operating cash flow.* The greater the future free cash flow anticipated, the more will be available for distribution to shareholders and the greater the market value of the business.

2. *Anticipated timing of cash flow.* Because cash received today is worth more than cash received tomorrow, the speed with which markets are penetrated and cash flow generated positively influences value. This is taken into account through the use of a discount rate.

3. *Anticipated sustainability of the cash flow.* The more lasting the cash flow, the greater the value created. This depends upon the durability of the firm's differential advantage and the perceived growth options it has available. The long-term ability to sustain positive free cash flow should be reflected in the firm's continuing value figure.

4. *Anticipated riskiness of future cash flow.* The greater the perceived volatility and vulnerability of the firm's cash flow, the higher the cost of capital used to discount the return. More predictable cash flows have a higher value.

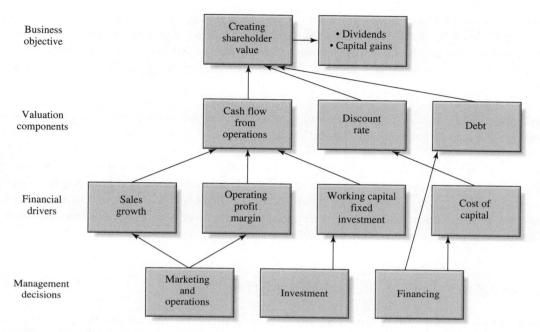

Figure 2.3   Financial Drivers of Shareholder Value

LEVEL OF OPERATING CASH FLOW

The most fundamental determinant of shareholder value is the anticipated level of free cash flow. Three core financial drivers determine this: sales growth, the net operating profit margin after tax (NOPAT) and the level of investment. Figure 2.3 shows how these determine shareholder value added. These govern cash flow which, when discounted by the cost of capital, give the estimated value of the business. Marketing critically influences each of these three financial value drivers.

SALES GROWTH

The most important way of increasing the level of cash flow and shareholder value is via sales growth. After all, additional cash flow is simply growth less the additional cost and investment to achieve it, i.e.

Additional cash flow = Sales growth − Added(Costs + Investment)

As long as the added sales are profitable, and do not require disproportionate investment, cash flow rises. Of course, it is possible in the short run to increase cash flow without growth, by cutting costs and investment. But such policies are one-off and will often lead to a decline in cash flow in the years ahead. Investors usually see through such policies in their valuations of companies.

Growth brings other benefits. Often it enables the business to gain economies of scale. This means it will be able to lower unit costs and increase the utilisation of its investment, further increasing cash flow. In a new market it may well pay to invest in growth even though the business is not yet profitable and additional sales do not increase cash flow. In many of today's growth markets it is important to obtain a critical mass of customers to achieve profitability. Unless it has critical mass, the business may not have the level of sales to secure adequate distribution or to spread its overheads over a sufficient volume to have a viable unit cost structure. Again, whether this type of market penetration strategy makes sense depends upon carefully forecasting cash flows over a long period ahead.

Growing companies also make it easier to attract and retain staff. Able people know that growing companies offer more security and opportunities for advancement.

How to build successful growth strategies is the subject of Chapter 6. Successful growth strategies depend upon building marketing assets. These intangible assets include marketing expertise inside the business that provides the knowledge base to recognise growth opportunities. They also include brands that customers have confidence in. Loyal customers are additional marketing assets that facilitate higher growth. Finally, strategic partnerships with other businesses enhance growth opportunities by providing additional resources and growth ideas.

NET OPERATING PROFIT MARGIN AFTER TAX

The amount generated for net investment and dividends is not determined by sales growth alone but rather by the balance after costs have been deducted. The net operating profit margin after tax (NOPAT) measures this relationship. Improving NOPAT has a crucial impact on shareholder value. There are three ways in which marketing can improve the operating margin:

1.   **Higher prices.** If the Beta Company has a NOPAT of 7 per cent, then if it could improve its average prices by as little as 5 per cent without losing volume, after-tax profits would rise by 50 per cent.[10] Even if it lost 5 per cent of its volume to competition as a result of this price increase, NOPAT would still increase by 20 per cent.[11] In Chapter 8 we will explore a variety of marketing strategies for raising prices without losing significant volume. These include developing strong brands, demonstrating value to customers, segmenting customers by price sensitivity, multibranding and creating exit barriers. But by far the most effective marketing strategy in the long run is innovation – developing new products and services which meet customer needs better than the alternatives currently on the market.

2.   **Cost decreases.** With global competition and increasing information available to customers, all companies are aware of the importance of becoming low-cost suppliers. With most businesses having pre-tax operating margins of 10 per cent or less, small cost cuts have disproportionate effects on the bottom line. Today's efforts to cut costs include improved approaches to more effective supply-chain management, business process reengineering, outsourcing and the more effective use of marketing resources.[12]

3.   **Volume growth.** Volume growth tends to improve the operating margin because overhead costs do not increase proportionately. In the short run the effect can be very big. For example, suppose a company with spare capacity increases sales by 30 per cent. If half its costs were variable – bought in materials, components and variable labour, then a current NOPAT of 7 per cent would be doubled to 14 per cent.[13] Over the long run, however, most costs are variable to a greater or lesser extent: capacity has to be increased, marketing and administrative overheads rise and the business needs to spend more on R&D to support its broader line of business. Nevertheless, the effect of market-led growth on the operating margin is generally positive. While bigger companies do have higher overheads in absolute terms, as a percentage of sales overheads are usually lower. Economies of scale normally occur across a broad area of costs.

INVESTMENT

Managers invest in tangible assets like equipment and stocks, and also in intangible assets such as brands, customer relationships, market research and training. Reducing investment produces an immediate jump in cash flow. But in the long run, such actions can be extremely counterproductive. The purpose of investment is to increase long-run growth and cash flow. The golden rule is that investment creates value if the net present value of the cash flow is positive. Or, expressing it in equivalent economic profit terms, investment creates value if the return on the investment exceeds the cost of capital.

As long as the return on new investment exceeds the cost of capital, investment increases shareholder value. This is illustrated in Table 2.4. Here a company earns a return on new investment of 20 per cent. Under the first scenario it invests 25 per cent of its profits; under the second it invests 35 per cent. With the conservative investment strategy, it has a higher cash flow over the first 8 years, and, indeed, over the whole of the 10-year planning period, the present value of the forecast cash flow is greater. Under the high-investment strategy, however, annual cash flow overtakes in year 9, and then the lead continually widens. For the reader who cares to work out the result on a spreadsheet, assuming an 11 per cent cost of capital, the high investment strategy generates a significantly greater shareholder value. This is reflected in the greater continuing value figure in year 10.[14]

Managers need to avoid wasteful investment in both tangible and intangible assets. However, as the example illustrates, not investing sufficiently in profitable marketing opportunities is equally value destroying.

The *threshold margin* is a useful tool for marketing managers. It shows the relationshhip between the three drivers of cash flow: growth, margin and investment requirements. The threshold margin is the pre-tax operating profit margin necessary to finance value-creating growth. It is the minimum pre-tax operating profit margin on additional sales necessary to maintain shareholder value. It is calculated as:[15]

$$\text{Threshold margin} = \frac{(\text{Incremental investment rate}) \times (\text{Cost of capital})}{(1 + \text{Cost of capital})(1 - \text{tax rate})}$$

Table 2.4 Cash Flow Projections with High and Low Investment Levels

Year	25% Investment rate			35% Investment rate		
	NOPAT	Investment	Cash Flow	NOPAT	Investment	Cash flow
1	100.0	25.0	75.0	100.0	35.0	65.0
2	105.0	26.3	78.8	107.0	37.5	69.6
3	110.3	27.6	82.7	114.5	40.1	74.4
4	115.8	28.9	86.8	122.5	42.9	79.6
5	121.6	30.4	91.2	131.1	45.9	85.2
6	127.6	31.9	95.7	140.3	49.1	91.2
7	134.0	33.5	100.5	150.1	52.5	97.5
8	140.7	35.2	105.5	160.6	56.2	104.4
9	147.7	36.9	110.8	171.8	60.1	111.7
10	155.1	38.8	116.3	183.8	64.3	119.5

Using the example of the Alpha company, the incremental investment rate totals 40 per cent, the cost of capital is 10 per cent and the tax rate is 30 per cent. Substituting into the formula gives:

$$\text{Threshold margin} = \frac{40\% \times 10\%}{1.1 \times 0.7} = 5.2\%$$

If the additional growth marketing is planning to generate gives an operating margin of over 5.2 per cent, then value is created. The threshold margin depends on the additional working and fixed capital necessary to finance growth, the cost of capital and the tax rate. The higher these are, the higher the margin that is required on additional sales.

This is illustrated below:

Threshold Margins for Varying Rates of Investment and Costs of Capital

Incremental investment per £ of sales (%)

Cost of capital (%)	30	40	50	60
8	3.2	4.2	5.3	6.3
10	3.9	5.2	6.5	7.8
12	4.6	6.1	7.7	9.2

In Alpha's case, since managers believe they can get an operating margin of 10 per cent, then value is clearly going to be created. The difference between actual (or expected) margin and threshold margin is called the *threshold spread*. In the Alpha illustration the spread is 4.8 per cent. The size of the threshold margin is a key determinant of value creation. More specifically, the value created by a strategy (SVA) in a given period *t*, is given by the following equation:

$$\frac{\text{Shareholder value}}{\text{added (SVA)}} = \frac{(\text{Incremental sales in period } t)\,(\text{Threshold spread in } t)\,(1 - \text{tax rate})}{(\text{Cost of capital})\,(1 + \text{Cost of capital})^{t-1}}$$

For example, using the above equation on Alpha for year 2 we have

$$\text{SVA} = \frac{£13.44 \times 4.8\% \times (1 - 0.30)}{0.1 \times (1 + 0.1)^1} = £4.11 \text{ million}$$

This is exactly the same figure as calculated earlier using the cash flow method (Table 2.2).

TIMING OF OPERATING CASH FLOW

Besides the amount of cash flow a marketing strategy generates, its timing also affects the value that is created. For example, if the cost of capital is 10 per cent, £10 million free cash flow received at the end of the first year of a product's launch has a value of £9.09 million; if it is not received until year 3, the value is only £7.51 million. Marketing strategies to accelerate cash flow therefore create shareholder value. There are several ways marketing can accelerate cash flow:

○ **Faster new product development.** *Many companies are redesigning their new product development processes to reduce the time from initial idea to final launch. Methods include using cross-functional teams, conducting development processes in parallel rather than in series, and cutting out unnecessary steps.*[16]

○ Accelerate market penetration. *Once a product is launched it needs to gain quick market acceptance. Marketing can speed up this process through the skilful use of pre-marketing campaigns, promotions to gain early trial, and leveraging the early adopters to obtain word-of-mouth advertising.*

○ Creating network effects. *Many new products can gain from network externalities. The bigger the installed base (achieved or expected), the more desirable the product often becomes. Customers want products that will be standard in the market. For example, Sony's Blu-ray DVD format won the battle against Toshiba's HD DVD technology when it launched the PlayStation3 in 2006, which also functioned as a Blu-ray Disc player. Marketing can leverage network effects by such strategies as licensing and aggressively building the installed base.*

○ Using strategic alliances. *Alliances can speed up market penetration by giving access to additional distribution. For example, US fast food chains Subway and McDonald's both have restaurants in different Wal-Mart stores. Alliances are particularly important in allowing companies to penetrate international markets more rapidly.*

○ Leveraging brand assets. *There is evidence that consumers respond faster to marketing activities when they trust the brand. They are more willing to try new products under the umbrella of a familiar brand and they respond more to the advertising and promotions of familiar brands.*

SUSTAINABILITY OF CASH FLOW

The third determinant of value is the anticipated sustainability of the cash flow. This determines the assumptions used to calculate the continuing value of a marketing strategy. Some products are fads, achieving rapid prominence but then disappearing after a few seasons. They fail to create continuing value because of changes in fashion, new competitors or substitute products. On the other hand, some brands, like Mercedes, Coca-Cola or Nescafé, last for generations. The share prices of the companies that own these brands reflect their high continuing values. Two factors affect the duration of the business's cash flow: the sustainability of its differential advantage and the options it creates.

Many companies come up with products or services that have a differential advantage, but do not succeed in creating enduring cash flow because the advantage is not sustainable. It is quickly copied by competitors, substitutes appear, or strong buyers use their power to squeeze the supplier's margins. A key task of marketing is to build barriers that enhance the sustainability of the differential advantage. Superior marketing expertise allows managers to track customers' needs and customer satisfaction, and then to build new sources of value for them. High customer satisfaction increases customer retention and loyalty, which are the most effective means of creating enduring cash flow. Later chapters will discuss how brand-building investments add layers of emotional values and confidence to the product, which make it more difficult for competitors to erode the customer franchise.

Investors' perception of the sustainability of cash flow is also affected by the options they believe the company possesses. Options are opportunities to enter new markets in the future. Investors may perceive options being created by technical research and development that the company is undertaking. This explains the high valuations attached to some biotechnology stocks. Options may also be seen in marketing ventures that the company is exploring in high growth markets. A loyal customer base also offers valuable options because such customers are also likely to be willing to try new products that the company may launch in the future. Of particular importance are strong brand names. Trusted brand names such as Virgin and Disney have been shown to offer options because they can be extended to cover different product areas to offer new growth opportunities. Nokia's share price has, over time, reflected not just its continued leadership in mobile phone handsets but also investors' beliefs that it is well positioned in the market for mobile Internet services. Companies that lack these marketing assets have future cash flows that are perceived to be less sustainable.

THE RISK ATTACHED TO CASH FLOW

The fourth factor determining value is the risk attached to forecasting future cash flows. Cash flows that are seen as particularly difficult to predict because of the volatility and vulnerability of the market in which the business is operating are penalised by a higher discount rate. Investors expect bigger rewards for investing in risky ventures than safe ones.

By reducing the volatility of the firm's cash flow, marketing can cut the firm's cost of capital and add value. The most effective way to reduce the volatility and vulnerability of a firm's cash flow is to increase customer satisfaction, loyalty and retention. High customer satisfaction and loyalty reduce the vulnerability of the business to attack from competitors. As we see in the next chapter, this also makes costs and investments more predictable. Loyal customers have lower and more foreseeable servicing costs. A high retention rate also means that less needs to be spent in chasing new customers.

Marketing has a portfolio of policies to increase customer satisfaction and loyalty. These include market research, initiatives to improve customer service and loyalty programmes. Chapter 3 shows how the effects of these initiatives on shareholder value can be measured. Programmes to build channel partnerships also reduce the volatility of cash flow. Sharing information with distributors and suppliers can reduce unpredictable fluctuations in requirements, reduce stocks and lead to more predictable costs and investments.

MARKETING VALUE DRIVERS

Shareholder value and its financial value drivers are the objectives of business but they are not the strategy. It is a big mistake to target these measures directly; instead managers need a strategy on how to influence them.

For example, in principle, raising prices increases the threshold margin spread. But if a company simply announces a 10 per cent price increase, it is likely to lose customers fast. Losing market share will erode profits, allow in new competitors and could fatally erode the long-term competitiveness of the business. Improving average prices and margins has to be achieved through a marketing strategy that might well include targeting different types of customer, introducing new products and changing the mode of distribution. Similarly, raising the return on capital employed is an objective, not a strategy. Achieving it requires a fundamental rethink about the effectiveness of how the company approaches the market. Simply targeting to cut capital employed will be counterproductive. It would be likely to lead to declining efficiency, eroding service levels and missed opportunities.

Marketing strategy lies at the heart of value creation. It is the platform on which are based growth, profitability and return on investment. Marketing strategy defines the choices about which customers the business will serve and how it will create customer preference. By targeting appropriate markets and creating a differential advantage the firm gains the opportunity to grow and create the margin spread that is the basis for value creation. If the firm is locked into markets where there are no opportunities to grow and if it lacks a differential advantage, no amount of financial engineering will create value for investors.

The main elements of marketing strategy can be summarised in four steps. The first step is taken at the group level; the other three are formulated at the level of the business unit.

CHOICE OF MARKETS

Most companies operate a portfolio of businesses – different industry sectors, technologies, countries or distribution channels. At the corporate level, the board has to decide which of these businesses it wants to be in and what priority they should have. Some of its business units may be in markets that do not have the potential to provide opportunities for growth or earn operating margins that exceed the threshold level. Others may offer tremendous opportunities but are not receiving sufficient investment and priority.

The mistake of many financially driven companies is to make this review static rather than dynamic. A static review focuses on the current profitability of the business units rather than their ability to create long-term value. Management must understand the need for continual change and evolution in today's rapidly changing environment. If the company is to survive it must move into new products, technologies, markets and distribution channels. To create value it must structure its portfolio dynamically. This means building a portfolio of three types of business units (Figure 2.4).

1. **Today's businesses.** These are the core business units that should be generating the bulk of today's profits and cash flow. Usually they have only modest growth potential left. The management goals will be high levels of current profitability and cash flow. The strategy is to extend and defend the core businesses through incremental extension, updating and cost reduction. Those businesses that are not generating economic profit should be quickly fixed or divested.

2. **Tomorrow's businesses.** These are the company's emerging stars: new businesses that are already demonstrating their ability to win profitable customers and grow. The success of these businesses is likely to be already having a major impact on the share price as investors recognise their long-term cash generating potential. The task here is to invest in the marketing infrastructure to capture and defend the market opportunities against competitors.

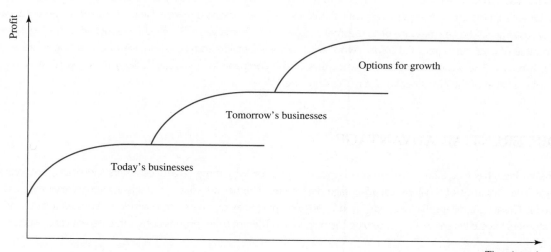

Figure 2.4 Building the Sustainable Business

3.   **Options for growth.** These are investments that seed tomorrow's businesses. These are market trials, prototypes, research projects, alliances or minority stakes that the firm undertakes to explore the market feasibility of new ideas. Many will fail, but without a bundle of options being continually explored, long-term growth will certainly stall. The task of management here is to decide which of the options to pursue, based upon their estimates of the profit potential of the opportunities and the probability of success.

Eventually a company needs businesses in all three categories. If it only has strong core businesses, then its current profitability and cash flow will be excellent, but its share price will disappoint because investors recognise the lack of long-term potential. On the other hand, if it does not have a strong core and only new businesses and options, management will lack credibility in their ability to extract value from the opportunities. The function of the board is first to weed out those businesses that fail to fit into any of these categories. Second, it needs to clarify to the unit managers where they fit in the portfolio, what their strategic objectives should be, and on what measures they will be judged. Third, it needs to identify the scope for synergies among the businesses. Can value be added by sharing technology, brand names, distribution systems or common services?

TARGET MARKET SEGMENTATION

The strategic objectives of the business units are set at the group level, but the marketing plans to achieve them have to be developed at the unit level. The basic marketing question is: what customers does the business want to serve? Targeting the right customers is fundamental to value creation. Research has shown that when the full costs of supporting customers is taken into account, the majority of customers are not profitable at all! Most companies make a loss on serving the majority of their customers.[17] The mistake is not being selective enough in seeking growth. It is invariably better to invest in developing long-term loyalty from a smaller number of high-value accounts than seeking to net everybody and anybody.

Customers that will enable the business to create long-term value meet four criteria. First, they should be *strategic* – the needs of the customers should match the company's core capabilities, so that it has the basis for creating a competitive advantage. Second, they should be *significant* – they should have the size or growth potential to have a substantial impact on the business's total revenue. Third, they should be *profitable* – after deducting all customer-support costs the operating profit should exceed the threshold margin. Finally, they should be potentially *loyal* customers. The key measure of a customer's value is the lifetime value. Research in recent years has highlighted the value of loyal customers. Customers who switch among suppliers to take advantage of current deals are rarely worth having. The value of a customer who stays with a company for ten years is likely to be worth at least 50 times the value of the customer who stays for only one.[18]

DIFFERENTIAL ADVANTAGE

The business has to create a differential advantage – a reason why these target customers should buy and remain loyal. The existence of a differential advantage determines whether a business sustains a return above the cost of capital. Creating a differential depends upon having competencies or assets not available to competitors. Different customers have different wants, so serving them requires different value propositions and different capabilities.

In most consumer or business markets there are four types of customers. Some want the latest, state-of-art products or services. Fashion or the desire for the most up-to-date technology drives their wants. Another segment buys primarily on the basis of low price and convenience. Quality might be important but they are unwilling to pay premium prices. Customers in a third segment want to express themselves through their purchases or want the assurance that brands provide. Finally, some are willing to pay more for a customised service that understands their specific wants and is willing to tailor-make solutions.

Each segment requires a different type of differential advantage and set of competencies to operationalise it. Differentiation for the first segment needs to be based on *product leadership*. Such companies as Apple, Intel and 3M have shown how capabilities in innovation and speed to market can deliver high margin growth. On the other hand, if a business is going to compete by offering low prices and customer convenience it has to differentiate itself by *operational excellence*. Such companies as Toyota, Wal-Mart and First Direct have shown that this depends on high levels of efficiency in processes that drive down costs, reduce investment requirements and tightly manage the supply chain. Differentiation in the third segment depends upon building *brand superiority* — creating emotional values that competitors cannot match. Companies such as Coca-Cola, Disney, Procter & Gamble and Virgin have shown the power of this type of strategy to generate shareholder value. Here the competencies lie in marketing research and strong and consistent communications.

Perhaps the fastest growing segment in today's information age is those customers wanting customised service. Information technology makes it possible to store data on the needs and buying behaviour of individual customers and to communicate directly on a one-to-one basis. New technology in production also makes it possible to tailor-manufacture products. Here the differentiation strategy is termed *customer intimacy*.[19] Profits and growth come from building loyalty through long-term, in-depth relationships aimed at improving the customer's performance and satisfaction levels.

Businesses have to focus on one differentiation strategy because each requires different competencies and operational processes. The appropriate value proposition is the one that matches the needs of the target customer segment. Yet, while the business must excel in one dimension to create a differential advantage, the others cannot be neglected. Customers today are increasingly demanding. They are conditioned to expect competitive prices, faster service and more innovative products. For example, while customers will not expect the same levels of technology or service from a price-orientated supplier as they would from a premium company, they do expect reasonable standards in these other dimensions. Rising customer expectations also mean that what is a great offer today will not be tomorrow. To sustain a successful position the business must be continually improving its business model faster than the competition.

MARKETING MIX

The marketing mix is the set of operating decisions that the firm makes to gain and retain target customers and pursue its differential advantage. It is often called the four, or five, Ps. The first P refers to the *products* the firm will offer. This includes decisions about the variety of products, brand names, quality, design, packaging and guarantees. *People* refers to the service and support the firm offers customers. *Price* concerns not only decisions about the list price but also discounts, allowances and credit terms. *Promotion* concerns advertising, sales force, direct marketing, web sites, PR and sales promotions. *Place* refers to how the firm distributes its offer, and includes choices about channels, coverage, locations, transport and stock levels.

The key point about the marketing mix is that all the decisions are derived from earlier choices about strategic objectives, target customers and the differential advantage. For example, if the business unit is targeted for rapid growth, management may be more aggressive in pricing and invest more in product variety, promotion and distribution. It may be prepared to sacrifice near-term cash flow for market share gains. The reverse will be the orientation for a mature business where current profitability and cash flow are the objectives. The target customers and differential advantage also shape decisions. Distribution and promotional decisions are governed by the characteristics and usage patterns of customers. The business will want to sell through distribution channels that fit the customer and promote through vehicles that they will use. Similarly, the differential advantage is the primary determinant of the opportunity to gain premium prices. In competitive markets, the firm will only be able to charge higher prices if customers believe its offer to be significantly better value than those of competitors.

ORGANISATIONAL VALUE DRIVERS

Achieving the objective of creating shareholder value requires a strategy – choosing high-value customers, formulating a differential advantage and planning an appropriate marketing mix. But it also requires the right organisation – having the capabilities and culture to operationalise the strategy. In most situations organisational capabilities and culture are more important than strategy. Looking at successful and less successful competitors in an industry at certain times – for example, Sony and Philips; Google and Yahoo!; BMW and Jaguar; Coca-Cola and Pepsi; Disney and Columbia – the real differences are not in their strategy but in how they have implemented it.

Delivering strategy depends upon the *core competencies* of the business. Core competencies comprise a set of skills and expertise that enable a business to deliver exceptional value to customers. Sony's product leadership in consumer electronics is based on its early mastery in miniaturisation. Google's leadership in search engine technology is based on its initial understanding of how to rank findings according to relevance. Singapore Airlines' success in service is based on skills in selecting, training and motivating staff. Toyota's success with low-cost, high-quality cars is based on its operational excellence in supply chain management and manufacturing. But it is more than just competencies that determine whether a business generates value – it is also about the *culture and attitudes* of people in the organisation. These determine whether competencies are applied appropriately.

IBM in the 1980s, for example, had outstanding competencies. It was at the forefront of computer technology, it had brilliant staff across all areas of the business, and had exceptional access to major customers. But it lacked the organisational drive to adapt to a changing environment and to deliver value to shareholders. The result was a collapse in its market share and in its share price.

The right form of organisation varies by market and over time. Competing successfully in high-value services such as management consultancy requires different capabilities and culture from basic industries such as steel or commodity chemicals. The former is about customised service and an intimate knowledge partnership between client and consultant; the latter is about organising to minimise production cost and meet delivery requirements.

In the past, major companies such as General Motors, Unilever, Siemens and Shell were about mass production and mass marketing. There was a high level of vertical integration from raw material to final distribution. Companies were organised hierarchically with information going up and head office decisions coming down. Employees were specialists; they worked in production, design or sales and interacted vertically with their boss or with their subordinates. This type of hierarchical structure was seen as the best way of harnessing economies of scale and expertise in the company.

The information age has changed all this. Intensifying global competition has forced companies to reshape their organisations to cut overhead costs and to provide for faster response to changes in market requirements. Rising customer expectations have led to an increasing demand for customised solutions rather than mass-produced products. Information technology has facilitated much faster and more direct ways of interacting among staff sharing responsibility for meeting customer needs. Finally, professional knowledge rather than capital resource has become the key source of competitive advantage. Unlike capital, knowledge is diffused throughout the organisation in the information individuals and groups have of technology, processes, supplier capabilities and customers' needs. Attracting, retaining and motivating knowledge workers is now recognised as much more difficult than utilising financial and physical capital.

INTERNAL NETWORKS

Increasingly, information-age companies are shifting from vertical hierarchies to horizontal, cross-functional teams. These teams have responsibility not for functional inputs, but for the key processes that add value for customers. Typically these processes are about new product development, operations, and customer service and support. Employees no longer communicate through formal hierarchies but use multiple, informal networks to connect with others who have knowledge which may be valuable to the process. Properly used, these internal networks cut overheads, speed processes and motivate knowledge workers by giving them responsibility and trust.

EXTERNAL NETWORKS

External networks have grown in importance alongside internal ones. The increasing need for knowledge about new products, new markets and new processes and for combining different technologies makes it difficult for organisations, however sophisticated, to operate autonomously. Networks – alliances, partnerships, joint ventures and outsourcing – have become the way to harness the disparate range of expertise and economic resources necessary to compete in today's changing markets. Many of today's fast-moving companies see the entrepreneurial task as being two-fold. First, they have to identify emerging opportunities in the market; second, they have to put together a network of companies with the collective set of capabilities to capitalise on the opportunity.

In the past companies aimed at vertical integration – performing for themselves as many of the processes as possible from raw material supply to final delivery. Networks, however, allow companies to unbundle their business and focus only on those particular activities where they have unique capabilities to add value. Increasingly, competition is not between individual companies but between networks.

THE 7-S FRAMEWORK

One of the most useful ways of auditing the effectiveness of the company's organisational value drivers is the 7-S framework developed by the McKinsey consulting firm (Figure 2.5).[20] The firm's analysis suggests that these drivers are essential for long-term performance. At the heart of the successful organisation is a set of *shared values* or vision that unites, challenges and gives direction to all the people working there. At British Airways it used to be to create 'the world's favourite airline'. Under the dynamic leadership of Lord King, the whole organisation was motivated to achieving this goal. Under subsequent, more financially-driven management, British Airways has become a much-maligned airline. Shared values are not financial goals but the motivational drivers that make the former achievable.

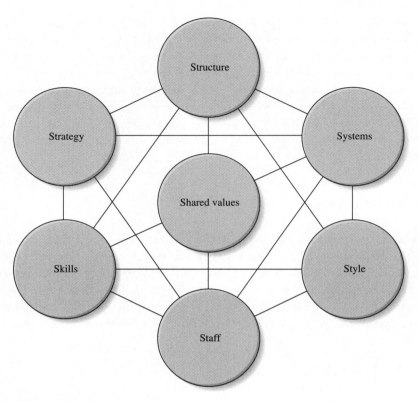

Figure 2.5　The McKinsey 7-S Framework

Statements of shared values are meaningless unless they are supported by other drivers that operationise them. The first of these is a *strategy*. Strategy has to be customer-led: a deep recognition, throughout the company, that achieving the vision depends on meeting the needs of customers more effectively than competitors. Primacy has to be given to listening to customers, understanding their operating processes and focusing on finding new ways to add value for them. *Structure* refers to how people are organised to work together. Today the emphasis is on empowerment, reducing functional barriers, delayering and encouraging knowledge workers to network widely. *Systems* refer to how information moves around the organisation and its network partners. Information technology which links customers, distributors and supply-chain partners has become a major source of advantage for companies like Dell, Wal-Mart or First Direct that use it to take out costs and achieve outstanding customer responsiveness.

Staff concerns the background and culture of people who work for the organisation. Successful companies generally attract and socialise staff so that they are relatively similar in attitudes. They share a common outlook that also reflects the company's values. Goldman Sachs attracts hyper-ambitious MBAs from the top business schools; Hewlett-Packard has an engineering culture; Abbott Mead Vickers BBDO attracts creative types. *Skills* are the distinctive capabilities that the people possess and which are the basis for the firm's ability to create a differential advantage. For example, Hewlett-Packard possesses outstanding skills in measurement and computing; Sharp in flat-screen technologies; 3M in adhesives and substrates; Procter & Gamble in branding. *Style* refers to the behaviour of top management and, in particular, how effectively they communicate the values and priorities of the organisation.

The 7-S diagram emphasises the interdependence of the organisational value drivers. An inspiring vision is valueless unless the organisation has the strategy, skills, systems and motivated staff to back it up. Similarly, outstanding skills are not enough unless the structure empowers people to make decisions, the strategy is geared to applying the skills to what customers want, and the systems can deliver fast, cost-effective solutions.

MARKETING APPLICATIONS OF SHAREHOLDER VALUE

The following chapters look in detail at how marketing and organisational strategies can be used to generate value for shareholders. But at this point it may be useful to highlight some examples of, first, how marketing strategies are essential for creating value and, second, how shareholder value analysis can be used to demonstrate to the board the contribution of marketing.

PORTFOLIO ANALYSIS

Strategy formulation starts with a company reviewing the prospects for its business units. Typically a business unit will be responsible for a market or product group. The board will want to ask which businesses have prospects for generating shareholder value and which do not. The former will be prioritised; the latter should be turned around or disposed of.

A popular approach to evaluating current unit performance is looking at whether the return on capital employed exceeds the unit's cost of capital, or equivalently whether it is making an economic profit. For example, suppose there are two business units, A and B each with £100 million of invested capital and the same cost of capital, 10 per cent. Suppose A makes an after-tax return on capital of 12 per cent and B 9 per cent. Then A makes a positive economic profit or EVA of £2 million and B makes an economic loss of £1 million.

The problem with ranking business units like this is that return on capital and EVA only measures current performance. They do not look at *future* returns and it is these that determine how investors value a business. Value is determined by discounting future cash flows, or equivalently, future economic profits, by the cost of capital. When this is done the rankings can look quite different. The first step requires unit managers to develop long-term strategies for their businesses and to forecast the resulting sales, operating margin and investment requirement over the planning period. The next step is for the board to evaluate whether the managers' forecasts match the

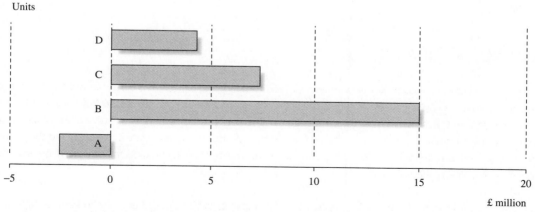

Figure 2.6   Economic Value Added by Business Unit

economic characteristics of the market. Do the assumptions make sense, given the likely growth of the market, the strategies of competitors and the power of customers to pressure margins?

Then once the strategies and cash flow forecasts have been agreed, the shareholder value added can be calculated and compared across business units as below. Here A turns out to add much less value than B, because A's market is rapidly commoditising and it faces losses in share and eroding margins. On the other hand, B's margins are expected to improve as it outsources production offshore and invests more in its brand. The result is that unit A's value is projected to actually erode by £2.5 million over the period, while units B, C and D add significant shareholder value. In contrast to what the original return on capital comparisons appeared to show, A rather than B is the problem unit.

EVALUATING REPOSITIONING STRATEGIES

In today's rapidly changing environment companies have to change strategy if they are to survive. Old concepts eventually become obsolete as consumer tastes change, new technologies appear and new competition enters the market. Marketing typically generates the new ideas, which are then evaluated in terms of their sales and profit potential. Shareholder value analysis provides a better approach that mirrors the way investors look at the options. Consider the following example:

> A chain of confectionery shops was considering changing its traditional format to a new 'continental' concept. A coffee bar would be added to most of the shops and a broader range of up-market gifts would be sold. From tests over the past year, the marketing department was projecting the new format would boost the group's sales growth from the current 5 per cent a year to at least 6 per cent and the operating profit margin would increase from 8 to 10 per cent. The marketing director believed that, since average store profits would rise by over 20 per cent – from £50 000 to over £60 000 per store – they should clearly go ahead.

> However, what he ignored was that the new concept had significantly higher investment requirements. The new concept demanded increased fixed capital needs to finance the new store designs. In addition, there were higher working capital requirements due to slower stock turnover and the suppliers of the new branded products demanding quicker repayment. As a result, while profits were higher over the planning period with the new concept, cash flow was lower. Worse, because demand for up-market products was more volatile than for the traditional lines, the cost of capital for the new format was up from 10 to 11 per cent. The result was that the traditional format generated almost 10 per cent more shareholder value than the new concept.

VALUING BRANDS

For many companies, such as Procter & Gamble, Unilever, Cadbury and Diageo, it is clear that most of their market value derives from the earning power of their brands. Brands are enormously valuable assets but they do not appear on the balance sheet. Besides giving a truer reflection of the size of a company's assets, there are other reasons for valuing brands. Brands are sometimes sold and are frequently licensed to associate companies and third parties. Management need to monitor whether their brands are increasing or declining in value and to determine how much to spend on supporting them.

There are various approaches to valuing brands. Some companies have valued them on the basis of how much they cost to create. But, as with most assets, current values are not related to historical expenditures. Another approach is based on estimating the royalty rate that would have to be paid if the company had to license the brand. Unfortunately, detailed royalty rates are not easily obtainable. The approach that is now increasingly used is the standard shareholder value approach. The brand value is calculated by discounting back to the net present value excess net earnings attributable to the brand.

This involves three steps. First, free cash flow is projected for a 5–10-year forecast period. Second, the percentage of this cash flow that can be attributed to the brand is estimated. Third, this brand cash flow is then discounted by the cost of capital, to give the value of the brand.[21]

EVALUATING ADVERTISING EFFECTIVENESS

Advertising agencies and brand managers tend to justify the effectiveness of advertising by looking at changes in awareness or attitudes to the brand. But to financially orientated board members there is little connection between these qualitative measures and the share price. They are unconvinced by arguments saying that advertising is necessary or that postponing or reducing it will do harm.

Accountants often challenge marketing management to justify advertising by showing how it increases profits in the budget for next year. But this is a trap marketing needs to avoid. Advertising rarely increases short-term profits. Indeed, cutting advertising generally increases profits in the short-run. Brand-building advertising is an investment and, as with any investment, its effectiveness should be based on whether it increases long-term discounted cash flow or economic profits.

To do this marketing needs to identify the effects of advertising on sales over the planning period. After-tax cash flow or economic profits have then got to be discounted to their present value. Whether value is created is then determined by comparing the shareholder value with and without advertising. Let us look at an actual example.[22]

Between 1996 and 1998 Orange Plc, a new UK mobile phone operator, spent £44 million on brand-orientated advertising. To estimate its effect on shareholder value, the first task was to estimate the impact of the advertising on sales over the planning period. Revenue growth in telecoms is a function of the number of subscribers attracted, the number retained from year to year, and the average amount spent. An econometric model was used to isolate the effect of advertising on these variables from the other factors affecting them, such as distribution, competitive activity, price, and seasonal and market trends. Cash flow for each year and the continuing value were then projected and discounted by the cost of capital.

The results are summarised in Table 2.5 (on page 68). Shareholder value was estimated to have increased by nearly £3 billion as a result of the advertising strategy and the implied share price almost doubled. Faced with such a comprehensive case, and presented in the same format as investors employ to evaluate strategy, the case for the effectiveness of the advertising campaign was hard to resist and the principles it illustrates still resonate.

ACQUISITIONS

The past decade has seen an enormous growth in the number of acquisitions. These have been triggered by deregulation, excess capacity in many industries and the drive to achieve global economies of scale. But making an acquisition can be a gamble and the evidence suggests that most acquisitions fail to add value for the acquirer.

Table 2.5 Orange Plc: Shareholder Value Summary

(£ million)	No advertising	With advertising
Cost of capital (%)	9	9
PV forecast cash flows	328	1035
PV continuing value	4172	6396
Total present value	4500	7431
Other investments	459	459
Enterprise value	4959	7890
Debt	1616	1571
Shareholder value	3343	6319
Shareholder value added	1198	1198
Shares outstanding (m)	80	80
Implied value per share (£)	2.79	5.28

Determining whether an acquisition is likely to make sense employs the same type of analysis used to evaluate any other strategy.

An acquisition adds value if the price paid is less than the maximum acceptable purchase price. The maximum acceptable price is the stand-alone value of the prospect plus the value of any synergies that are likely to arise from combining the two companies. The stand-alone value will be the market value, if the potential acquisition is publicly traded (provided no anticipated take-over premium has become impounded in the market price). The value of any synergies is calculated by projecting the cash flow of the prospect taking into account any benefits from the lower costs or enhanced differentiation that the company would gain from being combined with the acquirer. When the present value of the forecast and terminal value cash flows are added, the implied value per share can be calculated and this is the maximum acceptable price. If the company can be bought for less than this, value is expected to be created.

LIMITATIONS OF SHAREHOLDER VALUE ANALYSIS

The essence of the shareholder value approach is that managers should be evaluated on their ability to develop strategies that earn returns greater than their cost of capital. The advantages of this approach are that it maximises the value of the firm for investors and creates the cash flow to enable it to meet the claims of other stakeholders – employees, suppliers and the community. It is superior to traditional accounting approaches in that it avoids the short-termism inherent in targeting earnings, ROI or payback criteria. In an age where intangibles – brands, skills, customer and supplier relationships – are the primary assets, accounting or book value has little use for valuing businesses.

But like any technique, managers need to be aware of the assumptions and approximations needed to apply shareholder value analysis to real-world problems. Incorrect assumptions and inadequate estimates of the required data can, and will, lead to poor forecasts of shareholder value and incorrect decisions. The main areas of sensitivity are the following:

○ Forecasting cash flows. *The key inputs to the analysis are forecast of sales growth, operating margins and investment requirements for at least five years ahead. These critically depend upon good judgements about the evolution of the market in the future and, in particular, the firm's ability to sustain a competitive advantage. Such estimates can be far out due to biases on the part of the managers making them, inadequate knowledge of customers and competitors, and unpredictable events. Nevertheless, omnipotence is not a prerequisite for the use of scientific methods. In addition, most well-managed companies have made five-year forecasts of sales, profits and cash flow as part of their annual planning process. So shareholder value analysis does not require any new data.*

○ Cost of capital. *Calculating shareholder value requires discounting the cash flow stream of each business unit by the weighted average costs of debt and equity. Each business unit within the company will have its own cost of capital depending on its risk exposure and the amount of debt needed to finance the assets of the business. Estimating the cost of capital is not easy and different estimates will give different present values. Of particular difficulty is estimating the unit's risk premium. It is generally difficult to find similar publicly quoted companies to estimate share price volatility so indirect weighting systems are often used. These subjective indices mean that the cost of capital figures used can easily be a percentage point or two out.*

○ Estimates of terminal value. *Shareholder value calculations split the estimation into two components: the present value of cash flows during the planning period and a terminal value which is the present value of the cash flows that occur after the planning period. For growth businesses the overwhelming proportion of value arises in the terminal value. Unfortunately, it is difficult to be too confident about this value. There are a variety of methods for coming up with an answer, including the perpetuity approach, perpetuity with inflation, and the market value multiple approach. But each can give very different estimates of terminal value. In the end, the choice is a matter of judgement.*

○ The baseline. *The value created by a strategy is calculated by estimating the shareholder value if the strategy is employed, and then deducting from it a baseline shareholder value. The baseline or pre-strategy shareholder value is normally taken to be the current value of the business assuming no additional value is created or destroyed. This conveniently allows the present value of the business to be estimated by the perpetuity method of dividing net operating profit by the cost of capital. But this assumption that profitability will be maintained and any net investment will earn its cost of capital can be unrealistic. As the industry matures, excess capacity and competition will often put pressures on profits, leading to an erosion rather than a maintenance of value. In this case the value created by the strategy will be underestimated unless a more realistic baseline value is used. In some cases, where the baseline strategy amounts to harvesting the business, the pre-strategy value might be the business's liquidation value.*

○ Options for growth. *If a business is to be sustainable it needs to develop options which will allow it to explore new growth opportunities (see Figure 2.2). Some of these options will become tomorrow's businesses. Option theory plays a major role in capital markets but until relatively recently it was not used in business decision-making. An option is the purchase of an opportunity, but not a requirement, to go ahead with an investment at a later date. Innovative companies make many decisions like this. A European retailer makes a small acquisition in the USA to learn about the market before deciding whether to make a major commitment. Faced with technical and market uncertainties about its new product, a company can decide whether or not to build a £50 million new plant, or alternatively, it could build a £5 million pilot plant and then build the factory in a year's time if it looks successful. The £5 million investment represents the purchase of an option and may be a sound investment if uncertainty is high.*

Shareholder value analysis cannot directly handle options. If managers did not use this type of experimentation, then innovation and growth would certainly be deterred. Fortunately, most companies seem to make option decisions on a judgmental basis outside the normal capital appraisal frameworks. More recently, decision theory and financial options theory have been extended to give insights on how to evaluate these types of problems.[23] Options are unquestionably important and the high valuations the financial markets give to many growth companies clearly reflects the value being attached to the firm's options.

○ **Stock market expectations.** *Shareholder value analysis assumes that if a strategy increases the implied value per share this will be reflected in an increase in the actual or market share price. In other words, shareholder returns are a function of discounting future cash flows to their net present value. There is ample evidence that this is true in general. Earnings per share have virtually zero correlation with share price movements over time, while discounted cash flows explain around 80 per cent of price changes.*

Nevertheless, in the short term there can be significant discrepancies. Actual share prices are determined by investors' expectations; implied values are determined by the expectations of managers. These may differ on account of differences in the information available to investors and to differences in judgements about the implications of the information. To reduce these differences, it is important for the board to test the strategic and marketing assumptions behind their managers' forecasts. It is also important that they effectively communicate to the market the long-term rationale behind their strategies.

SUMMARY

1. The task of marketing strategy is to increase the value of the business for its shareholders. This is achieved by increasing the sum of all its anticipated future free cash flow, adjusted by an interest rate known as the cost of capital.

2. There are two common approaches to valuing marketing strategies: the cash flow method and the economic value added method. Both will produce the same result given similar assumptions. Using either method, it is crucial to remember that looking at one year's figures can be highly misleading. Value creation is a long-term phenomenon. Marketing strategies, in particular, can only be valued properly after the long-term cash flow is properly projected.

3. Shareholder value added depends upon four key financial factors: the level of anticipated cash flow, its timing, its sustainability and the risk attached to the forecast. The level of cash flow is determined by the strategy's ability to achieve growth and adequate operating margins and by the investment required. The speed, sustainability and predictability of the cash flow are primarily dependent on the company's ability to satisfy its customers and achieve a high retention level.

4. The financial drivers are the objectives of the business. But achieving the growth and profitability targets depends upon strategy – especially marketing strategy. Growth and profitability rest primarily upon choosing attractive target markets and creating a sustainable differential advantage. Implementing a strategy depends upon the firm's organisational value drivers – its core capabilities and the motivation of its people.

5. Shareholder value analysis is the most effective technique for evaluating the effectiveness of alternative marketing strategies in financial terms. Of course, it depends on the accuracy of forecasts but comparing like with like and identifying the sensitivities are a valuable part of the process. We are not trying to guess the future but only decide which marketing strategy to adopt. It also provides a powerful tool for valuing brands.

6.   Like any analytical method, the results depend upon the accuracy of the information used. In particular, it requires good judgements about future sales, operating margins and investment requirements. But such judgements are inevitably required from managers responsible for strategic decisions. The other particular inputs required from the analysis are estimates of the cost of capital and the continuing value of the business.

REVIEW QUESTIONS

1.   Describe the principles of shareholder value analysis.
2.   How can shareholder analysis be used to evaluate alternative marketing strategies?
3.   How could a business unit marketing manager use shareholder analysis to demonstrate to the board the effectiveness of his or her marketing strategy?
4.   How do the financial, marketing and organisational value drivers work together to increase shareholder value?
5.   Explain how marketing can increase shareholder value.
6.   What are the main assumptions required that could lead to poor estimates of the shareholder value added by a marketing strategy?

NOTES ON CHAPTER 2

[1] For a complete discussion of the valuation of bonds and shares see Richard A. Brearley and Stewart C. Myers, *Principles of Corporate Finance*, 6th edn, New York: McGraw-Hill, 1999.

[2] This is demonstrated more fully in, for example, Brearley and Myers, (note 1), pp. 59–62.

[3] For evidence see James M. McTaggart, Peter W. Kontes and Michael C. Mankins, *The Value Imperative: Managing for Superior Shareholder Returns*, New York Free Press, 1994. See also: Roger Mills, *Shareholder Value Analysis – Principles and Issues*, London: Technical Bulletin of the Institute of the Chartered Accountants of England and Wales, 1999.

[4] See for example, Andrew Black, Philip Wright and John Bachman, *In Search of Shareholder Value*, London: Pitman, 1998, p. 45.

[5] This section draws heavily on the standard text, Alfred Rappaport, *Creating Shareholder Value*, 2nd edn, New York: Free Press, 1998, pp. 32–58.

[6] For a comprehensive account of the sources of competitive advantage see John Kay, *Foundations of Corporate Success*, Oxford: Oxford University Press, 1993. See also: Michael Porter, *Competitive Advantage*, Free Press, 2004.

[7] For a detailed discussion see Tom Copeland, Tim Koller and Jack Murrin, *Valuation: Measuring and Managing the Value of Companies*, 2nd edn, New York: John Wiley & Sons, Inc., 1996, pp. 285–331.

[8] G. Bennett Stewart III, *The Quest for Value*, New York: HarperCollins, 1991. See also: Joel M. Stern, John S. Shiely and Irwin Ross, *The EVA Challenge: Implementing Value-Added Change in an Organization*, John Wiley & Sons, Inc., 2003.

[9] On this equivalence see Rappaport (note 5) pp. 121–128; G. Bennett Stewart III, EVA: fact and fantasy, *Journal of Applied Corporate Finance*, Summer 1994, 78.

[10] Assume initial sales are 100, costs are 90 and the cash tax rate is 30 per cent. With a 5 per cent sales increase and volume unchanged, sales rise to 105, costs stay the same, pre-tax profits rise from 10 to 15, and NOPAT from 7 to 10.5.

[11] Working on the same example, assume that half its costs are variable. With a 5 per cent volume loss on the new price, sales slip to 99.75, variable costs drop from 45 to 42.75, then pre-tax profit increases from 10 to 12 and NOPAT from 7 to 8.4.

[12] See for example, Michael Hammer and James Champy, *Reengineering the Corporation*, London: Brealey, 1993.

[13] Here sales rise from 100 to 130, variable costs increase from 45 to 58.5, fixed costs remain unchanged at 45, pre-tax profits go from 10 to 26.5 and NOPAT from 7 to 18.6 or to 14 per cent of sales.

[14] Under the low-investment strategy the present value of the continuing value is £754 million and the shareholder value is £1287 million. Under the high-investment strategy the continuing value is £894 million and the shareholder value is £1393 million.

[15] For detailed development of threshold margin see Rappaport, (note 5) pp. 51–55. Rappaport calls the figure used here the incremental threshold margin.

[16] George Stalk and Thomas M. Hout, *Competing Against Time*, New York: Free Press, 1990.

[17] Robin Cooper and R.S. Kaplan, *The Design of Cost Management Systems*, Englewood Cliffs, NJ: Prentice Hall, 1991.

[18] See the very influential research of Frederick F. Reichheld, *The Loyalty Effect: The Hidden Forces behind Growth, Profits and Lasting Value*, Boston, MA: Harvard Business School Press, 1996, 2001. See also, Frederick F. Reichheld, *Loyalty Rules: How Today's Leaders Build Lasting Relationships*, Boston, MA: Harvard Business School Press, 2003.

[19] Fred Wiersema, *Customer Intimacy*, London: HarperCollins, 1998. For a parallel discussion see Don Peppers and Martha Rogers, *Enterprise One-to-One*, New York, Doubleday, 1997. See also: Peppers and Rogers: *Managing Customer Relationships: A Strategic Framework*, John Wiley & Sons, Inc., 2004.

[20] For a fuller description see Richard Tanner Pascale, *Managing on the Edge*, London: Viking, 1990, pp. 37–50.

[21] For a detailed review of brand valuation methods see David Haigh, *Brand Valuation: A Review of Current Practice*, London: Institute of Practitioners in Advertising, 1996.

[22] This case is described in a paper written by the advertising agency, WCRS, 'The FTSE's Bright, the FTSE's Orange: how advertising enhanced Orange PLC shareholder value', published in the *IPA Advertising Effectiveness Awards 1998*, London: NTC Publications, 1999.

[23] For an introduction to option theory in business see Thomas E. Copeland and Philip T. Keenan, How much is flexibility worth? *McKinsey Quarterly*, no. 2, 1998, 38–49.

3 The Marketing Value Driver

'Increased customer loyalty is the single most important driver of long-term financial performance.'

Dave Illingworth, Lexus US

INTRODUCTION AND OBJECTIVES

This chapter looks at what managers need to know about marketing in today's information age. Marketing is about meeting customers' needs and developing their trust and loyalty. Only by creating such relationships can the firm achieve profitable growth and shareholder value. The starting point for successful marketing is understanding the needs of customers and developing a proposition that they will regard as offering superior value. The next step is to develop a service that customers will trust and want to continue to do business with. All this in turn depends upon having built within the organisation a level of skills, capabilities and commitment that enables the firm to deliver superior value than competitors.

In the past marketing was less important. High profitability could be achieved by operating in regulated markets, controlling scarce production resources or distribution channels, or acquiring and rationalising poorly performing businesses. But now with deregulation, global competition and the information revolution transforming communications and distribution, such opportunities are fast disappearing. Growth and profitability are increasingly based on the firm's ability at marketing.

This chapter looks at how successful marketing drives growth, profitability and shareholder returns. By the time you have read this chapter, you will be able to:

- ○ *Define marketing in terms of shareholder value*

- ○ *Understand how delivering value to customers is the basis for creating shareholder value*

- ○ *Explain the significance of the firm's differential advantage*

- ○ *Understand the increasing importance of measures of customer satisfaction, loyalty and trust in modern businesses*

- ○ *Describe the essential requirements for delivering customer value*

The chapter conceptualises value-based marketing in terms of four major steps. The first step is developing a deep understanding of the customer's needs, operating procedures and decision-making processes. This provides the essential information for determining what is of most value to customers. The second step is formulating value propositions that meet the needs of customers and create a differential advantage – propositions that are superior to the offers of competitors. The third step is moving from successful transactions with customers to building long-term relationships with them, whereby they continue to buy again and again. This entails developing a level of loyalty and trust based upon satisfaction and confidence with the supplier's commitment. Finally, managers have to understand that delivering superior value to customers requires more than just a customer focus: it also requires superior knowledge, skills, systems and marketing assets. Management has to invest and maintain a superior resource base from which great products and services can be produced to make superior marketing a reality.

A NEW DEFINITION OF MARKETING

Marketing has not had the impact on top management that its importance merits. Chapter 1 showed that this was largely due to it having objectives that were not aligned to management's central goal of maximising shareholder value. Chapter 2 went on to demonstrate how shareholder value analysis provides a powerful tool for proving the effectiveness of marketing. This concept of value-based marketing leads to a new definition of the field that will be amplified in this chapter. The new definition is:

Marketing is the management process that seeks to maximise returns to shareholders by developing and implementing strategies to build relationships of trust with high-value customers and to create a sustainable differential advantage.

This defines the objective of marketing in the business enterprise and the strategies that contribute to it. The objective is to maximise returns to the owners of the business, as measured by its long-term dividend stream and capital growth. The specific contribution of marketing lies in the formulation of strategies to choose the right customers, build relationships of trust with them, and create a differential advantage.

Choosing the right customers is important because some customers do not offer the potential to create value, either because the costs of serving them exceed the benefits they generate, or because the company does not have the appropriate bundle of skills to serve them effectively. It wants long-term relationships with its chosen customers because loyal customers make possible faster and more profitable growth. A firm's ability to earn a return above the cost of capital depends upon it maintaining a differential advantage – a reason why target customers perceive the firm as offering superior value to competitors. A strategy to create a differential advantage is based on understanding the needs of customers and the strategies of competitors.

CREATING CUSTOMER VALUE

Top management needs to be deeply committed to marketing because marketing drives growth and shareholder value. The essential idea of marketing is offering customers superior value. By delivering superior value to customers, management in turn can deliver superior value to shareholders. Indeed this formula – customer value creates shareholder value – is the fundamental principle of capitalism. In a free-enterprise system individual consumers choose how to spend their money. In turn firms compete with one another to attract the patronage of customers. Firms making offers that do not appeal to customers go out of business because they do not generate the cash flow to pay their suppliers of materials, labour and capital.

MEETING CUSTOMER NEEDS

The marketing approach to creating customer value is based on three principles. First, it recognises that in choosing between competing companies, the customer will select the offer that he or she perceives to be of best *value*.

Second, customers do not want products (or services) for their own sake, but rather for meeting their *needs*. These needs may be emotional (e.g. to look good), economic (e.g. to cut costs), or, more likely, some combination of both. Value is the customer's estimate of the product's or service's ability to satisfy these needs. Third, rather than having just a one-off transaction with a customer, the firm will find it more profitable in the long run to create *relationships*, whereby trust is established between them and customers remain loyal and continue to buy from the business.

To get into a position to offer superior value to customers, the company must first understand their needs. The basic idea of marketing is that whatever product or service the company produces, the customer does not want it! What the customer wants is to satisfy his or her problems. The young woman spends the whole of her Saturday shopping for a dress not because she needs clothes, but because she wants to look glamorous at the party. The chief executive signs a buying order for a new £1 million computer, not because he wants the product, but because he has been convinced that it will enable the company to improve its profitability.

Customers naturally want to deal with companies that they believe will solve their problems. Understanding customers and solving their problems better than they, or the competitors can, is a challenging task. Increasingly, superior knowledge of how to solve the problems of customers is the key capability for competitive success. Value today comes from knowledge, not products. Products (or services) today, whether they are computers, restaurants, banking, clothing, household goods, steel or chemicals, are increasingly low-margin commodities. Profit comes from solving problems customers find difficult. Products are only vehicles for offering customers solutions (see box, 'Delivering Customer Value – Knowledge Not Products').

Understanding customer needs and solving their problems requires research on the whole customer experience, not just the ordering decision. Figure 3.1 illustrates how marketing needs to understand the problems leading up to the purchase, the choice criteria the buyer has in mind, how the buyer will proceed through ordering, installing, learning about and using the product, and what after-sales support he or she should expect. It is this whole experience that determines the buyer's perception of value. Within each of these stages, depending upon the needs of the

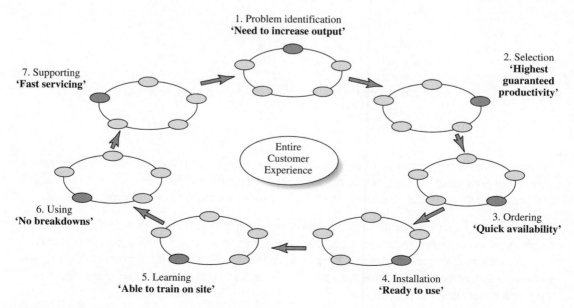

Figure 3.1   Understanding the Purchasing Process

individual buyer, there will be one or two critical interfaces between buyer and seller that will drive the customer's perception of value and the decision of whether or not to buy again. These may be the supplier's willingness to pull out all the stops when the customer needs fast repairs to the equipment, or their ability to put together effective training for the customer's operatives. These are often called *moments of truth*. Detailed knowledge of this process and management of these moments of truth are the foundations for a strategy to deliver customer value and create competitive advantage.

Delivering Customer Value – Knowledge Not Products

Commoditisation is a problem facing many suppliers today. This was certainly true for a leading producer of industrial sewing thread facing increasing competition from new low-priced entrants. It received a demand from one of its largest customers, for a 20 per cent price cut. The customer was a China-based contract manufacturer for two of the leading US sports shoe companies.

Rather than lose the business, the company sent in a team of experts to analyse the productivity of the customer's operations. It discovered that sewing thread accounted for only 2 per cent of its operating costs, but sewing activities accounted for at least 50 per cent of total costs. That is, most of the labour and machinery was absorbed in stitching operations.

Returns from customers for faulty products too were invariably due to poor stitching. The customer's operating statement is shown below. The team discovered that a major productivity problem was breaks in the thread during sewing operations. Such breaks resulted in lost output, wasted labour and materials, and lost machine time. The team found that thread breaks could be substantially reduced by better machine maintenance, improved operator training and the introduction of alternative sewing patterns.

Operating costs per 1 million shoes

	%	$000
Costs	100	10 000
Raw materials	35	3 500
Thread	2	200
Labour	30	3 000
Returns	10	1 000
Depreciation	7	700
Overheads	16	1 600
Profit	15	1 725

The customer's operating margin was 15 per cent. The company showed its customer that while a 20 per cent cut in the thread price would improve profits by only 2 per cent, a realignment of the sewing operation could reduce total operating costs by at least 7 per cent – improving its operating profits by over 40 per cent.

The customer was so impressed by the supplier's knowledge of sewing operations that the business was renegotiated. The company was appointed its customer's 'business partner' and paid a fee for managing the sewing operations. Instead of being paid for metres of thread, it was paid for its knowledge in improving customer productivity. It was a win–win situation: the customer made substantial gains in productivity; the supplier retained the account at a significantly higher margin.

DIFFERENCES BETWEEN CONSUMER AND BUSINESS-TO-BUSINESS MARKETS

Some companies produce for final consumers but most produce for other businesses. Needs, purchasing behaviour and product use differ in these two markets. Actually managers need to understand both markets and develop two separate strategies. Consumer goods companies generally must first sell to other businesses. The Procter & Gamble brand manager has to make toothpaste appealing not only to consumers but also to the big supermarket chains that will decide whether or not to stock the brand, and how much support they will give it. Similarly, the demand for all business goods is ultimately derived from the demand for consumer goods. The amount of steel bought depends on consumer purchases of cars and the type of cars they buy. A shift in consumer tastes, for example, could see aluminium or plastic substituting for steel in cars.

The sources of the differences between the two markets lie in the number of customers and the professionalism of the buying processes. Whereas firms in consumer markets count their customers in millions, in business-to-business markets four or five customers can account for 80 per cent of a supplier's profits. This results in larger customers with greater bargaining power. The supplier normally deals directly, one-to-one, with these major customers and has a detailed knowledge of their wants and buying processes. Purchasing is increasingly professional as buyers seek to construct efficient supply chains that will allow their businesses to compete effectively. Today buyers look for partnerships with a few chosen suppliers who can share responsibility for optimising key areas of the value chain.

While individual buyers will always be influenced by personal and social factors, in business purchasing, motives tend to be much more *rational* than in consumer buying. Suppliers are chosen more for their perceived value in improving the buying firm's economic performance.

In some ways consumer marketing is less sophisticated than business-to-business. Consumer marketers do not know their individual customers and they employ mass marketing techniques such as branding and advertising that treat all customers, or at least large segments of them, as alike. The huge numbers of buyers typical of consumer markets meant that the marketer usually dealt with them through intermediaries such as shops or dealers. They didn't have one-to-one communication with, or acquired knowledge about, the needs and buying patterns of individual consumers. Modern information technology, however, is changing this picture. The Internet is transforming consumer marketing from mass marketing to the type of one-to-one marketing that exists in business markets.

UNDERSTANDING THE DECISION-MAKING UNIT

Meeting customer needs is complicated because, except for the most routine decisions, buying is rarely the choice of a single individual. In consumer buying, the parents may book the holiday but other members of the family, and perhaps, friends, may influence their choice. In business buying, technical people, finance, marketing, shop floor and top management may influence the key purchasing decisions. In contrast, the influence of the manager formally responsible for purchasing may be slight. Studies suggest up to seven roles in the purchasing process: initiators, users, influencers, deciders, approvers, buyers and gatekeepers.

Understanding these roles in the buying process is important because the participants are likely to want different things from the supplier. For example, in buying breakfast cereals, the parent may want to choose a healthy brand for the family, but the kids want one that tastes sugary. In industrial buying, purchasing managers tend to be heavily influenced by price, technical people by product specifications and top management by overall impact on the bottom line. Marketing needs to understand the power relationships in these buying units and to communicate the appropriate messages to each of the important influences.

EXISTING, LATENT AND INCIPIENT NEEDS

The most obvious way to discover the needs of customers is to ask them. But sometimes simply asking customers what they want is not enough.

Wants or needs can be classified into three groups. *Existing wants* are those for which consumers consider satisfactory solutions already exist. Here opportunities for new products are limited since they will be competing head-to-head with similar products. *Latent wants* are wants that people have, which are not yet satisfied. Customers can easily articulate these needs in market research. People would like a cure for flu or cancer. Laptop users would like a battery with a longer life, and so on. Profit opportunities are much greater for companies that can meet latent wants since solutions represent innovations for which, temporarily at least, no competition exists.

Incipient wants are wants that people have, but which they do not know about until they see the solution. Customers were unlikely to articulate the desire for Post-It notes, iPods, Internet banking or automated teller machines. In areas of rapid technological and social change, buyers are likely to lack the foresight to predict the new products or services they would buy. Companies often have to follow up on novel technologies and the insights of their researchers without the benefit of direct consumer research. Rather than the classic marketing approach of first researching needs, in many situations the product breakthroughs occur first, and then the pioneering company has to find customers afterwards.

But it is a mistake to think that companies like Apple, Sony or 3M, which often proceed like this, *create* wants. Unless the invention meets an underlying customer need, and customers perceive it offering an advantage to current products on the market, it will not succeed. Such products as mobile phones, iPods and GPS car navigation systems were not suggested by consumers. But they succeeded because they offered them demonstrable benefits and advantages. Technology-led innovation is very risky.

THE MARKET-LED ORGANISATION

Many managers still do not understand today's necessity of being customer-orientated and confuse marketing with selling. A market-orientated business starts with understanding customer wants and then goes on to develop products and services to meet these wants. Production- and sales-orientated businesses work the opposite way.

PRODUCTION- AND SALES-ORIENTATED ORGANISATIONS

Many organisations – not only in manufacturing, but also in services and government – are production-orientated (Figure 3.2). They believe that if you have the necessary technical capabilities to produce good quality products or services at the right price, then, as in the case of the better mousetrap, 'the world will beat a path to your door'. If marketing is seen as having a role, it is about selling – using advertising, salespeople and PR to tell the public about your offer and to convince them to buy.

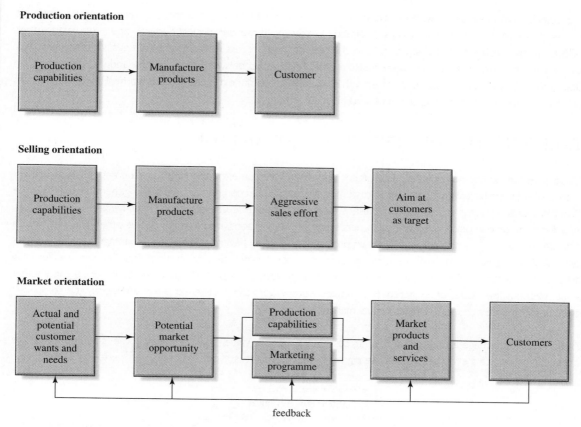

Figure 3.2   Production, Sales and Market Orientations

But in today's world these strategies cease to work. Because production- and sales-orientated companies design products or services with little or no input from customers, they are unlikely to be exactly what customers want. With overcapacity and intense competition in most industries, customers have plenty of choices and can usually do better. These businesses then can only find customers by slashing their prices. The results of ignoring customers are declining market shares and eroding margins.

MARKET-ORIENTATED ORGANISATIONS

Today's top companies are customer-led. This business orientation is often called the *marketing concept.*

The marketing concept states that the key to creating shareholder value is building relationships with target customers based on satisfying their needs more effectively than competitors.

A market-orientated company starts by looking for market opportunities created by unmet customer needs. These needs are identified by listening carefully to customers and closely monitoring technological and environmental changes that impinge on markets. From this set of opportunities it aims to select those which look to have the most potential and which best fit its competencies. The business then evaluates what production and marketing capabilities it will need, and how they should be resourced. Should it undertake these activities in-house or should it seek partnerships with other businesses already possessing these capabilities? Services and products are then tailored to the problems that customers have. Throughout the process management continually obtains feedback by listening to customers. The aim is to create a good relationship between the company and its customers such that both parties see value in doing business with one another over an extended period of time. Figure 3.2 contrasts production-, sales and marketing-orientated business.

BUILDING THE DIFFERENTIAL ADVANTAGE

Value-based marketing not only requires a focus on satisfying customer needs: it also has a competitive dimension. Management must be aware of both what customers want and what competitors are offering them (Figure 3.3). The firm must seek a value proposition that satisfies the needs of target customers more effectively than competitors. A differential, or competitive, advantage is necessary for two reasons, one marketing, the other financial. First, a differential advantage is necessary to maintain preference. Only by having a differential advantage can the business profitably attract new customers or prevent existing customers defecting to competition. Second, a differential advantage is necessary if a business is to maintain earnings above the cost of capital, i.e. to generate shareholder value. Without the barrier of a differential advantage, competitors can easily enter the market, copy the company's offer, and compete away its premium profits margins.

A differential advantage is created by offering customers superior value. Value is the customer's perception of the product's or service's effectiveness in meeting his or her needs. It is a trade-off between performance and cost.

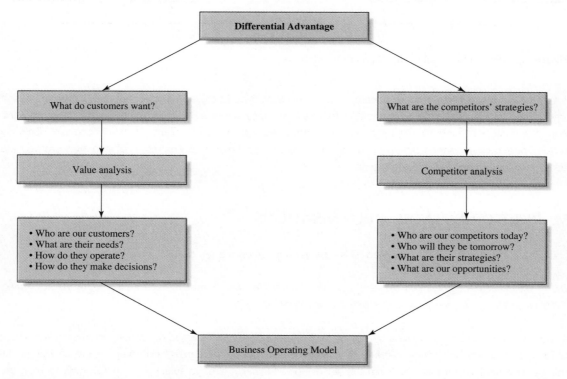

Figure 3.3   Developing the Differential Advantage

Value can be increased by offering customers more performance or benefits for the same cost, or the same benefits for a lower cost.

A differential advantage is a perceived difference in value that leads target customers to prefer one company's offer to those of others.

Since customers have different preferences and constraints, the optimum value will differ among them. Some customers will put a greater emphasis on benefits, such as innovative product features or services; others will place a greater weight on price or convenience. Hence, in any market there will be different viable value propositions, depending on the customers targeted. The choice management makes is called the company's *market positioning strategy*.

Market positioning strategy is the choice of target customers, which defines where the firm competes and the choice of value proposition, which determines how it competes

STRATEGIES THAT OFFER MORE

Some companies compete primarily on the basis of offering more benefits; others compete on cost and convenience. The former strategy reflects that some customers are primarily interested in selecting suppliers that offer the best solutions and are willing to incur more costs to get them. Four types of positioning strategy can be distinguished that compete on this dimension.

1. **Product leadership.** Some companies target customers who want the latest technology and products with the most innovative features. Examples include Apple, 3M, Sony, Microsoft and Intel. These companies invest heavily in research and development, prioritise hiring the brightest talent and build organisational cultures focused on creativity and innovation. The financial advantages of successful product leadership are the opportunities to achieve rapid growth and to obtain premium prices.

2. **Service leadership.** Some customers place a high value on outstanding service. Companies with a value proposition based on service include Virgin Atlantic, Four Seasons Hotels, American Express and the US department store Nordstrom. Businesses competing this way need first to identify the types of customers who will pay more to be pampered.

3. **Customer intimacy.** This strategy involves communicating with customers on an individual basis to learn about their needs and develop tailored solutions which directly improve the customer's performance or experience. It is now often called one-to-one marketing and promises to be one of the most successful strategies of the information age. Customer intimacy has been a common strategy for business-to-business suppliers with a small number of customers. Companies such as KPMG and Boeing have long seen this as their positioning. But today, led by such organisations as Amazon.com, Federal Express, Lexus and Hertz, we see it spreading into areas where previously advertising and mass marketing played central roles.

Category Management – Developing Customer Intimacy

The most significant development in recent years in the consumer goods area is category management. Suppliers of fast-moving consumer goods (fmcg), such as Unilever and Procter & Gamble sell to final consumers via supermarkets. To attract final consumers these companies seek to develop appealing brands. But supermarkets have different buying motivations to final consumers. The supermarket's objectives are to increase its own business turnover and profitability. Most of the sales activities suppliers undertake to increase their market shares, such as developing new brands, promotions and advertising, do not help supermarkets; they merely produce brand switching within the store.

This creates conflict between the increasingly powerful retail chains and suppliers. Retailers retaliate by demanding better margins and cash incentives, and by developing their own private label brands that switch sales from manufacturer brands. Leading suppliers have responded by introducing category management. Category management is a partnership between a supplier and a retail group designed to grow the retailer's sales and profits in a merchandise area. For example, a category management team from Procter & Gamble will work with Tesco to develop a plan to increase the supermarket's sales and profitability in the detergent category by 10 per cent per annum over the next three years.

Rather than trying to sell the reluctant retailer its variety of competing brands, the supplier uses its knowledge of the category to design a portfolio of brands, space layout, price points and promotions to maximise the client's growth and profits. Electronic data interchange can then link retail sales to the supplier's production line to cut inventories and optimise the supply chain. Category management aims to replace an adversarial relationship with a one-to-one partnership designed to increase the customer's performance.

The characteristics of a customer intimacy strategy are (1) the construction of data banks to hold information on the preferences and buying behaviour of individual customers, (2) the use of information technology to allow direct, one-to-one communication between the firm and the customer, (3) the organisation of marketing around customer managers rather than brand managers, and (4) the tailoring of individual product and services solutions. The stimuli for the growing popularity of this strategy are the increasing difficulty of maintaining uniqueness in products or services. This has resulted in competition shifting from delivering quality products and services to the provision of solutions that enhance the customer's overall experience or performance (see box, 'Category Management – Developing Customer Intimacy'). Finally, information technology is making it increasingly cheap and easy to store individual data and to communicate on a personalised basis.

4.   **Brand Leadership.** Consumer brands such as Starbucks, Coca-Cola and Gillette have emotional values beyond those that can be explained by their product or service performance. In business-to-business markets, brands such as McKinsey, IBM and Hewlett-Packard have similar values. Brands give consumers confidence that they can trust these suppliers. They reduce the personal, social or economic risks attached to making decisions. For the supplier, the benefit of strong brands is that it is easier to gain market share. Preference also means that strong brands sell at higher prices.

LOWER TOTAL COST: OPERATIONAL EXCELLENCE

Rather than delivering the customer more product, service or image benefits, a company can seek a differential advantage by offering lower total costs. Lower total cost for the customer can include several dimensions. The most obvious one is offering customers the guarantee of consistently lower prices. Wal-Mart is a good example of this. A second way of offering lower total cost is emphasising product reliability, durability and low running costs as

Caterpillar communicates on its web site. Another element of cost that operationally excellent companies stress is convenience – the absence of tangible and psychic costs stemming from irritation and delays. The strength of these companies lies in the delivery of swift, dependable service. For example, DHL promises to accept instructions from anywhere and to ship packages anywhere. It could not be easier or involve less total cost.

CRITERIA FOR A DIFFERENTIAL ADVANTAGE

Treacy and Wiersema, in reviewing the differential advantages of industry leaders suggested four rules:[1]

1. Provide the best offering in the marketplace by excelling in a specific dimension of value.

Different customers buy different kinds of value. No company can be the best in all dimensions, so it has to choose its customers and focus on offering them unmatched value on one dimension. Customers recognise they have to make choices – they accept if they buy from a supplier offering 'unbeatable prices', that they are not going to get personalised service.

2. Maintain threshold standards on other dimensions of value.

While outstanding performance is not expected on all dimensions, threshold standards are required. The lowest cost car on the market will not succeed if its reliability and service backup are unacceptable.

3. Dominate the market by improving value year after year.

Competition is continually raising the expectations of customers. What represents a differential advantage today will not do so tomorrow. Companies have to continually get better, faster than their competitors.

4. Build a well-tuned operating model dedicated to delivering unmatched value.

Developing a winning value proposition requires companies to structure their operations specifically to deliver on that dimension. A business focusing on a value proposition of innovation and product leadership will require a quite different operating model from a company focusing on price leadership.

A differential advantage, or winning value proposition, must meet the following criteria if it is to create value for shareholders:

- ❍ **Customer benefit.** *The difference must be seen by customers as of value to them in improving their performance or experience. Differential advantages must be founded on dimensions that consumers want.*

- ❍ **Unique.** *Customers must perceive the benefits to be different from those offered by other competitors.*

- ❍ **Profitable.** *The company must be able to produce the product or service with a price, cost and volume structure that makes it profitable to produce.*

- ❍ **Sustainable.** *The advantage must be difficult for competitors to copy. There should be some barriers to entry in the form of difficult to acquire skills, scale economies, branding or patents, to prevent the differential being rapidly eroded.*

BUILDING RELATIONSHIPS WITH CUSTOMERS

The first step in marketing is to understand the needs of customers; the second aims at creating a differential advantage; the third seeks to convert this understanding and advantage into a continuing relationship with customers so that they buy again and again. Managers really need to understand how such customer relationships are the fundamental key to creating value for shareholders.

THE ECONOMICS OF CUSTOMER LOYALTY

Shareholder value is determined by the company's growth rate and its ability to achieve an operating margin above its threshold level. *For most companies, customer loyalty is the single most important determinant of long-term growth and profit margins.* Customer loyalty refers to the customer's willingness to continue buying from the company. It is generally measured by the retention rate – the percentage of customers buying this year who also buy next year. A typical company – for example, a bank, car insurer or advertising agency – loses 10 per cent of its accounts annually. The average retention rate is therefore around 90 per cent.

LOYALTY AND GROWTH

The effect of the retention rate on a company's growth is greatly underestimated by managers because new customer acquisition masks the effects of a high defection rate. But a high defection rate makes profitable growth almost impossible to achieve. It is like a leaky bucket: the bigger the hole in the bucket of customers, the harder marketing has to work to fill it up and keep it full.

If management can increase the retention rate from the average of 90 per cent to 95 per cent, then it can massively increase the company's growth rate. Consider two companies, the first losing 10 per cent of its customers annually, the second losing only 5 per cent. If both companies are acquiring new customers at the rate of 10 per cent per year, the first will have no net growth; the second will have a 5 per cent net growth rate. Over 15 years, the first firm will be unchanged in size; the second firm will double. Table 3.1 shows the effects over a 10-year period of varying levels of customer retention in mature, moderate-growth and high-growth markets. In growing markets (i.e. 20 per cent new customers acquired annually), a 5 per cent improvement in the retention rate increases the total number of customers by between 55 and over 100 per cent over a 10-year period. In mature (0 new customers) or low-growth markets (10 per cent annual new customer growth), a high defection rate soon destroys the customer base.

Table 3.1 Growth in Total Number of Customers over 10-year period

Retention (%)	Growth of new accounts (% per annum)		
	0	10	20
95	−34	55	252
90	−61	0	136
85	−77	−37	55
80	−87	−67	0

LOYALTY AND OPERATING MARGINS

If the effect of customer loyalty on growth is high, the effect on operating profits is extraordinary. In many industries there are vast differences between companies in profitability, even though their prices are pretty much the same. The major cause of this difference is variations in the customer retention rate. Customers who stay with the company are assets of increasing value – each year they tend to generate higher and higher net cash flow. A customer who has been with the company say, seven years, typically generates six or seven times the amount of a new customer. Frederick Reichheld, a director of management consultants Bain & Company identified six sources making loyal customers more profitable:[2]

1.   **Acquisition cost.** Obtaining new customers is very expensive in terms of such costs as advertising, direct mail, sales commissions and management time. It has been estimated that it typically takes six times as much to win a new customer as to keep an existing one.

2.   **Base profit.** The base profit is the earnings on purchases before allowing for loyalty effects. Clearly, the longer a customer is retained, the greater the total sum of annual base profits.

3.   **Revenue growth.** Loyal customers increase their spending over time. They learn more about the company's product line and, because they trust the company, are more inclined to put more of their business with it.

4.   **Operating costs.** As customers become more familiar with the company, the costs of serving them decrease. Less time has to be spent answering questions and learning about each other's operations.

5.   **Referrals.** Satisfied customers recommend the business to others. Referrals can be a very important source of new business in many markets. In general, personal recommendations are more powerful persuaders than advertising or paid for communications.

6.   **Price premium.** Old customers are normally less price conscious than new ones. New customers are usually attracted by bargains and discounted offers that earn the company low margins.

Figure 3.4 illustrates how these factors shape the cash flow over a customer's lifetime.

The *customer lifetime value* (CLV) is the net present value of a customer – that is, the discounted value of the cash flow generated over the life of the relationship with the company. The cash flow is usually low or even negative at the beginning and then grows strongly over the years as a result of the factors described above. The major determinant of CLV is the retention rate. For example, for a credit card company, an average customer who only stays two years has a CLV of around £15, while one who stays 20 years has a CLV of over £600. Reichheld showed the effect on the CLV of a 5 per cent increase in the retention rate for typical industries (Figure 3.5). For example, if a personal insurance company increased its retention rate from 90 to 95 per cent it would increase the customer net present value by 84 per cent – from, say, £280 to £515. This occurs because with a 90 per cent retention rate the average customer stays with the company 10 years; with 95 per cent the average loyalty is 20 years.

GROWTH PLUS MARGIN EFFECTS ON SHAREHOLDER VALUE

Putting the two effects together demonstrates the enormous impact on shareholder value of increasing customer loyalty (see box, 'Findings on Customer Loyalty'). As shown above, increasing the retention rate from 90 to 95 per cent in a moderate-growth market would increase the number of customers by 55 per cent. So, for example, an insurance company with 100 000 customers would gain a net 55 000 over a 10-year period. This is the *growth effect*.

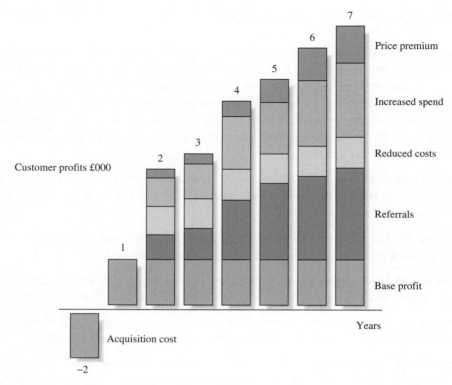

Figure 3.4   Cash Flow over a Customer's Lifetime

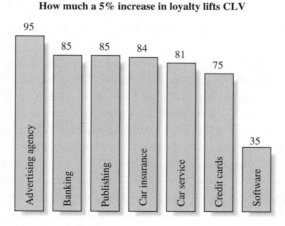

Figure 3.5   Effect of Increased Loyalty on Customer Lifetime Value

But in addition, the average duration a customer stays with the business would double. As a result of lower average acquisition and operating costs, more referrals, revenue growth and higher prices, the average lifetime value of a customer grows by over 80 per cent. Using the above example, this is from £280 to £515. This is the *margin effect*. The net result is to almost treble the value of the business from £28 million to £80 million, i.e.:

Value with 90 per cent retention:

Customers	100 000
Average CLV	£280
Business value	£28 million

Value with 95 per cent retention

Customers	155 000
Average CLV	£515
Business value	£80 million

Given the importance of customer loyalty on shareholder value, it is striking how few companies measure retention rates. Without such information, managers do not know the lifetime value of their customers and miss crucial opportunities to increase their company's growth and profitability.

Findings on Customer Loyalty

- *Loyal customers are assets.* A customer that generates a cash flow of £1000 for a supplier in its first year is likely to have a net present value (customer lifetime value) of around £50 000 if retained as a satisfied customer over 10 years.

- *Loyal customers are more profitable.* They buy more of the company's products, are less costly to serve, are less sensitive to price and bring in new customers.

- *Winning new customers is costly.* It costs up to six times as much to win a new customer as to retain an existing one. These are the costs of researching, advertising, selling and negotiating with new prospects.

- *Increasing customer retention.* The average company loses 10 per cent of its customers annually. Increasing customer retention by as little as 5 per cent can double the lifetime value of customers.

- *'Highly satisfied' customers repurchase.* They are six times more likely to remain loyal than customers who merely rate themselves 'satisfied'. Highly satisfied customers ('apostles') tell others about the company.

- *Dissatisfied customers (increasingly called vigilantes) tell others.*[3] It is estimated that, on average, dissatisfied customers tell 14 others. So if losing a single customer represents the loss of an asset with a lifetime value of say, £10 000, this might just be the tip of the iceberg. The total value lost might be 14 times as great.

- *Most dissatisfied customers do not complain.* While they tell their colleagues, only around 4 per cent bother to complain. For every complaint received, another 26 customers will have had problems, and about 6 will have serious ones.

- *Satisfactory resolution of complaints increases loyalty.* When complaints are resolved to the customer's satisfaction, these customers tend to be more loyal than those who never experienced a problem in the first place.

- *Few customers defect due to poor product performance.* Only 14 per cent defect for product reasons; two-thirds leave because they find service people indifferent or inaccessible.

CUSTOMER SATISFACTION

Fundamental to building loyalty is customer satisfaction. Customer satisfaction is defined as where the supplier's perceived performance is equal to the expected performance. Many businesses regularly measure, through surveys, customer satisfaction levels. The belief is that increasing customer satisfaction will increase loyalty and therefore future growth, profitability and shareholder value.

Unfortunately, research suggests that the link between customer satisfaction and loyalty is not so straightforward. Frederick Reichheld[4] has found that conventional customer satisfaction measures lack a consistently demonstrable connection to actual behaviour and growth. Instead, in most industries, there is a strong correlation between a company's growth rate and the percentage of its customers who are 'promoters' – those who say they are extremely likely to recommend that company to a friend or colleague.

Typically surveys measure customer satisfaction on a 1 to 5 scale where 5 is 'very satisfied' and 1 is 'very dissatisfied'.[5] Loyalty is measured by repeat buying behaviour or intention to repeat buy. The relationship often appears to be nonlinear (Figure 3.6). People rating at either extreme end of the scale tend to have *intense feelings* about the company. Those in the middle, scoring 2, 3 or 4, fall into a *zone of indifference* where there is little association between the satisfaction score and loyalty. One company, for example, found customers who rated the company 5 were six times more likely to repurchase than those who scored it 4.

The customers who score themselves at the very top end of the scale have been called *'apostles'*. They are so enthusiastic about the company that they are like unpaid salespeople, spontaneously telling others about the

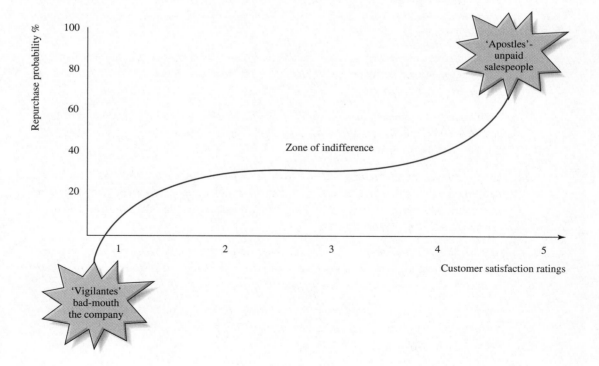

Figure 3.6   Customer Satisfaction and Customer Loyalty

company and recommending them to it. Those at the other extreme – sometimes called vigilantes – are so angry about the company's perceived performance that they actively 'bad-mouth' it and advise others not to buy.

Many marketing experts argue that in today's environment, faced with intense competition and buyers looking for the best values, companies have to do more than satisfy customers, they have to *delight* them. They have to try to convert as many as possible to apostles. A delighted customer is defined as one where the supplier's perceived performance exceeds expected performance. For example,

> When Richard Branson launched his new airline, Virgin Atlantic, he sought to do more than meet expected standards of performance and service. He aimed to delight his consumers by making their journeys exciting and romantic. He pioneered video screens behind every seat. Beauty therapists and a tailor were an occasional treat for passengers. A chauffeured motor cycle service to the airport was offered to business class passengers and champagne and birthday cakes for special occasions.

THE TRUST RELATIONSHIP

Customer satisfaction or delight measures how happy customers are with the company's product and with their recent transactions with the company. In the past few years, top marketing companies have moved away from focusing on products and transactions to building lasting relationships with customers. For suppliers, such partnerships are attractive because they replace the potential for destructive conflict with cooperation to achieve common goals. They shift the focus of negotiation from price to delivering total value to the customer. They also reduce the defection vulnerability. Increasingly, customers want partnerships too. Japanese manufacturers have taught Western companies that long-term cooperation with a small number of suppliers is a better way to reduce costs, enhance quality and boost innovation than playing off one supplier against another. Both parties should gain from successful partnerships.

The creation of a long-term relationship depends upon a *commitment* from both sides to make cooperation work. Such commitment depends on *trust* – defined as a willingness to rely with confidence on the partner. Trust is the belief that neither party will ever act opportunistically to take advantage of the other party's vulnerabilities.[6] The marketing emphasis among top companies like Federal Express, Hewlett-Packard, Johnson & Johnson, Xerox and GE is to move beyond satisfying customers with good products and services. The aim is to develop trust relationships with customers that focus on working in cooperation to enhance the customer's performance or experience.

Figure 3.7 summarises how to build a trust relationship and the benefits that arise from it.

IMPLEMENTING RELATIONSHIP MARKETING

In the previous sections we have presented the principles of successful marketing: understanding customers' needs, developing a differential advantage and building a trust relationship with customers. We now turn to how managers can plan to put such principles into action. The key steps in this planning process are shown in Figure 3.8.

DEFINING THE VALUE PROPOSITION

Management has to decide how the firm is going to compete. Is it seeking a differential advantage based upon a value proposition of product innovation, superior service, brand image or low costs? The choice is determined

**Trust-building
elements**

**Trust relationship
consequences**

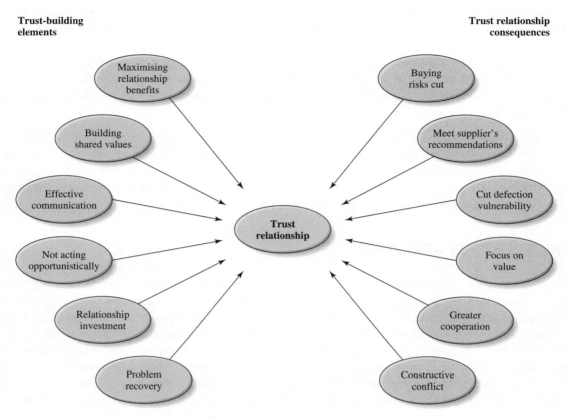

Figure 3.7   Building Trust Relationships. *Source*: Adapted from Christopher W. Hart and Michael D. Johnson, A framework for developing trust relationships. *Marketing Management*, Spring, 1999, 20

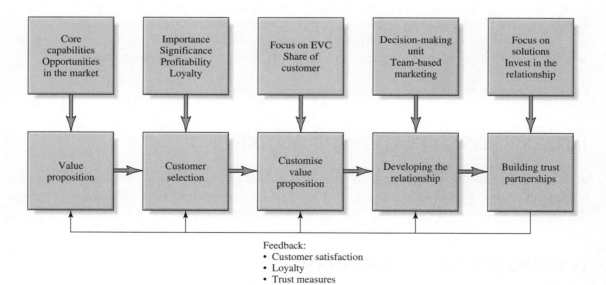

Figure 3.8   Customer Value-Based Strategy

by two key factors. The first is the firm's core capabilities – its unique combination of skills, assets and partnership relationships with customers and suppliers. These determine what the firm can do well. For example, a business is unlikely to be able to create a differential advantage based upon product innovation if it lacks a research and development base and experience in being first to market. Similarly, a firm today is not going to be competitive as a low-cost operator unless it has optimised the efficiency of each component of its supply chain.

The second determinant of the value proposition is the opportunities in the market. The value proposition has to match the wants of the customers. Of course, markets are segmented: some customers will want superior products, others will be more interested in services or low costs. But some market segments will offer more opportunities than others. The firm will need to research the size of the key customer segments, their growth, the amount of competition, average operating margins and investment requirements. It can then identify the profit potential of alternative value propositions.

SELECTING CUSTOMERS

In today's increasingly competitive markets, successful marketing is about focusing on key customers. Many companies are willing to do business with any customer willing to spend. Such companies end up with large numbers of unprofitable small accounts. They fail to develop the sophisticated partnering skills big accounts expect and so end up with low margins, big overheads and high customer turnover. Numerous studies have shown that the 80:20 rule – 20 per cent of customers account for 80 per cent of the profits – is typical. Professors Cooper and Kaplan of the Harvard Business School suggested, in fact, that the situation is often much worse. Using activity-based costing they found that in most companies, 80 per cent of customers were unprofitable. They proposed the 20:225 rule, which stated that in many companies 20 per cent of customers account for 225 per cent of the profits. This of course means that 80 per cent lose 125 per cent of profits!

To select customers who will have a high lifetime value for the company, four criteria need to be used:[7]

1. **Strategic importance.** Strategic importance has three dimensions. The company should seek customers who desire its value proposition and so fit its core capabilities. Second, customers are strategically important if they are expected to grow, either because they are in fast growth markets or because they have strong competitive advantages. Finally, a customer can be important if it is an opinion leader. These lead customers can open the door to other customers who are influenced by them.

2. **Customer significance.** Significance refers to the percentage of total revenue and gross profit the customer accounts for. For example, is the customer in the top 10 per cent of accounts? Size is not always correlated with profitability. Some large accounts demand big discounts and onerous levels of servicing, which shrink the operating profit they generate. But size should be significant. Big customers should offer more opportunities, they are very difficult to replace, and their loss can have a devastating impact on the business.

3. **Customer profitability.** The main reason why the majority of companies carry such a long tail of accounts is that they do not measure customer profitability. At best they measure contribution (revenue less variable costs). But contribution massively overestimates account profitability. Additional customers require more administrative support, warehousing, sales support, distribution and financing costs. Some firms employ activity-based costing, which attempts to charge costs to products, channels and customers for the resources they consume. When such estimates are made management is usually shaken by the losses that unfocused growth has brought. This inevitably leads to a strategy to refocus on the handful of profitable accounts and to make the others profitable or get rid of them.

4.   **The loyalty coefficient.** If the company wants to create long-term partnerships, it needs to identify customers who would be interested in such a commitment. Some customers are inherently more loyal than others. In business-to-business markets, some purchasers are spot buyers, focused solely on price, and they will switch from month to month according to which supplier is offering the best deal. For most companies, the lifetime value of these customers is very low. In consumer markets, too, some types of customer are inherently more loyal than others. In financial services, for example, there are striking variations in loyalty by demographic and social characteristics. In car insurance, loyalty is higher for married people, for homeowners rather than renters, and for those living in rural areas. In the credit card industry in the 1990s, for example, MBNA, now part of the Bank of America, became a very profitable company by avoiding mass marketing its cards and instead focusing its promotion on those specific professional groups with the highest loyalty coefficients.

CUSTOMISING THE VALUE PROPOSITION

Value-based marketing is about developing solutions that improve the customer's performance. The focus, in today's information age, is from doing a small amount of business with a large number of customers, to a large amount of business with a smaller number of high-value customers. This allows the firm to add value by customising the solution.

MOVING UP THE VALUE LADDER

Developing trust relationships with customers is based fundamentally on offering them value. Value is defined as improving the customer's performance or experience. Many companies do not offer value; they sell the products or services their company produces. Rather than understanding the customer's needs, the salespeople try to sell the features of their product, its quality or the services that accompany it. Such companies are production- or sales-orientated rather than market-led.

In most industries, competition leads to an evolution of value propositions (Figure 3.9). At the initial stage of the product life cycle the innovator wins customers on the basis of its successful new product or service. It is unique and, if successful, offers customers benefits that are superior to the old solutions. But soon competitors copy the innovation, allowing customers to choose among a variety of suppliers. The effect of competition is to reduce prices and margins. Suppliers then seek to avoid margin erosion by emphasising value propositions typically based on the quality of their products and then the services that are offered to support them. But over time these distinctions erode. Usually there will be a number of suppliers, all offering products of acceptable quality, and with similar support and service. Buyers then increasingly focus on price, and the margins of suppliers sink towards the threshold level where, at best, they are earning just the opportunity cost of capital.

Leading companies recognise that in the longer run, there is little profit to be made from selling products and services (see box, 'Companies Shift from Products to Solutions'). The real returns are made from solving customers' problems. We call this EVC, which in business markets normally means economic value to the customer. *Economic value to the customer* is created where the supplier finds ways of improving the customer's profitability by helping the customer increase sales, reduce costs, raise prices or lower its investment requirements. In consumer markets, EVC can mean emotional value to the customer. *Emotional value to the customer* is created where the supplier enhances the customer's experience by helping the individual obtain greater social, personal or psychological satisfaction. (EVC is discussed in detail in Chapter 8.) The fifth and final step on the value ladder is where the supplier can transform

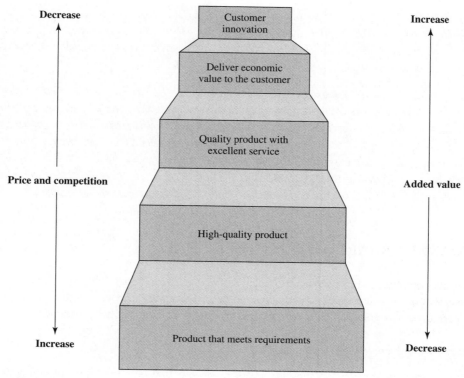

Figure 3.9   The Value Ladder

the buyer's business by finding it innovative ways to compete and grow. Focusing on solutions that offer customers EVC and innovation is a much more secure way to create trust partnerships than focusing on products.

Note that offering customers solutions requires different core competencies than those required from offering them products. Competing on products requires the company to be an expert on its own value chain – it must have outstanding skills in sourcing, producing and delivering its products and services. Competing on solutions requires the company to be skilled in the customer's business. It must have expertise on the customer's value chain to help the customer source, produce and deliver effectively to its own customers.

Companies Shift from Products to Solutions

Managers see a revolution sweeping through Western industry that has nothing to do with technology, the Internet or innovation. It is the switch that puts delivering solutions, rather than producing products, at the centre of the business.

Companies such as IBM, GE and Boeing are seeing manufacturing accounting for a smaller and smaller part of their profits. Global competition and excess capacity have made products and basic services increasingly low-margin commodities. Rather than selling products and components, these companies see profits and growth coming from taking direct responsibility for increasing the performance of their customers. Durr, for example, a world leader in painting systems for car plants, has only a very small proportion of its employees in production. The rest are working at the customers' premises operating the equipment and guaranteeing cost and quality targets. Castrol, a leader in industrial lubricant, offers its automotive customers a range of business services such as database management, aftersales consultancy and training.

Companies are positioning themselves as consultants, designing total solutions that will enable customers to increase their profits. They are also offering partnerships to deliver these results and give customers peace of mind. Boeing has set up a division to offer the airlines total fleet servicing. At IBM services now account for well over half of revenues. GE also gets over half its profits from servicing customers rather than selling products. Such a transformation requires a complete mindset change – from focusing on internal efficiency to understanding what drives the effectiveness of the customer's business.

FROM MARKET SHARE TO CUSTOMER SHARE

Earlier approaches emphasised brands, mass marketing and market share. Today's strategies focus on one-to-one marketing, partnerships and customised solutions. Rather than building market share by attracting large numbers of small customers, the new emphasis is on gaining a bigger share of the business of large customers.

The advantages of the share-of-customer strategy are:

1. Since they are existing customers they are already qualified on the selection criteria of strategic importance, significance, profitability and loyalty coefficient.

2. Experience with them will mean that they are low risk, there are no acquisition costs and they should be less costly to serve.

3. Since they are familiar, the supplier should understand their needs, know how they like to purchase and know their key personnel.

4. Since the basis of a trust relationship is already established, the customer should be more willing to consider proposals aimed at increasing its performance.

By contrast, the blunderbuss approach to growing market share by attracting new accounts leads to a large number of small customers, most of which have little potential. The net result is that focusing on a share-of-customer approach usually generates more profitable growth.

DEVELOPING AND CONSOLIDATING RELATIONSHIPS

Partnerships are not built between companies but between individual managers. Trust and confidence in the capabilities and commitment of the supplier have to be developed on a person-to-person basis.

THE DECISION-MAKING UNIT AGAIN

In business-to-business marketing, top management, middle management and the purchasing department all have a role in the development of customer partnerships. Normally companies do not sell directly to top management. But top management does control the purse strings, and their agreement is necessary before significant new investments can be made. The purchasing department is of course directly involved in buying arrangements. But the problem with purchasing executives is that they are generally transaction-orientated. Their focus is on getting the best deal in terms of price, product features and payment terms. Because they do not have profit responsibility, they are less interested in initiating performance-based partnerships.

The most useful focus for initiating partnerships is middle management, defined here as the heads of business unit profit centres and functional departments. The former are evaluated by their profit performance; the latter by their ability to reduce costs. These managers have the primary incentive to respond positively to suppliers who have the capabilities and commitment to generate continuing proposals to increase the performance of their businesses. They have the most to gain. They are also in the best position to make proposals to top management to get funding for supply partnerships. When business unit heads are convinced that their suppliers can become partners to generate EVC for them, these managers become *allies* in winning the support of the top management.

TEAM-BASED MARKETING

Developing partnerships generally requires a team-based approach from the company. Only a cross-functional team will have the expertise to put together a comprehensive plan to boost the customer's performance. Technical staff will be needed to understand the customer's operations, logistics people will be required to review the supply chain, development and marketing will be involved in putting together the offer, and financial staff in assessing the benefits to both parties. Teams also create an across-the-board commitment to the partnership. A successful ongoing relationship will depend on positive interactions between the businesses at many levels.

A team approach is also necessary in initiating the partnership. While the focus will be on the client's business unit manager, others in the decision-making unit cannot be neglected. Good communications need to be maintained with the purchasing management to align them to the objectives of the partnership. Top management also has to be brought alongside. Typically there will be multi-level communications: sales and purchasing people will be meeting, marketing will be leading the expert team negotiating with business unit management, and top management of the two companies will be in communication with one another developing trust and confidence.

CONSOLIDATING TRUST PARTNERSHIPS

Figure 3.7 suggests ways in which trust relationships are developed and consolidated. They can be divided into three types of initiatives. First, a partnership arrangement should be judged on its ability to deliver successful solutions for customers. Second, both parties need to invest time in understanding each other's businesses. Third, because problems and perceived breakdowns in trust are inevitably going to occur, it is important to have in place service recovery strategies that provide for investigating difficulties and resolving them to the satisfaction of both parties.

ORGANISATIONAL REQUIREMENTS

Managers cannot create a market orientation overnight. The organisation needs to have in place the assets and capabilities to provide unique value to customers. For example, Sony's ability to develop a successful value proposition based on product leadership rests on heavy investment and deep-rooted skills in microelectronics and

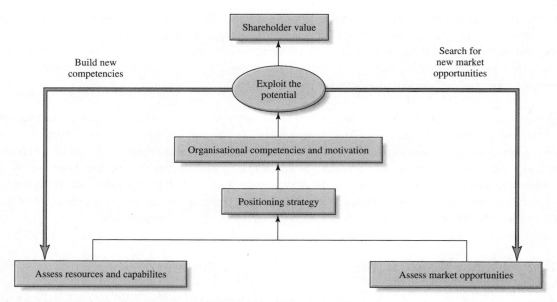

Figure 3.10   Developing and Delivering Customer Value

precision mechanics. Wal-Mart's ability to dominate American retailing with its low price value proposition is based on a huge investment in developing a unique low-cost sourcing and distribution system.

Developing and delivering a strategy to create customer value rests on the firm's resources and capabilities (Figure 3.10).

ASSESSING RESOURCES

A firm's resources and capabilities have to be assessed at several levels. First, firms possess at any one time bundles of tangible, intangible and human *resources*. But some firms succeed in combining these resources more effectively than others to create superior *capabilities*. There is a further stage. Today a firm's success in creating a differential advantage depends not just upon its own resources and capabilities but how well it *networks* with other firms to leverage their capabilities alongside its own.

A firm's resources can be grouped under three headings:

1.   **Tangible resources** are those assets that appear on the balance sheet: current assets, investments and fixed assets. Historically, the amount invested in such physical and financial assets and the firm's ability to manage them efficiently has determined its value.

2.   **Intangible assets** normally do not appear in the firm's financial statement but today they have become far more important in determining the value of the firm. They are of three main types. *Reputational assets* are brand names and other trademarks that give customers confidence in the firm or its products. This confidence results in higher sales and often price premiums, both of which translate into higher shareholder value. *Proprietary technology* consists of patents, copyrights and trade secrets that allow the firm to profitably exploit unique knowledge. *Strategic assets* are inherited advantages that give the firm a monopolistic or

unique market position. For example, the government gave British Airways a favourable position at Heathrow, Europe's busiest international airport hub.

3. **Human resources** are the valuable knowledge and skills possessed by the organisation's staff and their ability and willingness to work cooperatively with others in the organisation. In today's knowledge-based society, it is the organisation's ability to attract and retain highly skilled people that is increasingly valued by investors.

Of particular importance are the firm's marketing resources. These consist of *marketing expertise* – the knowledge staff possess of customers' needs and the managers' skills in developing marketing strategies and making decisions about products, pricing, communications and distribution. Then there are the *brands* that have been created through marketing investment over time and which offer the promise of future profits. *Customer relationships* are other intangible marketing assets that are highly valued by investors. Then there are other *partnerships* with suppliers, distributors and agencies that augment the organisation's resources with additional knowledge and skills.

ORGANISATIONAL CAPABILITIES

Marketing resources are not effective in isolation. To build value-creating strategies, resources have to be brought together in collaboration.

Organisational capabilities are the firm's capacity to exploit a particular marketing opportunity. They are determined by the firm's resources and management's ability to integrate them in pursuit of a marketing strategy. Of most interest are those special capabilities that enable the firm to create a differential advantage. In their influential book, Hamel and Prahalad called these the organisation's *core competencies*.[8] They defined core competencies as those special capabilities that make a disproportionate contribution to customer value, are relatively scarce, and provide a basis for entering new markets. Marketing is increasingly seen as the central core competency.

Harvard Professor Michael Porter proposed the *value chain* as a powerful tool for appraising the firm's capabilities to create a differential advantage (Figure 3.11).[9] A firm is a collection of activities to design, produce, market, deliver

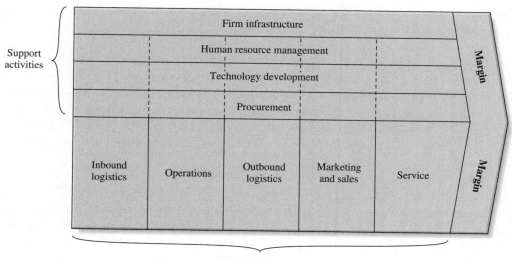

Figure 3.11 The Value Chain

and support its products. The value chain identifies nine strategically relevant activities that create value and incur costs. Five of these are termed primary activities and four are support.

The *primary activities* represent the sequence of bringing materials into the firm (inbound logistics), converting them into final products or services (operations), shipping out the products (outbound logistics), marketing them (marketing and sales) and servicing them (service). The *support activities* – procurement, technology development, human resource management and infrastructure – sustain the ability of the firm to conduct its primary activities.

The central task of management is to improve the firm's value chain by reducing the costs of these activities or improving their performance. The optimum structure of a firm's value chain will depend upon its market and its value proposition. For example, a company in the mainframe computer market will expect to operate on gross margins twice that of one in the PC industry, reflecting the higher investment it will have to make in sales, support and technology development. Similarly, a company with a value proposition based on price, such as Southwest Airlines, will have quite a different value chain from one competing on superior service, such as Singapore Airlines.

INTEGRATING CAPABILITIES: PROCESSES AND TEAMS

The value chain describes sets of specialist activities – procurement, marketing, logistics, and so on – but the key to generating shareholder value is to integrate these activities into *processes* that add value for customers. Having brilliant specialisms will not be enough unless they are brought together and combined to generate fast, innovative and efficient solutions for customers.

Capability comes from combining a competence with a reliable process. While an organisation conducts a multitude of processes, the core processes that add value for customers can be grouped into three (Figure 3.12). The first is the *innovation process*, which analyses potential market opportunities, researches for solutions and develops marketable products. Without a steady stream of new products the organisation will find its prices and sales being driven relentlessly down. Second, the business needs an efficient *operations process* – it has to be able to produce and deliver products that meet world-class standards of cost and performance. Finally, it must have an effective process for *customer creation and support*.

There have been significant changes in the way successful firms organise their value-creating processes. In the past, firms were organised hierarchically and functionally. Individuals saw themselves as specialists rather than team players. Inputs to processes were organised hierarchically and each function performed its tasks sequentially. For example, in the innovation process, researchers would first produce ideas, designers would then develop a prototype, it would then be passed on to production for manufacturing, and finally marketing would be involved to develop plans to sell it. Each of the specialist managers would report to his or her functional head rather than to the general process manager.

Today this type of functional organisation is increasingly giving way to *cross-functional teams*. The members of the team are chosen for their specialist skills but their duty is to accept joint responsibility for achieving process goals. Information technology has given added impetus to direct, informal networking between knowledge workers. Computers and open access to information make redundant the role of bureaucrats in collecting, filtering and passing on information. Cross-functional teams then permit the number of organisational levels to be cut back, reducing overheads and facilitating faster processes. Perhaps the biggest gain from effective team working is its

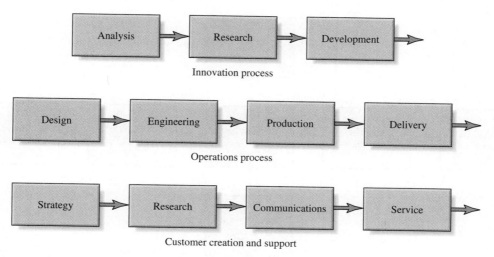

Figure 3.12   The Core Processes of the Business

motivational impact on employees. By breaking work down into tasks that can be accomplished by self-managing teams, management releases the energies of their people. Employees can throw off the debilitating blanket of bureaucracy, can set themselves ambitious targets, and can see the results of their contributions in new products, faster processes or higher levels of customer satisfaction.

NETWORKS: AUGMENTING COMPETENCIES

The competitiveness of a firm's value chain depends not only upon the effectiveness of its internal, cross-functional networks but increasingly upon its external networks. In the past, larger companies preferred to integrate the activities which contributed to value. For example, in the past a company like Ford had its own foundries casting iron and steel, its own factories making glass, tyres, engines and electrical components, and its own distribution business taking the assembled cars to its dealers. Today, however, most companies prefer to outsource non-core activities to a network of suppliers, distributors and partners. Procter & Gamble is a case in point. The company uses open-source innovation, collaborating with suppliers, competitors, scientists, entrepreneurs, and others. It scours the world for proven technologies, packages, and products that P&G can improve, scale up, and market either on its own or in partnership with other companies. [10]

The decline of vertical integration and the growth of networks are due to the changing business environment: notably, rapid technological change, the globalisation of markets and rising customer expectations. New technologies have meant that firms have had to rapidly obtain capabilities that were outside their traditional areas of competence. Sourcing such component products from outside is often the only practical route. Developing the capabilities internally would take too long, require too great an investment and be too risky. Similarly, globalisation has opened up new markets, but often firms lack the capabilities to exploit these opportunities. Finding business partners is an obvious solution.

Increasingly, the firm's value chain is part of a system for delivering solutions to customers (Figure 3.13). It is the effectiveness with which managers handle the whole supply chain and network of partnerships that determines the

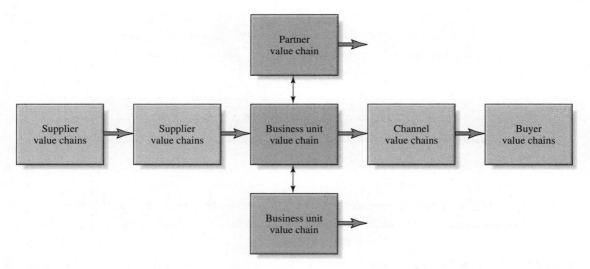

Figure 3.13   The Firm's Value Chain System

competitiveness of the firm. Again, information technology boosts the facility with which such networks can be managed.

THE CUSTOMER-FOCUSED ORGANISATION

The concept of the value chain allows management to explore how people can be organised internally to create greater value. But the external impacts of staff on customers also need to be optimised. In recent years leading firms have been putting great efforts into making their organisations customer-orientated.

In the past, customer focus was not the driving force behind the design of organisations. Instead organisations were designed bureaucratically to optimise the efficiency of capital and to reduce risks. Top management formulated strategy and those at the bottom of the hierarchy undertook implementation. Job roles were clearly defined and employees were organised into functional departments (e.g. production, marketing, purchasing). To ensure that strategy was implemented correctly, controls in the form of supervisors, centralised information systems, budgets and formalised reporting played a major role. Communication was vertical: information went up and orders came down. Lateral communication across functions was limited and was the preserve of senior staff.

In recent years three pressures undermined these bureaucratic organisations. One was the need to cut overhead costs as increasing global competition eroded the gross margins of many firms. Companies could no longer pay for the big head office staffs and the layers of middle management supervising and controlling the front-line staff. A second pressure was the need to accelerate the pace of innovation. While the formalised hierarchical structures worked well enough in steady-state industries, they were poor at stimulating innovation. Fast-paced innovation does not work well in organisations characterised by rules, rigid reporting procedures and tight job specifications. A third problem was that these organisations were not customer-orientated. The front-line staff who dealt with customers were at the bottom of the organisational pyramid. People with talent did not want these jobs because they lacked prestige and autonomy. Real decisions and power lay at the top of the hierarchy – far away from direct contact with customers and the front line. Not surprisingly, customers frequently found such organisations unresponsive and their front line staff unmotivated and unprofessional.

THE RIGHT-SIDE-UP ORGANISATION

The new, more demanding market environment created the pressures to change organisations; information technology provided the means for change. Three features stand out in the way leading companies are reorganising to enhance customer orientation and shareholder value:

1. Breaking into small, autonomous business units
2. Turning the organisation upside-down
3. Changing the role of top management

BREAKING INTO SMALL, AUTONOMOUS BUSINESS UNITS

Large organisations cannot help but become bureaucratic, slow moving and unresponsive to customers. To counteract these problems, companies are breaking themselves down into small business units that have profit responsibility for a specific market, product or process. They are trading off the old priorities of scale economies and cost efficiency for the new agenda that prioritises innovation and customer responsiveness. Companies like Procter & Gamble still enjoy the economies of scale from taking a global approach to purchasing, manufacturing and the like, but also benefit from a decentralised approach to regional and local markets.

TURNING THE ORGANISATION UPSIDE-DOWN

Today companies want to focus on customers – and those who are directly responsible for understanding and satisfying their needs – the front-line staff. Traditional organisations do not do this. The pyramid structure devalues the role of the front-line staff and promotes the importance of supervisory and staff positions. Power and rank go to those who can manipulate the politics of the organisation rather than those who satisfy customer needs.

Modern companies want to reverse this focus by turning the organisation upside-down and flattening it (Figure 3.14). The aim is to enhance front-line positions, improve knowledge about solving customer problems and enhance service. The new orientation recognises that the key to creating shareholder value is the loyalty of customers. This in turn depends on the skills and motivation of the front-line staff. To achieve this, companies have to recruit the best staff and invest heavily in their training and development. Finally, such staff have to be empowered to act on their own judgement about the right way of dealing with customers.

The new upside-down organisation emphasises that the role of middle and senior management is to support the front-line staff in satisfying customers. If managers are not assisting the front-line staff by providing the products, services and tools that they need, then these managers are not adding value. The philosophy has led to new approaches to evaluating managerial performance. Evaluating the performance of front-line staff is often straightforward – customers can be asked to rate the way they perform. But deciding who should evaluate, and how the performance of middle and senior management should be judged, has been more problematical. In the new

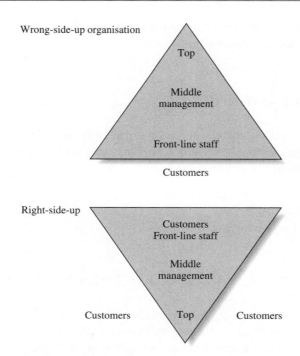

Figure 3.14   Wrong- and Right-Side-Up Organisations

customer-focused organisation the answer is clear – ask the front-line the question: 'Are these middle managers help-ing you serve the customer?' Such an approach changes the outlook of middle managers – instead of being controllers, they have to prove their value by becoming supporters and coaches, assisting the effectiveness of the front-line.

THE ROLE OF TOP MANAGEMENT

Today the roles of the chief executive and top management are changing. In the past the chief executive was the company's top marketing strategist. He or she would define the company's markets and how it would create competitive advantage. Once the strategy was formulated, top management would then design the organisational structure and systems required to implement the strategy. But this view of strategy is looking increasingly anachronistic.

It is no longer realistic to assume top management has the superior knowledge to develop strategy. Relevant knowledge now lies in the front line, not in the corporate office. The real job of top management today is not to strive to achieve the impossible goal of being the marketing guru defining strategy, structure and systems. Instead, it is to focus and release the knowledge and energy of the front line by developing and communicating a vision of the company's purpose, processes and people.

In large organisations it is all too easy for people to become disaffected by bureaucracy, cost cutting and the inevitable changes that threaten their security and careers. Shareholder value is not a goal that inspires staff. Work is more than an economic institution for people; it is also a social institution that involves a major proportion of their time, energy and relationships. To create involvement and motivation, top management needs to give the organisation a human *purpose* with which employees can identify. Both Ian MacLaurin and Terry Leahy as successive chief executives of Tesco have had as the driving principle for everyone in the company: to create value for customers to earn their lifetime loyalty. Today, the real role of the chief executive is to shape the culture of the organisation and give it a meaning that encourages people to willingly contribute their energies and skills.

SUMMARY

1. Marketing is the basis for creating shareholder value. Only by meeting customer needs, developing customer preference and building customer relationships can an organisation achieve profitable growth.

2. Marketing has not had the impact on top management that its importance justifies. This is largely due to its objectives being poorly defined. Value-based marketing redefines marketing as the central contributor to shareholder value and presents a clear framework for evaluating the success of marketing strategies.

3. The first step to successful marketing is a detailed understanding of customers: their needs, operating procedures and decision-making processes. Customers do not want products, they want solutions to their problems. Preference and value is created by solving customers' problems. Today it is increasingly difficult to make money from selling products.

4. Meeting customer needs is not sufficient. The organisation also has to create a differential advantage: a reason why it should be preferred to competitor businesses. A differential advantage may be based upon offering consumers superior benefits, lower costs or some combination of the two.

5. The ultimate goal is to build partnerships with high-value customers founded on loyalty and trust. Customer loyalty is the real source of sound business growth and profitability. Customers are assets: the longer they are retained, the more value they should create.

6. Building successful customer partnerships depends upon the firm having the resources and capabilities to build outstanding processes, particularly in innovation, operations, and customer creation and support.

REVIEW QUESTIONS

1. How does value-based marketing differ from the traditional definition of marketing?
2. Why is meeting customer needs the foundation for creating shareholder value?
3. Explain the significance of the differential advantage for marketing and shareholder value.
4. Explain and illustrate how customer loyalty affects a company's rate of sales growth and its operating margin.
5. What are the steps necessary for developing a relationship-marketing programme?
6. What resources and capabilities does an organisation need to develop a successful marketing strategy?

NOTES ON CHAPTER 3

[1] Michael Treacy and Fred Wiersema, *The Discipline of Market Leaders*, London: HarperCollins, 1995.

[2] Many of these findings are presented in an important book, Frederick F. Reichheld, *The Loyalty Effect*, Boston, MA: Harvard Business School Press, 1996.

[3] 'Consumer vigilantes', *Business Week*, 21 February 2008.

[4] Frederick F. Reichheld, The one number you need to grow, *Harvard Business Review*, December 2003.

[5] Thomas O. Jones and W. Earl Sasser, Jr, Why satisfied customers defect, *Harvard Business Review*, November/December, 1995, 88–99.

[6] For a complete review of this approach see Robert M. Morgan and Shelby D. Hunt, The commitment–trust theory of marketing, *Journal of Marketing*, **58**(3), 1994, 20–38. See also: Glen L. Urban, *The Trust Imperative*, MIT Sloan Working Paper, No. 4302-03, March 2003.

[7] For an example of the use of rating systems to evaluate prospective customers see John O. Whitney, Strategic renewal for business units, *Harvard Business Review*, **74**(5), July/August, 1996, 84–99.

[8] Gary Hamel and C.K. Prahalad, *Competing for the Future*, Boston, MA: Harvard Business School Press, 1994.

[9] Michael E. Porter, *Competitive Advantage: Creating and Sustaining Superior Performance*, New York: Simon & Schuster, 1985.

[10] Larry Huston and Nabil Sakkab, Connect and develop: inside Procter & Gamble's new model for innovation, *Harvard Business Review*, 1 March 2006.

4 The Growth Imperative

'When the rate of change inside the company is exceeded by the rate of change outside the company, the end is near.'

Jack Welch, Chairman of General Electric

INTRODUCTION AND OBJECTIVES

Growth is essential for creating shareholder value. Those companies that created the greatest shareholder value during the latter half of the 1990s and the early years of the 21st century, such as Microsoft, Dell, Vodaphone, Nokia and Wal-Mart, were all companies that grew turnover rapidly. Logically, this is easy to understand: shareholder value is created by discounting long-term cash flows. The primary determinant of cash flow is profitable sales. Of course, cutting costs and investment can temporarily boost cash flow. But such actions rarely increase the value of the business substantially, because investors recognise that these actions do not create long-term profit growth. Such measures simply produce short-term gains, often at the expense of long-term growth. In contrast, financial markets clearly recognise, in large share premiums, the value of those companies that create the potential for profitable growth.

Management should make growth a top priority. But the evidence suggests that this does not happen. The boardroom agenda is all too often crowded out with operating and administrative concerns that have little relevance to the key strategic issues of growth and value creation. This chapter focuses on how to develop and manage a growth strategy.

By the time you have completed this chapter, you will be able to:

- *Explain the link between growth and value creation*

- *Identify the alternative ways growth can be achieved*

- *Analyse when diversification outside the company's traditional products and markets makes sense*

- *Describe how to develop a growth strategy for a business*

- *Understand how to implement a growth strategy in a company*

The next section shows how growth increases the financial value of a company. We then turn to the growth ladder – nine pathways to accelerate growth, starting with maximising the potential opportunities offered by the company's existing customer base and culminating in the unconstrained search for growth outside the boundaries of the current industry. Finally, we show how a growth strategy should be organised. We explore how management can put growth at the top of the corporate agenda and implement an action plan to move up the growth ladder.

MARKETING, GROWTH AND SHAREHOLDER VALUE

WHY GROWTH?

Growth is the central determinant of shareholder value because of its potential for increasing the net present value of future cash flow. As shown in Chapter 2, shareholder value is a function of four financial drivers: (1) the level of cash flow, (2) the timing of cash flow, (3) the sustainability of cash flow and (4) the risks attached to future cash flow. Growth has the potential to impact positively on each of these drivers.

THE LEVEL OF CASH FLOW

A key rule is that *growth creates value for shareholders if the operating margin on the additional sales exceeds the threshold margin*. This minimum operating margin to create shareholder value increases with the level of investment required to fuel the growth, the cost of capital and the tax rate. Recall from Chapter 2,

$$\text{Threshold margin} = \frac{\text{Incremental investment} \times \text{Cost of capital}}{(1 + \text{Cost of capital})(1 - \text{Tax rate})}$$

For example, if the investment rate is 50 per cent of incremental sales, the cost of capital is 10 per cent, and the tax rate is 35 per cent, then the threshold margin is 7 per cent. So if managers expect the long-run operating margin to be above 7 per cent, growth adds value for shareholders.

Also, investors normally expect growth to increase the level of cash flow through improved costs and greater pricing power. There are three potential sources of cost improvements. *Economies of experience* are reductions in unit costs that result from the learning that accompanies growth. The Boston Consulting Group summarised its studies in its Law of Experience: doubling cumulative production typically reduces unit costs by 20 to 30 per cent.[1] *Economies of scale* are cost advantages that go with size. Typically these have been associated with manufacturing costs, but today marketing costs are equally, if not more, important. For example, the cost of a national sales force or advertising campaign is relatively fixed; it is the same whether a company has a 5 or a 50 per cent market share.

This means that bigger brands usually have much lower unit marketing costs. Research into the American soft drinks market during the 1990s (in Figure 4.1) illustrates the economies of scale between adspend and volume. Small brands like Schweppes had unit advertising costs 10 times greater than big brands like Coca-Cola. Finally, *economies of scope* arise from having a range of products. As a company grows and adds new products, savings will often come from sharing the same distribution network, IT system, sales force or R&D facilities. New products may also use existing brand names to lower marketing costs. Finally, economies of scope may arise from sharing the special managerial capabilities and skills that the company has built.

The level of cash flow may also be increased by higher prices. In general, companies that grow to become market leaders obtain better margins from the trade and from powerful buyers. Marginal brands suffer most from pricing pressures.

TIMING OF CASH FLOW

Because investors discount cash flows, the faster high positive cash flow occurs, the greater the shareholder value that is created. Companies that have managers skilled at developing growth strategies know how to accelerate cash

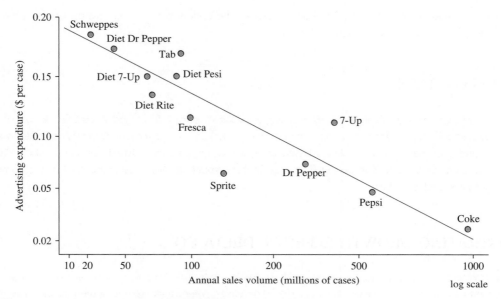

Figure 4.1 Scale Economies in Advertising: US Soft Drinks Industry

flow. Methods include fast-track new product development processes and pre-marketing campaigns to accelerate market penetration. Growth can also be accelerated by licensing and strategic alliances to gain rapid access to new markets, to obtain new distribution channels and to create standards. Finally, managers geared to growth opportunities know how to use their current strong brand names to leverage new products. New products launched under a strong umbrella name can generally achieve faster market penetration.

SUSTAINABILITY OF CASH FLOW

As discussed in Chapter 2, the majority of the value of companies lies in their continuing value – the cash flow that lies beyond that created in the five- or six-year planning period, over which most companies project. The value investors assign to the continuing value of a company depends upon their perceptions of three factors: the sustainability of its differential advantage, the company's ability to innovate and the options it possesses.

Growth extends the sustainability of a firm's differential advantage by offering the opportunity of taking the product or service into new markets. Much of the value in the McDonald's and Coca-Cola share prices, for example, has stemmed from the perceived opportunities of taking these brands, which are maturing in the USA, into new high-growth markets. The second factor is the company's potential to innovate. Growth and innovation are inextricably linked. Investors expect growth companies to be innovative. It is impossible to achieve long-term profitable growth without developing new products, new marketing concepts or new distribution channels. Future innovations promise long-term cash flow.

Closely related to innovation are the real options investors perceive in high-growth companies. Options are opportunities to invest in tomorrow's new markets, without the obligation to make big, high-risk investments if management changes its mind. For a pharmaceutical company, these options may be in the research and investment projects it has under development. For a web-based business the options could be the opportunity in the future to sell additional categories of merchandise through its portal. The options a firm is perceived to possess have a big effect on investors' perceptions of its continuing value.

CASH FLOW RISK

Growth can also create shareholder value by reducing the volatility of cash flows and so cutting the cost of capital. First, growth reduces dependence on a single product and market and so reduces the firm's vulnerability to specific shocks. Second, sustained growth is always based upon a growing core of satisfied customers who have been with the company for an extensive period. The greater the number of loyal customers, the less the company is susceptible to competitive activity.

ILLUSTRATING GROWTH EFFECTS: DELTA CO.

The effects of growth on shareholder value are illustrated in Table 4.1. Delta has a turnover of 20 million euros and a current estimated market value of almost 19 million euros, when capitalised using the residual value method (NOPAT divided by the cost of capital). This will be its value if it does not pursue profitable growth opportunities. To explore how growth affects shareholder value, the following assumptions are made:

Operating profit margin (%)	12.0
Cash income tax rate (%)	30.0
Incremental working capital investment (%)	20.0
Incremental fixed capital investment (%)	25.0
Cost of capital (%)	9.0

To keep the model simple, marketing and overheads are assumed to increase proportionately with sales, so that the operating margin remains at 12 per cent. Note, this is well above the break-even threshold margin, calculated at 5.3 per cent.[2]

A new management team introduces a marketing strategy that promises to boost growth to 10 per cent a year over the six-year planning period. As shown, because of the positive threshold spread, this strategy increases shareholder value by 34 per cent to over 25 million euros. Table 4.2 shows that if growth is accelerated to 20 per cent a year, shareholder value is increased by 86 per cent. The last two columns in the table also show how value is further enhanced if growth also leads to economies in costs or working capital. For example, 10 per cent growth associated with a similar reduction in unit variable cost would boost shareholder returns to 88 per cent. The figures in the growth columns illustrate why investors give such extraordinarily high share valuations to high-growth companies.

Of course, not any growth policy makes sense. If companies make excessive investments, and sales do not earn the threshold margin, then growth will be value destroying. In the 1970s and 1980s, many Japanese manufacturers made enormous investments in capacity in a vain effort to dominate their markets. The results in the 1990s were excess capacity, declining prices and massive losses, triggering a major recession and the collapse of many of these businesses. To create value, sales have to achieve a threshold margin determined by the company's cost of capital, its investment requirements and the tax rate.

Table 4.1 Illustrating Growth and Shareholder Value

Year	Actual 2000	Planning Period 2001	2002	2003	2004	2005	2006
Euros 000							
Sales (10%)	20 000	22 000	24 200	26 620	29 282	32 210	35 431
Variable costs	8 000	8 800	9 680	10 648	11 713	12 884	14 172
Marginal income	12 000	13 200	14 520	15 972	17 569	19 326	21 259
Advertising	500	550	605	666	732	805	886
Fieldforce	800	880	968	1 065	1 171	1 288	1 417
Marketing	1 000	1 100	1 210	1 331	1 464	1 611	1 772
Contribution after marketing	9 700	10 670	11 737	12 911	14 202	15 622	17 184
R&D	1 000	1 100	1 210	1 331	1 464	1611	1772
Overheads	6 300	6 930	7 623	8 385	9 224	10 146	11 161
Operating profit (12%)	2400	2 640	2 904	3 194	3 514	3 865	4 252
Tax (30%)	720	792	871	958	1 054	1 160	1 276
Net profit after tax	1680	1848	2033	2236	2460	2 706	2 976
Additional working capital		400	440	484	532	586	644
Additional fixed capital		500	550	605	666	732	805
Cash flow		948	1 043	1 147	1 262	1 388	1527
Discount factor ($r = 9\%$)	1.000	0.917	0.842	0.772	0.708	0.650	0.596
Present value		870	878	886	894	902	910
Cumulative present value		870	1747	2 633	3 527	4 429	5 340
PV of continuing value	18 667	18 838	19 011	19 185	19 361	19 539	19 718
Cum. PV + continuing value	18 667	19 708	20 758	21 818	22 888	23 968	25 058
Shareholder value added		1 041	1 051	1 060	1 070	1 080	1 090

TWO ROUTES TO VALUE CREATION?

Market-led growth has a clear causal effect on shareholder value by increasing the net present value of future cash flow. But many managers believe there is an alternative to market-led growth for creating long-term value. This is a strategy of rationalisation – a focus on cutting costs, raising prices and divestment. This is surprising since the stock market rarely rewards such a strategy in terms of significant value enhancement.

One reason for the belief in rationalisation is that many companies lack a market focus. They do not have long-term strategies in place to capitalise on emerging market opportunities. Managerial incentives also often conflict with a

Table 4.2   What Leverages Shareholder Value?

	Growth in shareholder value Sales growth rate p.a.			
	−10%	0	10%	20%
Growth	−22	0	34	86
−10% Variable costs	−4	33	88	181
−10% Overheads	−6	26	77	153
−10% Inventories	−23	5	35	89
+10% Price	−20	−6	46	107

focus on long-term growth. In many companies management bonuses are tied to annual profits. A failure to hit the year's budget is seen as penalising managers' pockets and possibly their careers.

Managers are also aware that rationalisation and growth strategies work differently in their effects on profits and cash flows. Cutting costs and investment usually works quickly to increase profits and cash flow. While cutting back on such investments as in service staff, brand support and R&D will hit sales, this tends not to happen for a considerable time. Often the negative effects do not show through until the managers responsible have moved on to other jobs. In contrast, creating profitable growth is costly immediately and it may take years before the positive results begin to show on the bottom line. In addition, rationalisation is relatively easy since it is about reconfiguring the firm's internal resources. Growth, however, is more difficult since its success is determined externally. It depends on convincing customers that your business offers them superior value to the other competitors in the market. Unfortunately, in career terms, rationalisation is often a more advantageous path than investing in market-led growth, especially when the firm's profits are under pressure and competition is fierce.

Figure 4.2 compares accounting-led rationalisation and market-led growth as approaches to creating shareholder value. Rationalisation focuses on cutting fixed and variable costs, reducing working capital and fixed assets, and price increases. Prices can be pushed up directly or by concentrating on high-value market niches or by price discrimination using regular and premium-priced products to serve different market segments.[3] Market-led growth focuses first on existing customers, reinforcing loyalty, increasing purchases and selling new products to them. Next, it looks to develop new customers with existing and new products. Finally, it aims to develop new business through new distribution channels, international markets and entering new industries.

Despite its managerial appeal, rationalisation is fundamentally flawed as a long-term corporate strategy. First, it sacrifices long-term investment for short-term improvements in profitability and cash flow. In the longer run, these companies fail to meet the emerging needs of their customers, miss new opportunities and are left marooned in declining markets with yesterday's technology. Second, even where there is waste, rationalisation can only be done once; it does not offer continual opportunities. Finally, investors see through these strategies and generally do not reward rationalisation with higher share prices. This is illustrated in Table 6.2 for GourmetFoods in Chapter 6. The first column shows that if sales are declining, no amount of cost cutting or price increases will prevent a decline in the future cash flow available to shareholders.

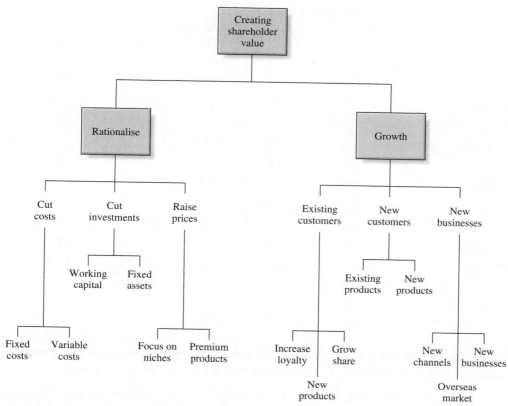

Figure 4.2 Two Routes to Value Creation

PATHWAYS TO GROWTH

SETTING OBJECTIVES

In a business geared to creating value for shareholders, the planning process will start with top management setting a shareholder value goal. For example, the new chief executive of Delta Company declares the goal of doubling the share price over a five-year period. As shown in Table 4.3, the current equity value of the business, using the perpetuity method to calculate continuing value, is £46 million. This was close to the current stock market value of the company. Management understood that growing the equity value of the company depended upon a strategy to increase the net present value of future cash flow and communicating this strategy to investors.

After a situation analysis of the industry and the business (as discussed in the next chapter), management believed it possible to set a three-part strategy to increase future cash flow, involving:

1. **Margin improvement.** By reengineering business processes, costs could be reduced sufficiently to drive up operating margins from 8 to 12 per cent over the next four years.

2. **Incremental investments.** The net increase in working and fixed capital to support sales growth was estimated at 40 per cent of sales, i.e. each £100 of additional sales would involve new investment of £40.

Table 4.3   Growth and Shareholder Value at Delta

Year		1	2	3	4	5
Sales	100.0	114.0	130.0	148.2	168.9	192.5
Operating profit	8.0	10.3	13.0	16.3	20.3	23.1
NOPAT (tax = 30%)	5.6	7.2	9.1	11.4	14.2	16.2
Investment (40%)		5.6	6.4	7.3	8.3	9.5
Cash flow		1.6	2.7	4.1	5.9	6.7
Discount factor ($r = 10\%$)	1.000	0.909	0.826	0.751	0.683	0.621
Present value		1.4	2.2	3.1	4.0	4.2
Cumulative PV		1.4	3.7	6.8	10.8	15.0
PV of continuing value	56.0	65.3	75.2	85.7	96.9	100.4
Cum PV + CV	56.0	66.7	78.9	92.5	107.7	115.4
Debt	10.0					23.4
Equity value	46.0					92.0

Most of the investment would have to be financed from profits. Management was willing to see the amount of debt increase from £10 million to around £23 million, but was not issuing more shares.

3.   **Sales growth.** Management then looked at what growth was necessary based on the above assumptions. As shown in Table 4.3, by a process of iteration, an annual sales growth of 14 per cent would double the value of the business, increasing it from £46 million to £92 million.

The next task was to consider whether and how such growth might be achieved. What was clear was that the company was stagnating. Sales had been static for a number of years. No strategies to grow were being considered. It was obvious that the new management team needed to develop growth policies and to change the organisation and culture of the business. Essentially, there was a 'strategic gap' between what sales were desired and what were likely under current policies (Figure 4.3).

THE GROWTH LADDER

To fill this gap the company must find new growth opportunities. A consultant introduced to management the concept of the growth ladder. The *growth ladder* conceptualises a company's growth opportunities as a nine-step progression that starts with consolidating the core customer base and then moving on to capitalise on less constrained opportunities for growth (Figure 4.4). Key to the concept is first establishing the fundamentals – ensuring that the business has the trust and loyalty of its existing target customers. The nine steps of the growth ladder are:

1.   Increase customer retention rate
2.   Grow share of customer
3.   Gain new customers
4.   Develop new products and services

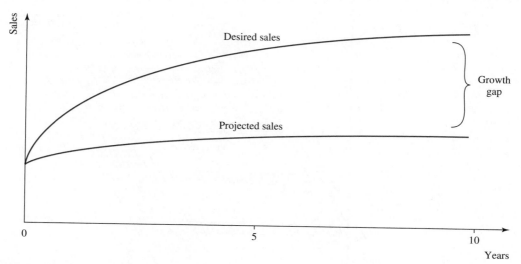

Figure 4.3   The Growth Gap

5.   Enter new markets
6.   New distribution channels
7.   International growth
8.   Acquisition and alliances
9.   Growth outside current industry boundaries

STEP 1: INCREASING CUSTOMER RETENTION

The first and most fundamental stage of building a growth strategy is ensuring that existing key customers have complete confidence and trust in the company. As shown in the previous chapter, a typical company – a bank, insurance company or retailer – has a customer retention rate of 90 per cent. That means it loses 10 per cent of its customers every year. Or, to put it in another way, the average customer stays with the company for ten years. As we have seen in Chapter 2, increasing the retention rate has an enormous impact in raising profits and growth potential.

Much of the research has focused on the effect of retention on increasing the *profit* or lifetime value of an average customer. But increased loyalty also has a powerful effect on the company's potential *growth* rate. Trying to grow without achieving customer loyalty is like trying to fill a bath using a bucket with a big hole in the bottom.

Consider three companies, A, B and C. Each begins with 100 000 customers and each succeeds in attracting 10 000 new customers each year over a 10-year period. However, they differ in their ability to retain customers: A's retention rate is 80 per cent, B's is 90 per cent and C's is 95 per cent. In other words, an average customer stays with A 5 years, B 10 years and C 20 years.[4] The consequences for growth are that despite attracting the same number of new customers, company A's customer base ten years later has shrunk to 55 000, B's has remained unchanged, but C's customer base has grown to over 140 000.

Without loyal customers it is almost impossible to grow. A high level of customer loyalty, on the other hand, makes growth much easier. If it wanted to double its customer base over the decade, company A would need to attract 42 000 new customers a year, while C would only need 17 000 a year.

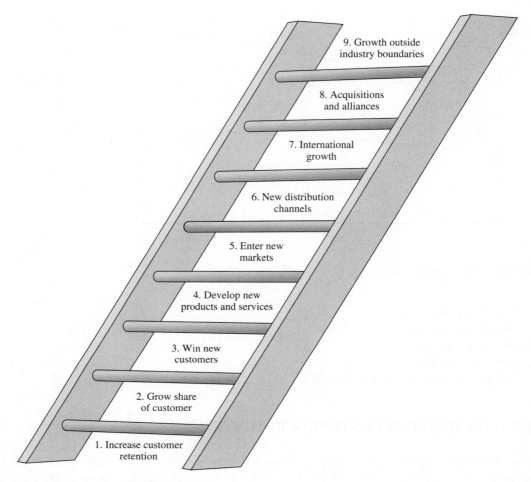

Figure 4.4   The Ladder of Growth

To increase retention rate management needs to put in place a number of steps, outlined in the following subsections.

1. CUSTOMER SELECTION AND PRIORITISATION

Managers need to understand that customers should not all be treated equally. It is worth investing much more in retaining some customers than others. Two criteria determine what priority they should receive: customer lifetime value and strategic fit. The potential lifetime value of a customer depends on its size, growth, profitability and loyalty potential. Strategic fit refers to the customer's need for the firm's distinctive capabilities and value proposition.

Managers should segment accounts along these criteria and respond accordingly. For example

A polymer company segmented its customers into three categories based on the size of the account, its expected future development and the type of business relationship. The categories were Partnership, Base load and Swing. A different product and service offering was developed for each customer category.

The company offered a formal *partnership* proposal to priority customers. If the customer accepted, it agreed to buy a minimum of 80 per cent of its requirements from the company. The agreement covered product, credit terms, consignment stocks, technical and laboratory services as well as advice on training on environmental, health and safety issues. For example, the company maintained consignment stock representing three weeks' average consumption by the partner. All partner orders were handled on the same day. Just-in-time deliveries meant that the customer did not need to maintain stock. All partners had an account manager who took personal responsibility for the smooth operation of the customer's business.

Base load customers did not have consignment stocks maintained for them. Laboratory and technical services had to be paid for. A more limited programme of training on environmental, health and safety issues was offered. Orders were handled within three working days.

Swing customers typically purchased most of their requirements from competitors. For these customers the business relationship was limited to little more than delivery, If services were requested they were invoiced at market rates. Swing customers were normally requested to open a bank guarantee before orders were accepted.

2. CUSTOMISE THE VALUE PROPOSITION

Fundamentally, increasing the loyalty coefficient depends upon meeting the needs of the individual customer. So the first priority is *listening to customers*. Only by researching customers can management discover their needs and problems. Business-to-business marketing will focus on offering customers superior profitability through lower costs or enhanced output. For household consumers it is often also about offering emotional value – confidence, prestige or trust.

Until relatively recently it was only possible to *customise* solutions when a company had a small number of customers. Most companies used variants of a *mass marketing* model. They designed products and services for a mass market, or at least a major segment of it. Consumers then had to choose the best approximation to their individual requirements. Loyalty was low because consumers would shift when a competitor came out with a better approximation to their requirements.

The reducing cost of information technology has changed this by making new capabilities affordable. First, powerful *databases* allow companies to tell customers apart and remember their individual interests and purchasing history, even when the numbers of customers run into millions. Second, *interactivity* through the Internet, telephone or direct mail means that individual customers can communicate information about their wants directly to the company. Third, *mass customisation technology* means companies can customise products to individual requirements. Companies like Dell and Amazon.com that pioneered this new mass customisation model found they could greatly increase the retention rate. What is the point of customers switching when their current supplier is giving them the exact product they want, when they want it, at a fair price? Especially when the company remembers what you bought last time and your billing details and can use this information to take the hassle out of ordering. It can even anticipate your requirements, suggesting new products that will interest you and keep you up-to-date. Customisation can be either in terms of how the offer is communicated to the customer or in terms of whether product attributes are personalised (see Chapter 10 for more on customisation).

3. ENHANCE THE VALUE PROPOSITION

However successful a company is today, it cannot afford to rest on its laurels. New competition is always closing the gap. Changes in customer requirements and new technology continually make existing solutions obsolete. To maintain customer loyalty, the company has to maintain leadership by updating its products, services and the quality of its relationships with customers.

Keeping one step ahead involves close monitoring of customers, competition and technological trends. It also means taking a long-term view of what is required to maintain customer loyalty. It may mean pursuing new products even when they offer low margins and risk cannibalising current winners. For example, Hewlett Packard pioneered cheap ink-jet printing technology even though it competed with its own high-margin laser technology. The company recognised that while in the short-run this cannibalisation reduced profits, in the long run it was the only way to retain customer loyalty.

4. MONITOR CUSTOMER SATISFACTION AND LOYALTY

Since customer loyalty is the first step on the ladder to achieving higher growth and profitability, it is amazing that so few boards of directors insist on regularly measuring and monitoring it and its determinants. Improving customer satisfaction with the quality of the service experience is the most direct way of increasing loyalty. Researchers have shown that there are normally five determinants of service quality that need to be monitored.[5] On average, customers weight them in importance as:

1. **Reliability.** The ability to perform the promised service dependably and accurately. (32 per cent of the total importance score)

2. **Responsiveness.** The willingness to help consumers and provide prompt service. (22 per cent)

3. **Assurance.** The knowledge and courtesy of employees and their ability to convey trust and confidence. (19 per cent)

4. **Empathy.** The provision of caring, individualised attention to customers. (16 per cent)

5. **Tangibles.** The appearance of the physical facilities, equipment, personnel and communications. (11 per cent)

Obviously, the relative importance of these factors will vary from product to product and market to market and firms need to conduct research with their own customers to establish how they rank them.

Customers are satisfied if the service they perceive they receive along these dimensions equals what they expected. Customers are delighted if the perceived service exceeds expectations. The model of Figure 4.5 describes the main determinants of customer satisfaction.

How should managers use customer satisfaction data? Movements in ratings are lead indicators of the ability to retain customers and hence achieve growth and profit goals. As discussed in Chapter 3, only the highest scores, i.e. delighted customers, really correlate positively with loyalty. Management should not be satisfied if large groups of key customers are not rating the service in the top box.[6]

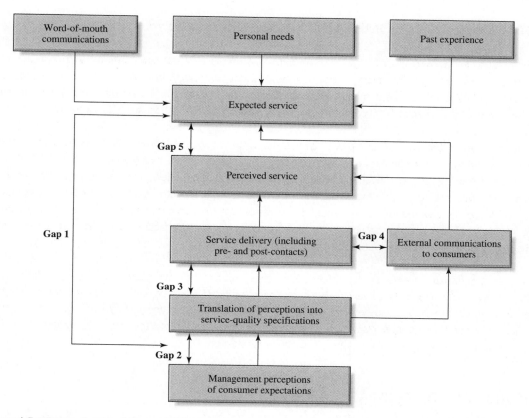

Figure 4.5 Determinant of Customer Satisfaction. *Source:* Reprinted with the permission of The Free Press, a Division of Simon & Schuster, Inc., from *Marketing Services: Competing through Quality*, by Leonard L. Berry and A. Parasuraman. Copyright ©1991 by the Free Press

To motivate performance, especially among front-line employees, customer satisfaction should form a part of the reward and incentive system for staff. The model also suggests where management should look to increase customer satisfaction. Figure 4.5 shows five 'gaps' which undermine service:

1. **Misunderstanding of customer requirements.** This occurs where companies have not researched customers properly and are focusing on the wrong things. For example, managers think customers want higher-spec solutions when in fact their priority is greater reliability.

2. **Poor specification of standards.** Management may not have set sufficiently clear specifications for staff to implement the desired standards. The managing director tells the switchboard to be customer-orientated but does not specify how.

3. **Lack of capabilities.** Staff may lack the training or motivation to meet the standards specified.

4. **Creating over-expectations.** Advertising and salespeople can promise too much, leading customers to have inflated expectations. The result is disappointed customers.

5. **Misperception of service.** Consumers can misperceive the company's attentions. Highly attentive staff at a restaurant are sometimes perceived by customers as hassling.

5. FOLLOW-UP ON COMPLAINTS AND DEFECTIONS

It is misleading for a company to rely on complaints as a measure of customer satisfaction. Most dissatisfied customers do not bother to complain. Even when they do, not surprisingly, front-line staff often do not pass the complaints upward to management. It has been estimated that on average only 4 per cent of dissatisfied customers complain. So if a bank receives 1000 complaints a year, it probably has 25 000 dissatisfied customers.

But it is important to follow up on complaints for two reasons. First, angry customers can easily become customers who actively bad-mouth the company to dozens of prospective purchasers. Such negative publicity can do enormous harm to a company's growth prospects, particularly with the ability of disgruntled customers to wreak havoc through anti-company web sites that can reach hundreds of thousands of prospective purchasers.[7] Second, complaints can generally be dealt with and customer confidence restored if the company responds quickly and generously. Some studies show that when complaints are resolved to the customer's satisfaction, such customers become more satisfied than those who never experienced a problem in the first place.

Companies should make it easy for dissatisfied customers to record their complaints. This way, problems can be identified early and dealt with decisively, before they become a tidal wave that washes away the company growth potential. *Defections analysis* is another very useful tool. Here companies interview or survey via email customers who have switched their business elsewhere. This gives direct, fresh insight into the causes of dissatisfaction, which is often more incisive than general measures of customer satisfaction.

6. BUILD CUSTOMER PARTNERSHIPS

Increasingly, companies see the best way to create loyalty is to shift from a transactional to a partnership relationship with customers. By offering a formal partnership contract to customers companies create a framework for mutual gain. Customers gain an organisational capability dedicated to improving their long-term performance. For the supplier partner, it means that it can trust in holding the account, gaining the majority of the business and the probability of increasing its sales with the client.

Normally creating a partnership will mean assigning a dedicated account manager to the customer to coordinate the development of the relationship. Partnering is about integrating the value chains of customer and supplier (see box, 'Building Partnerships with Customers').

Building Partnerships with Customers

Forging highly collaborative relationships with selected customers can deliver significant results, according to McKinsey. It suggests that an intelligent and well-organised approach can create and capture value at a time of mounting price pressures.

It cites two prominent examples:

○   *'In the mid-1990s, Alcoa's Wheel and Forged Products division began devoting more energy and attention to developing custom products for several auto manufacturers. The result was more*

> distinctive (and often proprietary) forged aluminum wheels for vehicles such as the Special Edition Jeep Grand Cherokee, Ford Super Duty truck, and GMC Hummer. Eventually, Alcoa extended its collaboration with original-equipment manufacturers (OEMs) beyond the development of new products, to include rollout, marketing, and post sales service. During the past ten years, Alcoa has expanded its share of this market to 35 percent, from 5.
>
> ○ About six years ago, Sonoco, a packaging supplier, intensified efforts to help the snack food maker Lance determine the ideal packaging for its product lines. One improvement involved the use of flexographic printed packaging film in Lance's single and multiserving Home Pack snacks for brands such as Toastchee and Captain's Wafers. Efforts like these drastically reduced Lance's packaging costs, and the company made Sonoco its "Supplier of the Year" in 2002. In an industry where most players were growing slowly or shrinking, Sonoco generated annual revenue growth of 7 percent and margin growth of 18 percent from 2001 to 2004 – thanks in part to this collaboration and others like it.'
>
> A survey carried out by McKinsey of more than 200 sales executives at Fortune 1000 companies found that for the leading sellers in the survey collaborative initiatives increased revenues and profits by more than 20 per cent on average. Success comes from a well-thought-out framework, including having a thorough understanding of the customer's economics, making sure the right personnel are in place on both sides, and carrying out regular audits of how the partnership is working.
>
> Source: Maryanne Hancock, Roland John, Phil Wojcik, "Better B2B selling", The McKinsey Quarterly, June 2005

Full partnerships only make sense where the client's potential lifetime value to the company justifies the investment required. But falling computing and communication costs have lowered the costs of interfacing with customers. Many companies find it effective to tier partnerships. For example, British Airways executive club members are designated gold, silver or blue tier members depending upon the value of the business they place with the company. Each tier offers a different level of benefits to the customer.

STEP 2: GROW SHARE OF CUSTOMER

Once managers have in place an effective programme to increase customer loyalty, the second rung of the growth ladder is to grow its share of the spending of these customers. Over the past few years there has been a major change of emphasis in marketing. Traditional marketing has focused on selling a single product to as many customers as possible; the new marketing focuses on selling as many products as possible to each, individual customer. It is a shift from mass marketing to one-to-one marketing.

Several factors are breaking down the old business model. One is that products are becoming increasingly commoditised. Virtually all industries have excess production capacity. Worse, in most of these industries it is proving impossible to retain significant technological or quality differences. Second, mass marketing, and particularly advertising, is increasingly costly. The average consumer is exposed to as many as 3000 ads a day. The fragmentation of television channels and print media makes it more and more expensive to obtain the required impact. The result is that gaining market share is more and more expensive. Also, without real differences between offers, market share once achieved is difficult to retain against aggressive competitors.

But the greatest cause of the change is new technology, which has opened markets to new competition by allowing the unbundling of the functions of providing information to consumers with that of the physical delivery of products. Consumers go to a retailer like Toys 'R' Us both to gain information about products and to physically obtain them. But they can also check information, compare prices from a number of suppliers, shop online and have the product delivered directly to their home. This is often more convenient for the consumer, and for the supplier it means economies because there are no expensive shops and much less working capital to finance.

Equally important, information technology allows customisation. Companies can communicate one-to-one with consumers, learning their individual requirements, storing this information and customising products and services. Until relatively recently the technology was simply not available, or prohibitively expensive, for companies with large numbers of consumers to learn about them individually. But this is quickly changing with the rise in Internet usage which means that companies can gather valuable information about customers, including their whole purchase history and their preferences.

The convenience, additional sources of differentiation and collaborative relationships resulting from information technology enable companies to increase their share of the customer's spend. Increasingly, successful companies are selling services rather than products. After all, it is services rather than products that ultimately meet consumer needs. For example,

> Successful airlines increasingly draw their revenues from the additional services they offer passengers. These include hotel bookings, car rentals, travel insurance and financial services. The airline has no need to own any of the other service providers: it simply brings them together under its brand umbrella to provide a convenient package for the customer.

> As it collects more information about customer preferences, it can offer other things that might be of interest. It could suggest a theatre performance to somebody travelling to New York, make all the bookings and throw in a limo at a bargain rate. It could get flowers delivered before arrival. And reserve a table at a favourite restaurant 15 minutes after curtain-down. If the customer's schedule changes, the airline will change not just its ticket, but all the other arrangements as well.[8]

Selling more to current customers means using technology to communicate individually with customers, retain the information obtained and customise products and relationships to meet their needs. Then it requires being proactive in proposing additional services and products that will further improve the customer's total organisational performance or the individual's personal experience.

STEP 3: WIN NEW CUSTOMERS

The first two steps get the basics right – they focus on delivering a value proposition that offers the quality of products, service and reliability that customers want. The result is a trust relationship with the individual customer that achieves a high loyalty coefficient and a growing share of the customer's expenditure. If this base is set properly, growing the number of customers is relatively easy. High performance on the first two rungs of the ladder leads to a strong reputation and brand image. New customers will want to do business with the company. Satisfied customers will also recommend the company to others. It is often more about selecting rather than winning new customers. For example,

> First Direct is one of Europe's leading direct banking operations. It deals with its customers by telephone, the Internet and through text messaging on mobile phones, with 80% of customer contact by electronic means.

The bank uses the technology to deal with customers as individuals and achieve high levels of service, 24 hours a day. Customer polls have consistently shown the bank to attract much higher satisfaction ratings than many of its competitors. One in three of its customers joins through personal recommendation from friends, relatives and colleagues. It targets busy professionals, who are described as 'money rich' but 'time poor'. It has been in profit every year since 1995.

The company can enhance the word-of-mouth effect by using the marketing mix or '4 Ps' to extend its reach and communicate its value proposition:

○ Product *refers to the tangible offer the firm makes to the market and includes quality, range, design and branding. It also includes services such as delivery, leasing, repair and training. The product range can be enhanced to bring in more customers. For example, smaller pack sizes may attract more low-income customers.*

○ Price *is the amount of money that customers pay for the product. It includes discounts, allowances and credit terms. The firm could attract more customers by lowering the price or offering distributors more allowances to push the product.*

○ Promotion *consists of all those activities used to communicate and promote the product, including the sales force, advertising, public relations, promotions, and direct and online marketing. For example, advertising and public relations can be used to increase awareness and comprehension of the firm's product and service range.*

○ Place *refers to the activities and partners involved in distributing the product and making it available to customers. It may include wholesalers, retailers, web sites and transport. Increasing the numbers of retailers and distributors carrying the product might attract new customers.*

STEP 4: DEVELOP NEW PRODUCTS AND SERVICES

Strategists often use the *Ansoff matrix* (Figure 4.6) to discuss the growth options available to the firm.[9] The first three rungs on the growth ladder refer to the top left box, which Ansoff called market penetration. This is growth by selling more of the firm's current products in its existing market by raising the retention rate, increasing customer spend or winning competitors' customers. The fourth rung moves to a new element of

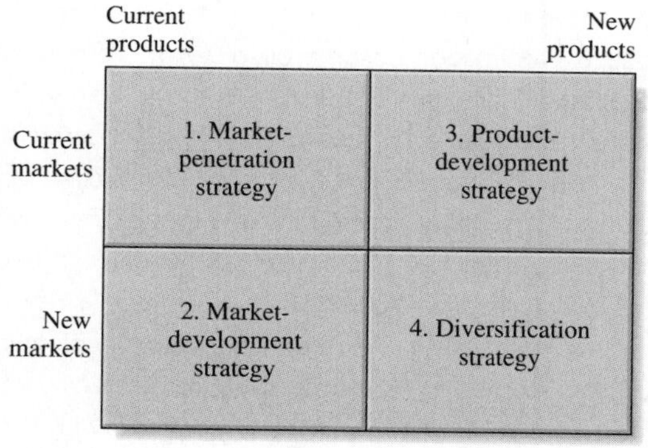

	Current products	New products
Current markets	1. Market-penetration strategy	3. Product-development strategy
New markets	2. Market-development strategy	4. Diversification strategy

Figure 4.6   The Product–Market Expansion Matrix

the matrix – the top right, developing new products and services. In today's rapidly changing environment it is an essential step. Technological change, new competition and changing customer requirements are continually shortening product life cycles. In most markets it is impossible to satisfy customers without an increasing stream of new products and services (see box, 'Accelerating Pressures to Develop New Products'). Without an effective new product development process, a firm will face declining customer loyalty, loss of customer share and declining margins on its products.

New product development has risen sharply up the corporate agenda. Top management has to champion innovation by continually asking three questions:

○   *Can existing products be improved to better meet customer aspirations?*

○   *Could extensions to the product range meet latent customer needs or attract new customers?*

○   *Are there new products that could be developed, purchased or licensed to complement the current range and enhance the firm's value proposition?*

Accelerating Pressures to Develop New Products

Pharmaceuticals is one of many industries being forced to radically ratchet up new product development. In the past, patents meant successful new products earned huge profits for an average of ten years. When the patent expired sales and profits usually collapsed under the onslaught of generic competitors. To maintain performance successful companies needed to develop a stream of patentable product improvements to extend the protection of their brands. But nowadays investors expect companies to launch several new drugs a year.

Expectations have been changed by three scientific revolutions – molecular genetics, informatics and automation – which are expected to lead to an explosion of new products. To survive, companies are looking at three strategies to ramp up their innovation activities. The first is outsourcing more of their R&D to new, niche companies with expertise in the new technologies. Second, they are boosting their own internal R&D budgets. The need to find bigger budgets has produced an explosion of mergers and alliances in the industry. Third, they are reengineering their new product development processes to accelerate the speed of development and launch and to ensure that they are closely linked to customer requirements.

Of the thousands of new products being introduced annually, less than 1 per cent are revolutionary, *new to the world products*. Many are *product improvements*, upgraded or redesigned versions of previous models. Without these continual facelifts, the products would soon become obsolete or unfashionable. Another major category is *line extensions* – new flavours, applications or types of the core brand to better fit special needs. These relatively low-tech marketing initiatives can be very valuable. For example, Coca-Cola Zero is a new flavour with zero calories designed to appeal to young adult males. Procter & Gamble's recent introduction of an active foam spray extension to its Fairy washing-up liquid allowed it to grow significant share in the 18–25 year old market. Another good example is Gillette, which continuously relaunches its products with updates. It became such a valuable company that Procter & Gamble paid £31 billion for it in 2006. Of this sum, only £4 billion was for tangible assets. £7 billion was paid for Gillette's innovative capability.[10] Another major category of new products are *new product lines*. These are a company's version of product lines already successively introduced by competitors. For example, Nestlé launched a cream-filled chocolate bar under its Kit Kat brand to compete with Ferrero's successful Kinder Bueno chocolate bar in New Zealand, Australia and the UK. Dell Computer Corporation followed the lead of Toshiba and Compaq in launching a line of notebook computers.

INVENTION VERSUS INNOVATION

Many people, especially scientists, confuse invention with innovation. An invention is a new product; an innovation is a new customer benefit. Many inventions fail to find profitable markets because customers do not see them as offering benefits in terms of improving their performance or experience. To be a successful innovation, a new product or service must be tested against five criteria:

○ **Benefit.** *Customers must value the new features. For example, a new watch, accurate to one second in a hundred years, would be a great technical feat, but would probably not be regarded as a substantial benefit by consumers.*

○ **Unique.** *The benefits offered by the new product must be seen as unique. If customers perceive that products already on the market provide the same benefits, the new idea will have little value.*

○ **Timely.** *Speed in developing and launching new products is increasingly critical. Products that are delayed usually cost more to develop, earn lower margins and obtain smaller market shares than those that are fast to market.*

○ **Sustainable.** *A new product may offer unique benefits but if it can be quickly copied, it will not create much value for shareholders. The innovator must try to develop barriers to entry. In some industries, patents may provide a barrier but more often it is achieved by brand building, superior marketing and speed to market.*

○ **Marketable.** *The company must have the capability to market the product. This includes designing a reliable and effective version of the product, producing it at a price customers can afford, and establishing an effective distribution system to deliver and support it.*

It is estimated that over 80 per cent of new products fail to generate a return to shareholders. They fail because they do not meet these criteria.

THE NEW PRODUCT DEVELOPMENT PROCESS

To guard against these causes of failure the business needs to develop processes and an organisational culture that increase the chances of successfully developing a stream of new products. The new product development process consists of the following steps (Figure 4.7):

1. **Business strategy.** Management needs to articulate a business strategy that sets out its ambition to innovate. For example, 3M makes innovation the core of the company's strategy by demanding business unit managers achieve a minimum of 25 per cent of their profits from new products. Most companies will have a mission statement that identifies the markets, needs and technologies that form the scope of its activities. New product ideas will normally be expected to fall within this ambit defined by the firm's core capabilities.

2. **Idea generation.** New ideas come from many sources. Customers and technical research are two basic sources. But competitors, overseas markets, distributors and licensees can also be extremely fruitful. Virtually all sources depend upon employees, and in particular front-line staff, identifying and championing the opportunities.

3. **Idea screening.** Once it has a stream of ideas, management needs to filter out those that are not worth pursuing. Companies often use screening techniques that rate ideas on their potential uniqueness, market

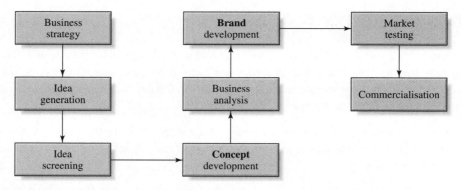

Figure 4.7   The New Product Development Process

potential and fit to their capabilities and business strategies. There are two types of errors in a screening process. Type I errors result from not screening out ideas that subsequently fail. They lead to financial losses from developing and marketing products that do not find profitable markets. Type II errors are harder to recognise, but can often be much more costly. These are mistakes in dropping ideas which could have been successful. (For some examples, see box, 'Type II Errors in New Product Development'.)

Type II Errors in New Product Development

'The telephone has too many shortcomings to be seriously considered as a means of communication. This device is inherently of no value to us.'

Western Union internal memo, 1876

'The wireless music box has no imaginable commercial value.'

David Sarnoff, 1923

'Who the hell wants to hear actors talk?'

H.M. Warner, WarnerBros., 1927

'I think there is a world market for maybe five computers.'

Thomas Watson, chairman of IBM, 1943

'We don't like their sound, and guitar music is on its way out'

Decca Recording Co rejecting the Beatles, 1962

'There is no reason why anyone would want to have a computer in their home.'

Ken Olsen, President of Digital Corporation, 1977

'The Web – it's not going to be that profound.'

Steve Jobs, President of Apple, 1996

---

4.   **Concept development.** Ideas that get through the initial screening have then to be developed as positioning concepts to assess their marketability. A *positioning concept* is a description of the product idea in terms of the

target market segment – who might buy it – and the value proposition – why they would buy it. The correct positioning is a crucial determinant of the product's potential market and its ability to achieve differentiation. It is generally a difficult problem because most new products could potentially be aimed at quite different segments and have different value propositions. For example, something as simple as a new cold remedy could be aimed at children or adults, severe or normal sufferers, those with headache or cough symptoms etc. Similarly, the value propositions could be built around efficiency, speed of action, length of action or fewer side effects. The choice of positioning concept will be the key determinant of the size of the market and the competition the product will face.

Positioning concepts should be tested for their appeal by researching:

○   **Market.** *What types of customers are most interested in the product?*

○   **Communicability.** *Do they understand the benefit being offered?*

○   **Believability.** *Do they believe the benefits claimed?*

○   **Need.** *Do they have a strong need for the benefit claimed?*

○   **Usage.** *How would they use it and how often?*

○   **Uniqueness.** *Are existing products already seen as satisfying the need?*

5.   **Business analysis.** Normally, the amount invested in the new product up to this stage is relatively low, but if it proceeds further costs and investment will now begin to accelerate. To make this go/no go decision management should require a detailed business analysis that will enable them to judge the potential rewards, risks and investments needed. In principle, this is the standard net present value calculation to determine whether the proposed project will create value for shareholders.

The first task will be to calculate the level and timing of cash flow over the planning period. This requires marketers to estimate the prices that can be obtained and the growth of sales over the period. Next the different functional areas will need to estimate the costs and investment requirements for developing, making and marketing the product. Since these estimates will be very uncertain, it is useful to produce optimistic and pessimistic estimates, as well as a median forecast of cash flow. Finally, management will need to choose the discount rate to be applied to the project. The more risky the product looks, the higher the discount rate that will be applied. The expected net present value of the project is then:

$$\text{ENPV} = \sum_t \frac{p_t C_t}{(1 + r)^t}$$

where ENPV is the expected net present value of the new product, C_t is net cash flow in year t, p_t is the probability estimate attached to cash flow in year t and r is the cost of capital.

The go/no go decision should not be based solely on the results of this financial calculation. Broader strategic considerations need to be examined. A failure to invest in a new product area could give a competitor a strategic opportunity to enter the market and build a beachhead for subsequent expansion. Similarly, a decision to invest may offer profitable growth opportunities that are not reflected in the basic discounting formula.

The theory of options is increasingly being used to value such strategic new product opportunities. Option theory calculates the net present value of a project by explicitly incorporating estimates of the value of the future options a new product may offer (see box, 'Using Options to Value New Product Proposals').

Using Options to Value New Product Proposals

The net present value rule can sometimes be misleading when applied to new products. When managers factor in the high levels of uncertainty about a new product's potential cash flows, the NPV will often be negative, indicating that the product proposal should be rejected. But such a decision may be wrong because management does not need to make a go/no go decision at the start of the new product development process. Instead, they can purchase an option by investing in research and deferring a decision until the results are known. This is an extremely common situation in developing new products and, indeed, in developing growth strategies generally.

Option theory was developed in finance in the 1970s. Essentially, options are a combination of decision tree analysis and NPV. A simplified example can illustrate the approach.

Management is considering a new product concept. The product will require a £100 million investment and if it succeeds it will be very profitable, generating an income stream with a present value of £150 million. The chances of success are put at 50:50. If it fails then the present value of the income stream is put at £10 million. A traditional NPV analysis would put the expected value of the project at £80 million. Since this is less than the upfront investment of £100 million, it has a NPV of minus £20 million, which leads to a rejection of the product proposal.

But in practice management will not put the whole investment upfront; instead, they will research the project. Suppose management takes an option to invest £10 million in research and consumer testing and delays a decision about proceeding further until the results are known after 12 months. If the development and testing are successful, management will launch the product and reap the profits of £150 million. However, since both the investment (£10m + £100m) and the returns are delayed by a year, they are discounted by the opportunity cost of capital, say 10 per cent, to £100 million and £135 million, respectively, or a net gain of £35 million.

The overall value of the new product, then, is £7.5 million (the average of £35 million and zero, less the upfront £10 million). Management should therefore proceed with further development and testing.

The technicalities in options analysis lie in calculating the discount rates to be used. Usually these are considerably higher than the normal weighted cost of capital. In summary, option valuation is most important in situations of high uncertainty where management can respond flexibly to new information, and where the project value without flexibility is near breakeven. If the NPV is very high, the project will go full steam ahead, and flexibility is unlikely to be exercised. Optionality is of greatest value for the tough decisions – the close call where the traditional NPV is close to zero.

Source: Thomas E. Copeland and Philip T. Keenan, How much is flexibility worth? *McKinsey Quarterly* no. 2, 1998, 38–49. Reproduced by Permission of McKinsey & Company.

6. **Brand development.** If the proposed product passes through the business analysis gate, the next stage involves developing a product capable of commercialisation and a marketing mix to complement and communicate its value. The brand development work demands the close cooperation of a cross-functional team, each member bringing in his or her specialist knowledge. A product has to be designed and developed to match the chosen positioning concept and be capable of efficient production and delivery. The brand

components – name, packaging, advertising and price – have to be generated and tested. There are a wide variety of market research techniques for developing and testing alternatives.

7. **Market testing.** After a brand has been developed and pre-tested, a company can test it further in a more authentic market setting, to get more reliable information about the size of the market and reactions to the elements of the brand, and to anticipate any problems that may occur in the full launch. The product can be tested in a sample of shops or distributors. Consumer goods are often tested in a representative geographical area.

8. **Commercialisation.** Once it is decided to commercialise the product then the really major costs and investments in manufacturing and marketing are incurred. By then management hope that all the problems have been anticipated. Speed to market is increasingly important. Being first – provided it is done right – often offers major advantages in terms of higher profits and long-run market share.

STEP 5: ENTER NEW MARKETS

The fifth step on the growth ladder is equivalent to the bottom left corner of the Ansoff matrix (Figure 4.6) – market development strategy, or entering new markets, using existing products or technology. This is an obvious and common growth strategy, but managers often underestimate the difficulties of executing it successfully. There are three stimuli for this growth strategy. One is the opportunity to build on the synergies from current know-how or products. For example, the success of the Apple iPod as a hand-held electronic device led the company to enter the mobile phone handset market with the iPhone, competing with established players like Nokia, Sony-Ericsson and Samsung. Also, many of the leading brands of women's perfumes have entered the market for men's cosmetics. Another attraction may be the emergence of new growth markets. Porsche, which holds a pre-eminent position in the upmarket sports car market, decided to enter the rapidly growing sports utility vehicle (SUV) market with the powerful four-wheel drive Porsche Cayenne. Caterpillar, which dominated the market for large bulldozers, decided to enter the small equipment market when the US heavy construction market matured. Glaxo (now GlaxoSmithKline) took its anti-ulcer drug Zantac into the over-the-counter market after sales peaked in the prescription-only market.

But the most common stimulus to entering new markets is the product life cycle. Initially, a new product, because of its high price and limited communication, appeals to a specialist market. Then, over time, awareness grows and prices fall, offering opportunities to sell the product to a succession of new markets. For example, when mobile phones were first launched, very high prices limited the market to senior executives, then after a few years the market expanded into the broader business community; later still, the household market offered growth opportunities, and finally young people became the fastest growing market.

Managers often think that moving into new markets is straightforward because it deploys current products or technologies. But this is a mistake: adapting to the needs of different markets is generally more difficult than developing new products. For example, in the mobile phones market, Motorola lost its leadership as it failed to adapt to the different requirements of the new markets. The problems occur because these new markets have different needs, different operating processes and different buying patterns from the initial customers. This means that the products require different positioning strategies, and pricing, promotion and especially distribution channels have to be dramatically changed. Seeking to sell to new markets with strategies that worked for the original market are almost bound to fail.

Top management need to check that the new market strategy is soundly based by ensuring proper research has been done on the following questions:

○   *Who are the new customers and what are their wants and aspirations?*

○   *How do these differ from those of our current market?*

○   *Who makes the decisions and who influences the buying process?*

○   *What is the positioning strategy and marketing mix that would ideally match the needs of these customers?*

○   *How different is our proposed strategy from this ideal?*

Market leaders often come unstuck by not adapting sufficiently to emerging markets. When this happens they are leapfrogged by new competitors, unencumbered by traditional strategies and channels, that can set up new market strategies that fit more effectively the needs of the new market.

STEP 6: NEW DISTRIBUTION CHANNELS

The sixth rung of the growth ladder is innovation in distribution channels. This has become one of the major sources of growth opportunities for businesses. The main drivers of change have been technological. In 1990 only 100 000 computers were connected to the Internet. By 2007 usage had soared, with over 1.3 billion people logged on. This has produced huge changes in the way customers buy. Both in consumer markets, and even more in business-to-business markets, sweeping changes have occurred in the ways suppliers sell and distribute their products and services.

REVIEWING DISTRIBUTION CHANNELS

The reasons why growth-orientated companies need to continually review their channels are:

1.   **Opportunities to innovate.** New distribution channels have offered the opportunity to create whole new markets. Lastminute.com created a unique concept using the Internet to sell exclusive last minute deals for flights, entertainment, gifts and hotel rooms (see box, 'New Distribution Channels Offer Opportunities to Create New Markets').

2.   **Accelerate growth.** A company can outgrow its distribution channel. For example, confectionery company Thorntons relied on sales from its own shops for two decades. To increase its growth opportunities, it began to sell to supermarkets and chain stores as well.

3.   **Changing customers.** New customers or changing customer needs can make existing channels obsolete. As customers become more familiar with a product, distribution tends to migrate from high-price, full-service retailers to low-cost channels such as mail order, telesales or online.

New Distribution Channels Offer Opportunities to Create New Markets

Two young British entrepreneurs set up Lastminute.com in 1999 to exploit the growing availability of the Internet. They recognised that for the first time the net offered the opportunity to publicise exclusive last-minute deals for a whole range of items including flights, entertainment and hotel rooms – even diamonds have been sold on the site.

> *Their target market was 'yuppies': the cash-rich, time-poor people who can take off at the last minute. This was the audience that was already online. By 2007, there were 2.5 million people logging on in the UK every week. The company was bought by two private equity groups in 2007.*

4. **New technology.** New technology can make current distribution channels obsolete. The impact of ATMs and telephone and Internet banking has meant rationalisation of the bank branch network, for example. With new low-cost technologies, competitors do not need to make enormous investments in bricks and mortar to compete.

5. **Poor performance.** Current distributors may not be performing inadequately. Perhaps they have more profitable alternatives or lack the skills and knowledge to exploit the supplier's product range.

Changing distribution channels is always difficult because it introduces conflict between the current distribution channel and the emerging one. For example, the early 1990s saw the growth of direct selling of personal insurance products. For the existing players this was a problem since they relied upon independent brokers to sell their products. Fearing the loss of broker support, they were deterred from selling direct to the public. As a result they lost a major share of the market to new entrants. Similar problems face many businesses today: locked into large investments in site locations, historical distribution networks or sales forces, they find it hard to slip into the new wave of low-cost, information-based distribution systems. Often the result is the emergence of a new generation of industry leaders.

SEARCHING FOR NEW DISTRIBUTION OPPORTUNITIES

By finding new and better ways of delivering products and services, companies can challenge the positions of industry leaders. Here are the questions managers should address:

1. **Are there additional channels?** The company can increase growth by adding *new distributors* to its current network to broaden or deepen its market coverage. *Piggyback* and *co-marketing* involve using the selling and distribution networks of other suppliers to create additional sales. Besides intensifying distribution, a company can add new channels. *Web sites* have become increasingly integrated into the growth strategies of firms. A company can also have *parallel distribution* by running two channels simultaneously. For example, beauty care company Avon sells its cosmetics online, by direct selling to individual households, by phone and by post.

2. **Are there substitute channels?** As the market changes and new technologies appear a company may have to look to change its channels. In the early 1990s, Compaq became the market leader in PCs through its dominant position in leading retail channels. But by the late 1990s, direct marketing had become the fastest growing channel. By cutting out the retailer, dealing directly with the individual customer over the telephone or Internet, and making to order, Dell was able to undercut Compaq's prices and build a closer relationship with consumers. By 1999 Compaq's channel leadership had become a liability rather than an asset. It merged with Hewlett-Packard in 2002.

3. **Can the channel be reengineered?** Often the current channel can be reengineered to reduce costs, take out investment and increase speed of response to customer demand. Information technology can be used to improve demand forecasting, reduce stocks and enhance the ability to meet customer expectations.

STEP 7: INTERNATIONAL GROWTH

Today even the smallest companies have to exploit the growth opportunities presented by the new global economy. Many companies are pulled into international marketing by the need to serve their customers. New stimulus is given by declining barriers to trade, deregulation of markets, global media and communications and new trading and political entities like the European Union. Virtually all companies now face foreign competitors in their domestic markets. Indeed, the concept of a domestic market is losing much of its meaning; markets are increasingly regional or global.

In developing an international growth strategy, management has to take a number of strategic decisions.

WHICH MARKETS?

A company can choose to focus on a small number of markets or spread its efforts over a large number of countries. For all but the most experienced businesses, focus is the best strategy. Concentration allows a company to build knowledge in depth about its markets and it can focus resources to build strong distribution systems, critical mass and market share. In deciding on which markets to concentrate, the company needs to assess their market attractiveness, its competitive advantage and the country risks.

HOW TO ENTER THE MARKET?

Companies can choose between low-cost, limited-commitment methods of entering and developing overseas markets, and high-investment, high-goal approaches. They face the usual trade-off between risk and reward. *Indirect exporting* – paying independent agents or merchants to find customers – is a low-risk entry mode. *Direct exporting* gives more control. *Licensing* is another relatively low-risk method of developing a market. This allows a foreign company to use the brand name, patent or manufacturing process in return for a fee or royalty. Coca-Cola's enormously successful overseas growth has been based largely on having overseas bottlers licensing the company's brand name.

When a company is ambitious for greater control but still wishes to draw on outside skills and capital it can look to *joint ventures*. Joint ventures are increasingly being created when it is necessary to quickly put together large investments and complex technologies. Finally, the ultimate form of foreign commitment is *direct investment* and ownership of overseas-based assembly or manufacturing plants. This gives the firm the greatest control and upside potential; the downside is the greater risk and resource commitment required.

HOW TO DEVELOP THE MARKET?

A key problem in developing an international marketing strategy is deciding on how much tailoring there should be to local conditions. There are two extremes. One is a *global strategy*, where a company uses, as far as possible, a standardised marketing mix everywhere. The other is a *multinational strategy*, where the marketing mix is adapted to the local conditions in each country. As examples, Sony, Panasonic and Coca-Cola have tended to follow the global standardised model; Unilever, GE and Nestlé more the multinational strategy. The ideal solution depends upon on how diverse are local consumption patterns and marketing systems. New electronics products are easier to standardise than traditional eating habits. However, the opportunities presented by globalisation and the desire to achieve scale economies have increased the pressure on companies to seek greater standardisation in their marketing. The ability to standardise varies with the different elements of the marketing mix. The basic product is often the most easily standardisable. With increasing transparency and fewer barriers to trade, there is also greater pressure towards convergence in pricing. Culture and language differences demand local adaptation in advertising, but again companies are tending towards sharing themes across countries and especially regions. Different historical developments make distribution patterns probably the most diverse element of the marketing mix today.

WHAT TYPE OF ORGANISATION?

Companies need to develop international organisations that reflect their commitment to international operations. An *export department* will be able to handle the limited commitments of a company involved in indirect or direct exporting. If the commitment grows to involve the firm in different types of overseas ventures and overseas sales become important, it will need to create an *international division* to control its operating units. In recent years, the largest and most experienced operators such as Procter & Gamble, IBM and Microsoft have switched to a *global organisation*. Management plan brands, manufacturing and logistics on a global basis to maximise the company's operating efficiency and effectiveness. Country managers then are constrained to develop their own strategies within the parameters set by the global strategy. This new global thrust is being shaped by pressures on companies to achieve economies of scale and lever new products and expertise more rapidly across markets.

STEP 8: ACQUISITIONS AND ALLIANCES

The next rung is acquisitions and alliances. Managers in high-growth companies assign these a major role.

The late 1990s saw record levels of mergers and acquisitions. One cause was the opportunities to boost efficiency created by the deregulation of such industries as telecommunications, transportation, financial services and the utilities. A second catalyst was overcapacity in many industries. Third was the race to become bigger. Companies saw markets and competition becoming increasingly global, and regarded becoming one of the top two or three players a necessity for long-run competitiveness.

Acquisitions have certain advantages over internal growth:

- *Acquisitions are a faster way to penetrate a market. Developing successful new products can take years; an acquisition can achieve the sales goal in weeks.*

- *Internal growth is costly. A competitive battle to win market share can be very expensive. Buying a business is less likely to cut industry margins.*

- *Some strategic assets such as well-known brands, patents and strong distribution channels are often difficult, if not impossible, to develop internally.*

- *An established business is typically less risky than developing a new one from scratch.*

HIGH FAILURE RATE

Despite the popularity of acquisitions, studies over the years have shown that most fail to add value for shareholders in the acquiring company. The findings suggest the following:

1.   The bid premium paid by the acquiring company averages between 40 and 50 per cent over the acquired company's pre-acquisition value. The premium is lower for a friendly merger and higher for a hostile takeover.

2.   Shareholders in the acquired company are the big winners, receiving the benefits of the bid premiums. In two-thirds of take-overs, the value of the acquiring company declined after the acquisition. Taking a longer run view, only around a quarter of acquisitions were judged successful in delivering satisfactory returns to shareholders. The higher the bid premium, the more likely the acquisition was to fail.

3.   The chances of an acquisition being successful were improved when the acquirer had a strong core business before the take-over. The success rate was also higher where the company being bought was relatively small and in a related business.

What accounts for the failure of so many merger and acquisition programmes to deliver profitable growth? The most important reason is that companies pay too much. With acquisitions costing up to 50 per cent more than the market valued the company, it is easy to see how this occurs. They overpay because they make overly optimistic forecasts of the market's growth potential or because they overestimate the synergies the acquisition will create. A second cause is poor post-acquisition implementation. Management fails to capture the potential synergies. Relationships with customers, staff and suppliers in the acquired company are eroded, damaging the value of the business. A third reason for poor acquisitions is the incentive systems in many companies. Often managers are compensated by the return they achieve on *tangible* assets. An acquisition adds to their top line, but the bid premium does not appear in the denominator. The result is that almost any acquisition increases the bonuses of managers even though shareholder value is being destroyed.

DEVELOPING A SUCCESSFUL ACQUISITIONS PROCESS

To increase the chances of acquisitions leading to profitable growth, a business needs a systematic acquisitions process. This should consist of five stages:

1.   **Strategic analysis.** The process starts with an objective assessment of what the company needs to do to generate continuing value for shareholders. Are acquisitions necessary or would organic growth be superior? What types of acquisitions might enhance performance? This analysis should identify whether the company needs acquisitions to strengthen its present core business, or whether it should be looking for companies that will take it into new technologies or markets.

2.   **Search and screen.** The next task is to generate a good list of acquisition candidates. The screening process then eliminates candidates that do not fit the results of the strategic analysis. Additional screening criteria should include company size, cultural fit, current market share and quality of management.

3.   **Strategy development.** For the handful of companies that remain after the screening process, management has to assess in detail how they could leverage value from the company if it was acquired. How much cost could be taken out? How could sales be ratcheted up? How could best practices be transferred from one company to the other?

4.   **Valuation analysis.** The next issue is determining how much it is worth paying for the acquisition candidate. This is discussed further below.

5. **Negotiation.** Effective negotiation is based on thorough preparation. In entering negotiations the management team should be clear on what is the maximum price they are prepared to pay. They should also have assessed the value of the candidate to the existing owners and other potential buyers. They need to have assessed the financial position of the current owners, their objectives, strategy and likely negotiating tactics.

VALUING AN ACQUISITION

How much should management be prepared to pay for an acquisition? The principles of valuation were described in Chapter 2. As with any asset, the value of an acquisition is based on the net present value of the future stream of cash flow that is anticipated. For an acquisition, the fundamental equation is:

$$\frac{\text{Maximum acceptable}}{\text{purchase price}} = \frac{\text{Pre-acquisition}}{\text{value}} + \frac{\text{Value of}}{\text{synergies}}$$

If the prospect can be acquired for less than the maximum price then the investment should generate a return above the cost of capital. The pre-acquisition value is the market value of the target before the prospect of the acquisition. This is the minimum the seller will expect. Invariably the seller will hold out for a premium above this pre-acquisition value. This will be rationalised in terms of other potential bidders or the belief by the managers that the market underestimates the company's potential.

The amount the buyer should be willing to pay depends on the estimate of the synergies involved. Each of these synergies has to be identified and valued. The main synergies are:[11]

○ Cost savings. *Cost savings may increase the operating margin in the combined business. These are likely to be greater where the acquired company is in the same industry. Savings may be from economies of scale in purchasing, from eliminating duplicate jobs, facilities and other expenses, and from transferring best practices.*

○ Investment savings. *Consolidation of the two companies may produce economies in fixed and working capital requirements.*

○ Taxes and cost of capital. *Sometimes a merger will reduce the combined cash tax rate and the company's weighted cost of capital.*

○ Sales growth. *This can occur when the acquirer introduces the target's products into a broader distribution channel. Sales enhancements are generally more difficult and uncertain to estimate than cost and investment savings.*

The maximum acceptable price for a target is then calculated by valuing it using these synergies to upwardly adjust the original cash flow projection. The present value of these cash flows should normally determine the maximum price to be paid.

However, there are occasions when a higher price might be paid. This may be the case if the acquisition is a necessary investment as part of a much broader long-term strategy to gain competitive advantage in the target market. Here, the whole strategy should be valued rather than any particular element forming a part of it. The specific acquisition can be thought of as purchasing an option allowing future opportunities to participate in the industry. Analogously, there are occasions when the company should pay considerably less than the maximum acceptable price. This is where there are other bid candidates that are cheaper, or where other initiatives such as joint ventures, strategic alliances or licensing could produce similar results more economically.

POST-MERGER INTEGRATION

Given the substantial premium an acquirer is likely to have paid, it is crucial that the post-acquisition implementation is handled effectively. In fact, studies show that most acquirers destroy rather than add value after the acquisition – acquired companies do worse after being acquired. To avoid this, a well-planned post-acquisition plan is required. Step one is to agree objectives. Management in both companies should be in harmony about the objectives and strategy of the new business. Step two is to communicate a plan to reassure customers, employees and suppliers. Step three is to develop and implement the strategy for quickly progressing the synergies in costs, investments and sales. The last step is to develop a long-term strategic and organisational change programme to leverage value from the merger.

ALLIANCES

Strategic alliances provide an alternative to acquisitions for accelerating profitable growth. Alliances differ in several ways from acquisitions. First, there is no bid premium involved so it should be easier to create value for shareholders. Second, alliances usually involve only parts of a company rather than the whole business as in the case of an acquisition. This should lower the overall level of risk. Third, alliances have to be carefully structured to allow for effective control. Finally, the motivation for alliances is often different from acquisitions. Acquisitions generally benefit from geographical overlap because of synergies from consolidating facilities, distribution networks and sales forces. Alliances, on the other hand, are usually intended to expand the geographical reach of the partners.

In an influential study of a large number of alliances in the 1990s, Bleeke and Ernst made the following findings:[12]

1.   Both acquisitions and alliances had roughly the same success rate in creating shareholder value.

2.   Acquisitions work better for core businesses and existing geographical areas. Alliances are more effective for edging into related businesses or new geographical areas.

3.   Alliances between strong and weak rarely work. When one partner has the major stake, it tends to dominate decision-making and put its own interests above those of the alliance. A 50:50 split works best.

4.   Successful alliances must be able to evolve beyond their initial objectives. This means they must have autonomy and flexibility to respond as markets and technology change.

5.   Alliances and joint ventures have a limited life span. More than 75 per cent of the alliances that terminated ended with the acquisition by one of the parents.

STEP 9: GROWTH OUTSIDE INDUSTRY BOUNDARIES

The last rung of the ladder involves opportunities for even more creative ways of achieving profitable growth. These involve growth outside the current boundaries of the company's industry. The most obvious alternatives are:

○   **Vertical Integration. Forward integration**, *where the firm takes over ownership and control of its customers, can offer opportunities. For example, PepsiCo began acquiring its bottlers in the 1990s to gain greater control over sales effort. Such investment may enable the firm to achieve greater differentiation and avoid its margins being squeezed by an increasingly concentrating customer base.*

Backward integration involves moving into a supplier industry. In the past, car manufacturers produced around half of their components internally. Today, with the increasing importance of getting close to customers, forward integration has become more popular than backward integration.

○ **Diversification.** Some companies have achieved enormous growth by transferring capabilities and intangible assets to quite disparate industries. The source of this creativity has often been based on taking a marketing view of the firm's business. Instead of defining it in product terms, management has defined the business in terms of meeting certain customer needs. For example, Gillette expanded from its core business of men's razors by redefining its mission first as men's grooming products. This took it into shaving creams, deodorants and aftershave. Later the mission was expanded even further to personal care, which took it successfully into dental products, small appliances and stationery. Virgin defined its markets even more broadly to include any area where its brand added value. This took it from its start in records to growth in the airline industry, financial services, cosmetics, clothing, railways, telecommunications and the Internet.

○ **Creating new businesses.** Creative companies that are alert to the opportunities created by today's rapidly changing technologies and changing consumer wants can create new businesses. Tesco identified the potential of using the Internet for home shopping early on. By 2001, it had emerged as the clear leader in the battle to become the UK's most successful grocery home delivery service. With over 65 per cent of the market and 95 per cent national coverage, it was taking over 100 000 weekly orders and offering more than 20 000 grocery product lines. By 2005 it claimed to be able to serve 98 per cent of the UK population from its 300 participating stores. In 2006 it launched a home shopping catalogue for its expanding non-food range, which has been integrated with its Internet channel under the banner of Tesco Direct.

○ **Leveraging relationships.** Some companies create whole new sources of growth by leveraging customer and supplier relationships to enter new markets. GE, one of the world's most valuable companies, is a good example. Until the early 1980s it was seen primarily as a supplier of industrial equipment and consumer appliances. But since then it has ratcheted up its growth rate by leveraging its relationships to move into a whole new set of growth businesses, especially in the service sector. Initially, it focused on financing the sale and distribution of GE products. Today, it is a leader in a broad array of financial and outsourcing services, ranging from railcar leasing and credit cards to reinsurance and equipment financing. It is regularly ranked as one of America's most admired companies.

○ **Exploiting industry convergence.** Today technological changes are leading to many industries converging. Examples are pharmaceuticals and genetic engineering, cable television and telecoms, and media, computers and the Internet. For industry leaders, such changes present opportunities as well as threats. Pioneers of new technologies tend to be small, making it financially feasible for current leaders to buy into them and dominate the newly converging sector. US telecoms provider Verizon is fighting back against cable competition by turning itself into a diversified communications company by offering voice and Internet tie-ups, as well as wireless and TV services.

DEVELOPING A GROWTH STRATEGY

To create continuing value for shareholders managers have to grow the top line. This means the company has to climb the growth ladder. Unfortunately, relatively few companies manage to do this; most fall away once the changing marketing and technological environment erodes their original core business. One reason is that many managers do not know how to grow their businesses; they have been over-preoccupied with the existing core. Another reason is the belief in the conventional wisdom of 'sticking to the knitting'. Managers believe that being tempted by new opportunities recklessly takes them out of their area of expertise. They do not understand that while innovation does involve risk, 'sticking to the knitting' in today's world brings certainty – of failure. Finally, many managers lack the flair for leadership. They have honed the ability to manage operating processes but lack the imagination and confidence to identify new opportunities, to communicate an inspiring vision to staff and to lead the company in new directions.

UNDERSTANDING GROWTH STRATEGY

To achieve long-term, continuing growth, managers have to understand the basic concept and its relationship to shareholder value. The objective of a growth strategy is to develop a pipeline of projects that will pour out a continuing stream of initiatives, some of which will create major new rivers of cash flow. A successful company's businesses and projects can be grouped into three types: today's businesses, tomorrow's businesses and options for growth.[13]

To understand their significance, we can work with a real example:

> Tesco is Britain's biggest supermarket group. Its revenue has grown from £37 billion in 2005 to £51.8 billion in 2008 (figures to year-end February 2008). In the early 1990s the retailer was caught between rivals Sainsbury and Asda – between quality and value. It has since outperformed the market consistently and expanded into telecoms, financial services, non-food and international markets and now enjoys a diversified business base. It has done this under the 'Every little helps' banner.[14]

> This initiative, introduced in 1995, means that everything is measured against whether it is helpful to customers and whether it makes shopping easier. Building its strategy on penetrating customer insight has enabled the company to extend its brand not only into a new range of services, but also to increase choice in its core products, such as its own-label *Value* and *Finest* food ranges. It also has an increasing international presence – results for 2007/2008 show that half of its growth in trading came from the overseas operations, which includes supermarkets in Europe, Asia and a foothold in the US, where its first shops opened in 2007.

TODAY'S BUSINESSES

These are the company's current core businesses and account for the bulk of the sales, profit and cash flow. At Tesco nearly 80 per cent of group sales and profits come from the UK business and provide all the cash to finance the growth of the other brands. Growth in the UK business comes from new space, extensions to existing stores and a multi-format approach. There are four different formats Tesco uses.

- **Express stores**, the first of which opened in 1994, are those of up to 3000 sq. ft and which offer a range of up to 7000 lines, including fresh produce, wines and spirits and in-store bakeries.

- **Metro stores** are approximately 7000–15 000 sq ft. They first opened in 1992 in town and city centre locations. These offer a tailored range of food lines, including ready-made meals and sandwiches.

- **Superstores** are between 20 000–50 000 sq ft. Tesco began opening superstores in the 1970s, and, during the 1980s and 1990s, built a national network. In recent years a number of new non-food ranges such as DVDs and books have been offered for sale in this format.

- **Extra stores** are approximately 60 000 sq ft and above. The first one was opened in 1997 as a one-stop destination store. This format offers the widest range of food and non-food lines, ranging from electrical equipment to homewares, clothing, health and beauty and seasonal items.

The problem with today's businesses is that they are inevitably maturing. For these established businesses management has three tasks. First, they want to get rid of any older businesses which are not generating adequate returns on capital and which cannot be turned around quickly. For those that remain, the focus is on operating efficiency, ensuring that these businesses are managed to optimise return on investment. The marketing task is to ensure that all profitable growth opportunities are explored. It is fatal to treat these successful businesses as cash cows: such attitudes will lead to a rapid erosion of market share. Instead the strategy must be to keep the brands up to date, focus on customer retention and retain the brands, for as long as possible, as thriving assets.

TOMORROW'S BUSINESSES

These are the company's star new businesses. They are already demonstrating their ability to win profitable customers and grow rapidly. For Tesco, this includes tesco.com, launched in 2001, and which rapidly became one of the UK's number-one Internet shopping destinations. Results to the year-end February 2008 show that tesco.com achieved a 31 per cent increase in sales to £1.6 billion and a 49 per cent increase in profit to £124 million (before initial operating losses on Tesco Direct – see below). A 20 per cent growth in new customers meant the web site had one million active customers by the end of the year.

Another source of tomorrow's profits is Tesco Direct, a general merchandise business launched in 2006 with over 11 000 products online and 7000 in the catalogue, from beds and sofas through to kitchenware, electrical goods, cameras and golf clubs, all of which can be ordered through the Internet, by phone or in selected stores. Management's job here is to capture critical mass and dominate the market in the same way they have done with their core business.

OPTIONS FOR GROWTH

These are investments in research, experiments and trials that seed tomorrow's businesses. They are low-cost options that give the company the chance to learn about new opportunities. Many of these experiments will fail, in which case they can be dropped without major damage to the company; those that show promise can be developed and exploited. Given the high failure rate to be expected with options, companies should always be pursuing a bundle of them simultaneously.

Many managers over-focus on today's businesses because they generate the bulk of sales and profits. But this is a big mistake. Not only will their companies lose out on tomorrow's growth, but today's investors will penalise them in terms of the values they attach to their businesses. It is important to understand that the value investors attach to tomorrow's businesses, and particularly an attractive bundle of options, can far exceed their current sales and profit contributions. Much of the shareholder value created by successful companies is based not on the success of their current businesses but upon expectations about the management's capacity to generate future profitable growth.

One of Tesco's options for growth is its ambitious international expansion programme. By early 2008 operations in international markets already generated 54 per cent of the growth in group sales and 50 per cent of the growth in group trading profit. However, the company is determined to see revenue from overseas markets account for more than half its annual revenue by 2017, a doubling of the proportion it currently achieves. One approach, for example, has been to form joint ventures with Sime Darby Berhad in Malaysia and Samsung in South Korea.

In 2008 the company also announced its move into online entertainment with Tesco Digital. While initially the service was offering the availability to download music for iPods and MP3 players, it was set to be just the beginning of a wider Tesco Digital strategy that would encompass TV, films and games in the near future.

How should management implement a growth strategy? We suggest developing a six-step process:

1.   Creating the mindset
2.   Setting strategy
3.   Making it happen
4.   Building momentum
5.   Fast implementation
6.   Organising for growth

CREATING THE MINDSET

Building a sustainable growth strategy requires management to understand that they need businesses in all three categories: today's businesses, tomorrow's and options. They first need to appraise the current situation. If today's businesses are generating good returns but they do not have any emerging businesses or promising options, the task of management is to focus on climbing the growth ladder. On the other hand, if the core business is not performing, the initial task is to sort this out.

SORTING OUT THE CORE

If the company's core business is unprofitable it is difficult to pursue a growth strategy. A profitable core is necessary to generate the funds to finance growth. It is also necessary to give investors confidence in management's ability to achieve profitable growth.

Making today's business perform depends upon achieving a strong strategic position in its market and efficiently executing a sound operational plan. For some businesses the chances of achieving a strong strategic position may look too formidable. In this case *strategic divestment* will be the appropriate action. Divesting those businesses that are seen as not offering adequate returns sends a decisive signal to investors about management's strategic intent.

For those mature businesses that are kept, the task is to quickly create cash flow. Since for most of these businesses growth potential is limited, restoring profitability usually focuses on reengineering to take out costs and reduce the amount of working capital and fixed assets employed. There is also often scope for improving margins by dropping unprofitable customers and targeting higher margin accounts.

SWITCHING TO GROWTH

Many experienced managers can handle the task of rationalisation but stumble when it comes to building growth. This is not surprising since the perspective and skills are quite different. Building a successful growth business normally takes longer than fixing an unprofitable one. Rationalisation is essentially internally focused on the company's assets and costs; growth, on the other hand, requires a marketing focus on customers and the environment outside the firm. Growth is more difficult because it is competitive; it is about getting customers to prefer buying from your business rather than the myriad of other companies all seeking to attract the same customers. This requires having core capabilities and a differential advantage that are perceived as superior by customers. Unlike rationalisation, which is usually about divestment, growth and the creation of competitive advantage require investment in skills, products and marketing. Finally, rationalisation can be directed from the top, but a growth strategy requires a commitment throughout the business. In particular, it needs the enthusiastic support from the front-line staff, who have the knowledge to generate ideas for growth and who have the task of implementing them.

The catalyst for change is almost always a new chief executive. Few companies can catalyse a growth strategy without the outside stimulus. Even with a new chief executive, building a growth orientation can take years since it requires a fundamental change in the company's culture. The task can be divided into three stages. The first is winning the commitment of the senior executive team. This requires an educational programme to teach executives about marketing and developing market-led strategies. Frequently the chief executive will need to bring in new blood to provide experience and support for the strategy.

The second stage will be to set ambitious goals which signal change and stimulate progress. Jack Welch, legendary CEO of General Electric, set the goal of doubling sales over a five-year planning period. Each GE division was asked to find two 'breakthrough' ideas that would significantly transform their growth performance. Sam Walton, founder of Wal-Mart, the world's biggest retailer, set the goal in 1990 of quadrupling sales, doubling the number of stores and increasing sales per square foot by 60 per cent by the year 2000. Such visible objectives signal what is expected from managers.

The third stage is removing any organisational barriers that restrict managers from focusing on growth. To generate growth options, the top team must sweep away a culture that penalises failure and mistakes. Fixed beliefs about what the company can and cannot do must also be challenged. Systems and budgets must be aligned to the new growth objective. For example, bonuses can be awarded for achieving top-line growth. Or, like at 3M, targets for new products can play a key role in the planning process.

SETTING STRATEGY

If the firm's growth is to be profitable it must be founded on a strategy to create a competitive advantage. A competitive advantage is developed by exploiting the firm's unique competencies. Management should look for growth opportunities that match its organisational capabilities. To set strategy the management team need to undertake three steps:

- ○ *Assess the organisation's resources and capabilities*
- ○ *Search for growth opportunities that exploit resources and capabilities*
- ○ *Develop the resource base*

The company cannot build a sustainable growth strategy from its current resource base alone. In developing strategy management will be made aware of resource gaps which need to be plugged. It will need to develop comprehensive training programmes, recruit new talent with specialist knowledge and skills, develop additional technologies and form new relationships with customers, suppliers and distributors.

MAKING IT HAPPEN

Having ideas is not enough; ideas only have value when they are transformed into options through the planting of a new business. This may be achieved by initiating an R&D project, setting up a pilot plant or a test market, or making a small acquisition.

The early business books on corporate planning saw developing a growth strategy in highly rational terms. Strategic decision-making was viewed as a logical process in which a plan is formulated through systematic analysis of the firm, its performance and the external environment. The strategy is then communicated to the organisation and implemented down through successive organisational layers.

Today few people accept this picture. The process in practice is much less structured and more diffused, and there is less of a dichotomisation between formulation and implementation. Mintzberg, one of the foremost researchers in this area, has made a useful distinction between intended, realised and emergent strategy.[15] *Intended strategy* is the strategy as conceived by top management. Even here, rationality is limited and the intended strategy is the result of a process of negotiation, bargaining and compromise, involving many individuals and groups within the organisation. *Emergent strategy* is the process by which managers adapt the intended strategy to changing external circumstances, their own strengths and weaknesses and their own learning. *Realised strategy* is the strategy that emerges. Mintzberg suggests this tends to be only 10 to 30 per cent of the intended strategy.

Drucker called this emergent process in successful growth companies a *piloting approach*.[16] A company takes small steps to learn more about the market opportunity and to gather the skills necessary to capitalise on it. Rather than a big, high-risk leap into a new venture, the piloting approach is a learning process. If they are going in the right direction managers can accelerate their steps; if it looks a dead end, they can abandon the option without too much being lost. For example, Johnson & Johnson's growth in contact lenses remains a vivid example of this piloting architecture (Figure 4.8):[17]

The original idea of entering the contact lens market came out of a 1980 strategic review and looked promising given the growth prospects, the lack of entrenched competition, and the potential fit with the company's distribution strength and reputation. To turn the idea into an option for growth, Johnson & Johnson took an exploratory first step. It acquired Frontier Contact Lenses, a small player in the US market, with the objective of learning about the contact lens business.

A year later it was able to buy the rights to a revolutionary new process developed in Denmark that had the potential to slash production costs. To improve the process it contracted NYPRO, a leader in precision injection moulding, to develop lenses to the tolerances required. Three years after its first move, Johnson & Johnson had learned enough about the industry to judge the potential of its idea. It had also acquired distinctive technology and manufacturing skills. Up to this point the sums at risk had been relatively modest, but over the next few years, it invested nearly $500 million to develop and launch its new ranges around the world. By the mid-1990s, it had built a highly profitable business with annual sales of over $600 million.

BUILDING MOMENTUM

A successful growth strategy depends upon putting together a difficult-to-imitate bundle of critical capabilities that make it possible to sustain a competitive advantage. A firm's capabilities depend upon its collection of resources:

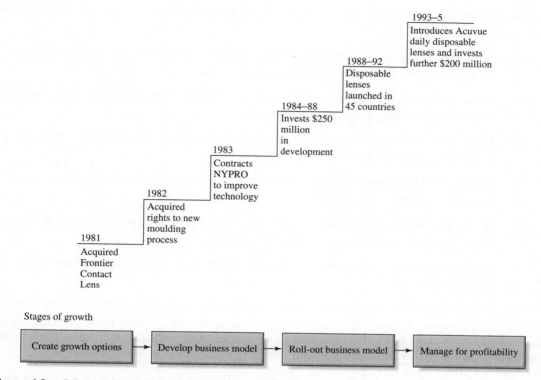

Figure 4.8 Johnson & Johnson's Contact Lens Piloting. *Source:* M. Baghi, S. Coley and D. White, *The Alchemy of Growth*, London: Orion, 1999, p. 83. Reproduced by Permission of McKinsey & Company

tangible assets, intangible assets and people. These resources, when integrated effectively, provide the firm with its special capabilities, which in turn form the basis of its ability to grow.[18]

Capabilities are not fixed; they can be acquired and developed. Indeed, it is the skill in acquiring and developing capabilities that determines an organisation's ability to develop a long-term growth strategy. Hence companies should not take too narrow a view of their capabilities when considering growth opportunities. A company does not have to limit the search for opportunities to areas where it presently has the full range of competency, it should have the confidence that it can develop and learn new competencies.

The essence of the piloting approach is that capabilities need to be built and developed. It makes sense for the company to develop the most critical capabilities internally so that it controls the key sources of competitive advantage. But capabilities that are not so critical can be outsourced. Outsourcing, alliances, partnerships, joint ventures and the formation of economic webs have increasingly become the ways in which today's companies access manufacturing, development and IT capabilities. The need to quickly learn about new products, technologies and local markets makes it difficult for any organisation, no matter how large, to develop all the necessary knowledge in-house.

FAST IMPLEMENTATION

Successful new business concepts are quickly copied. If the company is to profit from its innovation it needs to move fast and to establish critical mass. Speed may allow the company to establish a *first-mover advantage*. A first-mover advantage is access to resources and capabilities that later entrants cannot easily acquire. Such advantages include:

○ Patent and copyrights. *By establishing a patent or copyright, the first mover may possess technology, products or designs from which followers are legally excluded.*

○ Scarce resources. *When key resources are scarce, e.g. locations for new supermarkets or specialised employees, first movers can pre-empt these resources.*

○ Higher prices. *Prices are usually higher at the beginning of the market life cycle. The first mover can recoup higher margins before competition erodes prices.*

○ Reputation. *The first mover establishes a reputation with customers, suppliers and distributors that cannot initially be matched by followers.*

○ Standards. *When proprietary standards in relation to product design and technology are important, the first mover may have an advantage in setting the standard.*

○ Experience. *Economies of learning suggest that the first mover can obtain a cost advantage by virtue of its longer experience.*

Achieving first-mover advantage is not simply about being first but also about achieving sufficient scale to defend against ambitious followers. It requires heavy investment in marketing and product development. Strategic alliances and partnering are ways of sharing the costs of developing the market. Priorities in exploiting the growth opportunity will include:

○ Market development. *Initially a new product is bought by a specialist niche but if it is successful it will spread to broader markets. It is important for the innovator to lead in the development of these new market segments; otherwise it offers a beachhead for new competitors. For example, Xerox, inventor of the copier, did not develop the market for small machines, which allowed Canon to enter the market and become a major rival.*

○ Build the brand. *Creating a well-known and trusted brand name can give additional sources of defence. Even when competitors copy the product, customers may feel more confident buying a familiar brand. Much of the success of companies like Gillette, Coca-Cola and Marlboro is due to their investment in brand building.*

○ Line extensions. *Line extensions allow the product to be more finely tuned to the needs of specific customer segments. Such customisation makes it more difficult for competitors to find gaps.*

○ Overseas markets. *The erosion of barriers to trade has made it dangerously myopic for a company to neglect the opportunities presented by overseas markets. Exploiting such opportunities will often require the firm to find partners with experience and resources already in place.*

CONSUMER ADOPTION PROCESS

When launching a new concept it is important to consider how the market will develop. It is generally a mistake to aim at all customers. People and firms differ in their propensity to take up new ideas quickly. An important idea in marketing is the consumer adoption process.[19] Figure 4.9 shows the typical development of a market from launch to maturity. Researchers term the first $2\frac{1}{2}$ per cent of consumers buying the product *innovators*; these are followed by the *early adopters*, the *early majority, late majority* and finally the *laggards*.

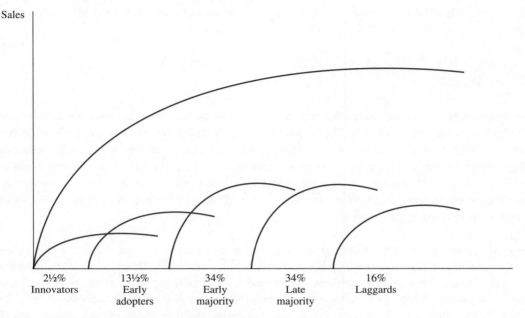

Figure 4.9   Adopter Categories in the Adoption of Innovations

For a new product it is important to focus on the innovators. The mass market will not buy until the opinion leaders have taken up the product first. The characteristics of innovators vary with the specific product, but in consumer markets they tend to be younger, more highly educated, more affluent and more cosmopolitan. In business-to-business markets innovators tend to be those customers who are more technically aware, who can gain most economic value from the new product, and who can manage the risks of trialling it.

The following characteristics of the new product or service also influence its speed of adoption:

○   Relative advantage. *The greater the perceived added value offered by the new product, the quicker it will be adopted.*

○   Compatibility. *If the new product does not disrupt the customer's current practices and processes it will be taken up more quickly.*

○   Complexity. *Adoption will be facilitated if it is easy to understand and use.*

○   Divisibility. *It helps if the customer can sample or trial the product before purchase.*

○   Risk. *The greater the economic or social risk attached to failure, the more reluctant buyers will be in buying it.*

○   Communicability. *Adoption is facilitated when the product's advantages are easy to show.*

ORGANISING FOR GROWTH

A growing business has to be organised differently from a steady-state one. They need different structures, systems, processes and, generally, different types of managers. At the same time they have to be linked to the centre if the company is to leverage the advantages of its size and its shared services, and exploit potential synergies across the group.

ORGANISATION

New businesses have to be organised differently from mature ones because their tasks differ. For mature businesses the priority is running them efficiently. The business is well understood; the company has the capabilities to run it and the market is familiar. The priority is to squeeze out more cash by controlling costs and investments and through marginal enhancements in the product and customer mix. For new businesses and growth options the priorities are different. They are about achieving rapid growth, speed and decisiveness. Market uncertainty is much greater: customers, competition, channels and positioning are all new and changing. Many resources and capabilities have still to be acquired by the business.

If new businesses are reporting to the same line managers as the core business, there is a real danger that the new ventures will fail to flourish. First, managers will not give them sufficient priority; invariably the new businesses will have tiny sales and often they will be making losses. Second, new ventures will have to conform to the same planning, budget procedures and performance measures as the mature businesses. If new ventures are held to the same profitability objectives as core businesses, the former will certainly wither away. Finally, speed is much more important in growing businesses. Tying managers in these ventures to the same approval processes found in mature business units would leave them floundering in the wake of more fleet-footed competitors.

Successful companies are responding in several ways to these problems. One approach is to assign responsibility to *autonomous, cross-functional teams*. Another approach often followed by companies like 3M, Johnson & Johnson and IBM is to create a *separate business unit*. Another approach is a *spin-out*. Spin-outs occur when the equity owners of the parent company receive equity stakes in the newly spun-out company. For example, the Hewlett-Packard shareholders received shares in Agilent Technologies when it was spun-out of HP in 1999. Here the company not only creates a separate unit, but establishes it as a separate company with some public shareholding. The senior management team enjoy the excitement and, with luck, the financial rewards of running an independent public company. At the same time, the group company, as the majority shareholder, can enjoy the benefits of keeping the unit connected to the larger enterprise. All these approaches focus on the need to create fleet-footed small business units, with managers totally orientated to successfully growing the new ventures.

MANAGING THE TALENT

Because the task of managing mature and growing businesses is different, so the management style has to be different. Most executives do not have the skills to create new businesses. Established businesses require managers who can optimise current operational processes and deliver consistent bottom-line results.

Tomorrow's businesses require managers to focus on top-line sales rather than bottom-line profitability. They need managers who are comfortable with ambiguity and changes in market requirements and operational processes. Managers who overemphasise consistency and discipline stifle risk taking and entrepreneurial flair. For managing options – explorations into new markets and technologies – the business needs visionaries. Commonly they are younger, less experienced and naïve in the wiles of organisational politics. They will need the support and sponsorship of a senior executive at the centre who appreciates their special skills and can reassure the organisation about the venture's importance.

Any company needs a mixture of these disciplined operators, business builders and visionaries if it is going to manage effectively its present businesses and capitalise on tomorrow's growth markets. Too many managers focusing on disciplined processes and budgets detract from the future. Too few focusing on the basics threatens the present. Individual business units benefit from cultural homogeneity, but the company as a whole needs to have cultural heterogeneity.

SYSTEMS AND PERFORMANCE MEASUREMENT

The type of planning used for mature businesses does not make sense for new ones. For emerging businesses there is much greater uncertainty about the market and a greater focus on accumulating the necessary capabilities. Detailed annual operating plans and budgets are simply counterproductive.

Budgets, performance measures and rewards need to be different, reflecting the different objectives. In mature businesses the budgets should focus on short-term profits and cash flow. Leading companies use cash bonuses to reward managers achieving short-term profitability goals. Managers who cannot achieve budgets are swiftly put aside. For growing businesses the focus is on long-term sales growth and value creation. Key measures are market share, customer acquisition and retention rates, the trend of profitability and expected net present value. Rewards need to reflect long-run value creation rather than achieving short-term budgets. To encourage an entrepreneurial culture, many companies offer executives equity participation. They are also more tolerant of failure than for mature businesses.

With options the focus is on estimating the potential rewards and the probability of success. In these businesses learning takes place through experimental projects. Performance and rewards can be based on achieving results from project-based milestones. Increasingly, companies are exploring option theory to value these opportunities. The number of initiatives being pursued and the proportion of them that lead to a business launch can measure the overall performance of the business in creating options.

AUTONOMY AND INTEGRATION

Growth and performance are best achieved by breaking big companies into small business units and giving their management teams as much autonomy as possible in running them. But if small businesses are best, what is the point of large companies? Surely investors would be better off if the company was broken up, the head office closed and the businesses floated as independent companies.

Large holding companies only make sense if they can add value through either shared central services or exploiting synergies between the businesses. Small businesses can buy services outside but sometimes it can be cheaper or more effective to have them internally. The most useful services the centre can offer growing businesses include acquisition skills, financing capabilities and legal and accounting support. The second possible source of added value are synergies. An emerging business may possess lower costs and investment through sharing the company's existing facilities. Marketing synergies may enable it to use existing sales force, channels and networks. Businesses may also be able to cooperate in cross-selling opportunities. Finally, technological synergies may enable the emerging venture to utilise knowledge lying in other areas of the company.

Such synergies can be realised only if ideas are readily shared across the company. For the corporate centre, the challenge is to devise sufficient coordination and exchanges that offer the benefits of size, but without eroding the value of the entrepreneurial flair and sense of ownership, that only devolved leadership can produce.

INSPIRING THE ORGANISATION

Many of the most exciting new businesses in the past decade or so have been start-ups. But it is important that large businesses learn how to create new enterprises. How can corporate headquarters in large corporations motivate their managers to hunger for the challenges of growth and entrepreneurial activities? One way successful companies do it is through setting ambitious goals, such as achieving double-digit growth or doubling market share. Ambitious goals help create a change in culture in the organisation by raising the profile of growth. They also stretch managers to be more imaginative by making them aware that the usual strategies will not be enough to reach the new goals.

The centre can also give managers the resources to achieve growth. These are not solely financial resources but also include sweeping away the barriers to growth such as bureaucratic planning and budgeting procedures. Top executives have to recognise that creating new businesses requires autonomous organisations and systems that prioritise entrepreneurial efforts.

Neither ambitious goal-setting nor adequate resourcing, however, is enough to inspire employees to great efforts year after year. It is hardly surprising that studies of the great growth companies like General Electric (GE), 3M, Procter & Gamble and Microsoft all show that they have guiding ideals of leadership that transcend financial numbers. Ghoshal and Bartlett express this as follows:[20]

Strategies can engender strong, enduring emotional attachments only when embedded in a broader organisational purpose. Today, the corporate leader's great challenge is to create a sense of meaning within the company, which its members can identify, in which they share a feeling of pride, and to which they are willing to commit themselves.

SUMMARY

1.   The companies that have created the greatest returns for shareholders have all been high-growth businesses. Top-line growth is the fundamental source of shareholder value.

2.   Rationalisation and reengineering can produce short-run increases in cash flow but investors recognise that such policies cannot produce enduring gains unless they are allied to gains in market performance.

3.   Growth creates shareholder value by increasing the future level of cash flow, accelerating the timing of cash flow, extending its duration or reducing the risks attached to future returns.

4.   Ascending the growth ladder must start with consolidating the current customer base: increasing customer retention and winning a growing share of their spending. This forms the foundation for going on to gain new customers and developing new products, markets and distribution channels.

5.   Any company that is to endure needs three types of businesses in its portfolio: today's businesses, tomorrow's businesses and options for growth. The first provide the bulk of the revenue and cash but the last two account for most of a company's market value.

6.   To grow, management has to create a growth mindset within the company, to build momentum and to sweep away the organisational barriers that constrain growth.

REVIEW QUESTIONS

1. Explain the links between growth and shareholder value creation.
2. Why has shareholder value become associated with rationalisation rather than growth?
3. Identify the different pathways to accelerate growth.
4. Why is customer loyalty seen as the foundation for building a growth strategy?
5. Describe how to develop a growth strategy for a business.
6. Discuss the issues in implementing a growth strategy in a company.

NOTES ON CHAPTER 4

[1] Carl W. Stern and George Stalk Jr. (eds), *Perspectives on Strategy from the Boston Consulting Group*, New York: John Wiley & Sons, Inc., 1998, pp. 12–23.

[2] The threshold margin is (20% + 25%) × 9% divided by 1.09 × 0.7.

[3] See the examples in Peter Doyle, *Marketing Management and Strategy*, London: Prentice Hall, 1998, pp. 65–68.

[4] Average customer tenure is calculated by taking the reciprocal of the defection rate. For example, if the retention rate is 90 per cent then the defection rate is 10 per cent annually. This gives a tenure of 1 divided by 10 per cent, or 10 years.

[5] Leonard Berry and A. Parasuraman, *Marketing Services: Competing through Quality*, New York: Free Press, 1991.

[6] Frederick F. Reichheld, The one number you need to grow, *Harvard Business Review*, December 2003.

[7] 'Consumer vigilantes', *Business Week*, 21 February 2008.

[8] Drawn from *The Economist*, 26 June 1999, 'Survey: business and the Internet', p. 14.

[9] Ansoff was the pioneer of the analytical approach to strategic planning. For his most recent work, see Igor Ansoff and Edward McDonnell, *Implanting Strategic Management*, 2nd edn, New York: Prentice Hall, 1990.

[10] Malcolm McDonald, Linking intangible assets to share price, *Intellectual Asset Management*, April 2008.

[11] For a useful discussion and recent examples see Robert G. Eccles, Kersten L. Lanes and Thomas C. Wilson, Are you paying too much for that acquisition? *Harvard Business Review*, **77**(4), July/August, 1999, 136–148.

[12] Joel Bleeke and David Ernst, *Collaborating to Compete: Using Strategic Alliances and Acquisitions in the Global Marketplace*, New York: John Wiley & Sons, Inc., 1993.

[13] This section borrows some of the ideas in Mehrdad Baghai, Stephen Coley and David White, *The Alchemy of Growth*, London: Orion Business, 1999.

[14] For more on this see Hugh Burkett and John Zealley, *Marketing Excellence: Winning Companies Reveal the Secrets of Their Success*, John Wiley & Sons, Ltd., 2006.

[15] Henry Mintzberg, *The Rise and Fall of Strategic Planning: Reconceiving Roles for Planning, Plans and Planners*, New York: Free Press, 1994. See also: Henry Mintzberg, *Tracking Strategies: Towards a General Theory of Strategy Formation*, Oxford University Press, 2008.

[16] Peter F. Drucker, *Management Challenges for the 21st Century*, Oxford: Butterworth-Heinemann, 1999, pp. 86–87.

[17] Baghai, Coley and White, *The Alchemy of Growth*, London: Orion, pp. 82–84.

[18] For a timely discussion of this topic, see Jean-Claude Larréché, *The Momentum Effect: How to Ignite Exceptional Growth*, Wharton School Publishing, 2008.

[19] Everett M. Rogers, *Diffusion of Innovation*, 5th edn, Free Press, 2003.

[20] Sumantra Ghosal and Christopher A. Barlett, *The Individualized Corporation: A Fundamentally New Approach to Management*, New York: HarperBusiness, 1997.

PART 2

Developing High-Value Strategies

5 Strategic Position Assessment

'Chance favours the prepared mind'

Louis Pasteur

INTRODUCTION AND OBJECTIVES

Part 1 looked at the principles of value-based marketing: the importance of shareholder returns as an objective; how to calculate the shareholder value added by a strategy; and the role of marketing and growth in creating value. Part 2 shows how to develop a value-based marketing strategy. This chapter examines the underpinning of strategy formulation: the assessment of the organisation's current business situation and the options available to it. The following chapter shows the steps in developing a value-based marketing strategy for a business unit.

By the time you have completed this chapter, you will be able to:

- ○ *Evaluate the performance of a business*

- ○ *Assess the causes of its present performance, distinguishing between external or industry factors, and internal or competency factors*

- ○ *Take a view on where the business is heading, if it maintains its current trajectory*

- ○ *Identify the internal and external opportunities to increase the value of the business*

- ○ *Set broad strategic objectives for the products and markets that make up the firm's portfolio of businesses*

The chapter begins by looking at how managers can assess the current performance of their business. It illustrates the difficulty of using purely financial or accounting performance measures to judge whether current actions are creating shareholder value. It shows how measures of change in the firm's strategic value drivers can be used to create a balanced scorecard for judging current performance. The chapter continues by showing how to analyse the causes of the successes or failures of the business. Third, it examines how managers can project the likely pattern of performance in the future. Finally, it explores the main strategic options managers have for enhancing the value created for shareholders.

AN OVERVIEW

During the 1990s most managers came to accept that the objective of the business was to maximise total returns to shareholders. If managers did not offer good returns to the owners of the business in the form of dividends and stock appreciation then they were likely to be replaced. It was also accepted that the way to increase shareholder returns was to maximise the net present value of long-run cash flow. This is a function of four factors: the level of cash flow, its timing, longevity and risk. Marketing plays a critical role in determining all four variables.

Maximising shareholder value requires each business unit to have a process that encourages managers to develop strategic options, to evaluate these options in terms of their effects on shareholder value, and to effectively implement the highest-value strategy. This process has three stages. The first is the *strategic position assessment*. This provides the basic information about the sources of value in the business and the drivers that create value in the business. The second stage is the *strategic marketing plan*. This uses the information from the strategic position assessment to decide on which markets to serve and how to win a competitive advantage in these markets. The third stage is *implementation:* the business needs the core capabilities and processes to achieve execution of the strategy.

This chapter presents the strategic position assessment. This assessment needs to be done at two levels: at the corporate and business unit levels. At the corporate level the focus will be on the value potential of the company's portfolio of businesses. At the unit level the focus will be on the value and drivers of the individual products and markets. The methodology is the same; the difference is in the unit of analysis. In both, the outcomes will be conclusions about the future of the business. Each business will be assigned one of five strategic objectives:

1.   **Divest.** Businesses will be closed or sold when it is judged that they do not offer good investment opportunities for the firm.

2.   **Harvest.** Some businesses will be run for cash when there are limited opportunities for further development but they are capable of generating healthy cash flow.

3.   **Maintain.** This may apply to businesses in mature markets where the firm already has an acceptable market share and where further share-building strategies are not seen as generating a positive net present value.

4.   **Growth.** This will apply to businesses in attractive markets where they possess competitive advantages.

5.   **Enter.** Managers should be generating new growth options for the firm to develop in the future.

The purpose of the strategic position assessment is to identify those parts of the business that are creating value and to identify the drivers of value in the different markets. A simple way of thinking about the structure of the assessment is in terms of four questions. First, how is the business doing now? Is the business creating value? Which are its strong parts and are there any parts that are destroying value? The next two questions seek to understand the drivers of value. The second question is: how did the business get here? What explains its success or failure in creating value? The third question projects these drivers to the future by asking: where is the business heading? What are the implications of its current trajectory? The final question asks: what needs to be done? What actions are necessary to enhance the value of the business?

ASSESSING THE CURRENT POSITION

The first step in the strategic position assessment is identifying whether the business is performing successfully at the moment. In principle this should be a straightforward question, but in practice, answering it is not simple at all.

WEAKNESSES OF FINANCIAL MEASURES

Unfortunately, financial measures do not give reliable indications on whether *current* performance is creating the long-term value shareholders expect. The problem needs to be explored at two levels: the company as a whole and its constituent units.

THE COMPANY OVERALL

For a publicly quoted company, the total return to shareholders in the form of dividends and share price appreciation is the natural way to judge the performance of its management. In the long run this is certainly the case. But as a short-run measure of performance it is often not a good indicator. This is because a company's share price is determined by investors' *expectations* of the value of future cash flows. This leads to a number of paradoxes, especially over the short term. If investors appreciate a well-run company's strategy, the value of future cash flows will be fully incorporated in the current share price. The future share price of this well-managed company will therefore not appreciate more than the stock market average. Investors can do better investing in poorly managed companies, if they believe that market expectations have overestimated how badly these companies are doing. In the short run, good companies therefore may not deliver better shareholder returns than bad ones!

Because of this problem, managers tend to judge performance using accounting measures such as return on capital or earnings per share. But such measures are even more unsatisfactory. Far from being objective, earnings and capital employed are subjective and easily manipulated by different accounting methods. But even more seriously, these accounting metrics are short-term and can be quite unrelated to the real job of creating long-term value for shareholders. Profitability can be easily boosted by cutting back on marketing, training and research to the long-run detriment of the business. New measures like economic value added may give a better measure of economic profit, but they in no way solve the problem of providing an indicator of long-term value creation.

OPERATING UNITS

Since the achievement of the company is the aggregate of the results of the operating performance of its individual businesses it is even more important to judge their results. Unfortunately, this is equally difficult. Since the operating units normally do not have their own shares quoted on the stock market, looking at the total shareholder return is not possible.

The theoretically correct method of measuring the performance of an operating unit over a year is to look at the value management has created. This means comparing the value of the unit at the end of the year with that at the beginning. The obvious problem is that these values are based on highly uncertain forecasts of long-term cash flows. Since generally the managers who make these forecasts will be the same ones whose performance is being evaluated, there is considerable scope for biased results.

So again, as at the corporate level, performance is generally assessed using conventional accounting measures such as return on capital, profits or economic value added. None of these gives a reliable measure of the long-term value being created by managers; indeed, they will often be completely misleading. In some ways, these measures are worse at the operating unit level because they encourage deceptive comparisons across business units. For example, expecting a promising new business in a high-growth market to show the same levels of profitability as a mature business unit would seriously erode the potential of the newcomer. Units at different levels of development need quite different objectives and measures of performance.

STRATEGIC VALUE DRIVERS

Because of the weaknesses of performance measures based on annual accounting measures and the subjectivity inherent in estimating directly changes in value, *indirect measures* have to be employed to decide whether current accomplishments are creating long-term value.

These lead indicators are termed the strategic value drivers of the business. *Strategic value drivers* are those organisational capabilities that have the most significant impact on the firm's ability to create shareholder value. For example, key strategic value drivers at 3M and Intel are their new product development capabilities; at Procter & Gamble brand management is a key driver; at Toyota operational efficiency is important. These drivers shape a company's ability to create and retain competitive advantage and continuing profitability. If managers' current actions are enhancing these value drivers, then long-term value is likely to be created. If these resources and capabilities are being neglected then the firm's competitive position and long-term value is likely to erode. To measure whether value is being created in any one year management have to (1) identify those organisational variables critically affecting competitive advantage and long-term cash flow; (2) set target levels of performance on these variables and (3) measure the performance achieved and compare this against target performance levels.

IDENTIFYING VALUE DRIVERS

To identify strategic value drivers the management team needs a fundamental understanding of their business. They need to be able to decide what are the most important factors determining the ability of the business to generate long-term cash flows. A strategic value driver should have three characteristics. First, it should be a *current* asset or capability that has a significant impact on the *long-term* value of the business. Second, it should be capable of being measured and communicated. Third, it should be capable of being influenced by management actions.

Most successful businesses will have a set of value drivers including financial resources such as strong operating margins and cash flow; marketing resources including brands, customer loyalty and distribution partnerships; operating capabilities such as efficient manufacturing and supply chain processes, and learning capabilities in the form of training and development resources.

TARGET LEVELS OF PERFORMANCE

Once the value drivers are identified, the levels of performance that are acceptable have to be determined. The best approach is to benchmark performance against a peer group or other companies that the business aspires to emulate.

It is important to recognise that the significance of a value driver and the appropriate level of performance depend on the nature of the business and its stage in the life cycle. For example, high returns on capital and positive cash flows are to be expected from mature businesses, whereas growth is a much more important measure of performance for a new business. Many new businesses will have high market valuations but little or no current profit. Here investors are valuing the future cash flows that they believe will occur once critical mass has been established.

MEASURING PERFORMANCE

To measure progress management has to set up the systems to collect regular, objective information on these drivers. These metrics are valuable if they form the basis for action. Targets have to be set, and individuals and groups have to be assigned responsibility for achieving results.

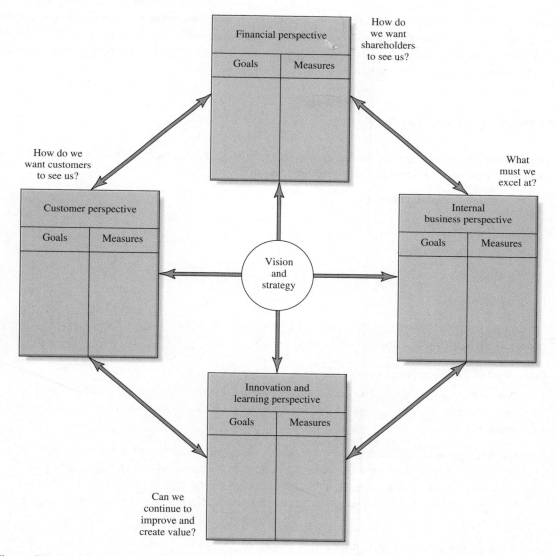

Figure 5.1 The Balanced Scorecard Links Performance Measures. Reprinted by permission of *Harvard Business Review*, Translating Vision and Strategy: Four Perspectives. From 'Using the Balanced Scorecard as a Strategic Management System', Robert S. Kaplan and David P. Norton, Jan.–Feb. 1996, Copyright ©1996 by the President and Fellows of Harvard College. All rights reserved

THE BALANCED SCORECARD

Successful companies are accepting that performance and plans cannot be built around a single measure such as return on capital or earnings per share. Instead they need a set of indicators to track performance and ensure that managers are achieving on the drivers of long-term performance. The most systematic and popular approach in recent years to developing such lead indicators has been the 'balanced scorecard' developed by Kaplan and Norton.[1]

The balanced scorecard was motivated by the recognition that companies cannot rely on short-run financial indicators to measure long-run performance. What is needed is a set of measures to link short-run achievement to long-run value creation. The way this is done is by getting managers to develop a model of their business (see box, 'Developing the Balanced Scorecard'). The model aims to identify what determines the business's long-run ability to generate cash. Each business will have its own key drivers and hence will have its own measures. But based on their research, Kaplan and Norton suggest most businesses will have four common sets of perspectives – financial, customer, internal and innovation (Figure 5.1).

FINANCIAL PERSPECTIVE

The financial perspective incorporates the financial drivers of shareholder value. Normally it will make sense for the business to set objectives for, and measure the performance of:

○ *Return on capital employed*

○ *Operating margins*

○ *Economic value added*

○ *Cash flow*

○ *Sales growth*

Developing the Balanced Scorecard

Developing the scorecard consists of eight steps.

1. **Preparation.** *The firm must define the business unit for which the scorecard is appropriate. Normally this will be a unit that has its own customers, distribution channels, production facilities, and financial performance measures.*

2. **Developing mission and strategy.** *The management team receives briefing materials on the scorecard concept and internal documents describing the company's vision, mission and strategy. The scorecard facilitator interviews the executives to obtain their perspectives of the firm's objectives and ideas about scorecard measures. Often a sample of customers and shareholders are interviewed to understand their expectations.*

3. **Agreeing the vision and what it means.** *In a workshop, the top team debates the vision and strategy until a consensus is reached. They then identify the strategic objectives that are required for shareholders, customers, internal processes and for the business's ability to improve, innovate and grow. Finally they try to draft a preliminary scorecard containing operational measures for the strategic objectives.*

4. **Drafting the balanced scorecard.** *The facilitator documents the output of the workshop and interviews the executives about the tentative scorecard. He also seeks opinions about implementing it.*

5. **Refining the scorecard.** *In a second workshop, involving a larger number of senior managers, the organisation's strategic drivers and draft scorecard is debated. Sub-groups are formed to review the proposed measures, link the various initiatives already underway to the measures, and start to develop an implementation plan. Finally, managers are asked to develop stretch objectives for each of the measures.*

6. **Final approval.** *The senior executive team meets to come to a final consensus on the strategy and scorecard and to agree stretch targets on the chosen measures. The team must also agree on an implementation plan including an action programme, communicating the scorecard to employees and developing the information to support it.*

7. **Implementation.** *A new team is created to implement the scorecard. This includes communicating it throughout the organisation, developing second-level metrics for decentralised units and a new, comprehensive information system that links top-level measures down through shop-floor and site-specific operational indicators.*

8. **Periodic reviews.** *Each month information on scorecard performance is reviewed. The balanced scorecard metrics are also evaluated annually as part of the strategic planning and budgetary processes*

The measures chosen and the target levels will depend upon the maturity of the products and services in the unit's portfolio. For businesses at the growth stage the primary financial objective will be sales growth. When the business reaches maturity profitability measures such as return on capital employed, economic value added and operating margins become more important. Finally, at the decline stage cash flow will become the key financial measure.

CUSTOMER PERSPECTIVE

Growth and profitability depend crucially on the ability of the firm to satisfy its customers. Measures of marketing performance are normally leading indicators of financial results. Goals and measurements will usually be required for:

- Market share
- Brand image and awareness
- Customer satisfaction
- Customer retention
- Customer acquisition
- Ranking by key accounts

Some businesses have different types of customers whose perspectives require separate measures. For example, financial institutions will need to monitor both savers and investors; fast-moving consumer goods companies will need to look separately at both their trade customers and final consumers.

INTERNAL BUSINESS PERSPECTIVE

The ability of companies to generate cash flow also depends upon the efficiency of their business processes: R&D, design, manufacturing, selling and distribution. The goals and measures should focus on those internal processes that have the greatest impact on customer satisfaction. They may include:

- *Percentage of sales from new products*
- *Manufacturing cost*
- *Manufacturing cycle time*
- *Inventory management*
- *Quality indices*
- *Technological capabilities*

INNOVATION AND LEARNING PERSPECTIVE

Long-run competitiveness depends on the firm's core capabilities and its ability to upgrade them over time. Many companies now have competency assessment centres to measure the skills and attributes of their employees. Others map out their key organisational competencies to identify strengths and weaknesses. Goals and measures can be set for competency developments in:

- *Product development*
- *Purchasing*
- *Manufacturing*
- *Technology*
- *Marketing and sales*

The balanced scorecard emphasises that in a complex business there are no single measures that can summarise performance in the short run. High levels of current profitability can easily disguise a decline in the long-term competitiveness of the business. The appropriate metrics also vary with the maturity of the business. The balanced scorecard and lead indicator approach encourages managers to think about the strategic value drivers that generate long-term value. The goal of maximising shareholder value is not itself an actionable objective or basis for strategy. To make it actionable managers have to think through what they need to accomplish and what competencies they will need to acquire.

EXPLORING THE PORTFOLIO

It is not enough to look at performance at the aggregate level. To really understand the picture, aggregate performance needs to be broken down into smaller units to identify the real winners and losers. A company will disaggregate its results into operating units such as major product lines or countries; operating units will then in turn disaggregate performance by individual products, customers or markets. One of the most pervasive phenomena in organisations is the Pareto principle: 80 per cent of the results come from 20 per cent of the activities. In other words, usually only one in five of the organisation's products, customers or businesses is really profitable.

One of the most common presentations by management consultants is the *profit waterfall* showing the percentages of the company's total economic profit and capital employed by each of its business units, products or customer groups. The results are invariably eye-catching. The Pareto principle invariably holds. Usually less than half of the company's invested capital is responsible for all the value created. Figure 5.2 illustrates a typical profit waterfall for a European chemical company. Here two major businesses accounted for 100 per cent of the company's economic profits. As much as 60 per cent of the capital was invested in business units that generated no profits.

The usual recommendation from the consultants is then to rationalise or sell the loss-makers and focus future investment on those businesses earning the highest profits. The implication is that the smaller, more focused company will have much higher profits and a smaller capital base. But such a conclusion is very dangerous. It is certainly true that managers should be aware of which products are profitable and that many companies are making the mistake of persisting with businesses that have no future. But to confuse current profitability with value is misleading. The stock market often values very highly businesses that currently exhibit no economic profit. Value is based on long-term cash flows, not current profits. Current profits typically account for less than 5 per cent of the equity value of businesses in growth markets. Over-reliance on the profit waterfall can be highly damaging to a firm's efforts to encourage innovation. It will generally overemphasise the value of mature businesses. Indeed, many of these mature businesses are profitable because they require little investment and brand building. Encouraging investment in them can be counterproductive because the incremental return on investment is low.

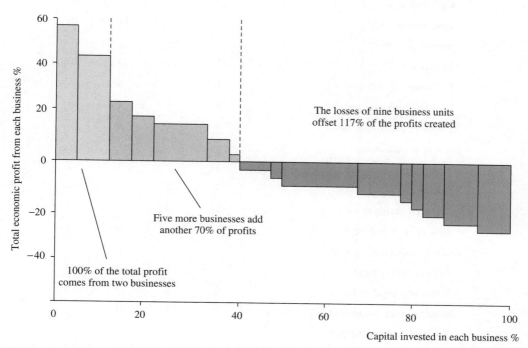

Figure 5.2 Profit Concentration in a Typical Portfolio

As for companies, the current performance of a product or customer group cannot be assessed from figures of current profitability alone. To judge their value managers need to explore performance on the full range of measures that are lead indicators of long-term value creation.

Table 5.1 presents a simple illustration of the lead indicator approach for a company with four business units. Overall the company looks to be doing well, with 18 per cent return on capital and a strong positive cash flow. But these averages disguise a more complex picture. Over 90 per cent of the profits come from the two business units, A and B. Unfortunately, these are declining businesses in mature markets. All the growth is coming from unit C and a recent acquisition, D. There is no straightforward answer to the question about which businesses are performing best. In accounting terms, A is best, generating over half the group's profits and most of its cash. But in terms of growth and from the perspectives of customers, operations, innovation and development it is doing poorly. It is probable that the value of A is declining, while the long-term values of units C and D are increasing with their high levels of customer satisfaction, technical capabilities and innovation.

Table 5.1   Lead Indicators to Evaluate Performance

		Operating units			
	Group	A	B	C	D
Financial indicators					
Return on capital (%)	18	24	22	10	0
Operating margin (%)	9	12	12	3	0
Cash flow (£m)	12	10	7	−2	−3
Sales growth (%)	2	−2	−3	11	25
Customer indicators					
Market share		24	20	14	10
Customer satisfaction		3	3	4	5
Customer retention rate		3	3	4	5
Customer acquisition rate		2	1	4	5
Operations indicators					
Manufacturing costs		3	3	2	2
Quality		3	3	4	4
Technical performance		2	2	4	5
New product performance		2	1	4	5
Innovation and development					
Product development		2	2	4	5
Purchasing capabilities		2	2	3	3
Manufacturing capabilities		2	3	4	4
Technological capabilities		2	2	4	5

Indicators based on 5-point ratings: 5, excellent; 4, strong; 3, average; 2, weak; 1, very poor.

If C and D can capitalise on their opportunities and establish critical mass they are likely to move into profit and become cash positive as the market matures. The task of the board is to ensure that the strategies are in place to achieve these goals. The board should be concerned about the threat to the value of units A and B from their mediocre performance in satisfying, retaining and acquiring customers and their weaknesses in development, innovation and operations.

EXPLAINING THE CURRENT POSITION

The first question asked: where is the business now? It sought to analyse the current health of the company. The second analysis seeks to diagnose it. It asks: how did we get here? What have been the *causes* of the current successes and failures? It is an essential preliminary step to projecting the future of the business and determining the actions necessary to enhance its value.

Diagnosis starts with the basic economic proposition that there are only two ways in which a business can earn profits that exceed its cost of capital. One is to find attractive markets where competition is weak. Lack of competition then allows the firm to earn *monopoly profits*. The other is to possess unique resources or assets that enable the business to create a competitive advantage – in the form of lower costs or a superior offer. These are called *Ricardian rents*, after the nineteenth-century economist David Ricardo, who explained why highly fertile land was able to earn high returns even though the market for wheat was competitive. In other words, success or failure can be explained by both (1) external factors – the attractiveness or otherwise of the market in which the firm is operating and (2) internal factors – the specific capabilities the business has inherited or developed, which allow it to develop a competitive advantage.

As with the assessment of performance, there are rarely simple explanations of the causes of success or failure. Managers tend to oversimplify and be biased in their analyses. A manager of a poorly performing business will invariably explain its failure in terms of external factors such as a declining market, excess industry capacity or aggressive competitors. A successful manager will usually explain performance in terms of internal factors such as superior products, excellent service or better marketing. Usually both sets of factors play a role, and it is important to disentangle these causes since their implications for strategy are quite different.

MARKET ATTRACTIVENESS

An attractive market can be defined as one where the average competitor consistently earns a return above its cost of capital, i.e. it is creating value for shareholders. Some markets do appear to be attractive for long periods of time, while in others it is much more difficult to earn economic profits. This is illustrated in Figure 5.3, which shows the average economic return on equity in different industries between 1976 and 1991. For example, companies in soft drinks and ethical drugs earned an average return of over 12 per cent above their cost of capital over the 15-year period. Companies in oilfield services, steel, textiles and mining were consistently unprofitable. Although the example is somewhat old, it nevertheless illustrates a point which is still valid today.

The most important factors determining the attractiveness of the market are:

1.   The size of the market
2.   Market growth

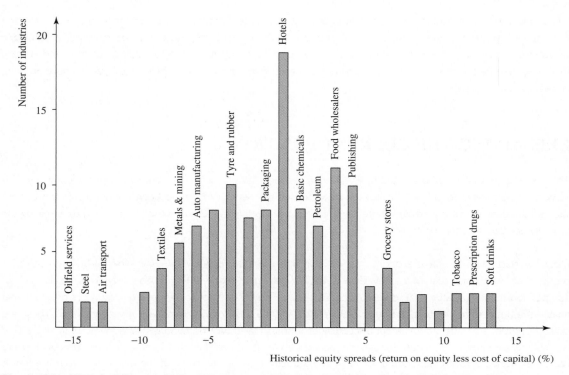

Figure 5.3 Historical Economic Returns Across Industries 1976–1991. Reprinted with the permission of The Free Press, a Division of Simon & Schuster, Inc. From *The Value Imperative: Managing the Superior Shareholder Return* by James M. McTaggart, Peter W. Kontes and Michael C. Mankins. Copyright ©1994 by the Free Press

3.   The competitive structure of the market
4.   The cylicality of the market
5.   Risk factors

SIZE OF THE MARKET

Big markets offer firms more opportunities to grow. For larger firms, only sizeable markets will have the potential to generate meaningful increases in value. Larger markets may offer smaller firms the opportunities to find profitable niches where they can prosper without competing head-to-head with the major players. Big markets can also enable ambitious companies to build economies of scale.

MARKET GROWTH

It is easier to grow if the market in which the firm is operating is also growing. Non-growth markets are zero-sum: a business can only grow by taking customers away from competitors. Growth under these circumstances is usually associated with declining prices and profitability. Growth markets are non-zero-sum: all the competitors can grow, which acts to reduce destructive price competition and margin erosion. In high-growth markets it is important to be ambitious. A firm's long-term competitive position can easily be undermined despite apparently satisfactory growth.

For example, a business might be growing at 10 per cent annually, but if the market is growing at 20 per cent, its market share is rapidly eroding. Within a few years it might be overtaken by competitors that are able to achieve economies of scale and power over the distribution channels.

THE COMPETITIVE STRUCTURE OF THE MARKET

The most important determinant of the average profitability of a market is its competitive structure. There are five main elements of competitive structure:

1. **Intensity of direct competition.** In some markets, competitors are much more aggressive in seeking to win or maintain sales. Where this occurs, prices and profits are invariably reduced. Intense competition is most likely in markets characterised by:

    ○   **Excess production capacity.** *The greater the excess capacity in an industry, the more likely competitors will cut prices and so erode profit margins in efforts to increase utilisation.*

    ○   **Standardised products or services.** *The more similar are the offers of competitors, the greater the chances of price-based competition and low margins.*

    ○   **Many competitors.** *The more players, the more likely is intense competition. With only a few competitors tacit collusion will often maintain higher prices.*

    ○   **Low growth.** *In rapidly growing markets, the intensity of competition is reduced since they do not have to take customers from each other. As growth slows, excess capacity triggers price competition.*

    In some industries such as steel or textiles all these characteristics are present, which act to eliminate profits for all but the most efficient producers.

2. **Buyer power.** The drive and ability of customers to reduce prices also has a major effect on the profitability of the industry. Buying pressure is a function of two forces: the price sensitivity of buyers and their negotiating power. The *price sensitivity* of customers is determined primarily by their profitability and the significance of the product's cost in their total expenditures. When times are tough for buyers and when they are spending significant sums with the supplier, there is a greater incentive to seek lower prices to restore their own margins.

    The *negotiating power* of a customer is high where there are few customers, many suppliers, little differentiation between suppliers, low switching costs, and opportunities for the customer to threaten to integrate backwards.

    Generally, as markets mature, customer pressure puts margins under increasing threat. Over time, as buyers obtain more information about product features and suppliers' costs, their leverage increases. When this is combined with high price sensitivity, as it is for example in basic chemicals or auto tyres, buying power can cause profitability to disappear for all but the lowest-cost competitors.

3. **Threat of new entry.** If barriers to new entry are weak then it will be impossible for companies to maintain monopoly profits. The major barriers to entry are:

    ○   *Patents and legal regulations*

    ○   *Economies of scale*

    ○   *High capital requirements to enter the market*

○ *Strong brands*

○ *Threat of retaliation*

○ *Access to distribution channel*

In some industries such as soft drinks and pharmaceuticals, such barriers are crucial in explaining the high profit margins that have persisted. On the whole, however, globalisation, deregulation and the Internet have reduced entry barriers in many markets (see box, 'The Internet Pulls Prices Down').

The Internet Pulls Prices Down

E-commerce has introduced a strong deflationary effect on prices. For customers, it has allowed them to quickly search around the globe for the best prices. For suppliers, e-commerce has meant savings from lower real estate and rental costs, and reduced outlays for advertising, inventory and transportation – items that can account for around 38 per cent of the consumer price.

---

4.   **Threat from substitutes.** Substitute products are indirect competitors that can undermine demand and prices. There are different types of substitutes:

○ **Alternative products.** *For example, if the price of steel rises constructors can build bridges from concrete.*

○ **New products.** *Innovation can erode demand, e.g. email undermined the fax, mobiles are replacing landlines.*

○ **Elimination of need.** *For example, new cars use less engine oil; eventually sealed engines may make replacement lubricant unnecessary.*

○ **Generic substitution.** *All products to some extent compete with one another. For example, producers of TVs, computers, cars and holidays all compete for the limited incomes of households.*

○ **Abstinence.** *Consumers can often decide to do without the product if the price is unacceptable.*

Some industries are more prone to substitutes than others. For example, it is more difficult for customers to substitute away from ethical pharmaceuticals than it is for them to find substitutes for glass packaging.

5.   **Power of suppliers.** Suppliers limit a market's profitability if they can drive up input costs faster than a market's customers will allow them to be passed on. Supplier power is likely to be high when:

○ *Few suppliers are available*

○ *Suppliers have unique products or strongly differentiated brands*

○ *Switching costs are high*

○ *Suppliers can threaten to integrate forward*

○ *There are large numbers of small customers with weak negotiating power*

Again, some industries, such as textiles or petroleum, are more affected by these forces than others.

Professor Michael Porter of Harvard Business School represented these factors that determine industry profitability in his now familiar 'five forces' diagram (Figure 5.4).

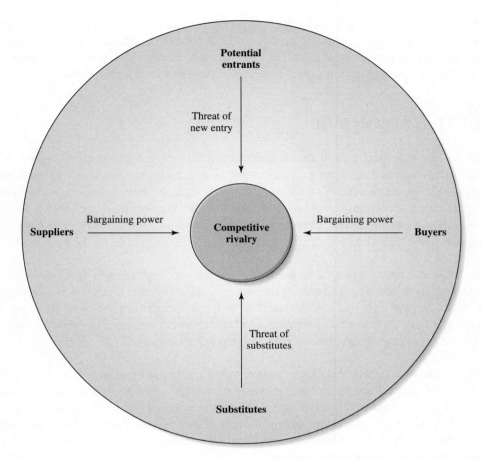

Figure 5.4   Five-Forces Analysis. Reprinted with permission of the Free Press, a Division of Simon & Schuster, Inc. from *Competitive Strategy: Techniques for Analyzing Industries and Competitors* by Michael E. Porter. Copyright ©1981, 1998 by The Free Press

THE CYCLICALITY OF THE MARKET

Some markets, especially those for commodity products, are highly cyclical, with prices 30 per cent or more higher at the peaks than in the troughs. This results in companies swinging from high profitability to substantial losses over the years. The cause of the cycle is usually over-investment when profits are high, which then triggers excess capacity and a collapse of prices. Prices are only restored when mergers, or companies exiting the industry, reduce capacity. The performance of a firm in such a market is therefore highly coloured by the stage of the industry cycle.

RISK FACTORS

The attractiveness of a market is also affected by the risks involved, since such factors affect the rate used to discount future cash flows or economic profits. Risk factors include political stability and monetary considerations in the primary markets, infrastructure and the possibilities of regulatory interference, availability of skills and resources, and possible economic and tax considerations.

It is important to analyse all these external market factors when diagnosing a company's performance advantages. They emphasise that high profits and growth are not solely a function of strong capabilities and good management. Some industries, for long periods of time, are just easier in which to achieve performance. In some industries, however well-managed the firm, it is just extraordinarily difficult to create value for shareholders.

COMPETITIVE ADVANTAGE

Generally, however, the firm's competitive advantage, or lack of it, has a more important impact on its value than the nature of its particular market. Even in the toughest markets, firms with a competitive advantage are usually able to invest at returns that exceed their cost of capital. Similarly, even in industries where the average company earns high economic profits, firms without any competitive advantage flounder. In other words, the variation of profitability within an industry exceeds the variation between industries. Ricardian profits are generally more important than monopoly profits.

To diagnose these internally generated sources of value creation, managers need to ask whether the business has held a value-creating differential advantage. If not, why not? As discussed in Chapter 3, the explanations of a firm's differential advantage or lack of it will be found in the firm's resources and the way they are integrated to form its core capabilities. If the firm has an effective set of lead indicators or balanced scorecard, which measures performance on the key value drivers, these should supply most of the answers.

When used in value-based marketing a differential advantage has a precise meaning. *A business has a differential advantage if it is able to sustain economic profits that exceed the average of competitors in its market.* This differential advantage can be based on either of two strategies. The first is an economic *cost* advantage, which occurs when a firm's total costs (including capital costs) are lower than those of the average competitor. The second is through a *differentiation* advantage, which occurs when customers perceive its product or services as superior, and are willing to pay a higher price than is charged by competitors.

COST ADVANTAGE

In many commodity markets building a differentiation advantage is very difficult. Of course, every marketing manager can find ways of differentiating the product by augmenting it with additional services and advertising. But, without real innovation, it can often be very difficult, or impossible, to get buyers to pay price premiums sufficient to cover the costs of these additional features. In such markets, superior profitability can only come through developing a cost advantage.

For value-based analysis a cost advantage has a precise meaning. *A business has a relative cost advantage if it has a lower total economic cost than the average of competitors in its market.* Total economic cost means the sum of operating costs plus a charge for capital, where the capital charge is the cost of capital multiplied by the amount of capital employed in the business.

Note that this definition of an economic cost advantage is different from the conventional accounting method that looks only at operating costs. Unless the business recognises the cost of employing capital, investing heavily to reduce operating costs can actually increase total unit costs. This occurs if the increased capital charge is greater than the decline in operating cost. An example of this is the Saturn programme at General Motors in the 1980s. GM spent billions on robotics and automation, only to find that companies like Ford, which focused on increasing the efficiency of its labour force, ended up with lower total economic costs per vehicle. This process has to be continuous, however; note how Japanese car manufacturers like Toyota have since succeeded through operational excellence. Today, even the Japanese are at risk from emerging nations such as Korea.

An economic cost advantage can create shareholder value in either of two ways. First, the business can charge the same price as competitors but earn a higher profit margin. Alternatively, it can charge lower prices and gain a higher market share.

Note that investing in a low-cost strategy may not always make sense. To create value any investment to gain a cost advantage must be more than offset by the improvement in profitability over time, or the gain in market share, depending on how management chooses to exploit the advantage. Many companies have over invested in efforts to gain a cost advantage only to find that innovation or competitive emulation quickly erodes the advantage.

DIFFERENTIATION ADVANTAGE

Differentiation occurs when there is a perceived difference in delivered value that leads target customers to prefer one company's offer to those of others. Generally, differentiation has been a more effective way of increasing returns to shareholders than cost-based strategies. This is illustrated in Table 5.2, which lists companies among the Standard & Poor's Europe 350 with the highest sustained return to shareholders. The list is dominated by firms that have pursued strategies based on innovation, superior service and brand loyalty. Cost-based strategies are more vulnerable for two reasons. First, rapid change has meant that cost advantages based on scale and experience are often undermined by competitors innovating in terms of even lower-cost processes or distribution channels. Second, low-cost technology and systems have often been speedily copied by competitors.

But developing a value-creating differentiation advantage is no easy task. Companies tend to overestimate the uniqueness of their offers. It is very common for managers to perceive their products or services as superior. Unfortunately, it is not their perceptions which count, but rather those of the customer. *Differentiation occurs only*

Table 5.2   Europe's Best Performing Companies: Total Shareholder Return 2001–2004

Company	Industry	Country	Total return
Continental	Automotive supplier	Germany	134.5
Autostrade	Industrial	Italy	127.7
Carnival	Leisure travel	UK	115.0
Imperial Tobacco Group	Tobacco	UK	108.3
Altadis	Consumer staples	Spain	87.3
Smith & Nephew	Healthcare	UK	80.3
Wolseley	Industrials	UK	79.2
Man Group	Financials	UK	79.2
Grupo Ferrovial	Industrials	Spain	76.9
Essilor International	Healthcare	France	71.5

Source: Business Week, June 28, 2004

if customers are willing to pay a price premium. If customers are unwilling to pay a price premium then the company does not have a differentiation advantage. The key requirement is customers being *willing to* pay more. If a business has such an advantage then management have three strategies to choose from: (1) charge the full price premium by increasing the price to the point where it just offsets the improvement in customer benefits; (2) keep prices at the level of competitors and use its advantage to gain market share; or (3) price above competitors but below the full premium to gain a combination of unit margin improvement and market share gain.

If management's claim about possessing differentiated products or services is to be proved they need to demonstrate that one of these three outcomes is occurring. The way in which this can be demonstrated is illustrated in Figure 5.5. Here managers believed that each of the five product lines had a differential advantage due to their superior quality and sales support. But the evidence from market research showed otherwise. Line A was perceived by customers as of lower quality than competitors; it sold at a lower price and still lost market share. Lines B and C charged premium prices, but customers obviously did not think these premiums were justified as market shares were also declining. Only D and E had a differential advantage. D charged higher prices and was holding market share; E charged parity prices but had gained over 5 per cent market share. Managers need to understand that being different is not the same as having a differential advantage. Unless the firm gains sufficient premium or additional share to cover the additional costs and investment there is no added value.

As described in an earlier chapter, the sources of differentiation can be grouped into three. The first is *product or service leadership* where customers perceive the company offer as of higher quality or more innovative (examples are Apple and Sony). The second is *customer intimacy*, or one-to-one marketing, where buyers see the company as being able to customise its offer to their personal requirements and deal with them on an individualised basis (examples are Federal Express and Lexus). The third is *brand leadership*, where the company's offer possesses emotional value beyond what can be explained by their product or service performance (examples are Coca-Cola and Mercedes Benz). As with cost advantages, successful differentiation is based on the firm's resources and capabilities. Progress in building these resources and capabilities should be monitored through the choice of lead indicators.

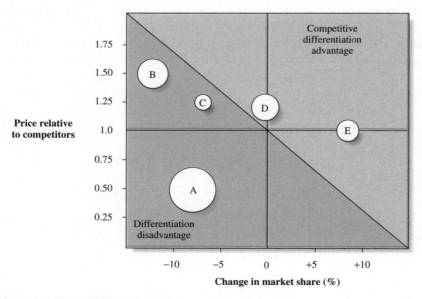

Figure 5.5   Measuring Competitive Differentiation

MARKET ATTRACTIVENESS AND COMPETITIVE POSITION

The analysis of the company's external and internal forces can be brought together in a *strategic characterisation matrix*.[2] This is illustrated in Figure 5.6 for a company with four business units with different strategic characteristics.[3] The radius of the circles is proportionate to the turnover of the business unit. A business like A, in an attractive market and with a strong competitive advantage, should always be creating value for shareholders. It may not currently be highly profitable if the market is new, but investment should earn long-run returns above the cost of capital. Ideally a company would like to have most of its business in this part of the matrix. Companies like Microsoft, Vodafone and Pfizer are examples of companies with the majority of their businesses in attractive markets and possessing competitive advantages.

Business B, on the other hand, has the opposite characteristics and will almost always be value destroying. It will produce economic losses and the return on investment will be less than the cost of capital. Outside the two extreme zones, for example for units C and D, the results are less clear cut. C will normally be in a better position than D because usually competitive advantage has a bigger impact on profitability than market attractiveness. Normally, when a business has a significant competitive advantage it can generate economic profits even though it operates in an unattractive market. Businesses such as D are usually value destroying because the attractiveness of the market does not compensate for the lack of competitive advantage. Even when they are generating positive economic profits, they are highly vulnerable to deterioration in the economics of the market.

To summarise, the past performance of a company is explained by a combination of the attractiveness of the market and its competitive advantage, with the latter generally the more important. To an extent, the two sets of factors

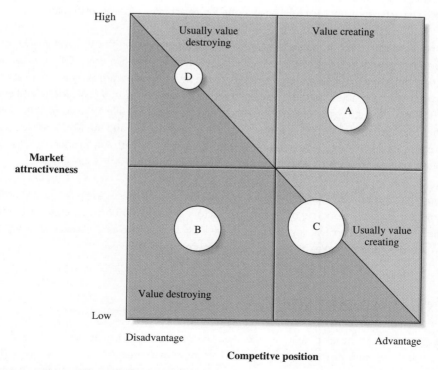

Figure 5.6   The Strategic Characterisation Matrix

overlap in that a competence of management should be in identifying attractive markets. Also, not all the features of the market are outside the control of managers. They can also develop strategies to improve the competitive structure of the market in their favour by, for example, building brands to create entry barriers, or by mergers to reduce capacity. But it is important to disentangle the two different dimensions since they shape how the future of the business is likely to develop.

PROJECTING THE FUTURE OF THE BUSINESS

The first part of the strategic assessment was aimed at obtaining a factual picture of the performance of the company. The second part sought to explain this performance in terms of the attractiveness of the firm's markets and its competitive advantages. The third question seeks to project where the business is heading under its present policies. It aims at predicting what the performance is likely to be, as a prelude to determining what new actions need to be taken.

Forecasting the future of the business on its present strategies requires projecting the characteristics of the market and anticipating the implications of the firm's competitive position into the future.

MARKET ATTRACTIVENESS

We have looked at how the characteristics of the market affected performance in the past. Now the task is to assess how these characteristics are likely to change in the future and affect future performance.

Each of the dimensions of market attractiveness has to be evaluated. First, on the size and growth of the market, managers have to estimate how the growth rate will change over the next five years. Of particular importance is determining how the market will be segmented and which customer segments are likely to be most attractive. The competitive structure of the market has to be evaluated and its impact on industry profitability. Will excess capacity be a problem? What are the strategies of the competitors and how will they affect the competitive intensity of the industry and the major segments? What implications will this have for prices and margins? Are customer pressures going to be a major issue? Are new competitors likely to enter the market? Are product substitution and new technology going to create pressures? Will suppliers be exerting significant cost pressures?

Similar projections need to be made about the industry cycle. Will cyclical pressures be favourable or not for prices and profits? Any new political, economic or societal risk factors also have to be considered. This research should lead to a profile of how market profitability and growth are likely to change over the next five years. It should lead to a conclusion on whether the market is likely to become more or less attractive.

DIFFERENTIAL ADVANTAGE

Alongside the projection of developments in the industry, management has to assess how the competitive advantage of the firm will shift over the coming years. If such an assessment is to be accurate and useful it will require comprehensive quantitative information, not only on the firm's products and services, but also on those of competitors and on the changing needs of customers. For example, to estimate the relative economic cost advantage of the business it will need to benchmark its costs against the major competitors for each stage of its value chain. Assessing the firm's differentiation advantage will require information on relative prices, market shares and consumer needs broken down by product and market segment. Since management is focusing on how these are likely to change in the future, it will also have to develop an understanding of the strategies of competitors and customers.

Figure 5.7 illustrates the results of such a competitive position assessment for a speciality chemicals company. The larger circles show the projected improvement of the business from the current year (2001) to the forecast position in 2006, resulting from a major rebranding plan and a cost reduction programme. The smaller points represent the changes in the competitive advantage projected for the business unit's individual products. Overall the forecasts show a modest enhancement of the differentiation advantage of the business together with a significant move towards competitive parity in costs.

The next step is to integrate this analysis with the market attractiveness projections, using the strategic characterisation matrix, as illustrated in Figure 5.8. This shows the strategic position of the business; most of its products are likely to improve from the projected enhancement of its competitive advantage. Its major weakness is in the continued unattractiveness of its markets, characterised by little growth, tough competition and strong buyers.

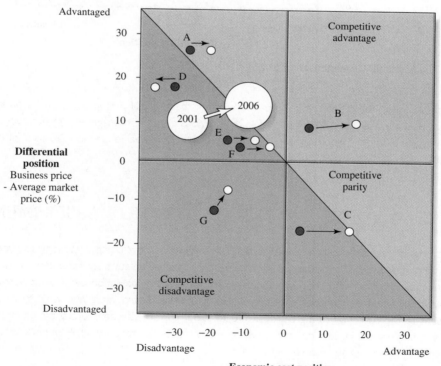

Figure 5.7 The Competitive Advantage Matrix. Reprinted with the permission of The Free Press, a Division of Simon & Schuster, Inc. from *The Value Imperative: Managing the Superior Shareholder Return* by James M. McTaggart, Peter W. Kantes, Michael C. Mankins. Copyright ©1994 by The Free Press

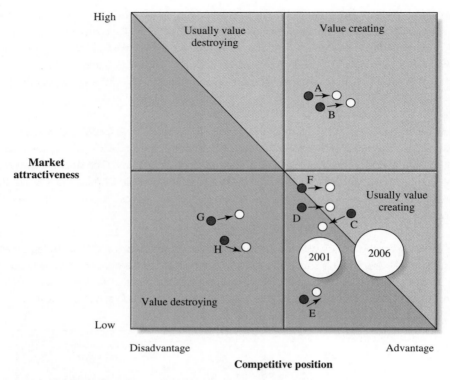

Figure 5.8   The Strategic Characterisation Matrix

The final step is to input these projections into a forecast of the financial performance of the business and the shareholder value added over the planning period. In the previous example, management forecast an improvement in its already positive economic return on capital employed, but modest value creation, on account of the lack of top-line growth.

IMPLICATIONS OF THE STRATEGIC POSITION ASSESSMENT

The strategic position assessment is a crucial tool for management developing a strategy to create value for shareholders. First, it provides the *information* for a valuation of the complete business under its current strategy. If the company is public, it will also show whether its current market capitalisation over- or undervalues it. It also shows which products and customers are creating value, which are destroying it, and why. More generally, the assessment leads to the collection of a great deal of data about customers, competitors, the internal efficiency of the business and its progress in developing its resources and capabilities that are vitally important for developing strategies to create profitability and growth in the future.

Second, it forces management to consider the *options* open to it to create more value. If the market is not attractive it encourages management to evaluate options to improve the average profitability of the industry. These might include efforts to improve industry capacity utilisation through mergers or joint ventures, and options to develop barriers to entry. Where the problems lie in a lack of competitive advantage, managers can develop strategies aiming to reduce costs or achieve product or service differentiation. When neither of these is sufficient it will energise managers to exit uneconomic businesses and search for new ways to grow.

The third benefit of a strategic position assessment is that it identifies the business unit's *strategic value drivers*. Considering strategic value drivers pulls managers away from a sterile focus on accounting measures of performance to an assessment of the real assets and capabilities of the business, which determine its ability to achieve differentiation and a competitive economic cost structure. A differential advantage is based on offering products that are perceived by customers as better value than those of competitors. This has to be matched by an economic cost structure that is capable of delivering economic profits from the offer. These are the two determinants of the ability of the business to create long-term cash flow. The main strategic drivers are knowledge of customers, capabilities to innovate and manage brands, operational skills, and the ability of the organisation to learn and develop.

Unless managers focus on the strategic value drivers they will not develop and adequately invest in them. Today, strategic assets that have in the past generated high returns soon become obsolete unless they receive attention and investment. Brands get dated, patents expire and skills become redundant. Tools such as the balanced scorecard ensure that this monitoring occurs and that the business continues to develop its assets and capabilities.

Understanding the strategic value drivers also encourages management to consider bold new strategies. IBM's turnaround in the 1990s, under Lou Gerstner, was based on the recognition that computer products were increasingly becoming low-margin, commodity items. Gerstner's team saw high-tech services and the Internet as the opportunities to find new sources of growth and profitability. To change the company, new options for acquiring Internet and servicing capabilities were developed, including closing manufacturing plants, a series of start-ups, investing in the service capabilities already existing in the different divisions, and all-out search for Internet and service companies that could be profitably acquired.[4]

Focusing on strategic value drivers rather than simply accounting numbers is also important because they can be leveraged to enter new markets and create new sources of profitable growth. Michael Eisner's success at Walt Disney was based on his leveraging the strategic assets of the business – its famous cartoon characters. This was the basis for Disney's successful moves into retailing, publishing, movies and hotel development, which grew shareholder returns at an annual rate of over 20 per cent during the 1990s. Similarly, Honda's skills in power train development allowed it to expand progressively into cars, lawn mowers, machine engines and generator markets worldwide. As discussed in Chapter 6, strategic value drivers are invaluable at both the business unit and corporate level, to the development of innovative product and market growth strategies.

THE VALUE-BASED PLAN

The result of the strategic position assessment should be a plan to increase shareholder value. The focus of such a plan is on what determines equity value – long-term cash flows, not short-term earnings. The perspective managers must take is that of the outside investor. This is a dispassionate approach that views businesses as investments in productive capacity that either earns returns above their opportunity cost of capital or does not. The units of analysis in the plan are the strategic business units, not the organisation as a whole. It is at the individual product-market level that competitive advantages are built and the strategic value drivers principally operate. The value and strategy of the company as a whole is primarily an aggregation of performance at the business unit level with a separate assessment of the value added, or otherwise, by the head office.

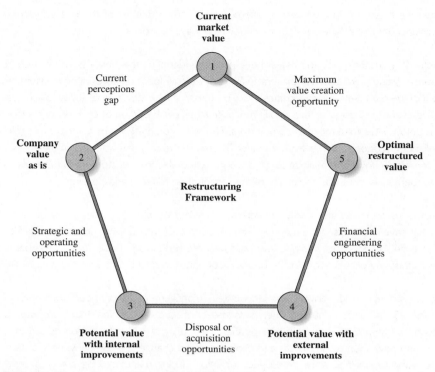

Figure 5.9   Restructuring to Create Value: The McKinsey Pentagon

THE RESTRUCTURING FRAMEWORK

The task of management is to develop and implement a plan to increase the equity value of the business. A useful framework for describing the steps in this process is the McKinsey pentagon.[5] Figure 5.9 shows how the process of restructuring to create increased value can be divided into five stages.

1. ESTABLISHING THE CURRENT MARKET VALUE OF THE COMPANY

The first step in the analysis is straightforward if the company is publicly quoted. The current market value of the company – its equity and debt – can be calculated from the *Financial Times* and other widely available information sources. This gives the estimate made by outside investors of the discounted net present value of the company's long-term cash flow. The market-determined value should be fairly close to the managers' own discounted cash flow valuation. If it is not the gap will be due to one of the following factors:

- ❍   *Management's perception of the future is based on unrealistic assumptions about the company's competitive advantage or the attractiveness of the market in which it operates.*

- ❍   *The management valuation may be higher if they have important information that has not yet been made available to investors (e.g. about new product breakthroughs or strategic alliances).*

- ❍   *The market's valuation might be higher than that of management if investors anticipate a successful take-over of the company at a premium.*

2. THE VALUE OF THE COMPANY AS IS

This stage examines *how* the company's market value is arrived at, and which are the company's most, and least, valuable businesses. It begins by breaking the company down into strategic business units. Cash flow projections have then to be developed for each of the units. These are based on projected sales growth, margins and investment needs, all of which should be available from the business plans. The finance staff will provide estimates of the cost of capital for each division. As described in Chapter 2, discounted cash flow valuations are then calculated.

This process is illustrated for a speciality chemicals company which we will call Ace Chemicals, in Table 5.3. The background is that Ace's recent performance had been disappointing, with little overall growth, stagnant profits and a sliding share price. A new chief executive had been brought in to improve the performance of the company. The company has three strategic business units, selling chemical products to the foundry, steel and aluminium industries. It also has a corporate headquarters costing some £10 million annually. The first task was to use the profitability and growth forecasts from the business plan to calculate the net present values of the cash flows for each of the three units. The present value of headquarters costs was calculated by capitalising projected after-tax annual costs.

To provide a simple benchmark to assess the validity of the current business plan, the finance staff also ran a valuation based on extrapolating the trend for the previous five years. The analyses showed that if the company continued on trend its value would be 13 per cent below its current market value. The planned strategy, on the other hand, was envisaged to bring about a 26 per cent increase in its equity value. This would put the value of Ace above its current market value, but only by 9 per cent – not a particularly exciting figure for investors in the light of the poor performance in the past.

The new management team saw that the vast majority of Ace's value was represented by the value of the foundry business's cash flow. Aluminium is a particular problem, showing a decline in value against its past performance. The plan also projected a cut in headquarters costs; even so, these would still represent a major drag on the company's equity value – almost 20 per cent.

Table 5.3 The Value of the Company 'As Is', January 2007 (£ million)

Ace Chemicals	Plan values (£)	Extrapolation values (£)	Difference (%)
Foundry	485	410	+18
Steel	120	105	+14
Aluminium	30	35	−14
Headquarters	−95	−110	+14
Total	540	440	+23
Debt	−50	−50	
Equity value	490	390	+26
Stock market value	450	450	
Value gap	40	−60	
Gap (%)	9	−13	

The results of the strategic position assessment that Ace had undertaken prior to developing the restructuring plan revealed the explanations of its position. The strategic characterisation matrix showed that the foundry's success was due to its strong competitive advantage based on leading-edge products and an outstanding reputation for quality and service. With steel and aluminium, however, Ace's products were not seen as differentiated and the markets were characterised by intense price competition and strong buying pressures. Conditions in the aluminium market were expected to deteriorate further and Ace had no expectations of significant breakthroughs in products or costs.

Ace had also developed a balanced scorecard to monitor performance on its strategic value drivers. The financial indicators confirmed investors' disappointment with the company. When total shareholder returns were benchmarked against a peer group in the chemicals sector, Ace had significantly underperformed the average. The consumer indicators, while good for foundry, were weak for steel, and especially for aluminium. The indicators for internal operations and learning and development highlighted the weak technology and lack of new products in the latter areas.

What was clear from the valuation exercise and strategic position assessment was that Ace was a vulnerable business. Even with the performance improvements envisaged in the plan, the equity value of the business was only 9 per cent above its current stock market value. Any deviations from the plan or unexpected developments in market conditions would risk a collapse of the share price.

3. THE POTENTIAL VALUE WITH INTERNAL IMPROVEMENTS

The new chief executive decided to develop a new plan that would more aggressively seek to increase long-term cash flows in the business. The four financial drivers of higher cash flows are increased sales, higher prices, lower costs and reductions in investment requirements. The core strategic value drivers that determine these dimensions of financial performance are increasing customer satisfaction, operational efficiency, quality management, the development of new products and the core capabilities that make possible further developments.

Action teams were set up for each business unit to undertake a fundamental reappraisal of the plan with the objective of significantly increasing the unit's value. In the steel products division management first did a simulation to see the leverage of the different financial value drivers. They found that a 5 per cent increase in sales would generate a 20 per cent increase in the present value of the long-term cash flow; a 5 per cent increase in average prices could add 48 per cent to the unit's value, and a similar reduction in investment would add 8 per cent. Next, they benchmarked steel's value chain against the best competitors to judge the scope for improvements in product performance, marketing and productivity. These analyses coupled with the strategic position assessment led management to believe that the business could perform at a significantly higher level. The major changes initiated were:

○ Sales performance. *The team was convinced that sales could be boosted without margin erosion by a modest increase in development spending on certain key projects, a new dealer partnership programme to build greater loyalty, and a refocusing of service staff around high potential customer accounts.*

   Management also decided to invest in three strategic alliances with high-tech businesses overseas to develop potential new areas for growth. It was anticipated that at least one of these pilots would create a significant new income stream after five years.

○ Price increases. *There was scope to reduce the high level and range of discounts the business was giving. A segmentation analysis also suggested that certain specialised customers were not price sensitive if high levels of service and support were guaranteed.*

○ Cost reductions. *Central buying and a vendor reduction programme could reduce material costs. Also, new information technology permitted further savings in office costs.*

○ Investment requirements. *Reducing the number of sites and a new logistics system would offer significant savings in working and fixed capital requirements.*

Similar analyses in the other two business units also produced corresponding improvements in future cash flow. On top of this it was also proposed to cut head office costs by half. Putting it all together, the Ace management team believed that the total value of the business could be increased by 40 per cent over the value in the original plan.

4. THE POTENTIAL VALUE WITH EXTERNAL IMPROVEMENTS

The next step is determining whether value can be created by external improvements. Such enhancements may be possible through either shrinking the business or expanding it. In the previous step management calculated what the units were worth to the company. Perhaps significantly more value could be created for shareholders if some, or all, were sold to other parties, spun-off and floated as independent businesses, or simply liquidated by selling their assets. Management can work with financial analysts to assess the price that might be obtained under each of these options. These sell-off options are often particularly attractive for unrelated businesses where other companies have more expertise, and could add more value than the current management. The cash received can then be returned to shareholders or reinvested to improve the core business if there are profitable opportunities available.

The alternative strategy is to consider strengthening the business through an acquisition. An acquisition might offer the potential to reduce costs or boost growth. While the overall success statistics for acquisitions are not high, the right combination can sometimes bring great rewards. Successful acquisitions depend upon being able to buy at a reasonable price and identifying genuine synergies in costs or marketing to justify the premium paid.

5. OPTIMAL RESTRUCTURED VALUE

The final stage of the restructuring pentagon is to determine the optimal restructured value – what it is worth with all the internal and external improvements. The final plan that was agreed by the board of Ace included selling off the aluminium business to a leading multinational for £60 million, halving the size of the head office, acquiring another foundry business in Taiwan, and a raft of new marketing initiatives that were projected to double Ace's growth rate over the next five years. The results of the value-orientated planning process are summarised in Figure 5.10. The new team was confident that the new strategy would increase the equity value of the company by 80 per cent more than its current value, offering shareholders the prospects of significant real returns on their investments.

STRATEGIC OBJECTIVES

The outcome of the strategic position assessment and the value creating planning process will be a set of strategic objectives, one for each of the business units. For example, in the case of Ace Chemicals the aluminium business was targeted for divestment, while the foundry and steel businesses were set growth objectives. The strategic objective assigned to a business unit sets the broad path management have to follow in pursuit of the company's

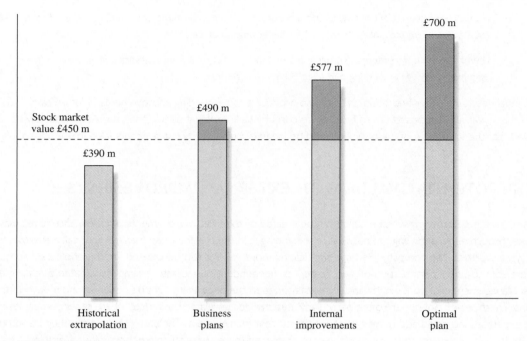

Figure 5.10   Ace Company: Creating Shareholder Value

overall value creating process. What the appropriate strategic objective is for a unit depends upon the assessment of the attractiveness of its market and the strength of its competitive advantage. Those in attractive markets and possessing strong competitive advantages are likely to be assigned growth as the objective; those in areas of limited attractiveness or where the business lacks the prospect of building a competitive advantage will be geared to divestment or harvesting.

Five broad objectives can be distinguished:

1.   Divest
2.   Harvest
3.   Maintain
4.   Growth
5.   Enter

DIVEST

An essential element of value-based marketing is exiting from markets or market segments that do not offer profit potential and rationalising unprofitable products. Divesting from such losers cuts costs and shifts resources from uneconomic activities. By pruning the number of activities it reduces complexity and allows managers to focus on those parts of the business that offer genuine opportunities for profitable growth. Many companies can double their value over a two- or three-year period simply by divesting from those products and customers that produce large, irreversible losses and increasing the growth of their most profitable units.

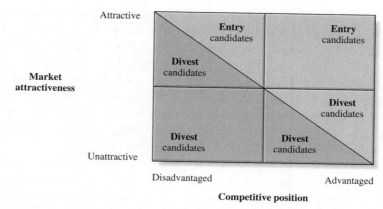

Figure 5.11 Characteristics of Candidates for Entry and Divestment

IDENTIFYING CANDIDATES FOR DIVESTMENT

Divestment should be considered under two circumstances. The first, and more common, is when the product or activity is not making an economic profit and where there is little prospect of the situation being turned around. The prospect of it turning into profit should be revealed in the strategic position assessment and, in particular, the assessment of the market attractiveness and the competitive position of the business (Figure 5.11). If the market is expected to remain unattractive – no growth, excess capacity, intense competition and powerful buyers – or if the company does not expect to achieve a genuine and significant competitive advantage in terms of costs or differentiation then an exit strategy should be proposed.

A second circumstance when divestment should be considered is where another company values the business more highly than the current owner. Capturing this surplus creates value for the company's shareholders. The outsider's superior valuation might be due to the synergies it could achieve through lower costs, increased sales or reduced competition. Another reason for the higher valuation may be that the outsider has a greater management capability to turn the business around. This is often the case when the business is not a core activity of the current owner. Finally, an outsider may be willing to pay more than the current value of the business because they are simply excessively optimistic, or using the wrong criteria (e.g. the effect on earnings per share) to judge the value of the acquisition. For example, Saatchi & Saatchi amazed the owners of the US advertising agency Ted Bates in 1986 by offering twice their most optimistic valuation of their business. Subsequent events proved that Saatchi & Saatchi had grossly overpaid, the cost being borne by its shareholders when the Saatchi share price subsequently collapsed.

PROBLEMS IN DIVESTMENT DECISIONS

Chief executives can be too accounting-orientated in their approach to divesting unprofitable products or businesses. Profitability and value are poorly correlated, especially in growth businesses. When new markets or technologies emerge, such as the Internet or mobile phones, entrepreneurial businesses are frequently unprofitable because of their high set-up costs, the need to build brands and the importance of developing critical mass. At the same time these unprofitable businesses are often highly valued by investors who are discounting their long-run ability to create profits. When executives divest such units they destroy, rather than create, value.

Economic profits are more closely related to value in mature businesses. But even here turning unprofitable businesses around may be a better option than divestment. The decision has to be based, in particular, upon management's ability to develop a competitive advantage in terms of costs or a differentiated offering to customers. It also needs a hard-headed analysis of the future attractiveness of the market. Managers have to assess what market conditions – capacity, competition and customer buying pressures – imply for average profitability in the industry. In cyclical industries taking a long-term view is particularly important. Depending upon where the business is on the cycle at any point of time, current prices and profitability can give very misleading signals of the trend. Managers need to look at the picture over a longer period to get an objective view of profitability and value potential.

Divestment and product rationalisation depend for their success on accurate data on economic profits. It is important that overhead costs and investment be allocated to products in a way that accurately reflects their usage. Without good economic information, the wrong products will often be sacrificed. Managers will often make rationalisation decisions based on volume, believing that low-volume products are less profitable than their high-volume counterparts. Once a proper allocation of costs and investments is made, it often becomes clear that many high-volume accounts are scarcely profitable because of the bargaining power of these customers. Many low-volume accounts are often discovered to be highly profitable because they are niche businesses, achieving higher prices, and selling to less demanding customers.

Another common problem in divestment lies in the links between the weak products and other parts of the business. It is common for the product under review to share costs, assets and customers with other more profitable products. Divesting the product will then mean reducing the profitability of the remaining businesses as they have to absorb the costs and assets. Often too there will be supply chain linkages. For example, shrinking the business unit's product line can reduce its level of influence over its dealers or retailers. Thus, the benefits of exiting one market or product must be weighed against the possibility of reducing the profitability of the whole product line.

Understanding of the linkages between products should not, however, be an excuse for inaction. Often the savings from divestment will more than compensate for the side effects. When side effects are a major issue there are often other options that can be considered. The business can source rather than manufacture products to maintain its product portfolio in a more economical manner. Alternatively, it may be able to find a strategic partner to share the costs of the business under review. In all circumstances managers have to decisively attack the problems caused by businesses that are not adding value.

Two other issues are common barriers to sensible divestment strategies. One is the use of marginal analysis to explore investment and divestment options. This assumes a product is worth keeping if it makes any contribution to overheads and profits. Such an approach is particularly tempting to management faced with substantial excess capacity. Unfortunately, such a criterion allows the business to drift into carrying a large number of products that do not make an economic profit because they are not held responsible for either the overheads or capital they incur. In the longer run, managers have to accept that all costs and assets are variable. Marginal analysis makes it too easy to sanction entry decisions and too easy to postpone exit decisions.

The second obstacle is the desire of managers for size and growth. Growth is of course a crucial way to create value for shareholders, but only if it is, over time, profitable growth. In many companies, ill-considered incentives bias managers to non-value-adding growth. These include the pattern of paying managers according to the size of the business they manage, the prestige attached to running the biggest unit, and incentives that reward volume rather than value. All these incentives encourage managers to add products and discourage them from sacrificing parts of their empires.

THE PROCESS OF DIVESTING

Management should review the business annually to identify candidates for divestment. Such a process involves four steps. First, identify divestment targets. These will be parts of the business that the strategic position assessment forecasts cannot earn economic profits over the planning period on account of the inability of the business to build a profitable competitive advantage or the unattractive nature of the markets in which they operate. Second, estimate the liquidation value of the business unit. This is the cash that could be obtained from selling off the fixed assets and releasing the working capital, less any exit costs (e.g. for environmental cleanup). Typically, liquidating a business and taking the tax loss will produce a cash amount of 40–60 per cent of the book value of shareholders' funds.

Third, estimate the highest operating value of the business unit under an optimal restructuring plan. As described earlier, this includes exploring all internal and external options to increase the long-term discounted value of cash flow that can be generated from the business. The final step is to determine the net divestment value. This is the present value of the after-tax proceeds from selling the business, liquidating it or spinning it off. If the net divestment value exceeds the highest operating value of the business then the decision should be to divest the business.

In summary, divesting parts of the business that do not add value is a crucial way of increasing returns to shareholders. It is also an important precursor to a growth strategy, by releasing management resources to focus on higher value activities.

HARVEST

A harvesting strategy is one that maximises the firm's cash flow from its existing assets. It is an appropriate strategy when two conditions hold. First, the net divestment value of the business is below its optimal restructured value. Second, the enhanced value from the restructured option accrues from increasing the cash flow from the current volume of sales rather than growth. Indeed, harvesting is often accompanied by declining sales volume.

Harvesting – or milking the business – is often appropriate when the competitive advantage of the business is in unavoidable decline or where market conditions are deteriorating. This may be because new technology is replacing the company's core product or because the market demand is falling. Harvesting is a common strategy in the pharmaceutical industry when a product's patent is about to expire. Tobacco companies in Western Europe faced with a falling demand for cigarettes also employ it.

STRATEGIES FOR HARVESTING

Companies pursuing harvesting strategies are willing to lose market share if this increases the cash flow. Cash flow can be increased in two ways. First, the company can *increase operating margins* by:

- ○ *Raising prices*
- ○ *Cutting variable costs*
- ○ *Cutting fixed costs*
- ○ *Focusing on premium market niches*

Second, it can *reduce investment* by:

- ○ *Reducing stocks and tightening up on payment terms*
- ○ *Pushing suppliers for extended financing*
- ○ *Reducing fixed assets*

Such policies can dramatically increase cash flow quite quickly.

DANGERS IN HARVESTING

The problem with harvesting strategies today is that excessive efforts to increase margins and prune investment can lead to very rapid losses of market share. If that occurs the market value of the business may fall precipitously. In such a situation selling off the business may generate a greater value than harvesting.

Successful harvesting will often require tactical investments in marketing and promotion to discourage new entry. It will also mean ensuring that value and service levels do not fall below market expectations, especially in those niches where premium pricing is possible. To compare the value created by harvesting versus divestment, management needs to project the cash flow from harvesting under realistic competitive conditions.

MAINTAIN

For some strategic business units an appropriate objective is to maintain market share. This objective is different from harvesting, where management normally accepts that market share will erode. On the other hand, management does not aim at a more aggressive strategy of market share growth. The conditions for a maintenance strategy are: (1) the business is earning healthy economic profits and marginal investments earn a return exceeding the unit's cost of capital, (2) the market is not expected to decline over the foreseeable future and the business has a well-established competitive position, (3) the market is dominated by only a small number of producers – usually no more than two or three – and (4) there are significant barriers to new entry.

In this type of market, a competitive equilibrium or implicit collusion often occurs. Each major competitor knows that an effort to increase market share will lead to a rapid response from competitors and prices and profits will tumble. Competitors earn higher profits by accepting the status quo. Such behaviour is apparent, for example, in UK detergents, where Unilever and Procter & Gamble have shared the market approximately equally for decades.

STRATEGIES FOR MAINTENANCE

The main objective in a maintenance strategy is to avoid price competition. Price competition is always the most damaging in its effects on value creation. For example, a price cut of 5 per cent for a company with a pre-tax operating margin of 8 per cent would see its profits drop by almost two-thirds. Price wars are what competitors fear most in these mature oligopolistic markets.

It is important for the established players to maintain barriers to entry since new competitors could quickly gain market share. Because lowering price is so unattractive for the incumbents, high levels of advertising and marketing support are often the best way to deter entry. Advertising and marketing are normally fixed costs and so offer the biggest competitors economies of scale that newcomers cannot match. In contrast, price cutting is like a variable cost: the bigger the company, the more it loses. A 5 per cent price cut costs a £40 million business, £2 million off its bottom line; a £4 million business on the other hand, loses only £0.2 million.

Besides high levels of marketing expenditures, companies also need to maintain a focus on innovation. Unless they keep their products or services up to date they will face market share erosion by either current competitors or new entrants. Maintaining market share does therefore require considerable proactivity from the incumbents to maintain the current position and keep out entrants.

Market signalling is another feature of a maintenance strategy. Signalling is defined as the selective communication of information to competitors designed to influence competitors' perceptions and behaviour in order to provoke or avoid certain types of action.[6] Signalling can be used to deter competitive entry. Procter & Gamble has developed a formidable reputation for defending its markets as this classic example shows.

> Clorox long dominated the bleach segment, a relatively small niche of the consumer soaps and detergents market. In 1990 it decided to extend into the mainstream US detergents market which was led by Procter & Gamble. Before Clorox's new product was even launched Procter & Gamble rolled out its Tide With Bleach, employing a massive promotional campaign. Clorox soon had to withdraw, nursing losses estimated at $50 million.

Signalling can also be used to discipline current players from aggressive moves. Alcoa, for example, deliberately over-invested in order to have available capacity to flood the market if the competitor did not toe the line on acceptable behaviour. Finally, it can be used to encourage mutual efforts to improve industry profitability. For example, the UK petrol market is characterised by price leadership. Before raising prices, the leader firm usually tests the water and builds a consensus by press releases that announce 'unsatisfactory industry margins' and 'expected price increases'.

GROWTH

The first three strategies – divest, harvest and maintain – should ensure that investors' funds are not wasted on economically unattractive investments. But to create outstanding returns for shareholders, it is essential to possess growth businesses. Investing to achieve high growth makes sense as long as the business can earn a return on the invested capital that exceeds its cost of capital. As long as this return is achieved, the faster the business grows, the greater the value that is created for shareholders.

Such growth opportunities depend primarily on the firm possessing a competitive advantage. Second, it depends on the attractiveness of the market. The most obvious high-growth opportunities are to be found in the north east quadrant of Figure 5.11. With high-growth businesses it is particularly important not to confuse profit or cash flow with value creation. Companies maximising value creation opportunities in high-growth markets will always have lower cash flows and generally lower profits in the early years than what could be achieved by reining back on growth. But holding back on opportunities for value creating investments to boost current cash flow and profits is a short-term strategy that erodes the value of the business and frequently means that the company fails to achieve the critical mass to be viable in the long-run.

STRATEGIES FOR GROWTH

In Chapter 4 we presented strategies for growth in terms of the growth ladder. The ladder has nine rungs:

1.   Increasing customer retention
2.   Growing the share of the customer's expenditure
3.   Gaining new customers
4.   Developing new products and services
5.   Entering new markets
6.   Developing new distribution channels
7.   Growing internationally
8.   Acquisitions and alliances
9.   Growth outside industry boundaries

DILEMMAS IN GROWTH STRATEGIES

Marketing managers often appear to think that any strategy that achieves growth is successful. Of course, this is nonsense. Anyone can grow sales if the price is low enough or if enough is spent on advertising and promotion. What the company needs is value-generating growth. These are additional sales that increase the net present value of the business. In other words, the additional sales must cover the investments, costs and the cost of capital incurred to generate the growth.

If marketers are often too optimistic about the value of growth, accounting-orientated management can be too conservative. One of the characteristics of many of today's markets is *network effects*, which suggest increasing rewards to companies that move fast and decisively in growth markets. A product has network effects or 'externalities' if the value to any one user rises with the total number of users of the product. A classic example is the telephone.[7] If you are the only owner of one in the country it is not much use. The more people with phones, the more valuable it is to the user. Such network externalities are a marked characteristic of many of today's information-based industries.

Network effects mean that the first company to gain a big installed base sets the standard that makes it difficult to displace. New customers want to buy the product that everyone else has. For strategy this has a number of implications. First, it stresses the importance of gaining a first-mover advantage. It also highlights the role of marketing and advertising to make customers aware that your product is going to be the leader. Often, too, there are opportunities to form alliances to boost credibility in the future leadership of the product. Most controversially, it suggests the importance of *penetration pricing* at the early stages of these markets. It is worth subsidising early adopters through low prices. Microsoft, for example, gave its browser away free to get people to adopt it, counting on establishing it as the new standard.

Strategies like penetration pricing are risky. It will normally mean losing money in the early years with the hope of becoming the next Microsoft and recouping it many times after it becomes the dominant player. Companies that are insufficiently aggressive in their marketing and pricing are still likely to lose money in the early years and lose everything in the long run.

ENTER

In today's rapidly changing environment, creating value is not just about rationalising uneconomic businesses and improving current activities, it is increasingly about innovation. Innovation can take several forms:

○ **New products.** *Sometimes these are blockbuster innovations, but more often they are new product lines, product improvements and line extensions, all of which can create value by adapting the company to a changing market.*

○ **New marketing concepts.** *These are solutions that meet new customer needs, without significant technical innovation being required. Examples are Diet Coke, which met the desire for low-calorie drinks, and Flora margarine, which met the desire for cholesterol-free spreads.*

○ **New marketing strategies.** *These are innovative ways of marketing products or services. For example, Castrol became the leading machine lubricant by charging workshops a monthly fee for maintaining their machinery rather than charging per litre of oil.*

○ **New processes.** *These are operational innovations that allow the same products to be delivered at lower cost or with higher quality. For example, Pilkington's invention of the float-glass process enabled it to capture much of the market for auto-glass.*

○ **New markets.** *A company can achieve new sources of growth through exploiting new markets or market segments. Swatch, for example, developed the market for watches as fashion accessories, significantly increasing the size of the total watch market.*

○ **New channels of distribution.** *Innovations in distribution channels are the most significant characteristic of the information age. Information technology and particularly the Internet have transformed industry after industry. Dell Computer Corporation catapulted to leadership in PCs in the 1990s by cutting out the traditional dealer and interacting directly with consumers using the telephone or Internet. Direct Line did the same in insurance, Amazon in book retailing, eBay in auctions, First Direct in banking, Google in search engines — the list is continually expanding.*

CRITERIA FOR ENTRY DECISIONS

There are three main criteria for deciding upon which activities to start or markets to enter. The first is the anticipated *market attractiveness*. As described above, this means forecasting the size of the market, its growth rate, the competitive structure of the market, in particular the intensity of competition and the power of the buyers, cyclical factors and the nature of the risks involved. If the industry is not going to be profitable on average — as industries like steel, airlines and textile manufacturing have been in the past — creating shareholder value is going to be very difficult, however good the company is. It is much better to swim with the tide than against it.

The second, and most important, criteria for entry is the firm's ability to create a *sustainable competitive advantage*. This means achieving a low cost structure or differentiated offering that will lead to customer preference, and a preference that can be sustained when competitors inevitably seek to emulate it. This base upon which such a competitive advantage rests is, of course, the firm's resources: the quality of the tangible and intangible assets it possesses, the skills and knowledge of its staff, and the drive and adaptability emanating from its organisational culture. Most successful innovations are, not surprisingly, based on leveraging the firm's current resources to enter new markets or develop new positioning strategies.

The third requirement is *overcoming the entry barriers* to the industry. Attractive markets are usually characterised by high entry barriers in the form of patents, capital requirements, economies of scale, strong brands or access to distribution channels. Their common feature is that they drive up the initial investment required to establish a viable position in the market. This means that the firm must have a really sizeable and sustainable competitive advantage to generate the margins that will achieve an economic return on this investment. Alongside barriers to entry, the prospective entrant must evaluate the likelihood of retaliation on the part of the incumbents, who will seek to deter entry. For example, the major airlines flying the London–North America route successfully used price cuts to drive the new discounter, Laker Airways, out of the market in 1982.

In general, the fiercest retaliation occurs when the total market is not growing. The odds are better for entrants in growing markets because increased sales are gained without necessarily reducing those of competitors. In mature markets, acquisition can be a more effective means of gaining entry since it does not add to industry capacity.

CREATING OPTIONS

Most managers do not understand the importance investors attach to a firm's ability to enter attractive markets. Much the greatest part of a company's equity value is based upon investors' expectations about the company's future products and markets rather than their current activities. As we have seen, on average cash flow over the next four years accounts for less than 20 per cent of a company's share price.[8] What investors are valuing are their expectations about long-term cash flow, which depends upon the options the firm has available and its ability to exploit these options.

Management accounting has not kept pace with our knowledge about how investors value companies. Accounting still overestimates short-term cash flows. It emphasises today's profit earners at the expense of tomorrow's. As we discussed in Chapter 4, the standard discounted cash flow analysis accountants use to evaluate investment projects discourages many new opportunities by overemphasising the risk and cost of failure. Financial options theory has presented a more effective way of judging new entry proposals. This approach reflects that entry decisions are not big, once-and-for-all choices, but rather a series of incremental investments, each one contingent upon the success of the previous one. If the feedback about the entry strategy is not promising, the company can usually pull out without further investment. Initial investments are options that allow the firm the opportunity to make subsequent investments if prospects look exciting at the end of the initial stage. Investors are valuing companies in terms of whether they have developed strategic positions to take up options in tomorrow's attractive markets.

SUMMARY

1.   To formulate a strategic plan management must first understand the firm's current position and the forces shaping the future of the industry and its competitive position within it. This is the role of the strategic position assessment.

2.   The first task is to assess whether management is currently adding value. This is often difficult to answer directly. Instead it is necessary to determine the strategic value drivers that act as lead indicators to long-term

value creation. The balanced scorecard is a useful framework for monitoring performance on these key capabilities.

3.   The success or failure of a business is caused by a combination of external and internal factors. The first is the attractiveness of the firm's market; the second is its competitive advantage. Competitive advantage is generally the more important determinant of value creation. Competitive advantage is a consequence of the strength of the firm's strategic value drivers.

4.   Value is determined by future cash flow, so it is the future attractiveness of the market and the future competitive advantage that must be projected. The purpose of a strategy is to shift the business towards attractive markets and build a sustainable differential advantage.

5.   The strategic position assessment provides the information for value-based planning. This is a framework for restructuring the business to optimise its value for shareholders.

6.   The end result of the value-based plan is that each business unit will be assigned a broad strategic objective that will form the basis of the marketing strategy. These objectives are divest, harvest, maintain, grow or enter.

REVIEW QUESTIONS

1.   How do you assess whether the management team has created value during the past year?
2.   Discuss the role of strategic value drivers in determining and assessing business performance.
3.   How might a company use the balanced scorecard in its planning process?
4.   What are the factors that shape a business's potential to generate value for shareholders?
5.   Show how the McKinsey pentagon can be used to restructure a business with the goal of creating greater value for shareholders.
6.   What determines the choice of strategic objective appropriate for a business unit?

NOTES ON CHAPTER 5

[1] Robert S. Kaplan and David P. Norton, *The Balanced Scorecard*, Boston, MA: Harvard Business School Press, 1996. See also: Robert S. Kaplan and David P. Norton, Using the balanced scorecard as a strategic management system, *Harvard Business Review*. Boston: Jul./Aug. 2007. Vol. 85, Iss. 7, 8, p. 150.

[2] The literature on strategy is replete with matrices which similarly try to characterise the attractiveness and competitive positions of business units. The best known are the Boston Consultancy Group's growth-share matrix, the General Electric matrix, the Shell directional policy matrix and the Marakon Associates strategic matrix. For a review see, for example, Gerry Johnson and Kevan Scholes, *Exploring Corporate Strategy*, London: Prentice Hall, 1999.

[3] The following sections draw on the work of James M. Taggart, Peter W. Kontes and Michael C. Mankins, *The Value Imperative: Managing Superior Shareholder Returns*, New York: Free Press, 1994, pp. 85–154.

[4] Doug Garr, *IBM Redux: Lou Gerstner and the Business Turnaround of the Decade*, New York: HarperBusiness, 1999.

[5] See Tom Copeland, Tim Koller and Jack Murrin, *Valuation: Measuring and Managing the Value of Companies*, 2nd edn, New York: John Wiley & Sons, Inc., 1996, pp. 327–358.

[6] For a review of signalling see O. Heil and T.S. Robertson, Towards a theory of competitive market signalling, *Strategic Management Journal* **12**, 1991, 403–454.

[7] For a good discussion of network effects and their strategic implications in information-based businesses see C. Shapiro and H. Varian, *Information Rules*, Boston, MA: Harvard Business School Press, 1999.

[8] See Kris Butler, Stephan Leithner *et al.*, What is the market telling you about your strategy?, *McKinsey Quarterly*, no. 3, 1999, 98–109. See also: Marc H. Goedhart, Bin Jiang and Timothy Koller, The irrational component of your stock price, *McKinsey Quarterly*, July 2006.

6 Value-Based Marketing Strategy

'Because its purpose is to create a customer, the business enterprise has two — and only these two — basic functions: marketing and innovation. Marketing and innovation produce results; all the rest are "costs".'

Peter Drucker

INTRODUCTION AND OBJECTIVES

This chapter shows how to develop a marketing strategy that will create value for shareholders. Creating long-term value is synonymous with achieving long-term competitiveness — the ability of the business to survive and prosper in a highly competitive global market-place. So a strategy that creates value for shareholders should also enhance the security of employees, creditors and the community at large. History has shown that firms cannot endure if they expand regardless of profitability, or if they do not adapt to changing markets.

A value-based marketing strategy is defined as the set of coherent decisions about the firm's approach to the market, which aims to maximise shareholder value. The decisions concern the choice of customers the business will seek to serve, how it will meet their needs, how it will create a sustainable competitive advantage, and the resources it will commit to these markets. As emphasised in earlier chapters, marketing is at the heart of the strategy for creating long-term shareholder value. Without an outstanding competence in marketing, shareholder value becomes merely an accounting tool focusing on short-run profitability and cash flow.

By the time you have completed this chapter, you will be able to:

- ○ *Understand why systematic strategic marketing planning is necessary*

- ○ *Recognise the important differences between strategic planning at the corporate level and at the level of the business unit*

- ○ *Understand the role of the strategic position assessment in developing strategic objectives*

- ○ *Use the key components of a value-based marketing strategy*

- ○ *Develop performance measures for implementing and controlling the strategic plan*

- ○ *Show how the results of the plan can be evaluated using shareholder value analysis*

- ○ *Outline the process for developing creative marketing strategies*

The chapter begins with the functions of planning at the corporate level. But marketing's most important role is not at the corporate level, but at the level of the individual market and product, and it is this — business unit planning – that forms the core of the chapter. A marketing plan is based first on the strategic position assessment, which evaluates the potential of the business unit and the broad direction by which shareholder value may be created. The strategic position assessment then leads to a definition of the unit's marketing objective. The chapter then unfolds the key components of strategy: the strategic focus, customer targets, competitor targets, core strategy and the marketing mix.

Once the strategy is formulated, management needs relevant performance indicators to ensure that the plan is kept on track over time. Finally, the financial implications of the proposed plan have to be tested through a shareholder value analysis to assess whether the marketing strategy looks likely to maximise value. The last section of the chapter looks at the dynamics of developing a marketing plan. It looks at how a cross-functional team can best work to come up with creative ideas to capitalise on the growth opportunities available and create a differential advantage.

WHY STRATEGIC MARKETING PLANS?

Developing a systematic marketing strategy is important, not because it will plot the future – no one can do that. It is impossible to forecast the future: there are too many unknowns in society, technology, economics and competitive reactions, to predict how the market will react to your company's efforts. The real functions of strategic market planning are:

1.   Facilitating the change process
2.   Forcing managers to ask the right questions
3.   Motivation and control
4.   Balancing the tyranny of accountants

FACILITATING THE CHANGE PROCESS

The process of developing a marketing strategy forces management to objectively confront the current performance of the business today and its likely performance in the future. The remorseless pressures of day-to-day operational problems often hide the real fundamental issues facing the company. The plan starkly reveals whether the business has been successful in generating value for shareholders, in satisfying customers, and creating a competitive advantage in the market. Strategic marketing planning also provides a vehicle for piloting change. It sets the framework for thinking about the future, developing more ambitious goals and identifying new options (see box, 'destroyyourbusiness.com'). Knowing that the business has a clear direction can invigorate employees and instil confidence among investors.

FORCING MANAGERS TO ASK THE RIGHT QUESTIONS

Managers cannot predict the future but they can plan for it. Most products that fail do not fail because of events that could not have been anticipated. Rather they fail because managers have not effectively analysed their customers and competitors. The marketing plan ensures that managers ask the key questions and do the vital analyses that determine success or failure. These centre on understanding the needs of customers, evaluating the competition and anticipating their likely strategies, and ensuring that the company can communicate a genuine competitive advantage. When managers have analysed the key questions, they are in a much stronger position to react effectively to the unexpected events that inevitably occur.

destroyyourbusiness.com

Few were surprised when Fortune magazine chose Jack Welch, chief executive of General Electric, as its 'businessman of the century'. Since taking over in 1981 he had increased the value of the company from $14 bn to more than $400 bn, quadrupled sales to over $100 bn and had grown profits six times to $9.3 bn.

Despite the applause, at the end of 1999, only a year from retirement, Welch was still not satisfied and wanted more. The particular challenge he identified was e-business, both as an opportunity and a threat to GE's dominance. His response was to launch a major new initiative called 'destroyyourbusiness.com'. Welch believed that only by getting his managers to imagine the end of their current businesses could they really create something radical and new enough to survive into the next century.

The initiative was based on the three key elements that lay at the heart of Welch's transformation of GE in earlier decades. It was iconoclastic — nothing was sacred: products, channels, practices and systems were all up for challenge. It sought to learn and borrow from the best practices of other leading edge companies. GE envoys who went out to study the new e-business pioneers came back with alarming demonstrations of how GE was still too slow, too internally focused and insufficiently customer-orientated for competing in 'Internet-time'. Last, the initiative sought to make determined use of GE's collective effort and intellect. A new set of 'workouts' was organised to stimulate all employees to challenge senior executives on current practices and to make recommendations for transforming the business and creating new ones. His strategy helped propel GE into what continues to be one of the world's most successful companies.

MOTIVATION AND CONTROL

Value-based marketing is based on two principles. First, the task of management is to create long-run value for shareholders. Second, its accomplishment depends on building relationships with customers founded on satisfying their needs more effectively than competitors. The strategic marketing plan brings these two principles together. The objective and test of the strategy is its ability to create shareholder value. The process of strategy formulation focuses on choosing profitable customers and developing a value proposition that will make them want to do business with the company rather than competitors.

The structure of the plan aims at ensuring managers do not pursue growth strategies that are not value enhancing. At the same time it encourages managers to invest heavily in growth if this will create long-run profits in the future. Investors are quite happy to forgo cash and profits today if they believe the company is investing in a strategy that offers great long-run potential. In particular, value-based planning should discourage arbitrary cuts in marketing budgets to boost short-term profits and cash flow. Investors look through such cuts and often react to the moves by selling their shares, knowing that future profitability and competitiveness are being sacrificed.

BALANCING THE TYRANNY OF ACCOUNTANTS

The great majority of company boards spend too much time on the monthly, quarterly and annual budgets produced by their accountants. Such a focus leads to an overemphasis on short-term profit performance and an underemphasis on the viability of the long-term strategy of the business. By delving into the details of the unit's costs and investments, the board demotivates management, discourages initiative and blankets the entrepreneurship it should be encouraging, under a stifling layer of bureaucracy.

The strategic marketing plan asks the board to consider what is important: will the strategy create competitive advantage? Will it maximise shareholder value? While accountants look backwards, the strategic plan looks forwards; and it is the future not the past that determines the value of the business.

CORPORATE LEVEL PLANNING

In discussing the strategic planning it is important to distinguish between the corporate or group plan and the business unit plans. Every company consists of business units. In big companies there can be a very large number of business units: GE, for example, has a number of business units grouped within six main businesses. A business unit may consist of a group of related products, a market or a distribution channel. Because a business unit serves a specific group of customers or meets a particular need, a tailored marketing strategy is required. It is the responsibility of unit managers to develop such a strategy with the aim of maximising long-run economic profits. It is this type of strategic planning which is the main focus of this chapter.

The corporate centre does not directly create value for customers; that is the task of the business unit. But headquarters can be very costly and absorb a substantial proportion of shareholder value. The largest companies spend on headquarters costs an average of 1.3 per cent of annual sales. This amounted to an estimated 39 per cent of their equity value.[1] Some companies had costs three times this average figure, implying that cutting headquarters costs could sometimes have a big impact on the share price. How can the corporate centre justify loading the business with this overhead cost burden? Would it not be cheaper if all their functions and staff were allocated to the business units that have the profit responsibility, and hence the incentive to manage costs more economically? Headquarters add value only if they enable the individual business units to generate additional profits that exceed the headquarters costs. In principle, headquarters can add value in three ways:

1. Driving organisational change
2. Managing the shared value drivers
3. Managing the business portfolio

DRIVING ORGANISATIONAL CHANGE

In successful companies, the corporate centre, and in particular the chief executive, is the catalyst for change. He or she communicates what the organisation's priorities should be. First of these is the belief that the central objective of all managers must be to develop strategies that will maximise shareholder value. Second is passionate understanding that in competitive markets shareholder value is derived from serving the needs of customers more successfully than competitors. Only by delighting customers and building strong, continuing relationships with them can the company build the revenue stream that is the basis for long-term cash flow. Third is the recognition that in today's rapidly changing environment the company must be continually sloughing off strategies that have worked in the past and finding new opportunities for growth.

An effective corporate centre puts in place a combination of formal and informal mechanisms for driving these priorities. The key mechanisms are:

1. **The strategic planning process.** In successful businesses strategic plans rather than accounting budgets become the focus for managers. Business units are required to develop strategic plans that demonstrate how they will create long-term value for shareholders rather than short-term profits. Top management also looks to see that these strategic plans are firmly grounded on convincing assumptions about customers' needs and

competitor reactions. The plans give management the information to question whether the business units are being sufficiently radical in responding to the problems and opportunities being created by today's rapidly changing markets and technologies and whether they are creating sufficient growth options.

2. **Resource allocation process.** The centre is responsible for allocating resources among the business units and for creating new businesses and making acquisitions. Over time these decisions will lead to a major reshaping of the company. Companies that manage for value allocate resources to businesses and new ventures when they promise a return that exceeds the cost of capital. There is no rationing problem. It makes sense for investors to forgo dividends and bring in new capital if management can earn returns that exceed the cost of capital. In this case a business is earning a better return than investors could earn if they invested the money themselves. An effective resource allocation process acts to continually reposition the company towards markets that have attractive economics (where market conditions allow the average company to make economic profits) and where the business has a sustainable differential advantage.

3. **Performance measurement and compensation.** Managers need feedback and incentives that motivate behaviour consistent with the objectives of creating shareholder value, customer orientation and growth. The first requirement is to give managers of the business units clear responsibility for strategy. As far as possible, each unit should be able to act as a separate profit centre and have total autonomy over how it buys, operates and markets its products or services. Ongoing performance will be judged on the balanced scorecard measures, which have been identified as the strategic value drivers. These in turn should be the basis of the compensation and rewards managers receive.

4. **Creating a sense of purpose.** In today's complex, knowledge-intensive organisations strategy is not enough. Employees need a sense of purpose with which they can identify if they are going to be truly committed to the firm. Increasingly the role of the chief executive is seen as providing this catalyst. Leaders such as Richard Branson of Virgin and Anita Roddick of The Body Shop, for example, articulated strong business philosophies, which created an unusually strong alignment between company and employee beliefs.

MANAGING THE SHARED VALUE DRIVERS

The ability of a multibusiness corporation to outperform a single business firm lies in whether the former can exploit economies from sharing resources or from transferring special capabilities which exist in one business to other businesses within the group.

SHARED SERVICES

All multibusiness companies have shared services. Typically these will include accounting and tax, treasury, legal, human resources and information systems. But shared services rarely create a differential advantage for the company in terms of either lower cost or superior quality. The key problem tends to be a lack of incentive within the centre to reduce costs or to meet the needs of their customers within the business units. The lack of customer focus often leads to the units duplicating corporate services. In dealing with corporate services, management needs to answer two questions. Which services are best done centrally to minimise costs? Which should be decentralised to best match the requirements of their business unit customers? For those services that continue to be offered centrally, management needs to find the least costly way to provide them, subject to quality standards. Sometimes it will be possible to do this by creating an internal market, in which central services have to 'sell' their capabilities to the business units, in competition with independent suppliers.

LEVERAGING RESOURCES

Much more important for creating shareholder value and, in particular, for creating new growth opportunities, are the opportunities the centre has to catalyse the transfer of resources across businesses and, indeed, to create new ones. As discussed in Chapter 3, every successful business has resources that form the basis of core competencies, giving it unique opportunities for growth and profitability. These resources may be tangible assets such as first-class factories or equipment, intangible assets such as brands or patents, strategic assets such as licences and natural monopolies or finally human resources in the form of highly skilled staff.

The centre can add value in a crucial way by leveraging these resources across its business units. Hamel and Prahalad have shown how much of the growth of such companies as 3M, Sony, Canon and Honda has been due to the way they leveraged technical skills across their business units to create entirely new products.[2] For example, a classic case is how business units at Canon developed core competencies in the early 1990s in precision mechanics, fine optics and microelectronics (Figure 6.1).

The centre continually encouraged the discovery of new products and markets that can draw on the entire range of the company's skills. This allowed Canon to move into a range of new opportunities from cameras, to calculators, printers, faxes, copiers and so on. For instance, when Canon identified an opportunity in digital laser printers, it created a new business unit and gave management the right to raid other units to pull together the required talent in engineering, optics, microelectronics and imaging.

Product	Precision mechanics	Fine optics	Micro electronics	Electronic imaging
Basic camera	X	X		
Compact fashion camera	X	X		
Electronic camera	X	X		
Video camera	X	X	X	X
Laser printer	X		X	X
Colour printer	X		X	X
Bubble jet printer	X		X	X
Fax	X		X	X
Calculator			X	
Copier	X	X	X	X
Laser imager	X	X	X	X
Cell analyser	X		X	X
Excimer laser aligners	X	X	X	X

Figure 6.1   Deployment of Canon's Core Competencies. Reprinted by permission of Harvard Business School Press. From *Competing for the Future* by Gary Hamel and C.K. Prahalad. Boston, MA 1994, p. 228. Copyright ©1994 by the President and Fellows of Harvard College. All rights reserved

Besides technical skills, marketing assets such as brands and customer relationships are becoming increasingly important sources of leverage across business units. Virgin, for example, has built a brand name symbolising innovation and genuine value, which has enabled it to move into businesses as diverse as record shops, airlines, soft drinks, railways, mobile phones and financial services.

To create these dynamic synergies across businesses, top management at the centre has to ask four key questions. First, what are the key strategic value drivers that can be leveraged across units? To preserve the autonomy and responsibility of business unit managers, the list of such shared drivers should be a short one. To meet the criteria a resource must offer access to multiple markets. For example, 3M's special competency in coatings and adhesives gave it the opportunity to start new markets in Post-it notes, magnetic tape, photographic film and pressure sensitive tapes. Second, it must offer a customer benefit. The Virgin brand name, for instance, gives customers confidence in products bearing the name. Third, it must be hard for competitors to copy, otherwise any advantage is short-lived.

The second question is: are these shared resources receiving sufficient investment? Because the benefits of these value drivers are shared there is a disincentive for any individual business to make sufficient investment. Unless the centre counteracts this, these capabilities will wither away. The third question is: are any of the units exploiting the shared resource to the detriment of the company as a whole? For example, if a shared brand name is used on poor-value products or promoted using an inappropriate campaign, the residual damage to the company as a whole may be severe. The centre has to act as the guardian of the shared resource. The final question management at the centre should ask is whether these resources are leveraged to the fullest extent possible to generate growth. This means encouraging managers to look for growth opportunities in the form of new products and new markets, where the company's special capabilities can form the basis of a competitive advantage.

Exploiting shared value drivers is an extremely critical function of the centre in the strategic planning process. Unless these drivers are proactively and aggressively managed the company will lose major opportunities to create value and leave itself exposed to new competition.

MANAGING THE BUSINESS PORTFOLIO

The centre shapes the value-creating potential of the company through the way it allocates resources to the business units, funds new ones, and makes acquisitions and divestments. A review of the company's opportunities should start with the strategic position assessment described in Chapter 5. This involves examining each business unit and assessing the future attractiveness of its market and its competitive advantage. This then enables management to produce, for each business unit, a forecast of its future cash flow and the shareholder value it can create. When the value a unit can create is less than can be obtained from selling or liquidating it, then it is in the shareholders' interest to divest the business. The general rules for managing the business portfolio are:

1. **Invest in strategies that increase shareholder value.** This then puts the onus on managers to look for attractive markets, to focus on developing differential advantages and testing that their plans create cash flow with a positive net present value.

2. **Encourage managers to look for new growth opportunities.** The centre should act as a catalyst challenging business unit managers to explore opportunities on each rung of the *growth ladder* (see Chapter 4): increasing customer retention, growing share of customer wallets, winning new customers, and developing

new products and distribution channels. They should also be triggering the creation of new business units to take advantage of emerging opportunities that build on key value drivers within the current business.

3.   **Fund value-creating acquisitions and strategic alliances.** Not all new market opportunities can be exploited through internal development; sometimes it is faster or more economic to acquire or make alliances with other companies. The role of the centre is to help the search for candidates that may exploit the firm's strategic value drivers.

4.   **Divest businesses that cannot create value for shareholders.** When, even after restructuring, a business unit looks incapable of generating value, management should divest it. Since the initiative is unlikely to come from the business unit managers themselves, this is a task for the centre.

THE CORPORATE CENTRE: DIFFERENT APPROACHES

The role of the corporate centre varies considerably across companies. Michael Porter identified four types of roles.

1.   **Portfolio management.** Portfolio management is where the parent company simply acquires a group of companies that it believes are attractive and allows them to continue operating autonomously, linked only through an internal capital market. This is often termed a *holding company* structure. One successful example has been Berkshire Hathaway. Holding companies will normally have a very small corporate centre focused on monitoring financial performance.

2.   **Restructuring.** While holding companies like Berkshire Hathaway buy well-managed companies, others, like private equity group Apax Partners and US leveraged buy-out operators such as KKR, created value by restructuring poorly-run businesses. Here the centre intervenes to change managers, dispose of underperforming assets, cut costs and restructure liabilities.

3.   **Transfer skills.** Some companies have corporate centres that seek to add value by transferring skills across business units. Philip Morris has focused on creating competitive advantage in newly acquired businesses by bringing in people with proven marketing and branding skills. To be successful this policy requires similarities between businesses such that skills learned in one market will be valuable in the new one.

4.   **Sharing activities.** The most important sources of value arise when the centre can exploit economies of scope from shared strategic value drivers such as brands, technical resources, R&D, distribution and service networks. Porter suggests such sharing is facilitated by:

     ○   *a strong sense of shared purpose*

     ○   *a mission statement that emphasises integrating business level strategies*

     ○   *incentives for cooperation across businesses*

     ○   *inter-business task forces and other vehicles for cooperation*

Changes in the role of the centre in leading-edge companies have paralleled changes in management more generally. This is a shift away from a controlling role to one more about encouraging and supporting. The key features of the transition can be summarised under four headings:

     ○   *A view of corporate headquarters less as the apex of the pyramid and more as a support service for the business*

     ○   *Less emphasis on formal systems and techniques, and more on relationships and informal interaction*

     ○   *Greater decentralisation and delegation of decision-making to the business units*

     ○   *Emphasis on the role of the centre, and the chief executive in particular, as a catalyst and driver of organisational change*

BUSINESS UNIT PLANNING

Strategic marketing planning takes place at the business unit level. Marketing strategy has to be bottom-up because the centre lacks the detailed knowledge of customers and competitors to develop practical options. The centre's role is to act as a catalyst and a facilitator.

The business unit strategic marketing plan consists of nine components (Figure 6.2). The rest of this chapter is an exposition of these components.

STRATEGIC OBJECTIVES

Every business unit needs a broad strategic objective. The fundamental objective for every business unit is to maximise shareholder value. But such an objective is not actionable without more definitive guidelines. For innovative business units – new Internet businesses such as Amazon, eBay and Priceline – shareholder value creation meant focusing on rapid sales growth, ignoring current losses and cash flow. These start-up companies were deemed extraordinarily valuable by investors even though they were not expected to show a profit for five years or more. Behind the valuations were investors' expectations of enormous growth potential and good profit margins once the start-up costs were out of the way. This proved to be somewhat of a costly mistake when many of the young dot.com companies collapsed (see box, 'How Investors Valued an Internet stock'). For other units – mature businesses in commodity-like markets might be an example – shareholder value creation might be best achieved by allowing the business to decline and focusing on maximising short-term cash flow.

As described in Chapter 5, a business unit and individual products or markets within it can be assigned one of five objectives: (1) divest, (2) harvest, (3) maintain, (4) growth or (5) enter. The assignment depends upon whether

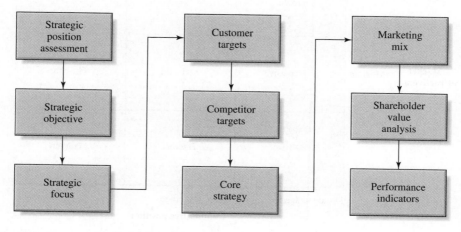

Figure 6.2 Elements of a Value-Based Marketing Strategy

investment in the unit is likely to generate a positive net present value. The strategic determinants of this are the attractiveness of its market and, most important of all, the possession of a competitive advantage.

Pruning the Portfolio

Low volume products may be dropped in order to create the slack necessary to develop and launch a new product. Current examples would be the frozen food market in the UK, which is generally viewed as being in long term decline. Although there are still large numbers of consumers who buy frozen food, Unilever announced in 2005 that it would drop its Bird's Eye brand which, although turning over £500 million per year, was seen as being a drain on resources that would hinder its growth into growth markets of the future. Bird's Eye was eventually sold to a private equity firm in 2006 for £1.2 billion.

Taken from: Baker, MJ and Hart, SJ, *Product Strategy and Management*, 2nd edition, Pearson, 2007, p. 40

Consultants and academics have come up with various matrices to portray businesses along these two dimensions. The best known include the Boston Consulting Group, the GE–McKinsey matrix and the Arthur D. Little model.[3] Our approach is the *strategic characterisation matrix*, described in Chapter 5 and illustrated in Figure 6.3. The previous models were presented as capital rationing models: cash had to be funnelled from 'cash cow' business units to 'stars' and 'problem children'. But today, companies geared to shareholder value recognise that there are no capital constraints if a business has strategies that will generate returns above the cost of capital. External finance is available to fund any and all businesses capable of delivering economic profits.

What most of these matrices agree on is that business units in attractive markets and with a strong competitive position are much more likely to generate good returns than units without an attractive market or competitive strength. Figure 6.3 suggests possible strategic objectives depending on the position of the business unit on the two dimensions. The objectives are clear at the two extremes; where they are more ambiguous is when one dimension

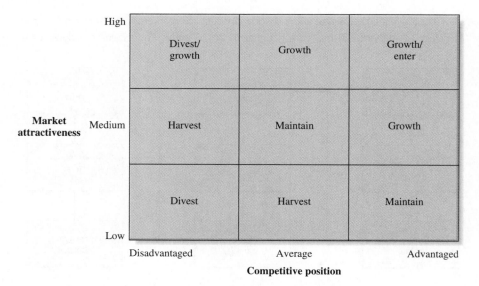

Figure 6.3   Strategic Objectives and the Strategic Characterisation Matrix

is positive and the other is negative. Most problematical is a unit in a highly attractive market but with a weak competitive position. These situations are often termed 'double or quit' – the business has to invest very heavily, often over a long period, to remedy its competitive weakness, or get out because of this weakness.

But these techniques should not be applied mechanically. Their real utility is to help managers analyse and organise information about the business, its market and the competition it faces. The skill in applying these matrices is projecting what will happen to these markets over time and how the business's position will be affected by the strategies of current and new competitors.

How Investors Valued an Internet Stock

It is instructive, particularly in light of the collapse of so many dot.coms in the early 2000s, to examine how investors valued an Internet stock.

In 1999, Amazon.com had five years of big losses but had a market value of $10.8 billion, far higher than much larger and more profitable companies such as Heinz, Nike and Kellogg's. How could this huge valuation have been put on an unprofitable business be understood? The explanation lies in the explosive sales growth investors were predicting for Amazon.

To arrive at the valuation, start with what was known at the time: sales were $588 million; the share price $214; and the number of shares outstanding 50 million. Then use the basic financial equation:

Market value (MV) = Current operation value (COV) + Future growth value (FGV)

First, the COV is calculated. This is what Amazon would be worth if there were no further growth. COV is net operating income after taxes (NOPAT) divided by the cost of capital – as discussed in Chapter 2. Because the heavy start-up costs meant that Amazon had no profit, start-up costs are taken out. An assumption is made that a normal NOPAT would be 7 per cent of sales, or $41 million on current sales. If the cost of capital on this volatile stock was 15 per cent, this implies a COV of $273 million, or a mere $5.46 per share.

The bulk of the $214 share price is therefore represented by the FCV. This is calculated by simply deducting the $273 million from the current market value of $10.8 billion, to give a FCV of $10.5 billion. The question then is: how fast do sales have to grow over the next ten years to give this future growth value? Assuming margins remained at 7 per cent and the cost of capital is 15 per cent, the answer was 60 per cent a year. Investors were expecting sales to grow from the current $588 million to $63 billion, ten years on.

In fact, Amazon is one of the few original dot.coms to have survived, although, with revenues of just under $15 billion in 2007, investor expectations pre the dot.com crash were highly optimistic.

Source: Adapted from Business Week, 14 December, 1998, 59.

THE STRATEGIC FOCUS

Once managers have conducted the strategic position assessment and determined the strategic objective, the next step is to determine the marketing direction for achieving this objective. This direction setting is termed the strategic

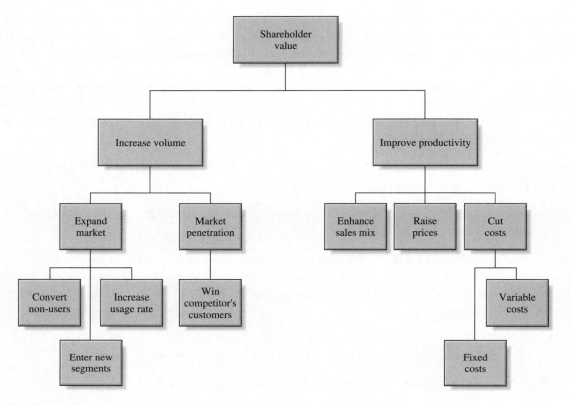

Figure 6.4 The Strategic Focus

focus. Figure 6.4 shows that shareholder value can be thought of as being created in two ways: through increasing sales volume or through increasing productivity. The latter means getting more value from the same, or even a lower, volume.

The primary focus – volume or productivity – depends upon the strategic objective. If the objective is to enter the market or grow the business the focus will be on *increase volume*. If the strategic objective is to maintain market share, harvest or divest, the focus will shift to *improve productivity*. As a market evolves, a business unit's focus is likely to change from volume to productivity.

THE VOLUME FOCUS

At the beginning of a market's evolution, or when a business has developed a product with a strong differential advantage, the focus is on increasing volume. Marketing strategy normally develops in a fairly predictable way as the market evolves. The main tasks over the market's life cycle are:

1.   **Convert non-users.** Initially a market has to be created for a new product or service. While an innovation, such as the mobile phone or broadband might eventually have a mass market, it is invariably a mistake to aim at the whole market at the beginning. The initial focus is to convert the *innovators*. These are the potential customers who will perceive the greatest value in the new product and have the resources to buy it. These are normally a small niche, perhaps only 2 or 3 per cent of the potential market. But these are important because they will be the first to adopt and will be the opinion leaders, whom the rest will follow.

2.   **Enter new segments.** As the market evolves several key changes occur: the innovator segment becomes saturated; knowledge and interest in the innovation spreads to broader groups of potential buyers; more competitors enter the market; and the price falls, broadening the size of the market. The key move then is to enter new segments of the market to maintain growth. For instance, business people initially purchased mobile phones. Then the growth rate was maintained by household consumers entering the market attracted by lower prices and the appeal of the product.

3.   **Increase the usage rate.** The first two stages expand the market. The next stage seeks to increase the usage rate among current or new customers. For example, Swatch made watches a fashion item and succeeded in getting many of its customers to buy several, in different styles and colours. Apple spread the appeal of the iPod with a range of different features, sizes and prices.

4.   **Win competitors' customers.** As the market matures, marketing strategy is increasingly a zero-sum game: growth has to be won directly at the expense of competitors. Rather than espousing the benefits of the product, the battle is about the superiority of the brand over competitive products that perform very similar functions. At this stage, operating margins usually come under increasing pressure as buyers become more price sensitive.

THE PRODUCTIVITY FOCUS

As a market matures two important changes usually take place. First, competition tends to consolidate with a small number of large players dominating the market. Second, customers become more sensitive to price as they perceive that a number of competitors are offering adequate products. In this situation, strategies to chase volume often cease to be value-generating. Aggressive moves trigger swift reaction as competitors seek to maintain capacity utilisation and the battle for market share leads to eroding profits and cash flow. For this reason, a better strategy is often to look to increase the cash flow from the volume the company has already achieved. There are several ways to do this:

1.   **Reduce costs.** With the shift from a priority of volume to one focusing on profits, more effort can be put into reducing costs and investments. The supply chain can be reappraised to cut variable costs and overheads and to achieve savings in working capital and fixed investment.

2.   **Increase prices.** The new focus should allow managers to be more confident in pushing for higher prices. With volume growth no longer the main objective, it may pay to trade-off the loss of some customers for higher average margins.

3.   **Enhance the sales mix.** Improving the product, customer and sales mix is a particularly important way of boosting profits in mature markets. The first step is usually to segment the market according to the price-sensitivity of customers. Greater focus is then given to higher margin accounts. Often, line extensions and additional services aimed at less price sensitive customers can push average prices up. For example, Johnnie Walker pushed up the average price per bottle of its whisky by introducing a premium whisky to sell alongside its familiar Red Label brand. The mobile phone market is another good example of this.

CUSTOMER TARGETS

The third component of the marketing plan defines target customers in more detail. This is a crucial stage since only by knowing exactly who the customers are and how they operate can a business meet their needs. The target market is also a key determinant of the marketing mix: how one designs the product and service, what price is charged, what distribution channel is employed and how the offer is communicated and promoted. There are two important aspects of customer targeting: segmentation and market dynamics.

MARKET SEGMENTATION

Market segmentation is at the core of all marketing problems. The task of marketing is to meet the needs of customers. But customers differ in their needs; consequently, meeting the needs of customers in a market effectively will require many different types of offer. Offering a single undifferentiated product or service to the market leaves a supplier highly vulnerable to competitors making differentiated offers to particular market niches. This is why, for example, Nike offers so many varieties of trainer and Boots carries dozens of different toothbrushes in its range.

One-to-one marketing aims at tailoring individual offers for each customer. Modern technology has increased the opportunities for such mass customisation. But in most cases, especially in consumer markets with millions of potential customers, to achieve scale economies and develop strategies, it pays to group customers in terms of similarity of need. This process is called *market segmentation*. The reasons for segmenting markets are fundamental:

1.　　It permits products and communications to be tailored to the needs of customers

2.　　By closer matching to customer needs, it leads to higher customer satisfaction

3.　　By focusing on customer needs it avoids commoditising the product and a consequent focus on price

4.　　Since customers differ in price sensitivity, it facilitates different pricing strategies and higher average margins

5.　　It encourages growth and customer relationships through different offers over the customer life cycle

6.　　It allows the company to pre-empt competitors by developing discrete offers customised to each segment of the market

7.　　It stimulates innovation by focusing product development around the specific needs of customers

The tasks of management with respect to market segmentation are summarised in Figure 6.5.

- ○　　Segmenting the market. *Finding the most revealing way to segment a market is more of an art than a science. There are always a number of alternatives and often several criteria will be used together. For example, car buyers can be segmented by age, sex, income, lifestyle, business or personal use etc. An advertising agency might segment prospective clients by size of budget, industry, local or global, profitability, attitudes to creativity, loyalty etc. The right choice will depend upon the specific market, its degree of maturity and the company's own core capabilities. Any useful segmentation scheme will be based around the needs of customers and should be effective in revealing new business opportunities.*

- ○　　Selecting target segments. *Managers then have to decide which segments will be profitable to serve. This requires estimating the size of each segment, its growth rate, competition, profit potential and its fit to the core capabilities of the company. The aim will be to choose groups of customers who will have a high lifetime value for the company (see Chapter 3).*

- ○　　Market positioning. *After choosing the segments, management then needs to determine what value or differential advantage to offer each segment and how to tailor the marketing mix to implement the*

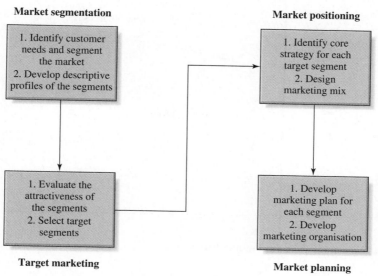

Figure 6.5 Segmentation, Positioning and Planning

strategy. Market positioning is the combination of the choice of target market segmentation, which defines where the business competes, with the choice of differential advantage, which determines how it competes.

○ Market planning. *A separate marketing plan needs to be developed for each market segment in which the business decides to compete. Normally each segment will have a manager responsible for coordinating the resources of the business and tailoring them to these customers.*

DYNAMICS OF MARKET SEGMENTATION

It is crucial for managers to appreciate that market segments are not fixed but highly dynamic: new segments are continually emerging and old ones disappearing. Capitalising on these dynamics is one of the most important avenues for companies to achieve growth and value creation. Two forces affect these market dynamics: changes in the environment and the evolution of the market.

○ Changes in the environment. *Over time the demographics of markets change, new customer needs appear, novel technologies emerge, competition increases, markets deregulate and taxation policies change. All of these alter how markets are segmented. For example, in recent years customers have become more concerned with diet and health. The result has been an explosive growth of health-orientated segments and the emergence of low-fat and low-cholesterol brands in the food and beverages market. Increasing computer literacy has led to the rapid growth in the number of customers banking and shopping online.*

   Managers who are alert to environmental changes and identify the opportunities they create can tap enormous value-creating opportunities. It is invariably easier and more profitable to capture market share by pioneering new segments than fighting head-to-head with competitors over established ones.

○ Market evolution. *One of the great confusions among managers is that between the product life cycle and the market life cycle. The product life cycle describes how total sales of a product evolve over time. The market life cycle describes how the customers buying the product change over time. The market life*

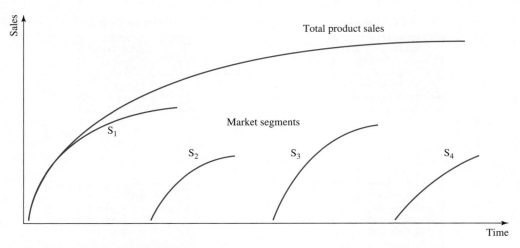

Figure 6.6   Market Dynamics over the Product Life Cycle

cycle is a much more important determinant of strategy. The key point is that markets do not grow in some uniform fashion; instead they grow by adding segments. The critical implication of this is that a business can only continue to grow by radical and often difficult changes in its positioning strategy. Failure to make these changes explains why once dominant players in a market, such as Hewlett Packard in calculators or Compaq in personal computers, lost out to new competitors with similar products but different marketing strategies.

Figure 6.6 illustrates the relationship between the product and the market life cycles. Growth is spurred by new segments entering the market. Initially the product is bought only by a small group of innovators (segment S_1). For a new prescription pharmaceutical product these would be hospital consultants; for mobile phones they were business managers. Innovators are those who first perceive the value of the product and have the resources to buy it. As awareness increases and prices fall, growth is taken on by a new segment of early adopters (segment S_2). Later, new segments emerge and repeat buyers take an increasing share of the market. For a company to maintain a leading position in the market it has to change its focus, switching resources out of maturing segments into emerging ones.

Switching segments is normally quite difficult because the new segments have different needs and operating characteristics. The problems are not generally about adapting the technology, but rather about adapting the market positioning strategy. One of the most challenging problems is shifting distribution channels. For example the small, high-price innovator segment is often served by a direct sales force; for segment 2 distributors might be the most appropriate channel; for segment 3 mass retailers might be the answer; finally, for segment 4, with customers familiar with the product and price sensitivity high, the Internet might be the lowest cost and most effective channel. Channel conflict often handicaps such changes in an organisation. The difficulties of throwing off the past explains why many of today's market leaders are relatively new companies like Amazon, Cisco, Wal-Mart and eBay. They have not had to be concerned with cannibalising existing businesses or upsetting current channel partners.

Who is the customer today? Who is it tomorrow? Developing a value-based marketing strategy therefore requires business unit managers to ask two questions. First, who are the target customers *today*? This is the easy question. A thorough analysis of the market should be capable of determining what target segments are the most profitable to serve today. But the second, and more difficult, question is more vital to the ability of the business to generate long-run value – that is, who should your customers be *tomorrow!* Unless the business can anticipate, or at least respond rapidly to, the newly emerging market segments, with their own specific needs and channel requirements, it will see its value erode.

COMPETITOR TARGETS

Developing a marketing strategy is not just about seeking to satisfy customers, it is also about beating competitors who are playing the same game. In formulating a plan managers need to analyse competitors around five questions.

WHO ARE THE COMPETITORS?

The easiest competitors to identify are the firm's *direct competitors*, who are offering similar products to the same market. So, for example, Nokia competes directly against Sony Ericsson and Motorola in the mobile phone market. But this can be too narrow and static a definition of the competition (see Figure 6.7). The basic insight from marketing is that a competitor is someone meeting the same need, not necessarily with the same product. *Indirect competitors* are firms offering different products that meet the same need.

A striking example of indirect competition was the effect of the PC on the demand for encyclopaedias. Parents bought the *Encyclopaedia Britannica* in the belief that they were maximising the educational opportunities for their children. But in the 1990s the PC became the product for meeting this need among aspiring parents. *Britannica's* traditional market was lost not to competitive encyclopaedias, but to a completely different product and technology that met the same need online.

There are also *potential competitors* that do not currently compete in the company's market segment, but may do so in the future. In the early stages of a market, different market segments often have different sets of competitors. But as the market matures, the more successful of these niche players drive into adjacent segments until they cover the entire market with differentiated offerings. Smaller niche players, lacking economies of scale and scope, get pushed out of the market by larger and more aggressive competitors. Finally, there are *incipient competitors* who may become competitors as alternative technologies converge. For example, convergence in communications

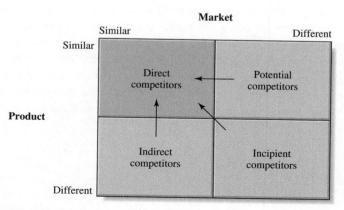

Figure 6.7   Different Types of Competitors

has transformed the industry, with competitors emerging from cable, satellite, wireless and traditional telecoms companies. To summarise, in looking ahead at the strategy, managers again have to focus on the market dynamics and ask who are the competitors *today* and who might they be *tomorrow*.

WHAT ARE THEIR LIKELY STRATEGIES?

Second, management will need to anticipate the strategies of the key competitors and their likely reactions to the business's own plans. This includes assessing how aggressive they will be in seeking to gain market share, which market segments they will focus on, and whether their positioning will be around price, service or innovation. Insights into these questions will be obtained from looking at their past behaviour, the strategic significance of the business to them, their financial position, and the focus of their recent investments and R&D spending.

WHERE ARE THEY VULNERABLE?

Developing a strategy to beat competitors requires identifying any weaknesses that can be exploited. The weaknesses may lie at the corporate level or at the level of the business unit. Two leading low-cost airlines, Laker and Debonair, were crushed by the majors (in 1982 and 1999 respectively) who had identified the precarious nature of their corporate finances. Their high levels of debt and low operating margins meant they were fatally vulnerable to relatively small erosions in price and market share.

More often it will be operating and marketing deficiencies at the business unit level that can be exploited. Glaxo was able to catapult Zantac into leadership in the huge anti-ulcer therapy market by exploiting the side effects said to affect patients using SmithKline's Tagamet. British Airways began to lose market share when rivals focused publicity on its very high prices. Tesco made gains when rival supermarket group Sainsbury introduced a poorly perceived advertising campaign. Dell won leadership by exploiting Compaq's weakness in direct marketing channels. Marks & Spencer lost its market-leading position when it had a poor year for fashion.

WHERE ARE WE VULNERABLE?

The fourth question reverses the previous one. It asks: what are our weaknesses that could threaten our long-run position in the market? This involves projecting the implications of changes in the socio-economic, technological and market environments. Changing customer needs and the evolution of new segments have to be explored. The competitiveness of the company's differential advantage and marketing mix have to be objectively assessed. Questions that need to be asked are: how competitive are our products and services in range and quality? Do our prices offer genuine value? Are our promotional and marketing channels right for the consumers of today and tomorrow? Nowadays any holes in the company's defensive wall are quickly exploited by aggressive competition.

WHAT SHOULD WE DO?

Finally, management need to decide on an action plan that anticipates and responds to the competitive threat. The plan will seek to reduce the company's own vulnerability and attack the competitor's own area of weakness.

CORE STRATEGY

Just as target customers and competition changes over time, so must the core strategy or differential advantage. A company's differential is soon obsolete unless continually upgraded. Managers again have to consider the market dynamics by asking: what is our core strategy today? What should it be tomorrow?

Chapter 3 introduced the concept of the *value ladder*. It described how managers can anticipate the requirements for maintaining a competitive advantage. Initially, at the innovation stage, the product concept forms a generic advantage. For example, AOL initially had no real competition as an Internet service provider. It was able to grow by offering customers a gateway to the Net and merged with Time-Warner in 2001. But then competitors enter the market and to maintain leadership the innovator has to show it is a *better* alternative. AOL was unable to show that it was a better gateway, with the resulting erosion in its market position and profit margins. Quality often becomes the next battleground. But soon quality ceases to differentiate and to prevent commoditisation, a new differential or core strategy is required. The third level of competition is often the provision of added services to augment the basic product.

The ultimate stage of competition moves away from the product completely and focuses on solving the customer's problems directly. Products increasingly play a marginal role in the core strategies of leading-edge companies such as GE and IBM. They see themselves as winning and retaining high-margin customers by offering customised solutions that have direct and measurable effects on the customer's bottom line. Today, managers have to realise that competitive advantage is about information rather than hardware. Value is created by providing information that enables customers to solve their problems better than before.

This requires turning the business into a learning organisation. In particular, it means that knowledge of the customer's business and operations ranks in importance with knowledge of one's own operations and business. To sell computing systems or merchandise to retailers, the supplier needs to know as much about what creates value for the retailer as it does about its own computing technology or baked beans. Without such information, computers and baked beans are just commodities that can no longer generate value for shareholders.

THE MARKETING MIX

The marketing mix is the set of operating decisions the business uses to pursue its marketing objectives in its target market. These decisions are often referred to as the four Ps: product, price, promotion and place. The four Ps are a simple – perhaps over-simple – reminder of the classes of decisions managers have to make to implement the marketing strategy.

PRODUCT DECISIONS

In commodity markets a supplier's product is a simple idea: it is a physical item produced or sold by the firm. But in today's marketing environment this concept of a product is less useful for describing the firm's options. One reason is that the business increasingly customises its offer so that there is no standard 'product'. The customer defines the product as much as the supplier. Also the firm increasingly augments its product with a range of services and supplementary products to increase its market competitiveness.

To capture these issues, marketing defines a product more broadly: a product is anything that is intended to meet a customer need or want. This means products can be *physical goods* (iPods, Nintendo Wii), *services* (holidays, meals), *people* (David Beckham), *organisations* (British Lung Foundation) or *ideas* (anti-smoking, safer driving). Equally importantly, they can be a combination of these concepts.

To understand the implication of this we start with the fundamental point that customers attach value to a company's offer in proportion to its perceived ability to help solve their problem or meet their needs. Customer needs can be separated into core needs and potential needs. A *core need* is the basic functional attribute a customer requires. For example, a core need of a car manufacturer is to buy sheet steel of a certain quality. A *potential need* is the ultimate goal of the customer. For example, the potential need of the car company is to increase the profitability of its business by either selling more cars or getting more profit from the volume currently sold. The closer a supplier gets to meeting customers' potential needs, the more value it can provide to customers and the greater their ability to differentiate its offer.

The *product hierarchy* describes how a company can build the level of a product to enhance the value it offers its customers (Figure 6.8). The *basic product* is the level of product offer that meets the core need of the customer. For the steel supplier this is a specific grade and quality of steel. But buyers expect more than a basic product; they also expect hassle-free delivery, specific prices and payment terms, and technical support if necessary. The *expected product* is the set of product attributes and services that buyers normally expect when they purchase this product. But a supplier can go even further than this by augmenting the product to exceed what the customer was expecting. This is called the *augmented product*. For example, the steel supplier might offer steel coatings and finishing, or services such as machine maintenance on site and just-in-time delivery. Finally, there is the *potential product*, where the supplier offers a total solution to the customer's ultimate or potential need. For example, the steel supplier

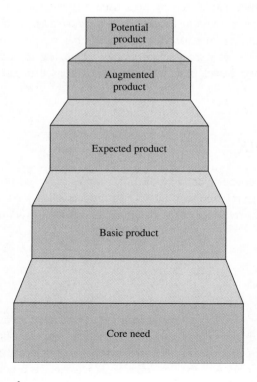

Figure 6.8   The Product Hierarchy

could offer a partnership that guarantees to take 5 per cent a year out of the car company's body manufacturing costs, so increasing the customer's bottom-line profitability by a defined and significant amount.

Today it is more and more difficult to earn economic returns from offering basic or expected products. Increasingly competition has shifted to the augmented level, whereby suppliers offer more services and features to differentiate themselves and seek to gain preference. But ultimately the best way of forging enduring relationships with customers is to focus on *their* ultimate or potential problems and offer them solutions which have direct value, rather than offering them more of *your* products and services.

In developing product policy, business unit managers have three broad decisions to make. The first is how much to invest in augmenting the product and seeking to meet the potential needs of customers. The manager has to ask whether customers will pay enough to generate an economic return on the additional investment. The second question is how much to invest in the brand – to create awareness and add emotional values that will build confidence in the company and its products. This important question we will explore in detail in the next chapter. The final question concerns the product mix: how many products should the business be offering to the target market? The broad answers to all three questions lie with the strategy: the strategic objective of the business, its focus, target customers, competitor targets and core strategy.

The product line is defined in terms of breadth, length and depth. *Breadth* refers to how many different product lines a business unit carries. *Length* refers to the number of items within a product line. *Depth* refers to the number of variants of each item.

The first determinant of these decisions is the business unit's *strategic objective*. In general, the more ambitious the growth objectives of the business unit, the greater the breadth, length and depth of its product mix. For example, a business like Amazon.com whose share price was originally dependent upon achieving truly enormous sales growth (see box 'How Investors Valued an Internet stock'), predictably increased the breadth of its product line. It started with books, but then added CDs to double its potential revenue sources, then auctions, and later a whole range of retailing lines. Without broadening its product line beyond books it could never have achieved its sales of over $14 billion by 2007 since the entire book market was valued less than that. Similarly, in its push to dominate its categories, the length of its product lines was expanded. For example, the number of different books offered has increased significantly. It also increased its depth, offering hardback, paperback, audio books, e-books and gift variants of most books. If such a company had become 'accounting-orientated' and sought to increase profits by pruning the product mix and focusing only on areas that were currently profitable, its potential growth would have been curtailed, triggering a fatal collapse in the share price. Instead, the company made its first profit in 2002.

The second determinant of the product mix is the *strategic focus*. Where a business shifts from a volume to a productivity focus, the product criteria change. Here the product mix is designed for more immediate profits than long-term sales growth. The length of the product line is likely to be reduced to cut costs, to save on working capital, and to focus on the more profitable items. Management should explore the possibility of introducing premium-priced versions of the more successful products to trade up customers and to capitalise on the higher margins that can be made from less price-sensitive customers.

Customer targets also have an important influence on the product mix. As the market develops, it becomes increasingly segmented. It is vital to introduce products to match the needs of each segment if the company is to retain customer loyalty. For example, once consumers simply bought trainers. Nike built a dominant presence by identifying that the market was segmented: players of tennis, basketball and squash, joggers, serious runners and those who 'hang out' could all have targeted products. It was no contest between Nike's customised offerings and the mass-marketed products of their old-fashioned rivals before they began to catch up. If a company has different customers with different needs – and that is virtually always – then it will need different products. Of course, the ultimate level of segmentation – increasingly possible in today's information age – is one-to-one marketing: a different 'product' for each customer.

Competitive targets can also influence the optimal product mix. Some products are introduced to thwart the strategic ambitions of competitors. Xerox had its position undermined in the copier market after it declined to produce cheap, low-volume copiers for smaller offices. This allowed Canon to first exploit the small market and then use this opening to move up into the larger product heartland of Xerox. Rover's position in the middle range sector of the car market was undermined when the luxury car makers, Daimler-Benz (now Daimler) and BMW moved downmarket with mid-level cars. To prevent competitors threatening the core businesses, companies need to consider *line stretching*. Downward stretching occurs when a company located at the upper end of the market stretches its line downward to block a segment that would otherwise attract a new competitor. Upward stretching is where a company at the lower end shifts into the higher end.

When a company is attacked by low-priced competition, it often resorts to launching *fighter products*. These are products added to the line and targeted at price-sensitive accounts most at risk from the new competition. The aim is to segment the market and limit as far as possible the overall decline in margins caused by price competition. Fighter products will often be withdrawn if they succeed in eliminating the competitor.

The last strategic influence on the product mix is the *core strategy* of the business. The core strategy will determine how much resource is put into augmenting the product and positioning the business as a solution provider rather than a product supplier. If the value positioning is around low price, then the necessity of minimising costs will lead to a 'basic product' positioning. If the value proposition is around service the business will invest in an 'augmented product' strategy. If the proposition is customisation then the company will be creating a 'potential product' positioning.

Information technology has made a significant impact on the approach to product decisions. Online marketers recognise that customers want not more choice, but less. They want a single offer that is tailored to their exact requirements rather than having to choose among a plethora of imperfectly fitting options. Personalised communications and customised solutions made to order is a response that makes more sense for both customers and companies.

PRICING DECISIONS

Pricing is covered in detail in Chapter 8. Pricing has a crucial impact on both the cash flow and growth potential of the business. Broadly, pricing decisions flow from the same set of five strategic parameters described above i.e. strategic objective, focus, customer targets, competitor targets and core strategy. The first determinant of the price is the strategic objective. If rapid growth is the goal then penetration pricing – pricing below current full-cost – may well be a viable option. Its justification could be that it is necessary to pre-empt competition and gain critical mass, without which long-run viability is not possible. Also, volume growth is likely to reduce average costs through economies of scale, so that while the price is unprofitable at the beginning it may be profitable in the longer run. Pricing to achieve short-run profit targets can destroy a business's future in young, dynamic markets.

When critical mass is achieved, the strategic focus may shift the pricing objective to margin improvement. For example, when the Japanese had captured large market shares in many of the world's car markets, they raised their prices upwards to improve their margins. The target customer segment also plays an obvious role in the pricing decision. The price points in the luxury car segment will be much higher than those in the economy segment. Different market segments have quite different price elasticities because of their spending ability and specific choice criteria. Competitive strategies are also important. The prices charged by competitors will constrain the pricing options available for the business.

Finally, the core strategy has a crucial bearing on the price that the company can charge. Fundamentally, the price a customer will pay for a product or service is determined by its perceived value, relative to competition. If a company is pursuing a 'basic product' or 'expected product' strategy then its price will have to be similar to the competition. If the core strategy is based on offering superior economic value to the customer, then the upper limit on the price will be the additional value this represents. For example, if a steel company offers a fabricating solution that saves a car company $1 million a year, then this, in principle, is what it should be willing to pay at the limit. How close to this limit the steel company is actually able to price depends on its negotiating skill and the sustainability of its competitive advantage.

Note that online markets bring in many innovations in pricing. Interactive communications can reverse the locus of the pricing decision. Conventionally, businesses have set the price to customers, but now we have, in addition to B2C, C2B and C2C. In C2B online intermediaries like Priceline allow consumers to state what they will pay for cars or airline tickets and companies have to respond. On C2C auction sites such as eBay, the company can be left out entirely as consumers sell unwanted goods to other consumers.

Online marketing facilitates much greater price discrimination. Using data banks that rank customers by anticipated value to the company or following web chains that indicate the customer's price sensitivity, suppliers are increasingly offering customised prices to online shoppers. Used effectively, such individualised pricing can capture the consumer surplus and maximise profitable sales.

PROMOTION DECISIONS

Promotion decisions cover advertising, sales promotion, public relations, personal selling, sponsorship, event marketing and the increasing array of online marketing techniques, as well as direct mail, telemarketing and TV shopping. The key decisions are how much the total promotion budget should be, how to allocate it across these promotional channels, and what message the firm should try to get across to the audience.

Again, these decisions are all consequences of the prior strategic decisions. The size of the promotional budget is mainly a function of the strategic objective management has determined for the business unit. If it is a new business with an objective of rapid growth, it is likely to require a large budget. While accountants treat this spending as a current expense, much of it is in fact an investment that builds up an intangible asset in the form of brand equity. The benefits of the current spending, in terms of positive awareness and attitudes to the business, carry over well into the future. In many of today's new markets, it is crucial to build a brand quickly to pre-empt competition. This means a high promotional spend is an essential entry requirement.

The strategic focus will determine the objective of the promotion. The focus may be on converting non-users, entering new segments or increasing the usage rate. When the strategic focus shifts from volume to productivity the task of communications will change from winning new customers to maintaining the existing base. Its function will move from persuasion to reminding customers about the benefits of the product.

The characteristics of the target market segment play a central role in every aspect of the communications strategy. Their behaviour will determine the most effective communication channels. Their attitudes to the business, its products and competitors will determine the most appropriate message. Thorough audience research is a prerequisite to effective promotion planning. Finally, the core strategy will have a major influence on what is communicated. The message will be designed to communicate the value proposition of the business.

A significant trend has been the growth of online media. The explosion of access to the Internet has given this an even greater impetus. This form of direct marketing has a number of advantages. It is easier to customise the message to specific market segments than 'mass media' like advertising and sales promotion. This enables it to match the message more effectively to the needs of individual customers. Second, it is more convenient for customers: they can often order 24 hours a day, 7 days a week, right from their homes or desk. Third, it allows more choice by separating the physical goods from the information about them. Unlike, say, shops where the presentation and storage of the goods take place in the one location, direct marketing can present a huge catalogue of choices, which do not have to be stored at multiple locations. A central warehouse and direct marketing offer economies of scale with maximum variety.[4]

The online medium has the additional advantage of allowing two-way communication, which is richer and more effective than one-way messages. For marketers, it offers often dramatically lower costs, continually updated information about customers, greater flexibility, and the ability to build relationships with customers by storing and retrieving information about their preferences.

Technology has spurred the trend towards greater efforts to produce *integrated marketing communications*. This means seeking to combine all forms of promotion in a synergistic way, to produce greater clarity, consistency and effectiveness in the way the business communicates to its target markets. The problem until now has been that each of these tools has usually been controlled by different managers and different external agencies that have set their own objectives. Much can be gained by bringing these together and developing integrated, multi-stage, multi-vehicle communications campaigns.[5]

PLACE DECISIONS

Place is concerned with the channels of distribution the business employs to reach the target market. Most companies do not sell their goods directly to final users; instead they use intermediaries such as agents, distributors, wholesalers, transport companies and retailers. They use intermediaries to perform channel functions when this is a more efficient or effective alternative. The advantage of intermediaries may lie in their superior access to the target market, their experience, or the economies of scale and scope that they possess. A higher return may be achieved from investing in expanding the firm's core business than in establishing its own channels.

The functions channels perform can be grouped into four:

- ○ **Information.** *The marketer needs information about what customers want, or might want. Customers need information about what the company can offer*
- ○ **Selling.** *The company has to promote its products and negotiate on prices and terms*
- ○ **Delivery.** *Goods have to be stored and transferred from the company to its customers*
- ○ **Financing.** *Inventories, accounts receivable and associated risks have to be managed and financed*

The question is not whether these four functions have to be performed, but who can perform them most efficiently and effectively. The key channel decisions management must make are who should perform these activities? Should they be done internally or through independent organisations? Then, how should the people or organisations be selected, trained, motivated and controlled? Most companies employ a multi-function, multi-channel approach. Different organisations are chosen for different functions, and some functions are handled by several intermediaries simultaneously. A computer company might use a market research company to gather information, a transportation company to handle delivery, banks to finance receivables and inventories, and then sell through its own sales force to large accounts and use independent retailers and a web site to sell to smaller customers.

A major problem today for many established companies is the way distribution channels have changed. The optimum channel structure is significantly influenced by the stage of the market. As a market evolves most products and services shift from high-service to low-cost channels. Personal computers, for example, were first sold by manufacturers' sales forces, later office equipment distributors became a lead channel, then retailers, and now mail-order firms and the Internet are the fastest growing channels. Information technology has also had a major impact on channel design decisions. In particular, the Internet has increasingly led to *disintermediation* in some markets as consumers order directly. In other markets, intermediaries called *infomediaries* have been created to help shoppers find the best deals from among the multitude of companies selling online.

Channels once established are not easy to change. Long-term relationships, contracts, infrastructure and systems linking channel partners cannot be quickly altered. This dilemma makes channel strategy an increasingly key factor affecting the company's long-term potential.

Channel decisions are influenced by the familiar marketing strategy parameters. Ideally the unit's channel configuration should create a differential advantage by matching the service needs of customers more effectively than competitors. So planning starts with research into the service needs of target customers and into the effectiveness of the competitors' channels. The amount a business should be willing to invest in channels will depend on the strategic objective. The strategic focus will also shape the appropriate channels. If the focus is to convert new customers to the business a more aggressive channel will be required than if the focus is on maintenance or cash flow. As the market evolves and becomes more segmented, the business will increasingly be pulled into developing multiple channels to cover the market and match the different needs. Similarly, the core strategy will be an important influence. If the strategy is around customised solutions to the potential problems customers are facing, a more direct channel will be required than if the business is simply selling basic or expected products and using low prices as the value driver.

VALUING THE STRATEGY

Once the strategy has been developed, management have to demonstrate that it is the best strategy for creating shareholder value. Typically companies adopt planning processes that culminate in projected (often five-year) accounting statements. These show the sales, operating profits and the return on capital employed the business is projected to earn if the strategy is adopted. But such statements do not demonstrate that value will be created for investors. Value-based planning looks at marketing plans from the viewpoint of investors and asks if the strategy will generate a return that exceeds the investors' opportunity cost of capital. The strategy valuation process should enable business unit managers to answer such questions as:

○ *Does the proposed marketing strategy create value for the company's shareholders?*

○ *Would alternative marketing strategies create more value?*

○ *How sensitive is the strategy to the marketing assumptions and to unexpected changes in the industry environment?*

Let us consider an example of the strategy valuation process. A company we will call Fine Wines Ltd was an established family firm selling wine to customers through a direct mail catalogue, which was sent out quarterly. In recent years sales and profits had stagnated due to increased competition from both retailers, other direct mail operators and the growing presence of online competitors. With net operating profit after tax of £5.3 million, and a cost of capital of 12 per cent, the business was valued at £44.17 million (i.e. using the perpetuity method, continuing value equals NOPAT divided by the cost of capital). A new managing director proposed to relaunch the business as an Internet operation, GourmetFoods.com. An *executive summary* of the marketing strategy is as follows:

Strategic objective. To create shareholder value by establishing market leadership online. The business would be launched initially in the UK and then rapidly developed throughout Europe. In the first year the product line would be limited to wine. But then a range of gourmet foods would be added and later a range of other luxury branded products.

Strategic focus. The focus would be on volume growth by attracting customers to switch from conventional retail channels to the Internet.

Target market segment. The initial market would be high-income householders aged between 30 and 45. Later the market would be broadened, as more online buyers were attracted to it.

Competitive targets. The competition would be conventional retailers, wine merchants, direct mail operators and other online marketers.

Core strategy. To develop the leading brand name in the sector. Key attributes associated with the brand will be excellent service, competitive prices and a broad range of high quality products.

Marketing mix

Product. A broader assortment of wines and gourmet foods than are available in supermarkets and other competitive outlets. Expert online advice to help customers with their selection. Delivery within five working days.

Price. Prices to be at least 5 per cent below high-street prices. Creative use of promotions to encourage seasonal purchasing and create consumer interest.

Promotion. Heavy continuous advertising campaigns in national press. Promotion on major Internet portals, including Google and Amazon.

Distribution. State of the art warehouse located at Dover. European warehouse to be located outside Brussels. Distribution through the leading overnight delivery operator.

Because this was a new market and one that would require heavy initial investment, management used a 10-year forecast horizon in assessing the value-creating potential of the strategy. As shown in Table 6.1, management believed that their strategy could drive sales growth of 30 per cent a year. They anticipated a normal operating margin of 15 per cent, but saw very high start-up costs over the first five years, particularly in advertising. £10 million annually was set aside to create critical mass in brand awareness and market penetration. Net investment and fixed and working capital was put at 40 per cent of incremental sales. Because of the higher volatility of Internet businesses, the financial director calculated a cost of capital of 15 per cent, as against 12 per cent currently. To finance the expansion, the board planned an initial public offering, selling up to 20 per cent of the shares on the stock market, and a borrowing facility of £10 million.

Table 6.1 shows a typical profile of an entrepreneurial business in a rapidly growing market. In the first year operating profits fall due to the high start-up costs. Cash flow does not recover to the current pre-strategy level until the ninth

Table 6.1 Shareholder Value from GourmetFoods' New Strategy

Year	Sales	Normal costs	Start-up costs	Operating profit	NOPAT	Net investment	Cash flow	Discount factor	£ million Discounted cash flow
Initial	50.0	42.5	0.0	7.5	5.3	0.0	5.3	1.00	5.3
1	65.0	55.3	10.0	−0.3	−0.2	6.0	−6.2	0.87	−5.4
2	84.5	71.8	10.0	2.7	1.9	7.8	−5.9	0.76	−4.5
3	109.9	93.4	10.0	6.5	4.5	10.1	−5.6	0.66	−3.7
4	142.8	121.4	10.0	11.4	8.0	13.2	−5.2	0.57	−3.0
5	185.6	157.8	10.0	17.8	12.5	17.1	−4.6	0.50	−2.3
6	241.3	205.1	0.0	36.2	25.3	22.3	3.1	0.43	1.3
7	313.7	266.7	0.0	47.1	32.9	29.0	4.0	0.38	1.5
8	407.9	346.7	0.0	61.2	42.8	37.6	5.2	0.33	1.7
9	530.2	450.7	0.0	79.5	55.7	48.9	6.7	0.28	1.9
10	689.3	585.9	0.0	103.4	72.4	63.6	8.7	0.25	2.2

Cumulative present value	−10.22
Present value of continuing value	119.27
Value of debt	10.00
Shareholder value	99.04
Implied share price (10 m shares)	£9.90
Initial implied share price	£4.42

year. But after year 4, operating profits are projected to grow rapidly. Over the whole ten-year period cumulative cash flow is negative, but this is greatly offset by the ongoing value of the business at the end of the planning period, when the present value of the continuing business is estimated at £120 million. After subtracting debt, this results in the strategy being predicted to more than double the value of the business to its shareholders.

SIMULATING ALTERNATIVE SCENARIOS

Before the board agrees to invest in this strategy they are likely to want to test management's assumptions. For example, how sensitive is the result to the 30 per cent growth forecast? The board might also want to explore alternative strategies to check whether they have found the optimal strategy. For example, what would happen if the high launch marketing spend was reduced? Or, how would a more aggressive pricing strategy affect shareholder value?

To explore the strategy's sensitivity to the growth assumption, management can rerun the spreadsheet, with say 20 rather than 30 per cent sales growth. This indeed halves the value created (Table 6.2). While the result is still better than the 'do nothing' strategy by £5.38 million, the implied share price falls from £9.90 to £4.96. This conclusion once again emphasises the importance of growth as the key to shareholder value in entrepreneurial businesses.

Other strategies can be considered. Management believed that if the high marketing spend in the early years was cut from £10 million to £5 million, growth would be cut by 20 per cent, i.e. from 30 to 24 per cent annually. The

Table 6.2 GourmetFoods: Sensitivity of Shareholder Value (£ million)

Strategy	Shareholder value	SV added	Share price (£)
Proposed strategy	99.04	54.87	9.90
20% growth	49.55	5.38	4.96
Cut start-up costs	70.94	26.77	7.09
10% price cut	57.11	12.94	5.71

analysis shows that the effect of this would be to reduce shareholder value by nearly 30 per cent to £71 million. Finally, management explored an even more aggressive strategy of cutting prices by 10 per cent. They believed this would reduce the operating margin from 15 to 10 per cent, but boost revenue growth to 40 per cent annually. Unfortunately, the higher investment requirements and the lower operating margin make this an unattractive option. As Table 6.2 shows, this is materially worse than the proposed strategy, reducing shareholder value by over 40 per cent.

THE PLANNING PROCESS

We now look at how management can introduce this type of value-based marketing planning in their companies. In most companies it will start with an educational process: a workshop to develop an understanding of the principles of value-based planning, the objectives of the process, and the importance of a marketing orientation.

A VALUE FOCUS

It is also important to make sure that managers understand why creating shareholder value is their principal task. They need to be familiar with the principle of creating shareholder value – that the task of management is to develop a business unit strategy that maximises the net present value of long-term cash flow. Value-based planning is quite different from conventional planning built around budgets. Budgets focus on accounting profits; value-based planning focuses on value creation. In today's dynamic markets there is no correlation between profits and the share price. Investors are looking at the potential of the business to create long-term cash, not short-term profits. Finding new growth opportunities from meeting new or unmet customer needs is the way to create long-term cash flow.

UNDERSTANDING THE OBJECTIVES

Managers need to understand the objectives of the planning process. The first objective is to drive business *growth*. This means clearing away the dead wood in the portfolio and exploring the growth ladder to find new opportunities to expand the business. Without growth it is impossible to build sustained increases in shareholder value. The second objective is to find a formula that will allow the business, and the people who work there, *to win*. Winning is about developing strategies that will give the organisation a lasting differential advantage in its target markets. Finally, implementing a strategy successfully depends upon *building core capabilities* that can result in meeting customer needs efficiently and effectively. These core capabilities are assets, skills and systems, which make possible customer benefits and are difficult for competitors to emulate.

BEING CUSTOMER DRIVEN

Managers also need to appreciate that the foundation for growth and profitability is solving customers' problems more effectively than competitors. Customers do not want products – they want relationships with organisations that can give them solutions to their problems. The performance of a business depends on its knowledge of customers, their operations and problems, and its ability to innovate by bringing out new and superior solutions. The task of the planning process is to bring this knowledge and problem-solving outlook to the fore. Without this knowledge and outlook the company becomes a commodity business, forced to compete largely on price. Commodity-based competition makes earning economic profits virtually impossible over a long period.

DEVELOPING THE PLAN

The recommended process for developing the marketing strategy is outlined in Figure 6.9.

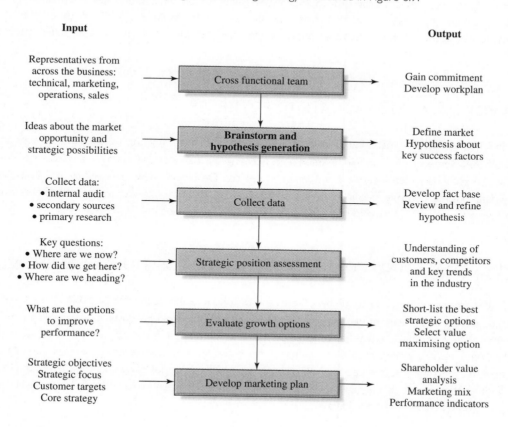

Figure 6.9   The Process of Value-Based Marketing Planning

FORM CROSS-FUNCTIONAL TEAM

The marketing department alone should not develop the marketing strategy. Genuine innovation relies on inputs from across the business – from technologists, market researchers, sales force, country managers etc. Involvement from across the organisation creates enthusiasm, accelerates the process and facilitates implementation.

BRAINSTORMING AND HYPOTHESIS DEVELOPMENT

Marketing is a creative process. Brainstorming is a good way of generating ideas from across the organisation and obtaining fresh insights about how to stimulate growth. The ideas that seem to be most relevant should then be formulated as hypotheses that in principle can be tested against data. For example, in a food company a hypothesis might emerge that there is a big marketing opportunity for a fat-free range of desserts, or that prices could be raised across the current product line by 10 per cent without affecting volume. One of the tasks of the leader is to steer the team to develop hypotheses across the range of issues relevant to the plan.

Hypothesis-orientated planning is valuable because it leads to a focus on the critical issues affecting performance. It also helps in developing a consensus because hypotheses provide clarity about what is under debate. Finally, once the critical hypotheses are agreed, they provides guidelines on what is the key information to collect and how it should be analysed, so that these hypotheses can be evaluated. Without hypotheses it is all too easy to get drowned in excessive amounts of data and for the whole process to suffer 'paralysis by analysis'.

COLLECT DATA TO EVALUATE HYPOTHESES

Once the critical issues have been identified data will have to be brought together to analyse the issues and test the hypotheses. Some of the data will be internal, concerning the business unit's current and past performance. Some will be secondary data available from published sources. Developing new ideas will almost always require primary data: original, purpose-specific information from surveys and focus groups to gauge customers' attitudes and problems. Good data is critical to make the plan rigorous and fact based.

ANALYSE DATA AND CONDUCT STRATEGIC POSITION ASSESSMENT

The data is then analysed to evaluate the hypotheses and to conduct a thorough strategic position assessment. This will include looking at the current performance of the business and its main products. It will enable an analysis of the internal and external factors that have shaped performance in the past. It should provide the facility to project the growth and profitability implications of the unit's current strategy. Inputs to the assessments will be information about how markets can be segmented and analyses of the probable strategies of competitors. Finally, the team will judge whether the present strategy is likely to fit the future environment and whether the results are likely to be satisfactory to the board and shareholders.

EVALUATE GROWTH OPTIONS

The team should then identify the best strategic options for generating shareholder value. For example, a pharmaceutical company looked at the possibilities for one of its major products, at a mature stage of the product life cycle and with its patent about to expire. It identified five strategic options:

- Maximise market share *over what was left of the product's life by aggressive spending on promotion.*

- Hold market share *by taking competitive actions only where required to maintain the current position.*

- Create life-cycle extensions *and migrate customers to higher priced newer products with better patent protection.*

- Divest *by licensing or selling the product to another company.*

- Launch a generic *and aim for leadership in the new market that will open when the patent expires.*

Members of the team will have to debate and value the options and prioritise the alternatives.

DEVELOP MARKETING STRATEGY

Here the team develops its main conclusions and investment recommendations. The strategy will summarise the key issues emerging from the strategic position assessment, the overall strategic objective and focus, how the business unit's value proposition will be positioned and the marketing mix. The shareholder value analysis will then be presented based on the sales, costs and investments forecast.

IMPLEMENTING THE STRATEGY

Bartlett and Ghoshal reviewed how 20 large, successful European, US and Japanese companies implemented strategy. [6] They found little similarity in their strategies, structures and systems, but a surprising consistency in how their leaders sought to implement strategies. They described it as a softer, more organic model built on the development of purpose, process and people. The overriding goal was to create a shared sense of commitment, belonging and common values throughout the organisation. The implementation style can be summarised under three headings:

1. Defining the organisation's mission
2. Building on the organisation's value
3. Giving meaning to employees' work

DEFINING THE ORGANISATION'S MISSION

Outside the ranks of top management it is difficult to make strategies to increase shareholder returns an inspiring goal. Maximising the returns for outside investors is unlikely to enthuse inside staff, who have their own goals and interests. What motivates employees is a sense of belonging and personal fulfilment. Successful leaders build on this by seeking to create a sense of organisational mission that employees can identify with. Generally a mission statement should provide focus by defining *what* business the firm is in. It should state its core strategy, which describes *how* it is going to be successful. Finally, it should contain an inspiring goal to *motivate* staff and other stakeholders to commit themselves to the organisation's plans (see box, 'Selections from Company Mission Statements').

Selections from Company Mission Statements

Vodafone

We will be the communications leader in an increasingly connected world.

Nike

To bring inspiration and innovation to every athlete in the world.

Google

Google's mission is to organise the world's information and make it universally accessible and useful.

Microsoft

At Microsoft, our mission and values are to help people and businesses throughout the world realize their full potential.

Estée Lauder

The guiding vision of The Estée Lauder Companies is 'Bringing the best to everyone we touch'. By 'The best', we mean the best products, the best people and the best ideas. These three pillars have been the hallmarks of our Company since it was founded by Mrs. Estée Lauder in 1946. They remain the foundation upon which we continue to build our success today.

Matsushita

Seven Principles

- *Contribution to society*
- *Fairness and honesty*
- *Cooperation and team spirit*
- *Untiring effort for improvement*
- *Courtesy and humility*
- *Adaptability*
- *Gratitude*

BUILDING ON THE ORGANISATION'S VALUES

When management invent mission statements that are meant to inspire employees, but which are unrelated to the organisation's history or culture, all they inspire is scepticism and cynicism. Most companies should build their mission around the strengths and values the company already possesses. Ian MacLaurin turned around Tesco, to make it Britain's largest, fastest growing and most profitable supermarket group in the 1990s, by building on its historic reputation for competitive pricing. But he realised that this value focus had to be supplemented with a new emphasis on quality and innovation if Tesco were to meet the needs of increasingly affluent and demanding shoppers. 'Being the UK's number one for quality, innovation and value' was a mission to which staff could subscribe.

Creating a sense of purpose and commitment to the strategy involves more than inspiring speeches and mission statements. It requires getting the organisation involved in interpreting, refining and making it operational. This means tapping into the reservoir of knowledge and expertise that is widely distributed throughout the organisation. Tesco's MacLaurin had store managers, buying groups and operations people engaged in dozens of projects to operationalise the mission and get buy-in. He also sanctioned a major programme of management education, training and organisational development to give the staff the knowledge and skills to move the organisation forward. Finally, implementing the mission also means developing indicators that measure progress. MacLaurin, for example, employed a market research company to provide regular feedback on how Tesco's brand name was perceived by consumers and how its image for quality, innovation and value was progressing, benchmarked against key competitors.

His successor, Terry Leahy, built on MacLaurin's legacy with the 'Every Little Helps' strategy, which revolved around the core purpose of creating value for customers to earn their lifetime loyalty. That included regularly asking customers and staff what the retailer could do to make shopping and working with Tesco that 'little bit better'.

GIVING MEANING TO EMPLOYEES' WORK

Successful leaders intent on implementing their strategies consider how to gain the commitment of individual employees. Three initiatives stand out as encouraging such commitment. First, successful organisations recognise and celebrate individual accomplishments. People want to feel part of the team: not cogs in a huge machine. It is not just about recognising the organisation's stars but also the efforts of all those who sustain the organisation. This has to be done in a meaningful way: front-line staff see through PR gestures as meaningless attempts at manipulation. At retailer John Lewis, for example, where all employees have a stake in the profits and all workers are called 'partners', the staff turnover is well below the national average.

Second, organisations need to be committed to developing employees. This is more than just skill training; it is also about educating them and helping them to realise their full potential. KPMG, for example, topped the *Sunday Times* 2008 'Best Big Companies to Work For' league table, which is voted on by employees, largely because of its commitment to developing its people.[7] By developing its employees' potential, management shows that it recognises commitment has to be two-way. Last, effective leaders foster individual initiative. Since the 1920s, when 3M was turned around, it has always shown that it recognises that innovation and growth depend on the initiative of individuals. Its processes recognise this, for example by the '15% rule' that allows employees to spend 15 per cent of their time on their own projects. Individual initiative can be stimulated by open information sharing in the organisation, by cooperation and by operating transparent and open decision-making, allowing all with relevant knowledge to contribute.

To summarise, strategic marketing planning is a key process in creating value for the organisation. But its implementation depends on engendering the cooperation and commitment of employees throughout the business. This requires creating a sense of organisational purpose that people can identify with, and feel a sense of pride in its accomplishment.

SUMMARY

1. The purpose of strategic marketing planning is not to forecast the future – that is an impossible task. Instead, it is to encourage managers to ask the critical questions about their changing markets so that they can identify the trends that are occurring and capitalise on the opportunities they offer.

2. Corporate level planning focuses on driving organisational change, managing the company's shared value drivers and adapting the business portfolio to the changing marketing and technological environment.

3. Marketing strategy has to be formulated at the level of the business unit. Business unit managers have the detailed knowledge of changing customer needs and competitive activities that are essential components for developing a growth-orientated marketing strategy.

4. A value-based marketing strategy consists of six parts: strategic objective, strategic focus, customer targets, competitor targets, core strategy and the marketing mix.

5. Once a strategy is formulated management have to test whether it looks likely to generate value for shareholders. It also has to consider whether there are other marketing strategies that would offer even greater returns.

6. The planning process and its successful implementation depend upon the involvement and commitment of the staff. They are the people with the detailed knowledge of the market and who have to make the strategy work.

REVIEW QUESTIONS

1. Why do companies develop marketing strategies?
2. What is the centre's role in the planning process?
3. What are the components of a value-based marketing strategy?
4. Illustrate how shareholder value analysis can be used to assess the potential of a strategic plan.
5. Describe the process of strategic marketing planning.
6. What additional considerations affect the successful implementation of marketing strategies?

NOTES ON CHAPTER 6

[1] Tom Copeland, Tim Koller and Jack Murrin, *Valuation: Measuring and Managing the Value of Companies*, New York: John Wiley & Sons, Inc., 1996, pp. 336–339.

[2] Gary Hamel and C.K. Prahalad, *Competing for the Future*, Boston, MA: Harvard Business School Press, 1994.

[3] For a summary see Peter Doyle, *Marketing Management and Strategy*, London: Prentice Hall, 1998.

[4] For an excellent discussion of the implications of this separation of the economics of information from the economics of physical items, see Philip Evans and Thomas Wurster, *Blown to Bits: How the New Economics of Information Transforms Strategy*, Boston, MA: Harvard Business School Press, 2000.

[5] For detailed examples of integrated communications, see Stan Rapp and Thomas L. Collins, *Beyond Maximarketing: The New Power of Caring and Daring*, New York: McGraw-Hill, 1994; Ernan Roman, *Integrated Direct Marketing*, Lincolnwood, IL: NTC Business Books, 1995.

[6] Christopher A. Bartlett and Sumantra Ghoshal, Changing the role of top management: beyond strategy to purpose, *Harvard Business Review*, November/December, **72**(6), 1994, 79–98. See also: Jim Collins and Jerry Porras, *Built to Last: Successful Habits of Visionary Companies*, Collins, 2004.

[7] *The Sunday Times*, '100 Best Companies to Work For', March 9, 2008.

PART 3

Implementing High-Value Strategies

7 Building Brands

'If this company were split up I would give you the property, plant and equipment and I would take the brands – and I would fare better than you.'

John Stuart, CEO of Quaker

INTRODUCTION AND OBJECTIVES

In today's information-based economy, intangible assets are usually much more important than the tangible assets that appear on corporate balance sheets. In the industrial era that ended somewhere in the early 1960s, possession of valuable property or efficient plant and equipment accounted for the stock market dominance of such companies as General Motors, Westinghouse, ICI and Unilever. They could turn out the cars, machinery, chemicals and foodstuffs the world clamoured for. But few of today's most valuable companies – Microsoft, GE, Wal-Mart, Google – rely for their profits on making things. When they do sell goods, their manufacture is often outsourced. Most of these top companies are predominantly service businesses whose major assets are knowledge, brand names and relationships with customers and partners. In these companies, the value of their tangible assets represents only a small percentage of their market value.

Intangible assets are of various forms, but in many industries the equity in the company's brands is the most important. The value arises from the trust that customers place in the company's brand. This trust creates a relationship between the brand and the customer that encourages preference, brand loyalty and a willingness to consider the new products and services that the company may offer in the future under its brand name.

There is clear evidence that strong brands create value for shareholders as well as for consumers. A study done by Millward Brown Optimor found that strong brands continuously outperform the market (Figure 7.1).[1] Other evidence lies in the high market value to book value ratios that usually occur for companies with strong brands. Finally, there is evidence in the high prices paid – typically five or six times book value – when branded goods companies are acquired.

A key question is who controls the brand and the relationship to the consumer. Most producers do not sell direct to the end consumer. So, for example, someone shopping for toys could think first of the supplier's brand (e.g. Mattel), a retailer that stocks toys (e.g. Toys 'R' Us), an e-business (e.g. eToys) or a search engine such as Google that finds and may even recommend the best choice. In recent years the power of the retailer's brand, whether bricks-and-mortar or online or both, has grown at the expense of the suppliers. The growing dominance of search engines and recommendation sites must also be taken into account. If a business loses control of its brand, it risks

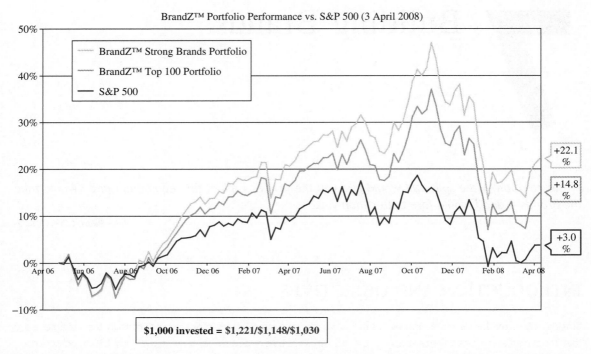

Figure 7.1   Strong Brands Continuously Outperform the Market. Reproduced by permission of Millward Brown

being commoditised and its value migrating to whoever has the customer's preference. Creating and sustaining the brand is therefore the key to shareholder value in many industries. This chapter covers these issues. By the time you have completed this chapter, you will be able to:

○   *Describe what a brand is*

○   *Understand how brands create value for shareholders*

○   *Explain how to build a successful brand*

○   *Assess the value potential in developing brand extensions*

○   *Explore the opportunities from updating brands and developing markets internationally*

○   *Show how a portfolio of brands can be structured systematically to control costs and maximise its effectiveness*

○   *Describe how brands are valued using discounting cash flow analysis*

The chapter begins by looking at the different types of intangible assets and how they contribute to value creation. It then goes on to examine how brands are defined and how they add value for consumers by simplifying the choice process and increasing satisfaction. By creating customer value, brands make possible enhanced shareholder value. The chapter explains how, through successful brand management, managers can increase the net present value of the company's cash flow. It goes on to look at the steps in building a brand identity and the ways it can be communicated to consumers to create the desired brand identity. The chapter continues by exploring some of the most important issues in developing a branding strategy – the contribution of brand extensions, repositioning and updating brands – and organising the brand portfolio for maximum effectiveness. Finally we look at using discounted cash flow analysis to measure brand equity and the value of a brand.

THE ROLE OF INTANGIBLE ASSETS

The three core business processes, or marketing, can be seen as: (1) the product development process, which aims to create solutions that customers want, (2) the supply chain process, which acquires the inputs for those customer solutions and efficiently delivers them and (3) the customer relationship process which identifies customers, understands their needs, builds relationships and shapes the perceptions of the organisation and its brands.[2] The first two processes lead to the sale but the third is essential for continuity, i.e. future sales. The effectiveness with which the firm undertakes these processes determines its ability to create a competitive advantage.

Whether this competitive advantage translates into profitable long-term growth is affected by two other factors. One is the *sustainability* of the firm's competitive advantage. In some markets even strongly advantaged firms do not earn high returns because low entry barriers mean that the competitive advantage is quickly copied. A second factor is the *appropriability* of the value of the advantage. Sometimes parties other than the shareholders appropriate this value.

These may be powerful customers, who are able to use their buying power to drive down the company's prices and so appropriate the value themselves. Sometimes suppliers may appropriate the value. Star employees can occasionally use their specialised skills or fame to leverage the full value of their added value to the firm. Movie stars and football players are examples. Wage demands may then make even organisations or products that lead the market only marginally profitable as value migrates from shareholders to the suppliers of skills.

Conventional balance sheets show only the firm's tangible resources or assets. Tangible assets consist of its financial resources and physical assets such as plant and equipment, land and locations. But in today's information age, tangible assets represent only a fraction of the value of major companies. For example, the ratio of market value to book value for the world's top 20 companies averaged 15, and for the *Fortune 500* it averaged 8, implying that tangible assets represented between only 5 and 12 per cent of a company's total assets.

Most of the resources a modern company uses to build strong core business processes and value for customers and shareholders do not appear on the balance sheet. These intangible assets can be classified into five types:

1. **Technological assets.** These are proprietary technology in the form of patents, copyrights and trade secrets, or special know-how in the application of technology.

2. **Strategic assets.** These are licences, natural monopolies or other privileges that restrict competition from other firms.

3. **Reputational assets.** These are the name of the company and its brands, which convey the reputation of its products, services and fair dealings with customers, suppliers, the government and the community.

4. **Human resources.** These are the skills and adaptability of the firm's employees.

5. **Organisation and culture.** These are the values and social norms inside the firm that shape the commitment and loyalty of employees.

The firm's brand (or brands) represents its major reputational asset. A brand is different from a label. The brand [equity] is an asset; a label is what goes on the bottle. A label is a name, symbol or design that is used to distinguish the firm's product or service. But in marketing a brand has other elements besides being recognisable, for example, the promise of added values to the customer – advantages not possessed by competitors (although the label can also signify the promise). A strong brand is more desirable to its target customers. This affects each of the core business processes. It facilitates the product development process by giving customers more confidence in the quality and attributes of the products. Strong brands aid the supply chain process by attracting suppliers and channel interest. They also enhance customer relationship management by creating emotional links over and above the functions of the product.

Table 7.1 lists the world's strongest brands as valued by Interbrand, a leading international brand consultancy. Interbrand also looked at the importance of intangible assets and brands by industry (Table 7.2).[3] In utilities and heavy industry, brands and intangible assets generally are not very important. In pharmaceuticals, technological assets, in particular patents, are the most important intangible assets. Brands are very significant in luxury goods and

Table 7.1 The World's Top Brands 2007

Brand	Brand Value $ millions	BV/Mkt Cap
Coca-Cola	65,324	54%
Microsoft	58,709	20%
IBM	57,090	36%
GE	51,569	13%
Nokia	33,696	29%
Toyota	32,070	16%
Intel	30,954	24%
McDonald's	29,398	48%
Disney	29,210	42%
Mercedes	23,568	25%
Citi	23,442	9%
Hewlett-Packard	22,197	18%
BMW	21,612	49%
Marlboro	21,282	14%
American Express	20,827	27%
Gillette	20,415	10%
Louis Vuitton	20,321	36%
Cisco	19,099	12%
Honda	17,998	28%
Google	17,837	11%

Source: Interbrand

Table 7.2   The Relative Importance of Brands and Other Assets

	Tangibles (%)	Brand (%)	Other intangibles (%)
Utilities	70	0	30
Industrials	70	5	25
Pharmaceuticals	40	10	50
Retail	70	15	15
Information technology	30	20	50
Automotive	50	30	20
Financial services	20	30	50
Food and drink	40	55	5
Luxury goods	25	70	5

Source: The World's Greatest Brands. Reprinted with permission from Interbrand.

grocery products. Even within an industry there are sharp differences among competing firms. Some companies build strategies around brands, counting on price premiums and higher market shares to give an economic return on the brand-building investments; other companies compete on price and do not invest in brands. While there is no simple answer, in most industries companies that possess strong brands perform better than those that do not.

THE ROLE OF THE BRAND

THE PROBLEM OF CUSTOMER CHOICE

Brands create value for customers by helping them navigate the choice process. Today customers are faced with an increasing array of competitive suppliers and products promising to meet their needs. Making the right choice often involves *risk* because the products are new and complex, or because the customer has not had to make this type of decision before. Even if the buyer is willing to spend time evaluating the alternatives, judging products can still be tough. Goods and services that are hard to evaluate before purchase are said to be low in 'search qualities'. Services, like those offered by consultants, hairdressers or repair shops, are examples: it is difficult to know what the end result will be like until the service has been performed. Many of them have high 'experience qualities': their quality can be evaluated after purchase. Some products and services are, however, difficult to evaluate even after purchase, for example a medical check-up or a survey on a new property. These are said to be high in 'credence qualities'. Buying them can be an act of faith. As the economy becomes more hi-tech and services become more dominant, consumer decision-making gets more difficult as these tend to be high in experience and credence characteristics and low in search qualities.

Decisions are particularly challenging when *complex criteria* come into play. Particularly in consumer markets, decisions are often not based solely or even largely on economic or functional criteria of value. As Freud and Maslow showed, products fulfil more than functional needs: they are also purchased to meet social needs, to seek status or for self-actualisation. In choosing clothes or a car customers are looking for far more than functional values. They are looking not only for what the product will do for them but what it will mean for how others see them.

The consumer's anxiety is increased where the decisions are *important* ones. This is where the wrong decision entails significant financial or social costs. Of course, many decisions are not important in this sense. Buying the 'wrong' chocolate bar or magazine is generally not an important mistake. But most decisions absorb *time*. As people get more affluent the value they assign to their time increases and they look for mechanisms to save time. Brands are one of the mechanisms to take time out of the purchasing process and to reduce risk.

BRANDS AS BELIEFS IN ATTRIBUTES AND EXPERIENCES

Successful brands create a relationship of trust with the customer. They reduce perceived risk, simplify the choice process and save time. This relationship is based on the image customers have of the brand. A *brand image* is a set of beliefs about a brand's attributes and associations. A customer's image of a brand is built up from four types of source:

○ Experience. *Often customers will have used the brand before. They will frequently have well-formed beliefs about its reliability and character.*

○ Personal. *Friends, acquaintances and others seen using it communicate beliefs about the brand's attributes and associations.*

○ Public. *The brand may have appeared in the mass media or been analysed in consumer reports.*

○ Commercial. *Advertising, display, packaging and salespeople are important in communicating messages about the brand's features and values.*

There are three main types of brands and brand images:

1. **Attribute brands.** An attribute brand possesses an image that conveys confidence in the product's functional attributes. Because it is often difficult for customers to assess quality and features objectively from the vast array of offers, they will often choose brands that appear to confirm their qualities. For example, Volvo's brand proposition is about a safe car, manufactured to high quality standards. Wal-Mart's brand image is of the lowest prices for nationally advertised products. Starbucks strives to be the 'undisputed coffee authority'. The McKinsey brand promises the highest quality strategic consulting. These are all 'beliefs about attributes' brands.

2. **Aspirational brands.** An aspirational brand conveys an image about the types of people who buy the brand. The image says less about the product and more about a desired lifestyle. The belief is that acquisition of these brands associates the buyer with the rich and famous. Louis Vuitton suggests it is the luggage choice of sophisticated jet-setters. Rolex watches are shown on the wrists of leading professionals. The desire to create such images reflects the recognition that many products are bought not just to meet people's functional requirements but to buy status, recognition and esteem.

3. **Experience brands.** An experience brand conveys an image of shared associations and emotions. It goes beyond aspirations and is more about a shared philosophy between the brand and the individual consumer. Successful experience brands express individuality, personal growth, and a set of ideas to live by. Examples are Nike with its 'just do it' attitude, or Google with 'don't be evil' in terms of how it tries to behave in every aspect of its business. Coca-Cola's brand proposition is about sharing the experiences and values of the young generation. The Timberland brand expresses the experience of rugged, outdoor-tested environmentally-conscious clothing. For these brands, no claims are made about the superiority or special features of the product – the promise is about experience and shared associations.

Table 7.3   Famous Business-to-Business Brands

Accenture	GE	John Deere
Boeing	GlaxoSmithKline	McKinsey & Co
Boston Consulting Group	Goldman Sachs	Merck
Du Pont	Harvard Business School	Microsoft
The Economist	Hewlett-Packard	Motorola
FedEx	IBM	Reuters
Financial Times	Intel	Canon

The most effective brand image varies with the nature of the market. In business-to-business markets, where purchasing tends to be more functional, attribute brands are more important (see Table 7.3). In luxury markets, aspirational brands play a big role. In consumer markets, many companies have been trying to create experience brands. Experience brands have a number of advantages over attribute and aspirational brands. The problem with attribute brands is that with today's sophisticated technologies it is virtually impossible to retain unique product features or qualities for any length of time. The availability of more objective information sources heightens the problem of attribute claims. For example, customers might read on the Internet about consumer tests that demonstrate that Volvo cars are not safer than other models, or that other retailers are as cheap as Wal-Mart.

Aspirational brands are threatened by increasing affluence, the declining influence of social class, and the growth of more individualistic lifestyles. In the West, people no longer feel the same need to imitate their betters or keep up with the Joneses. Consumers are becoming more individualistic, preferring to spend money on what makes them happy than on trying to impress the neighbours. Experience brands are more robust because they do not depend on a product or a 'look'. Another advantage of experience brands is that, because they are about personal values, they are often capable of greater extendibility than attribute or aspirational brands. The latter tend to be restricted to their category or closely related markets. By contrast, experience brands can stretch to wherever a buyer's personal philosophy can be made relevant.

The archetype of an experience brand is Richard Branson's Virgin brand, which stands for an unstuffy, irreverent, us-against-them attitude. This has been stretched from music and entertainment to transport (airlines and trains), financial services, media, cosmetics, clothing and mobile phones.

The most important thing about successful brands is that they differentiate. Today even the newest and most complex products can be copied within weeks. It is not difficult to produce a drink that tastes like Coca-Cola, an MP3 player like the iPod, a suit like Armani, or a microprocessor that functions like Intel's latest Pentium. But people will not buy these products in the same numbers and certainly not at the same prices. People buy the well-known brands because they have confidence in their quality, aspire to their status, or because they personally identify with the brand's philosophy.

The added values provided by strong brands in the form of risk reduction, confidence and experience are often demonstrated. Bartle describes how a parity performance on taste, when two food products are tested 'blind', becomes a clear preference for one brand (brand B), when the two products are labelled (Figure 7.2).[4] In another example, for a household product, a clear performance deficiency is removed when brand identities are revealed

Percentage preferring

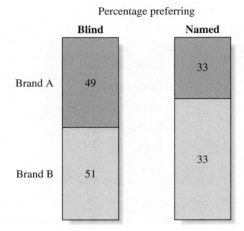

Figure 7.2   Blind versus Named Product Test: Food Product

Percentage preferring

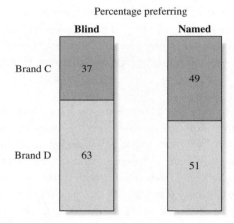

Figure 7.3   Blind versus Named Product Test: Household Product

(Figure 7.3). Blind product tests normally show a clear preference for Pepsi over Coke, but when the brands are labelled the preference changes overwhelmingly to Coke (Table 7.4).[5]

The result of these added values is customer preference. Economically this means that strong brands obtain higher market shares, higher prices or, usually, a combination of the two.

BRANDS AND SHAREHOLDER VALUE

This section explores how strong brands directly contribute to creating shareholder value. Brands are resources that contribute to the firm's capabilities in running its core business processes of managing its product development, supply chain and customer relationships. The effectiveness with which it runs these processes determines its ability to create value for customers and shareholders.

Table 7.4 Blind versus Named Product Test: Coke versus Pepsi

	Blind (%)	Branded (%)
Prefer Pepsi	51	23
Prefer Coke	44	65
Equal/don't know	5	12

Source: de Chernatony and McDonald, 1992.

As we have seen, the value of a business is determined by the present value (PV) of its future free cash flow:

$$PV(Business) = PV(Cash\ flow) = PV(Revenues - Costs - Investment)$$

$$= \sum_{t-1}^{\infty} \frac{CF_t}{(1+r)^t}$$

From this we can deduce that the value of the business can be increased in four ways:

1. Increasing cash flow now – by raising revenues, cutting costs or reducing investments.

2. Accelerating cash flows: earlier cash flows are an advantage because risk and time discount the value of later cash flows.

3. Adding to the long-term value of the business through profitable investments in tangible and intangible assets which will enable an increase in cash flow later.

4. Lowering the firm's cost of capital by reducing the risks and volatility of the anticipated cash flow, i.e. 'r' in the formula above becomes smaller.

INCREASING CASH FLOW

Strong brands can increase cash flow in four ways.

1. **Obtaining higher prices.** Because customers have confidence in the attributes and quality of brands, or because brands offer desirable associations and experiences, customers usually pay a brand premium to purchase them. Brands like Mercedes, Microsoft and Marlboro sell at substantial premiums to their rivals. A survey by Broadbent found leading grocery brands sold at a price premium averaging 40 per cent above retailer own-label.[6] Other studies have shown that the price elasticity of strong brands is lower – implying that price increases result in smaller volume losses than for unbranded products. Of course, developing brands implies higher marketing costs so that incremental revenue is necessary to make brands economic. But price premiums are perhaps the most important way that brands create value for shareholders.

2. **Higher volume growth.** Instead of taking the full price premium that the brand may justify, a company can instead sell at, or close to, the average market price and use the brand's reputation to build higher volume. McDonald's and Dell are examples of companies using their brand power this way. Most really strong brands such as Marlboro, Coca-Cola and Intel are both leaders in share *and* sell at a price premium. Leading brands can gain scale economies in marketing and outspend smaller competitors to build growth. Another way in

which strong brands increase growth is via line and brand extensions, which enable them to cover the market more fully or move into additional markets.

3.   **Lower costs.** Brand leaders gain economies of scale that often result in lower costs. Buying power can mean lower variable costs. But it is in fixed costs, especially marketing and distribution costs, where brand leaders have their biggest advantage. Most marketing costs are fixed. For example, the minimum cost to run a national advertising campaign or national sales force is the same whether the brand share is 5 per cent or 50 per cent. This means that while brand leaders generally spend more in absolute terms than their smaller competitors, their unit marketing cost is lower.

4.   **Higher asset utilisation.** Strong brands often have more opportunities to economise in fixed and working capital. They can obtain scale economies in plant and distribution. Suppliers and distributors also have a greater incentive to integrate their supply chains with companies possessing strong brands. This can lead to significant reductions in inventories, manufacturing and distribution assets.

Table 7.5 illustrates how these four factors operating together can augment the cash flow of a strong brand. Here the brand leader sells three times the volume of the follower and also has a brand premium of 10 per cent. Its buying power gives it a 5 per cent advantage in unit variable costs. The brand leader's fixed costs are £18 million more, yet in terms of fixed cost per unit, the follower is 20 per cent more costly. Both brands are assumed to have been growing sales by 5 per cent annually; the leader's investment rate is 40 per cent of additional sales and the follower's is 45 per cent. The result is that the brand leader's market share advantage of 3:1 turns into a free cash flow advantage of 8:1. In addition, with its much higher marketing spend, the brand leader is in a strong position to increase even further its market dominance (see box, 'The Importance of Market Share').

ACCELERATING CASH FLOW

Brands can increase shareholder value by generating cash flows sooner than otherwise. The faster the company receives cash flow, the higher is its net present value. There is considerable evidence that consumers respond quicker to marketing campaigns when they are already familiar with the brand and have positive attitudes towards it.

Table 7.5   Brand Strength and Cash Flow

	Brand leader	Brand follower
Volume (m units)	100	33
Price (£)	1.00	0.9
Revenue (£m)	100	29.7
Variable costs (£m)	40 (0.4/unit)	13.86 (0.42/unit)
Fixed costs	30 (0.3/unit)	12 (0.36/unit)
Operating earnings	10	1.86
Tax	3	0.56
NOPAT	7	1.3
Net investment	2	0.67
Free cash flow	5	0.63

This is likely to be particularly important for new products. Strong brands can also get access to the major distribution channels faster. To the extent that brands lead to faster responses and stimulate earlier purchases, then cash flow is accelerated and shareholder value is increased.

The Importance of Market Share

In both consumer and industrial markets companies attach great importance to market share. For example, both GE and Heinz have set their strategies around exiting from all markets where they cannot be number one or two. There is considerable evidence that in many markets only the top two brands in a category make an economic profit. As markets become increasingly global, these brand leaders become truly mega-brands.

The profitability of the brand leaders arises from three sources. First, brand leaders usually have lower unit costs as a result of economies of scale and purchasing power. Second, they can afford to spend more on marketing, enabling them to have a greater share of voice in the market and so boost sales even further. Third, they can obtain higher prices. Distributor economics pressure retailers and dealers to reduce the number of competing brands that they carry in a category. The brands most at risk are small-share brands, which have to resort to giving higher margins to distributors to maintain support.

The PIMS study of 2600 businesses found that on average brands with a market share of 40 per cent generated three times the return on investment of those with a market share of only 10 per cent. For grocery products the relationship appeared even stronger. Studies in both the UK and the USA indicate that, on average, the leading brand in a category earns around 18 per cent return on sales, the number two brand only 3 per cent, and the others are unprofitable.[7]

In recent years, 'network effects' have become important in adding to the critical significance of obtaining a high market share. For many products and services, especially those that are IT related, customers want to buy the brand leader. Buying the market leader gives them the assurance that the product is not going to be made obsolete by the emergence of new standards and that applications and networking with others will be facilitated.[8]

INCREASING THE CONTINUING VALUE OF CASH FLOW

Continuing value is the present value of a business attributable to the period beyond the planning period and, as shown in Chapter 2, it generally accounts for the majority of the value of the business. The continuing value reflects investors' views of the long-term ability of the business to keep generating cash. A strong case can be made for the importance of brands in enhancing continuing value. Striking evidence lies in the longevity of leading brands. Most of the world's leading brands, aside from those in completely new sectors of the economy like Google and eBay, have been around for over 25 years. Brands like Coca-Cola, Nescafé, Persil, Heinz, Kit-Kat, Cadbury and Kellogg's have been around for up to a century.

Brands have longevity because consumers believe in them. Consumers are confident about their attributes and values and so continue to buy them, as long as they go on being managed properly. Users of early versions of the product not only buy later versions but also often buy new line and brand extensions. Equally importantly, they contribute to continuing value by referring the brand to other potential users and new generations. Creating strong brands is one of the most important ways of increasing the long-term value of the business.

REDUCING THE COST OF CAPITAL

The company's cost of capital is influenced by the risk attached to its cash flow. Cash flows that are more stable and predictable will have a higher net present value and consequently create more shareholder value. Strong brands reduce a company's vulnerability to competitive attack. While products are easy to copy, the evidence suggests that strong brands are not. Brand identity is a significant barrier to entry and so acts to reduce the vulnerability of cash flow.

The volatility of cash flow is also often reduced for strong brands because brand loyalty promotes stability in operations. With a loyal customer base the company does not have to risk major investments in winning large numbers of new customers. This is important because the cost of winning new customers is much greater than the cost of retaining existing ones.

HOW TO BUILD BRANDS

FROM PRODUCTS TO BRANDS

A successful brand image B_S can be thought of as the combination of three elements: a good product (P), a distinctive identity (D), and added values (AV):

$$B_S = P \times D \times AV$$

The relationship is multiplicative, indicating that all three elements are necessary to create a successful brand. Developing a brand starts with having an effective product. Product effectiveness can normally be measured in blind product tests. Next, the product has to be given a distinctive identity so that customers can recognise it and ask for it by name. This is usually measured by prompted and unprompted awareness. Finally, and most crucially, a successful brand has to have added values that elicit confidence in consumers that it is of higher quality or is more desirable than similar products from competitors. Added values can be measured through market research into attitudes and preferences.

Having an effective product alone is not sufficient to earn economic profits. Competition only at the product level eventually makes it a commodity-type business and price becomes the major factor in customer choice. Most companies attach their names to their products so that they become recognisable, but again this is insufficient to create preference. Being distinctive is not the same as being seen as better. Preference depends upon the last ingredient: added values that give customers confidence that this product has qualities, status or associations not possessed by alternative choices.

The process of brand building is often described as a series of layers (Figure 7.4). The starting point is a product (or service) that meets a customer need. But however innovative or effective the product, it rarely forms the basis of a sustainable advantage. First, competitors can usually rapidly copy new products. For example, Gillette spent three years and over $1 billion developing the first version of its Mach3 razor which it launched in 1998. But one month after it was launched a retailer own-label copy of it had been introduced. In most markets today, there are no major quality differences among the leading competitors. Because manufacturing is often such a low-value activity, even the most innovative companies increasingly outsource making the product to third parties. A second

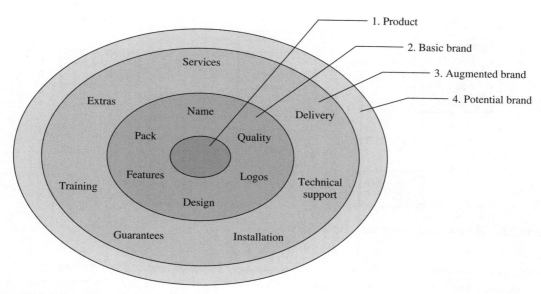

Figure 7.4 The Process of Brand Building

problem is emphasised in the basic marketing concept – people do not want products, they want solutions to their problems. Products are not bought for their own sake, but for the satisfaction they provide. In particular, emotional values – confidence, perceived status and personal fulfilment – are all major influences on choice.

The second layer builds a *basic brand* around the product. The primary function of this stage is to differentiate the company's product from competitors and to make customers aware of it. At the same time management will want to ensure that the differentiators are consistent with the added values they want to associate with the brand. The most obvious ways in which the basic brand is built, differentiated and customers made aware of it are through the choices of brand name, packaging, design, advertising and promotion.

The third layer of branding is the *augmented brand*. The objective here is to make the brand more desirable and differentiated by adding benefits. These typically include additional services such as free delivery, technical support, training, guarantees, credit and other financial terms. The final layer of branding is the creation of the *potential brand* whereby it succeeds in possessing the added values of emotional associations of confidence, status or identification that secure brand preference and loyalty. The potential brand status achieved by such brands as Sony, McDonald's and BMW is usually the result of a long period of sustained investment in marketing communications allied to a strong concern for the quality and consistency of the products and services that are offered.

DEVELOPING BRAND IDENTITY

THE BRAND COMMUNICATIONS PROCESS

Brand management centres on creating perceived added value for the company's offer among customers. The manager does this by shaping the brand's identity. The *perceived* brand identity is what the customer perceives; the *intended* brand identity is the message about the brand that the marketer wants customers to receive. This brand

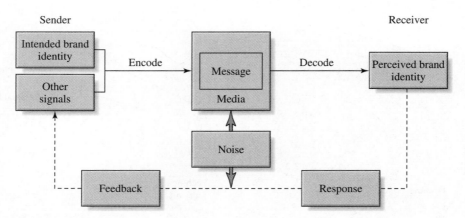

Figure 7.5 The Process of Building a Brand Identity

communications process is illustrated in Figure 7.5. The customer's perceived brand identity is the result of how he or she decodes (interprets) all the signals emitted about the brand. The company's task is to get its message about the brand identity across to produce favourable feedback and responses in the form of purchase and brand loyalty. The figure suggests why this is difficult and why a perceived brand identity may not match the identity the company intends.

The major problems in creating the desired brand identity and feedback are:

1.   **Competitive messages.** Customers are exposed to thousands of messages a day, of which only around 5 per cent are noticed and less than 1 per cent provoke some form of reaction. Without enormous expenditures, or luck, it is very difficult to get a message about your brand across (see box, 'The Cost of Sustaining a Brand').

2.   **Ineffective brand identity.** Target customers may not see the brand positioning as matching their needs. They may not believe the claims or want the attributes that are advertised. If attitudes to the message are negative, customers reinterpret it or reject it. Generally brand identities are likely to be more effective when they are close to current perceptions of the brand.

3.   **Other brand signals.** The company cannot control all the information being received about the brand. Customers obtain information from the Internet, from past experience with it, from seeing others who use it, from other actions of the company and elsewhere. For example, McDonald's has been under assault from numerous sites on the Internet attacking its alleged damage to the global environment.

4.   **Ineffective messages.** The creativity of the message can have a big impact on the effectiveness with which a brand identity is transmitted. The content of the message, the nature of the appeal, its presentation and the format of the communication can all affect the number of people noticing and responding to the message.

5.   **Wrong media.** Messages are communicated through personal media such as a sales force and impersonal media such as TV, newspapers and the Internet. The choice of media has a significant effect on the reach of the message and the confidence customers have in it.

6.   **Other constraints.** Whether the brand identity delivers the desired response and feedback from customers depends also on other elements of the marketing mix, such as price and level of availability in the major distribution channels.

The Cost of Sustaining a Brand

Building a brand is generally very costly. But without creating awareness and confidence in the brand's performance, there is little chance of it taking off in the market. In established categories such as drinks, breakfast cereals and household products most leading brands have been around for generations. The goodwill invested in these brands makes it very difficult for newcomers to gain entry.

For the new Internet businesses in the late 1990s, the cost of building a brand was also the major barrier to new entry. Start-ups routinely devoted as much as 90 per cent of the capital they raised in public offerings to advertising and marketing. It is estimated that new net brands cost hundreds of millions of dollars to create. Even for those new net brands that successfully broke through the clutter, the cost of sustaining brand leadership remained high by traditional standards. For example, in 1999 Amazon.com was still spending over $400 million on sales and marketing to maintain its brand, over 25 per cent of its revenue.

Rank	Brand name	Brand value ($ million)	1999 Marketing budget ($ million)	Marketing as % of revenue
Established brands				
1	Coca-Cola	83 845	4000	20.5
2	Microsoft	56 654	3752	16.7
3	IBM	43 781	1000	1.1
Internet brands				
35	American Online	4329	807	16.9
53	Yahoo!	1761	206	35.9
57	Amazon.Com	1361	402	25.9

Source: Business Week, 15 November 1999.

THE FACETS OF IDENTITY

To build or manage a brand effectively one needs a model. A model identifies the variables constituting a brand, defines the relationships between the variables, and predicts the effects of changes on consumer response. Developing a model of a brand is more difficult than modelling a product. The dimensions of a product are real and functional, e.g. speed, weight, size. However, those of a brand are often emotional and perceptual, making it harder for managers to agree on what the attributes are and how they can be measured. But brands are so important to the business that managers and investors need models.

A model provides a language for executives to discuss brands in a meaningful and precise way. Without a common framework it is difficult, for non-marketing managers in particular, to contribute to discussing the value and potential of a brand. When people do not contribute to the debate they tend to undervalue the importance of the brand, which can lead to weak management and inadequate investment. A model assists people to evaluate whether a brand is being managed effectively. Managers need to be able to judge, for example, whether an advertising campaign or a new design is consistent with the identity of the brand and leverages its strengths. Finally, a model contributes to developing branding strategy. It illuminates the important issue of how to extend the brand to capture new growth opportunities.

Kapferer has presented one insightful model of a brand.[9] He suggests that the identity of most brands can be captured in six dimensions. Each dimension has to be managed to influence the customer's perceived identity of the brand. The six dimensions are:

○ Physical. *This is the appearance of the brand in terms of its chosen name, colours, logo and packaging.*

○ Reflection. *This is the image of the target audience as reflected in the brand's communications, e.g. Coca-Cola reflects young people in its ads, even though the actual market is much wider.*

○ Relationship. *This refers to how the brand seeks to relate to the customer. An experience brand like Virgin positions itself as the customer's friend. An aspirational brand like Louis Vuitton invites you to join an exclusive club.*

○ Personality. *This is the character of the brand, e.g. IBM's personality is seriously professional, while Apple's is young and creative.*

○ Culture. *This refers to the background and values of the brand, e.g. Mercedes personifies German values, Nike celebrates the virtues of individualism.*

○ Relevance. *This is how the customer sees herself or himself in relation to the brand (meets my needs or for people like me). For example, customers buying from Body Shop may see themselves as expressing their concern for the environment in choosing this brand.*

In addition to the variables making up the brand identity, there is also the concept of the *brand core*. The core is the very essence of the brand: its DNA or guiding principle. The core of the Virgin brand is the irreverent championing of 'us against them'. For Intel, it is advanced technology made effective. The model is described in terms of a brand pyramid (Figure 7.6). The physical, relationship and reflection dimensions are termed *brand themes*, which are likely to be changed over time and which may well vary across sub-brands. Culture, personality and self-image are the *brand style*, which should change only very gradually. Finally, the *brand core* should be permanent and guide the consistent evolution of the brand's style and themes. Figure 7.7 illustrates the application of the brand identity model to IBM and Apple.

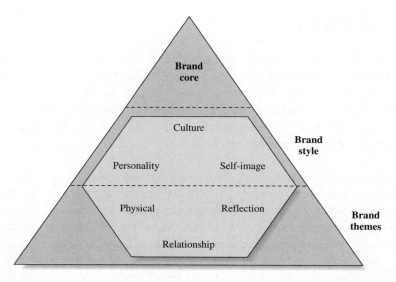

Figure 7.6 Brand Identity and the Brand Pyramid. *Source:* Adapted from Jean-Noel Kapferer, *Strategic Brand Management*, London: Kogan Page, 1997. Reprinted with permission from Kogan Page Ltd

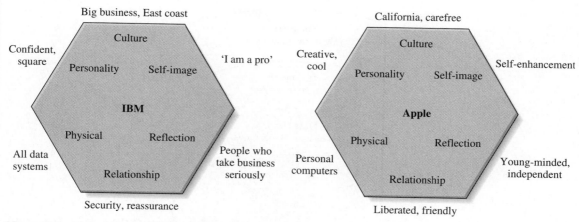

Figure 7.7   Brand Identities for IBM and Apple

ISSUES IN BRANDING

BRAND EXTENSIONS

For many years the most admired branding companies such as Procter & Gamble and Unilever employed a product branding philosophy. Each product was given an individual brand name and a unique market positioning was sought for it. This allowed each brand to be strongly differentiated and permitted the company to cover the market with individual brands targeted to each segment. It also reduced risk: a failure of one brand would not damage the rest of the business. Some Asian companies still favour this route: for example, Mitsubishi operates through a host of not obviously-connected products.

But increasingly companies are shifting to extending brands: using the *same* brand name to cover new lines in the current product category, i.e. *line extensions*, such as Diet Coke, and to new products in different categories altogether, i.e. *brand extensions*, such as Virgin radio. One major reason is to reduce marketing costs. With costs of perhaps £50 million or more to develop a new brand, it is simply too expensive to launch different brand names. Companies increasingly want to focus their brand support around a smaller number of 'power brands'. A well-known brand name also facilitates new product acceptance among consumers and distribution channels who have been satisfied with the performance of the brand in the past, and will be willing to try its new offerings.

The changing concept of a brand also encourages brand extensions. Successful marketers are seeing that brands based around a shared experience are more resilient than attribute or aspirational brands. Experience brands break the tie between the product and the brand. In buying an experience brand such as Body Shop, Virgin or Coca-Cola, consumers are not buying into a specific taste or design but rather into a particular personal philosophy. As long as the brand maintains its core values, consumers can accept its extension into different markets.

This is illustrated in Figure 7.8. Product brands are limited in the perimeter of their brand extension possibilities to line extensions around an inner core. It is difficult to imagine the Persil brand stretching much beyond the washing area or the Whiskas brand being stretched beyond cats. Consumers would find such brand names attached to chocolate bars or financial services laughable. But aspirational brands and, in particular, experience brands have fewer constraints. Often the experience brand can extend out from line extensions, to an outer core where consumers

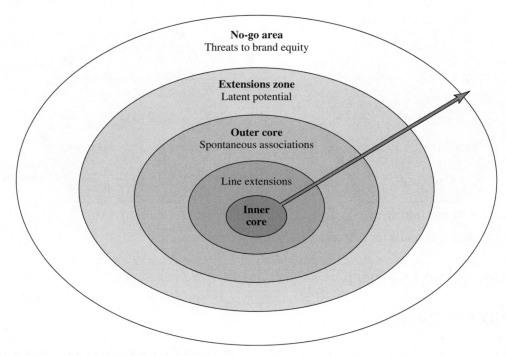

Figure 7.8   The Perimeters of Brand Extension

can make spontaneous associations with it, and then on to vast areas of latent potential that are consistent with the brand's core, yet are still outside the no-go area.

Companies such as Virgin have become highly diversified businesses. The synergies arise not from financial controls, as in the old conglomerates such as ITT or Hanson, nor from core technological competencies as at Canon or 3M, but rather from the synergies of sharing the same core brand. Until recently, strategists would frown on such diversification and advocate that companies should 'stick to their knitting'. This usually meant keeping to markets that utilised the same technological competencies. But in today's world, companies increasingly rely on networks and outsourcing arrangements to supply these technical competencies. For example, Singapore Airlines maintains Virgin's planes, MBNA supplies the Virgin credit card in the UK and T-Mobile its UK mobile phone facility. Production and technology skills are ceasing to be a constraint on the growth direction for companies with innovative ideas, strong brands and the new skill of managing networks.

The potential for brand extension is a key to the continuing value of companies. Strong brands give the company an option into new growth opportunities. Managers need to ask two questions. First, how strong are our principal brands? Second, are they principally attribute, aspirational or experience brands? Then, if the company has a strong brand, it can consider what new products could be built or acquired to leverage this brand strength.

UPDATING BRANDS

Unilever's philosophy is that brands should have an infinite life. This may be correct, but what is certainly true is that products, brand campaigns and even markets can erode quickly. What makes brands fail? The foundation of any brand is its product. If the firm allows the quality of the product to erode or become outdated or competitive, the brand will fail (see box, 'Revitalising the Jaguar Brand'). Even if the quality remains acceptable, technological advances, new competition, changing needs and new fashions invariably date products over time. No brand name can save a product that has become obsolete or irrelevant to consumers.

Revitalising the Jaguar Brand

Founded in the 1920s, Jaguar was one of the greatest car brands, admired for its sporting successes and distinctive classic styling. But Jaguar failed to match the rising product quality standards that occurred in the car industry during the 1960s and 70s. Disenchanted by the cars' unreliability and poor finish, consumers switched to other brands, such as Mercedes and BMW.

Eventually the loss-making company was acquired by Ford. The first task was to improve Jaguar's quality and technology. But the new management recognised that these were entry requirements and were not enough to restore Jaguar to health. Chairman Walter Reitzle recognised that by the late 1990s 'there were no bad cars on the market; quality is now given, not a matter of differentiation'. Technology faced the same problem. Technology in the car industry was converging as the systems-supply industry consolidated.

Today, if a car maker gets a lead on a new component, that advantage is fleeting. You might enjoy exclusivity on a breakthrough in technology for 12 months, maximum, says Reitzle. But because of the ramp-up curve involved in using technology, all your competitors will have it almost before the customer even realises that there is something new out there.

Although Jaguar continued to lose Ford money in the late 1990s, improvement in design carried on and, even as Ford sold the marque in 2007, one of its new models won a car of the year award in the UK. This is expected to be the salvation of Jaguar.

Brand presentation is also likely to get dated. The physical presentation of the product, including its packaging, colours and logos, will need to be updated if they are going to mirror current lifestyles. Similarly the brand's spokesperson and reflection need modernising as time progresses. Sometimes the brand's market may erode, requiring radical repositioning. For example, warmer winters and the spread of central heating sapped sales of Damart thermalwear. Consumers were less willing to sacrifice aesthetics for practicality. The brand had to be revitalised with new products, new themes and new relationships to fit today's fashion markets and is now a multi-channel specialist in women's clothing, including thermal wear.

If a brand, or set of brands, ceases to generate value for shareholders then management has four alternatives: repositioning, revitalisation, improving brand productivity or brand elimination.

BRAND REPOSITIONING

Repositioning the brand is a viable alternative if the brand has a weak position in an attractive market. There are several ways to do this:

- ○ **Real repositioning.** *Managers may need to update the product by improving its quality or updating its technology, functions or design. This is how Jaguar was turned around at the end of the 1990s.*

○   Augmenting the brand. *Offering additional products and services alongside the core product can increase the brand's value. Hotels have added leisure facilities, bars, and entertainment on top of their core product, accommodation.*

○   Psychological repositioning. *The company can seek to change buyers' beliefs about the quality of the product's attributes, the status of the brand or the philosophy behind it. Unfortunately, people's beliefs, once formed, are difficult to alter.*

○   Reweighting values. *Sometimes buyers can be persuaded to attach greater importance to certain values in which the brand excels. Lexus, for example, emphasised quietness as a factor in choosing a luxury car.*

○   Neglected values. *Occasionally new attributes are introduced. Unilever's new Radion detergent was positioned on the claim that it removes odours as well as dirt, an attribute not previously considered relevant in the market. The brand, however, did not have staying power (some blamed it on the strident advertising): it disappeared after 10 years by being rolled into another detergent brand, Surf.*

○   Changing preferences. *Sometimes buyers can be persuaded to change their preferences. Scare stories in the media created a preference for non-genetically modified foods and ingredients.*

○   Competitive depositioning. *In some countries it is possible to use comparative advertising to undermine the value of competitors' brands.*

BRAND REVITALISATION

Brand revitalisation is a strategy for when the brand is potentially strong but its current market is not sufficiently attractive to offer adequate profit opportunities. There are four ways forward:

○   Find new markets. *Developing new international markets has been a key means of maintaining the growth of strong brands such as Coca-Cola, McDonald's and Starbucks after they reached maturity in their US home market.*

○   Enter new segments. *Developing new segments is one of the most important ways to expand the market for a brand. Growing awareness in the market and falling prices are important stimuli, particularly in hi-tech markets. Line extensions are a flexible way to push into new market segments.*

○   Find new applications. *Companies can find new applications for the brand. The classic example is Arm & Hammer Baking Soda, which increased its sales significantly over the past 25 years by finding new applications as a deodoriser and cleaner for refrigerators, sinks, animals and even in toothpaste.*

○   Increase the usage rate. *The average consumption rate can be increased, for example by making the product easier to use (instant tea), reducing the disincentives to use (decaffeinated coffee), providing incentives for use (frequent flyer discounts), and finding new ways to increase the quantity consumed (large bottles).*

IMPROVING BRAND PRODUCTIVITY

When the market matures it makes sense to take a harder look at profitability. First, costs – fixed and variable – can often be cut. However, management must recognise that reducing marketing spend may well lead to a long-term erosion of the brand's market share. Second, cash flow can be boosted by reducing working and fixed capital requirements. For mature products it can pay to outsource production to contract manufacturers with lower cost structures. Third, raising prices will often boost short-term profits, even if volume declines. For example, if a brand has a contribution margin of 50 per cent and an operating margin of 8 per cent, then pushing up prices by 10 per cent will boost operating profits by a half, even if volume declines by 10 per cent.

Finally, in mature markets it will often be possible to reduce the number of brands and product lines in the portfolio. Cutting off the tail of low-volume items will have a disproportionate benefit on working capital, with little volume loss. Nevertheless, all these measures produce benefits that are essentially short-term and one-off. Management needs to simulate their long-term effects and value implications to check that long-term results are not being sacrificed.

BRAND ELIMINATION

Many companies have too many brands. Sometimes it is because there is no longer a viable market for the brand and investing in repositioning or revitalising it does not look to be economic. Another common cause is where the company has grown by acquisitions and mergers. This frequently results in the company having a portfolio of overlapping and competing brands with no strategic rationale. With too many brands it then becomes impossible to support them adequately and marketing spend is spread too thinly to enable any of them to become genuine power brands. The result is that market share is undermined by smaller rivals which can focus their marketing investment behind a single brand to obtain critical mass. A 1999 report by KPMG found that two-thirds of mergers and acquisitions resulted in a net loss of market share and more than 80 per cent led to erosion of shareholder value.[10]

Companies such as Procter & Gamble and Colgate-Palmolive have shown that consolidating overlapping brands can cut costs, increase market share and boost shareholder value. This is illustrated in Figure 7.9 where a company consolidates two of its competing brands into one new brand. Market share by volume increases from 40 to 42 per cent because marketing spend is focused, effectively doubling the absolute level of brand support. Greater distribution power allows it to cut the level of trade discounts, which adds 1 per cent to the net price. Cost of goods is reduced because of greater buying power, and duplicated overheads are stripped out, resulting in a doubling of profits.

What prevents companies consolidating brands is fear over the loss of sales. How serious this problem will be depends upon the degree of brand overlap and how the company implements the consolidation. Consolidating two

	Initial P & L		New P & L
	Brand A	Brand B	New brand
Market share %	20	20	42
Cost of goods sold %	50	52	45
Gross margin %	50	48	55
Marketing %	25	25	25
Overheads %	15	15	12
Operating margin %	10	8	18

Figure 7.9   Realising Value through Brand Elimination

brands into one is easier where the brands serve similar market segments, have overlapping brand images and when one is relatively weak. The problem is more complex where both are strong brands and they are serving different segments or distribution channels.

In implementing consolidation a company has four routes to choose from:

○ **Phasing out the brand** *is the appropriate approach if the brand to be eliminated has substantial brand value and a significant base of customers. This policy keeps the old brand as long as necessary but focuses promotion and development on the new brand. Effectively it seeks to reduce the cost of carrying duplicate brands, with the objective of eliminating the overlap over time.*

○ **Quick kill** *means the immediate dropping of a brand name. This is a high-risk strategy but may become necessary if competition is ratcheting up the cost of supporting brands. It requires a very heavy investment in marketing and trade support, if a loss of market share is to be avoided.*

○ **Co-branding** *is the most common transition strategy. Both brand names are kept on the new brand, giving consumers time to adjust. When Whirlpool bought Philips' household appliances business, the brand was marketed as Philips Whirlpool for the first six years.*

○ **Sale.** *Procter & Gamble and Unilever have sold off the lower performing 'tail' of brands and some specialists have now entered this secondary market. Sometimes the competition authorities require sales, as Diageo had to dispose of Dewar's whisky, Bombay gin and Malibu.*

TAKING THE BRAND INTERNATIONAL

Taking a brand into overseas markets is an obvious strategy for enhancing growth and shareholder value. Indeed, in today's globally competitive environment it is an essential strategy to achieve scale economies and to justify the investment in the new products that will ensure the continuity of the company.

In developing overseas markets a company can pursue one of three strategies. The first is *multinational* branding. This means developing different brands for each country and tailoring the marketing mix to local markets. This has been the approach broadly followed by Unilever, for example, which markets its brands under a variety of names and product formulations. The second approach is *global* branding where the brand name is standardised and the strategy is as far as possible similar in each country. Coca-Cola, McDonald's and Microsoft are obvious examples. The intermediate approach is *regional* branding, whereby the company tries to build common brands and strategies in certain areas, for example in the European Union or the Americas. Ford has pursued such an approach in the past.

LOCAL BRANDS

The primary case for local brands rests on the great differences in language, culture and market conditions that still exist between most counties. A brand of breakfast cereal like Sanitarium that has meaning and broad appeal in Australia will rarely have the same resonance in Belgium or Finland. It seems obvious that an approach that designs the brand identity to the local language, preferences, traditions, climate and competition will do better. Another advantage of local branding is that it facilitates higher prices to be charged in less competitive markets. With common branding, parallel imports makes differential pricing more difficult and this can lead to a significant loss of operating profit. A final important reason for local autonomy is that it encourages initiative, pride and responsibility for performance. Nothing destroys commitment like a faceless headquarters second-guessing local decisions and imposing strategies that the local management has not participated in developing.

GLOBAL AND REGIONAL BRANDS

However, in most leading companies there has been a significant shift towards regional and global branding. The drive to eliminate duplicate costs has been one reason. The cost of producing a TV commercial can easily amount to £1 million. The advertising agency McCann-Erickson claims to have saved Coca-Cola almost $100 million over a period of 20 years by producing commercials with international appeal. A global strategy facilitates a faster international launch, which reduces the danger of the brand being pre-empted by competitors. It also enhances shareholder value by accelerating cash flow.

On top of this, a number of forces in today's information society encourage a move towards global or regional branding. These include the growth of international business, the emergence of global media such as CNN and SkyTV, the explosion of tourism and international business travel, and the development of common standards like the Internet and GSM. All of these encourage the emergence of international lifestyles, or more accurately the emergence of market segments that transcend geographical boundaries. Scientists in different countries want the same brands of equipment, teenagers the same clothing, and those with aspirational lifestyles the same symbols as their peers abroad. Finally, the pace of technological progress and innovation has meant that people are increasingly spending on new products that have fewer cultural heritages to hinder global branding.

Global brands can make more efficient use of the new international media and the Internet. They can also uniquely exploit the growing popularity of international events such as the World Cup, the Olympics and Formula One, and the sponsorship of international stars such as Tiger Woods, Madonna or Manchester United. International brands often also obtain a premium status from the glamour they possess. Finally, an international reputation facilitates brand extensions and entry into new markets. Global brands often have a stature that gives customers confidence in trying their offerings.

CONSTRAINTS ON GLOBAL BRANDING

The constraints on global branding are external and internal. Some markets are still so idiosyncratic that global brands have limited potential. Often a brand name does not make sense in another market. Snuggles fabric softener has to be translated as Cajoline in France, Kuschelweich in Germany, Cocolino in Italy, and so on. Culture and tradition also prevent common approaches. For example, a basic product like cheese plays different roles in different countries: in Holland it is mostly consumed at breakfast; in France it is served after the main course at dinner; in the UK it is mostly consumed at lunch in sandwiches. Different laws, climates and traditions can all create constraints on a common brand identity.

Factors internal to the organisation also have an important influence on the development of global brands. A key factor is history. The first international companies were European and were well established by the beginning of the 20th century. Then the slowness of international travel and rudimentary international communications forced these companies to delegate decision-making to the local markets. Distance made central control from European headquarters simply impractical. Many companies like Unilever and Nestlé have maintained much of this pattern of *multinational* marketing. Global branding is much more associated with US companies and later the Japanese. US companies, which became prominent internationally after the Second World War, pursued an *ethnocentric* approach – they sold to a willing overseas market the products that had been successful in the home market, usually with only the minimum necessary adaptation. In the 1960s, Japanese companies such as Toyota and Sony introduced the first real *global branding* strategies. These were uniform products with a global brand name, designed to match the needs of international markets.

In recent years, the tendency has been to shift towards what is called *transnational* marketing. This might be loosely defined as seeking to standardise those elements of the brand where this is possible, but recognising that often it makes sense to adapt to local conditions. Generally this approach leads to asymmetrical, pragmatic strategies; companies will invest in adapting to local conditions in the biggest markets such as the USA, Japan and Germany, but not in smaller countries. Traditional brands that are part of the culture and heritage of a market will be left as they are. New products, particularly those in new categories or using new technology, will be much more geared to a global approach.

The elements of the brand's marketing mix also vary in the degree to which they can be standardised. Generally the core product is standardised across countries. Product functionality and use (e.g. how people listen to music or drive a bulldozer) tend to be fairly similar internationally. Also economies of scale are important here, as product development and manufacture are high-investment areas. The features of the basic brand – design, packaging, logo and name – can also often be standardised across countries, if planned systematically.

At the next level of branding – the positioning and communications – the difficulties begin to mount as culture, attitudes, language and economics impinge on the interpretation of the brand's meaning. The degree of standardisation possible varies with the market and the product. National values and traditions are still very important in food, but less so in electronics. Culture is less important in youth and more affluent markets than it is in mature, low-income ones. Moving further down the marketing chain to selling, promotion and distribution, these decisions are invariably specified locally because of sharp differences that normally occur in market and institutional characteristics across countries.

The shift from national to transnational branding and marketing is reshaping how companies are managed. Many of the biggest multinationals such as Ford, Unilever and Procter & Gamble have restructured to create international product divisions to replace the old country business units. Strategic decisions about brands are increasingly taken with a view to leveraging their full international potential and looking for global efficiencies in production and marketing. Most companies have sought to avoid building large central bureaucracies and rather aimed to use teams of local managers cooperating to develop international branding strategy. Often this has been accompanied by making certain countries lead managers for specific brands.

CONTROLLING THE BRAND FRANCHISE

Today competition is not between single companies but between networks. A network consists of all those companies in the supply chain that contribute components, services or knowledge to the ultimate product bought by the final customer. So Hewlett-Packard and its network of suppliers, partners and retailers compete with those of Dell to design and deliver desirable brands of personal computer to consumers. Tesco's network competes with that of Sainsbury to develop and execute the best retail concept.

WHO CONTROLS THE BRAND?

All companies participate in networks. A key issue to participants in a network is who controls the brand. In general, the participant that controls the brand that consumers value makes the greatest economic profit. Traditionally the manufacturer, such as Ford, IBM or GE, has usually controlled the brand. The manufacturer normally tries to commoditise suppliers' inputs to push down costs and stimulate competition among them. But manufacturers do not always succeed and sometimes the supplier succeeds in wresting brand power from, or at least sharing it with, the manufacturer. Intel and Microsoft are striking examples of this phenomenon. The images of Intel and Microsoft are so powerful among final consumers that computer manufacturers are forced to purchase their components. The result is that much of the profit in the industry has migrated to these two component suppliers.

The distribution channels – wholesalers, retailers or the Internet – can also control the brand power. One of the major trends in the past few decades has been the growth of retailer own-label brands. The large supermarket groups have succeeded in substituting their own brands for manufacturers' brands over an increasing percentage of their shelf space. Again, this has led to a transfer of value from manufacturer to retailer as the former's output has become increasingly commoditised. Today e-commerce has brought new participants to the struggle for who controls the consumer brand franchise. On the one hand, e-commerce has enabled the manufacturer to restore the power of the manufacturer by allowing it to 'disintermediate' – cut out the retailer and go direct to the end consumer, as Dell did so successfully in the 1990s. On the other hand, e-commerce has brought in a new breed of retailer like Amazon and eToys that can offer customers product ranges far superior to any that have been offered by retailers in the past. Other threats to traditional brand hegemony are the Internet navigators, including search engines such as Google and Yahoo!, evaluators such as Consumer Reports, databases such as Auto Trader and software programs such as Quicken. All of these can become, and indeed are becoming, the brands in which more consumers are placing their trust. When this happens, power in the network changes in favour of the organisation that controls the most trusted brand.

The implications of a loss of brand control are severe. If a company's product is seen as a commodity or a mere label it loses its ability to drive profitable growth. Customers will buy on price and there will be no barriers to switching to alternative suppliers. This is what happened to the personal computer manufacturers when they effectively ceded brand power upstream to the suppliers of their operating system and microprocessors. Computers became little more than low margin commodities while their suppliers, Microsoft and Intel, became immensely profitable. The same problem occurred with many textile and grocery goods manufacturers that became own-label suppliers to powerful branded retail groups. The enhanced bargaining power of the retailer often enabled them to appropriate all the economic profit of the manufacturers.

MANUFACTURING OR BRANDING

Companies increasingly have to choose between investing heavily in brands or becoming contract manufacturers for other branded businesses. The problem facing many firms is that they have got 'stuck in the middle' as the tide of global competition has washed away established relationships.

Contract manufacturing has become a rapidly growing area of business as companies increasingly outsource production. But global competition and global sourcing have made contract manufacturing much more demanding than it was in the past. To be a profitable contract manufacturer, a company has to minimise its cost structure on a global scale. Generally, this will mean locating production facilities in countries with the cheapest facilities and lowest labour costs, or where valuable resources are most abundant. It means minimising overheads and tight operational control.

Developing a strategy based on building strong brands leads to a different philosophy and organisation. A contract manufacturer focuses on production and costs; a branded business focuses on marketing and innovation. A contract manufacturer produces to a customer's specifications; a branded company has to discover what specifications consumers will want. The former has very low marketing costs; the latter needs to invest heavily in marketing to understand consumers and to build and communicate the brand. The personnel of a branded goods company have to be close to the market; those of the contract manufacturer have to be located where costs are minimised.

Given these completely different orientations, it is not surprising that trying to be both a low-cost manufacturer and a sophisticated marketer is a strategy that is difficult to make work. The danger is that in striving to be both, the company's philosophy and organisation becomes fatally compromised. It lacks, on the one hand, the cost structure to compete with global contract manufacturers and, on the other, the creativity and investment in branding to compete with those companies like Virgin and Amazon that focus entirely on innovation, marketing and branding.

ORGANISING THE BRAND PORTFOLIO

When a company goes beyond marketing one product, it has to decide how its products and brands should be related. It can market all its additional products under the same umbrella brand, as for example Canon does with its cameras, printers and office equipment, or it can do the opposite, developing a separate brand name for each new product, as Procter & Gamble has traditionally done. In between there are various other alternatives, including line brands, range brands and source branding strategies.[11]

A dilemma arises because management has to balance three partly conflicting goals. One goal is to differentiate the product from others it already markets. Generally, it only makes sense to introduce another product if it will do something differently, or appeal to a different group of customers. From this point of view, separate brand names are attractive. The second goal is to leverage the strengths and associations of the current brand name. This implies an advantage in using the existing brand name. Thirdly, cost factors have to be considered: the objective is not to maximise sales but to increase long-run economic profits. This again leads to an orientation to sharing brand names.

The right brand architecture should result in a system that makes sense to consumers. The branding system should indicate to them how products are differentiated from each other. Managers inside the company should also understand the logic of the system and when a new product should have a separate name or when it should share an existing name. Finally, the architecture should facilitate the growth in value of the brand portfolio as a whole, by enabling it to be effectively communicated and promoted.

BRAND ARCHITECTURE

The main difference between branding strategies is in the way they make the trade-off between differentiation and shared identity. There are six main brand strategies:

❍   **Product brands** *exist where the company assigns a unique name and positioning to each of its products. So, in the detergents market Procter & Gamble in the UK has Ariel, Bold, Dreft, Fairy and Lenor brands,* *each with its own target market segment and differential advantage. The Accor Group has developed multiple brands of hotels each with its own positioning strategy: Novotel, Ibis, Formula 1, Sofitel etc. The corporate name plays no role in the marketing of the brands to consumers: the focus is entirely on differentiation rather than shared identity.*

○ **Line brands** *are when a company has several complementary products sharing the same brand concept. For example, rather than individual product brands, L'Oreal sells a shampoo, hair spray, gel and lacquer under the L'Oreal Paris line of hair products. Selling a brand line rather than individual brands can reinforce the brand's selling power and reduce marketing costs.*

○ **Range brands** *include a broader array of products than with line brands, but still limit the extension of the brand name to the same area of competence. For example, Nestlé uses the name Lean Cuisine for its range of frozen food products in North America and Australia; Heinz uses the Weight Watchers Smart Ones brand for its diet range in the US.*

○ **Source brands** *are double-branded with a corporate or range name plus a product brand name. Examples are Kellogg's Corn Flakes, Castrol GTX and Johnnie Walker Black Label. The corporate name conveys identity and associations; the product brand focuses it to a particular segment.*

○ **Endorsing brand** *is a weaker association of the corporate name with the product brand name. Here the product brand is the dominant name; the umbrella endorsement merely aims to guarantee the brand's quality. Nestlé, General Motors and Johnson & Johnson follow this approach in endorsing, for example, their brands Kit-Kat, Opel and Pledge, respectively. An endorsing brand strategy is often an intermediate step as companies seek to shift away from product branding to range or umbrella branding strategies.*

○ **Umbrella brands** *are when one brand supports several products in very different markets. For example, Philips sells computers, phones, hi-fi, televisions, electric shavers and office equipment using the same name. This is the opposite strategy to product branding. Here the focus is on shared identity at the expense of differentiation. The main advantages are sharing brand-building costs. The main threat is what is called the 'rubber band effect' – the more the brand is stretched across different categories, the more likely the brand's identity is going to be weakened until its credibility and meaning are broken.*

CHOOSING A BRANDING STRATEGY

Competing companies often adopt quite different branding strategies. In the hotel market, Accor uses product branding, while Holiday Inn uses source branding. What are the criteria for deciding the right approach?

History again plays a big role. Many firms would not have the current number of product brands if they were starting afresh. Companies such as Procter & Gamble adopted a product branding approach in an era when competition was less fierce and margins were high enough to cover the heavy marketing costs involved in this strategy. Change today is difficult. For example, the Procter & Gamble name has no equity with consumers and so the type of umbrella branding favoured by Sony or Virgin is just not practicable.

A second factor is the power and type of brand. An umbrella or source branding strategy is not possible if the brand does not have strong added values, if it is little more than a label. Here, if a new product is thought to have potential, it is best launched under an individual brand name. Experience brands usually have more potential for umbrella or source branding than do attribute or aspirational brands. For example, British Airways aims to be an aspirational brand, so when it launched a budget brand in 1998 it did so under the name Go (since merged with EasyJet) in order not to risk weakening its core values. In contrast, Virgin is an experience brand – 'us against them' – with core values that shift easily into a budget offer. However, if the brand is exceptionally strong it is possible for aspirational brands to stretch downwards as long as the new product's status is indicated. For example, Daimler indicates the positioning of the different Mercedes models by affixing letters such as S, E, C and A to the appropriate ranges.

If a product is truly innovative in its attributes or concept, then product branding is attractive to highlight its originality. BP wisely decided not to risk diluting the equity in the Castrol brand by source branding when it was acquired. Product branding is also a way of reducing risks when there are hazards with a product's technology or side effects, which could be the subject of damaging publicity. Pharmaceutical companies selling novel medicines invariably use product branding.

A third factor is the attractiveness of the market. Developing separate brands is hugely expensive and most of the costs are fixed. Such an investment can only generate an economic return if the revenue and profits available are large enough. Umbrella branding can be the most effective way to enter smaller markets or where the opportunities to gain a high market share are limited. However, note that there is a risk that umbrella branding might dilute the main brand, and there could be conflicts with other brands under the umbrella. On the other hand, the other brands under the umbrella may help. Finally, product branding may be more expensive but also lead in the long term to higher profits and marketing assets.

VALUING THE BRAND

The issue of whether brands should appear as assets on the balance sheet has become controversial but is, as we shall see, irrelevant. A spate of hostile take-overs and asset stripping of brand-rich companies led to the accusation that, because brands were excluded from the balance sheet, these companies were undervalued and easy prey to corporate raiders. Conventional accounting treats investment in brand-building as costs to be set against current profits. The treatment of brands acquired externally was more equivocal and differed in countries around the world. Equated to the 19th century concept of 'goodwill', the cost might be carried permanently on the balance sheet (if the value was maintained or amortised against profits over a number of years, or written-off against shareholder funds). This need not divert us now because brand values can be annually reported by companies to shareholders in the narrative sections of their annual reports, if not the balance sheet sections. Note that the valuations of brands, internally grown or acquired, can *never* be shown on balance sheets but only the acquisition costs, downwardly adjusted if value has declined.

So, balance sheets apart, we still have the issue of whether companies should (a) value their brands and (b) report those values to their shareholders.

THE PROS AND CONS OF VALUATION

The pros and cons of brand valuation largely reflect the views of enthusiasts and conservatives. The conservatives argue against brands being reported. First, any valuation of brands is highly subjective. Different methods and different valuers will give very different valuations. Second, it may be difficult to separate the earnings that are created from the brand name from those generated by the company's other tangible and intangible assets. Can one really separate the value created by the Cadbury's brand from the values created by its other intangible assets [Note: the product differentiation and therefore the quality is part of the brand] including specialist skills and long-standing supply chain relationships? Third, the arbitrary assumptions needed to come up with brand valuations would make reported value open to the criticism of being mere 'window dressing', devoid of a factual basis. Finally, it is argued that brand valuations are unnecessary since market values demonstrate that investors make their own forecasts of the future cash generating value of the business that clearly take into account all its tangible and intangible assets. It is better that investors take responsibility for their own judgements than for the company's accountants to publish their subjective estimates of the future.

The positive case for valuing brands can be summarised under four headings. First, there is a clear conceptual case for treating brands as assets. Strong brands do offer their owners an enhanced and more secure cash flow than they would have without the brand. This is because they create a greater degree of customer preference and loyalty than weak – or non-branded – products. Second, new methodologies permit brand earnings to be separated and valued in ways that are conceptually sound and practical to use. Third, the financial authorities, such as the Accounting Standards Board in the UK, now recommend the inclusion of brand information in annual reports in the interests of transparency and forward-looking information. Finally, there are many situations where brand valuations are not a matter of choice; their use is a business requirement.

USES OF BRAND VALUATION

In recent years brand valuations have become essential for a wide variety of purposes.

○ **Mergers and acquisitions.** *Up to 90 per cent of the price an acquirer pays for a branded goods company is represented by intangible assets, most of these being brands. Brand valuations play an important role in assessing whether such acquisitions can be justified.*

○ **Investor relations.** *Companies such as Diageo and L'Oreal state as their central objective the creation of a portfolio of powerful brands. Brand valuations are an important way in which these companies can signal their strengths to the stock market.*

○ **Internal management.** *Brand valuations are being used internally to judge the performance of different business units. They also encourage managers involved in budgeting decisions to assess the long-term impact on brand performance and not just the short-run effects of decisions on profits.*

○ **Licensing and franchising.** *Companies often allow subsidiaries or third parties to use their brand name. An accurate valuation of the brand is necessary to arrive at a fair royalty rate.*

○ **Securitised borrowing.** *As brands have become increasingly recognised as valuable assets, companies have been able to use their valuations as specific backing for loans.*

○ **Legal arguments.** *Brand valuations are often used in legal cases involving such issues as damage to the brand caused by piracy, or in asset valuations for insolvency proceedings.*

○ **Tax planning.** *Some tax authorities demand companies charge royalties to their foreign affiliates for the use of their brand names or valuations as evidence of arm's length pricing.*

KEY ISSUES IN BRAND VALUATION

Any brand valuation methodology has to deal with three issues.

1. **Forecasting free cash flow.** The value of an asset is given by the net present value of its future free cash flow. This means forecasts have to be made of sales, operating profits, actual taxes to be paid, and net investments

in working capital and fixed assets. It is important that the forecast only refers to the sales of the brand being valued. If unbranded goods or other brands are also being produced their figures must be excluded.

2. **Calculating the brand value added.** This is a two-step process of identifying first the incremental cash flow generated by the intangible assets of the business, then separating the proportion of this additional cash flow that can be attributed to value provided by the brand name. In practice we see logical inconsistencies where brand valuers claim to separate the profits due to the product (goods and/or services) from those attributable to the brand name alone but then lump the two together because of the difficulties of making that separation. The problem can be resolved by defining the brand to include the underlying product(s).

3. **Determining the discount factor.** Future cash flows have to be discounted to their present day value. The discount rate that should be used depends upon the vulnerability and volatility of the brand's cash flow.

ALTERNATIVE VALUATION APPROACHES

Assets can be valued using different assumptions and methods. If assets are being valued for tax purposes the taxpayer will want to use assumptions that will produce a low value. Someone selling an asset will take an opposite approach. The method may also vary with the purpose of the valuation: the method that may be acceptable in a legal case may not be useful in an acquisition analysis. There are four main 'traditional' brand valuation methods, as described next, and the modern approach, based on estimating the discounted value of future brand cash flow, is described in detail in the following section.

1. **Cost-based valuation.** This values a brand on what it cost to create. Here past advertising and other brand-building expenditures are converted into today's prices and added together. Such a method is sometimes used in legal cases to calculate compensation. But the fundamental problem with this method is that historical costs bear no relation to current values. In theory a brand could also be valued on a replacement cost basis, i.e. what it would cost to recreate now. But the problem is that a strong brand is by definition unique, so finding its replacement value is not normally a practical exercise. This is rarely, if at all, used.

2. **Market-based valuation.** This values the brand on the basis of recent sales of comparable brands or businesses. For example, if a comparable company was sold at a multiple of four times book value, then this multiple can be used to value the current business. Tangible assets are then deducted from the implied stock market value to arrive at the value of intangible assets, and the proportion of these intangibles represented by the brand is estimated. The problems with this approach are that in practice it is complicated by companies often having several brands as well as some unbranded production, and that finding comparable companies and brands is very difficult.

3. **Royalty relief valuation.** This values the brand by estimating what the company would have had to pay in royalties to a third party if it did not own the brand name. The theoretical royalties that would be paid in the future are then discounted to arrive at the net present value of the brand. A number of the top accountancy firms regard this as the most effective valuation method. One problem with the approach is determining the royalty percentage to be applied to forecast sales. In practice, detailed information about rates is difficult to obtain, and they vary considerably according to arrangements about using patents, copyrights and shared marketing costs, as well as with the expected profits and market circumstances. Rates also tend to vary according to the industry and country being licensed. This method is used in legal and tax cases.

4. **Economic use valuation.** This values the brand's net contribution to the business by using a representative multiple of historic earnings attributable to the brand. So, for example, if a weighted average of the past

three years post-tax brand earnings was estimated at £15 million and the earnings multiple is 10, then the brand is valued at £150 million. This was the original method used by Interbrand but most companies now use discounted cash flow. The basic problem with this method is that historical earnings produce brand valuations that are highly volatile because they are so dependent on profits earned in the year the valuation is made.

DISCOUNTED CASH FLOW VALUATION

Like the economic use method, the discounted cash flow (DCF) method estimates the return shareholders receive from owning the brand name. The advantage of this method is that it mirrors the approach investors use to value a company's assets and so it links brand values to share values. The approach deals explicitly with each of the three issues in brand valuation: forecasting cash flow, separating the value created by the brand from that attributable to tangible and other intangible assets, and identifying the appropriate discount rate. This approach to brand valuation was popularised by the Interbrand consultancy.[12]

FORECASTING CASH FLOW

As with standard shareholder value analysis, the approach starts with managers forecasting sales and operating margins over a reasonable planning period, usually 5–10 years. Care has to be taken to eliminate any sales and earnings due to other brands or unbranded products. Cash flows after the planning period are estimated by a continuing value approach, usually the perpetuity method, which assumes that the brand continues to earn its cost of capital in perpetuity. The first two rows of Table 7.6 show forecast sales and operating earnings for an illustrative brand.

Table 7.6   Valuing the Brand (£ million)

Year	Base	1	2	3	4	5
Sales	250.0	262.5	275.6	289.4	303.9	319.1
Operating profits (15%)	37.5	39.4	41.3	43.4	45.6	47.9
Tangible capital employed	125.0	131.3	137.8	144.7	151.9	159.5
Charge for capital @ 5%	6.3	6.6	6.9	7.2	7.6	8.0
Economic value added	31.3	32.8	34.5	36.2	38.0	39.9
Brand value added @ 70%	21.9	23.0	24.1	25.3	26.6	27.9
Tax (30%)	6.6	6.9	7.2	7.6	8.0	8.4
Post-tax brand earnings	15.3	16.1	16.9	17.7	18.6	19.5
Discount factor ($r = 15\%$)	1.0	0.87	0.76	0.66	0.57	0.5
Discounted cash flow	15.3	14.0	12.8	11.7	10.6	9.7
Cumulative present value						58.8
Present value of residual						64.8
Brand value						123.5

ESTIMATING BRAND EARNINGS

There are two approaches: direct and by subtraction. The direct method relies on the widespread modern internal practice of attributing profits both to brands and to customers. The double counting involved in that can be simply resolved for the combined profits. The 'by subtraction' process is a two-step approach: (1) separate earnings due to tangible assets from those due to intangible assets, and (2) separate intangible earnings into those attributable to the brand name and those attributable to other intangibles such as patents, special skills or monopolistic advantages.

- ○ *Earnings on intangibles. These are the residual earnings after the return on tangible assets has been deducted from total operating profits. First, the tangible assets employed in the business – for example, plant, warehousing, creditors and stock – are calculated. These assets are valued at their realisable market value. Because they are included at realisable values ownership risk is minimised, so a reasonable return is the risk free borrowing rate, usually taken as the yield on ten-year government bonds, currently around 5 per cent. Operating earnings less the capital charge gives economic value added. This residual profit is the return on intangible assets.*

- ○ *Earnings from the brand. The next step is to judge the percentage of these intangible earnings that can be attributed to the brand. For some consumer goods, such as perfume or fashions, the brand is the major intangible item. For others, such as speciality chemicals or prescription pharmaceuticals, patents, technical know-how and personal relationships with key customers are more important than the brand name. In other words, they would sell almost as well under another name. Interbrand's approach involves two distinct steps. First, analyse the brand and its market to identify and rate the importance of the key strategic business drivers. Second, assess the extent to which each business driver is dependent upon the brand. If the driver would be just as effective without the brand, then the brand makes no contribution.*

Table 7.7 illustrates the approach for Esso's retail petrol business in the UK in the 1990s, where the branding index was estimated at 26 per cent.[13] This percentage varies by country. In this case it was 43 per cent in Chile and 37 per cent in the USA. It also varies by activity. For example, the brand name was more important in lubricants than petrol, and higher in the retail market than in marine. By applying the weighted average branding index to residual earnings, brand earnings were calculated. In the example of Table 7.6, the branding index indicates that the brand contributes 70 per cent of residual earnings.

DETERMINING THE DISCOUNT FACTOR

Future brand earnings have to be discounted to arrive at their present value. The discount factor depends upon the volatility and vulnerability of these future earnings. Interbrand has developed a technique called the 'brand strength index' to determine the discount rate. A brand is rated on seven attributes that are taken to indicate the strength of the brand. Each attribute has the maximum score shown in parentheses.

1. **Market** (10). Brands in stable growing markets with strong barriers to entry are the most attractive. So food brands will score higher than high-tech brands on this attribute.

2. **Stability** (15). Long-established brands that command consumer loyalty score better than new ones, or brands that have been erratically managed in the past.

3. **Leadership** (25). Strong brand leaders score better than brands with small market shares.

4. **Internationality** (25). Brands that have proven international acceptance and appeal are inherently stronger than national brands.

Table 7.7   The Branding Index: The UK Retail Petrol Market

Strategic value driver	Weighting	Relative importance (%)	Dependence on the brand (%)	Role of branding (%)
Location	100	31	0	0
Network	40	12	80	10
Price	80	25	0	0
Design of site	10	3	60	2
Cleanliness of site	10	3	40	1
Car services	10	3	20	1
Other services	20	6	20	1
Promotions	20	6	20	1
Advertising	15	5	100	5
Product quality	10	3	100	3
Credit cards	5	2	40	1
Premium petrol	5	2	40	1
Brand index	325	100		26

Source: The World's Greatest Brands. Reprinted with permission from Interbrand.

5.   **Trend** (10). Brands demonstrating consistent volume growth score higher.

6.   **Support** (10). Brands that have a record of receiving systematic and focused investment have a stronger franchise.

7.   **Protection** (5). Brands with registered trademarks and strong legal protection score higher.

Brands can score up to a maximum of 100 points. The higher the strength score, the less risk is attached to the brand and the lower should be the discount rate. Interbrand has developed an 'S' curve chart with the brand strength score on the y-axis and the discount rate on the x-axis. So a perfect brand (scoring 100) has a discount rate of 5 per cent, somewhat higher than the long-term real rate of return on a risk-free investment. An average brand with a score of 50 has a discount rate of 15 per cent.

A variation of the Interbrand approach, called 'Brand Beta Analysis' has been proposed by Haigh.[14] This calculates the appropriate discount rate from four factors:

1.   **Risk-free rate of return,** taken as the 10-year government bond yield.

2.   **Equity risk premium,** the extra return investors expect for investing in companies rather than 'risk-free' government bonds.

3.   **Specific market sector risk** adjusts the equity premium. For example, the equity risk premium is generally lower in a stable food market than in a high-tech sector.

4.   **Brand risk profile** is then used to adjust the average discount rate to the vulnerability of the specific brand.

For the brand risk profile Haigh presents a scoring method, based on a list of factors analogous to the brand strength index, to produce a brand beta score, which is again marked out of 100. For example, Coca-Cola can expect a much lower risk rating than, say, Virgin Cola. The beta score varies from 0 for a perfect brand to 2 for an unbranded product. In the example of Table 7.6, the risk-free rate at the time is 5 per cent, the average equity risk premium is 7 per cent, the specific market sector risk is averaged at 1.0, and it is a relatively new brand with an above-average beta calculated at 1.43, so the discount rate is then $5 + (7 \times 1.0) \times 1.43 = 15$ per cent.

The brand is valued in Table 7.6 at £123.5 million. Of its forecast total earnings, approximately 17 per cent is attributed to earnings on tangible assets, 83 per cent to intangible assets, and 58 per cent to the associations created by the brand name. Of the £123.5 million brand value, £58.8 million was due to cash flow added in the planning period; the remainder was its continuing value at the end of the period. This continuing value is estimated by the familiar perpetuity method, described in Chapter 2. The continuing value reflects the fact that well-managed brands can last indefinitely.

SUMMARY

1.   Today a firm's intangible assets are more important than its balance sheet assets in creating value for customers and shareholders. In many companies, the brands represent one of the most valuable of these intangible assets.

2.   Brands create value for customers by assisting them to reduce risks and by simplifying the choice process. Brands offer customers confirmation of their quality, status or the promise of shared experiences.

3.   Brands create value for shareholders by increasing the level of cash flow, accelerating its timing, extending its duration or reducing the cost of capital.

4.   Brand identities once communicated have to be periodically updated by brand repositioning and revitalisation. Improving brand productivity and eliminating redundant brands can also sometimes increase shareholder value.

5.   Today companies compete within a network of suppliers, distributors and partners. A critical issue is who controls the brand. Value in a network tends to migrate towards the organisation that holds the brand name.

6.   Brands can be valued using discounted cash flow analysis. This links brand values directly to the company's own market value.

REVIEW QUESTIONS

1.   Describe how brands create value for customers.
2.   How do brands create value for shareholders?
3.   How are successful brands built?
4.   Show how brand extensions can be a means of creating value.
5.   Describe how a multiproduct organisation can structure its portfolio to control the costs and maximise the effectiveness of its brands.
6.   Describe how brands can be valued. What uses can brand valuations have? How confident can you be in a brand valuation?

NOTES ON CHAPTER 7

[1] Millward Brown Optimor, BrandZ Portfolio Performance, 4 April 2008.

[2] Rajendra K. Srivastava, Tasadduk A. Shervani and Liam Fahey, Marketing, business processes and shareholder value: an organizationally embedded view of marketing activities and the discipline of marketing, *Journal of Marketing* **63**, Special issue 1999, 168–179.

[3] Raymond Perrier, ed., *Brand Valuation*, London: Interbrand and Premier Books: 1997, p. 44.

[4] John Bartle, 'The advertising contribution', in Leslie Butterfield (ed.), *Excellence in Advertising*, Oxford: Butterworth-Heinemann, 1999.

[5] Quoted from Leslie de Chernatony and Malcolm H.B. McDonald, *Creating Powerful Brands*, Oxford: Butterworth-Heinemann, 1992, p. 9.

[6] Simon Broadbent, Diversity in categories, brands and strategies, *Journal of Brand Management*, **2**, August, 1994, 9–18.

[7] Robert A. Buzzell and Barney T. Gale, *The PIMS Principles: Linking Strategy to Performance*. New York: Free Press, 1987; The year of the brand, *The Economist*, 25 December 1988, 93.

[8] See, for example, Larry Downes and Chunka Mui, *Unleashing the Killer App: Digital Strategies for Market Dominance*, Boston, MA: Harvard Business School Press, 1998.

[9] Jean-Noel Kapferer, *Strategic Brand Management*, 2nd edn, London: Kogan Page, 1997.

[10] KPMG, *A Report Card on Cross-Border Mergers and Acquisitions*, London: KPMG, 1999.

[11] This section draws heavily on Jean-Noel Kapferer, *Strategic Brand Management*, 2nd edn, London: Kogan Page, 1997.

[12] Raymond Perrier (ed.), *Brand Valuation*, London: Interbrand and Premier Books, 1997.

[13] Perrier, *op. cit*, pp. 43–53.

[14] David Haigh, Brand valuation methodology, in Leslie Butterfield and David Haigh, *Understanding the Financial Value of Brands*, London: Institute of Practitioners in Advertising, 1998, pp. 20–27.

8 Pricing for Value

'The majority of the public will buy on price but some will pay a slight premium. In our case a 5 per cent premium translates into an extra £250 million profit a year.'

Sir Colin Marshall, Chairman of British Airways

INTRODUCTION AND OBJECTIVES

In many ways pricing is the most important determinant of shareholder value. For the typical company a 5 per cent price increase can boost operating profits by more than a half. In many industries, such as pharmaceuticals, management consulting or drinks, the purpose of marketing is considered as primarily about obtaining higher prices. This is because the results of successful innovation, brand building or adding value should be a willingness on the part of customers to pay more. Pricing affects shareholder value through its impact on the company's margin and the volume it sells. Ideally a company wants to charge higher prices without this being offset by weak volume performance. Companies such as GlaxoSmithKline, McKinsey and Microsoft have shown how this can be done.

Price is the only element of the marketing mix that directly produces revenue; all the others produce costs. The short-term impact of price changes on both profits and sales is usually much greater than advertising or other marketing mix changes. Price is also a highly flexible tool: while new products or changes in channels or communications policies can take years, prices can usually be adjusted very rapidly. In spite of its importance, few companies are good at pricing strategy. Most do not collect adequate information and rely on rules-of-thumb that lead to decisions that are very costly in shareholder value terms.

Today's dynamic markets increase the need for better methods of pricing. In the last century consumers became used to sellers and retailers offering one price to everyone. But the information revolution and the Internet have destroyed the simplicity of uniform pricing and have brought back individually negotiated prices and haggling. Web sites like PriceScan.com specialise in comparing the prices of sellers across the market; intelligent shopping agents like Kelkoo find the best deals for customers; online auction sites like eBay enable buyers and sellers to negotiate prices individually, and business models like Priceline reverse the normal process by having buyers name the price they will pay and inviting sellers to respond. The information revolution makes markets more price-sensitive, placing greater pressure on suppliers' operating margins.

Pricing decisions are also becoming more critical due to the increasing complexity of markets. All markets are becoming more segmented, which has resulted in firms having to broaden their product lines with different products aimed at different types of customers. Gone are the days when Coca-Cola could offer a single brand to everyone: today it has Coke, Diet Coke, Cherry Coke, Coke Zero, etc. Successful business-to-business marketing is similarly shifting from commodity selling to speciality products. The result is that firms do not price products in isolation but have to develop product-line pricing strategies that take into account interdependencies within the range.

Another area of complexity is international pricing. Globalisation has meant that prices charged in one market affect the prices that can be charged in others. Finally, competition has also become more complex and diverse. The days have passed when Coke simply had to compete against Pepsi. Nowadays, competition comes also from retailer brands and a range of products such as mineral water brands and sports drinks that capture the imagination of today's consumers.

By the time you have completed this chapter, you will be able to:

- ○ *Show how pricing decisions affect shareholder value*

- ○ *Explain the weaknesses of the pricing approaches commonly used in business*

- ○ *Describe the principles of developing value-based pricing*

- ○ *Propose a more effective approach to making pricing decisions*

- ○ *Outline the key issues in designing product-line pricing strategies, customised pricing, international pricing and promotional pricing policies*

- ○ *Plan price changes*

- ○ *Manage prices to ensure effective price realisation*

The chapter begins by exploring the different effects price has on sales, profits and shareholder value. It shows that the price that optimises shareholder value is likely to be very different from that which maximises sales or profits. Different perspectives on pricing objectives is one reason why pricing is done so badly in practice. Four principles underlying effective pricing are discussed. These are the need to base prices on what value is being offered to the customer, the need to customise prices to individual consumers, the importance of anticipating competitor reaction, and the role of business strategy in shaping pricing decisions.

Next, the chapter describes an effective methodology for making pricing decisions. It starts with defining the long-term strategy for the brand. Next, the business has to collect information about the price sensitivity of the market and the structure of its costs, and predict the behaviour of competition. This then generates options for pricing strategy that can be evaluated in shareholder-value terms.

This fundamental approach is applied to the complex pricing decisions that characterise today's markets. We look at customising pricing to different types of buyers, pricing a product line, international pricing, and the use of sales, discounts and price promotions. In a changing economy, prices have to be adapted from time to time if economic profits are to be optimised. The issues in raising and lowering prices to customers are analysed. Next the difference between list price and realised price is emphasised. Care has to be taken to ensure that satisfactory list prices are not discounted away to produce inadequate realised prices.

PRICE AND SHAREHOLDER VALUE

The basic objective in pricing is to choose a price that maximises the discounted value of the product's free cash flow. Free cash flow (CF) in any year i, it will be recalled; is:

$$CF_t = P_t Q_t - C_t - I_t$$

where P is the product's price, Q is the volume of units sold, C is total cost and I is the investment in fixed and working capital. In a classic study of over 2000 companies, price had the most significant impact on operating profits (see box, 'Comparison of Profit Levers'). For example, consider a company selling 100 million units at a price of £1, with a contribution margin of 50 per cent and an operating margin of 5 per cent. A 5 per cent price increase would double profits if volume remained unchanged. Even if the volume sold dropped by 5 per cent, profits would still rise by 45 per cent because of the reduction in variable costs.

Effect of 5 per cent price increase		£ million	
	Now	Volume unchanged	5% Volume loss
Sales	100.00	105.00	99.75
Variable costs	50.00	50.00	47.50
Contribution	50.00	50.00	52.25
Fixed costs	45.00	45.00	45.00
Operating profits	5.00	10.00	7.25

Other ways of increasing profits tend to be less powerful. For example, while a 5 per cent increase in prices can double profits, a 5 per cent volume increase, or a 5 per cent cut in fixed costs has only half that effect on the bottom line. To put it another way, a 5 per cent price cut could eliminate profits altogether, while a 5 per cent volume loss would only halve profits. Price competition can have a devastating effect on profitability. The implication is that it often makes more sense to defend prices than to defend volume.

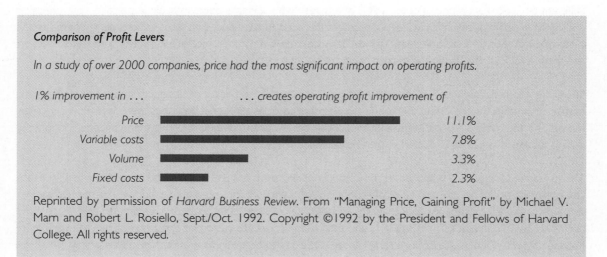

Comparison of Profit Levers

In a study of over 2000 companies, price had the most significant impact on operating profits.

1% improvement in . . .   *. . . creates operating profit improvement of*

Price	11.1%
Variable costs	7.8%
Volume	3.3%
Fixed costs	2.3%

Reprinted by permission of *Harvard Business Review*. From "Managing Price, Gaining Profit" by Michael V. Marn and Robert L. Rosiello, Sept./Oct. 1992. Copyright ©1992 by the President and Fellows of Harvard College. All rights reserved.

Pricing has not had the attention its importance merits. In seeking to improve profits and cash flow a great deal of attention has been given to reducing costs and capital employed. These have been the primary goals of reengineering and supply chain management in recent years. Sales and marketing people have focused their efforts on increasing sales and market share. But the fourth variable in the cash flow equation, price, has been relatively neglected. Managers often appear to be under the mistaken belief that this is determined by the market and outside their control.

BASIC PRICE RELATIONSHIPS

To discuss pricing it is important to understand four general relationships:

1.   **The demand relationship** relates price to the number of units sold. Almost always this is negative: the higher the price, the fewer units are bought. The degree of negativity is called the elasticity of demand. One of the key objectives of branding is to reduce the elasticity of demand, so that consumers will not so readily desert when prices rise.

2.   **The revenue relationship** shows how sales revenue varies with price. This tends to be a bell-shaped curve: raising prices initially increases revenue but eventually the decline in units sold outweighs the price increases and revenue declines.

3.   **The cost relationship** describes how total costs vary with price. This will tend to be linear: the lower the price, the greater the volume sold and the higher the total cost. The exact shape will depend upon the mix of fixed and variable costs.

4.   **The investment relationship** describes how working and fixed capital vary with price. Lower prices mean higher volumes and greater investment. This tends to rise step-wise, as fixed investment tends to be added in large, discrete amounts.

These four patterns lead to the key relationships of price to profits and shareholder value. Both *profits* and *value* have a U-shaped relationship to price – in other words, there are optimal prices that maximise profits and value. The various relationships are illustrated in Table 8.1. The first two columns show the demand relationship: as prices increase, volume declines. Often sales people believe that the firm should maximise sales, but, as can be seen, that means selling at the lowest price and incurring big losses and negative cash flow. Whereas the volume maximising price is £1, if the objective is to maximise revenue then the price should be £3. However, maximising revenue or volume ignores the costs and investments needed to support these sales. If the objective is to maximise profits – as assumed in most textbooks on pricing – then the price should be £5.

Table 8.1   Illustrating Price Relationships

Price (£)	Volume units (m)	Revenue (£m)	Cost (£m)	Profit (£m)	Investment (£m)	Cash flow (£m)	Value (£m)
1	**17.0**	17.0	27.0	−10.0	21.3	−31.3	50.0
2	16.0	32.0	26.0	6.0	24.0	−18.0	150.0
3	14.0	**42.0**	24.0	18.0	24.5	−6.5	220.0
4	9.0	36.0	19.0	17.0	18.0	−1.0	**250.0**
5	7.5	37.5	17.5	**20.0**	16.9	3.1	200.0
6	5.0	30.0	15.0	15.0	12.5	**2.5**	100.0
7	3.0	21.0	13.0	8.0	8.3	−0.3	50.0
8	2.0	16.0	12.0	4.0	6.0	−2.0	10.0
9	1.0	9.0	11.0	−2.0	3.3	−5.3	−50.0
10	0.0	0.0	10.0	−10.0	0.0	−10.0	−70.0

The problem with maximising profits this way, however, is that it is a short-term solution. By selling only to customers who will pay £5, much of the market is left unsatisfied and this presents an open invitation to competition. The long-run result of short-run profit-maximisation is likely to be declining market share, loss of scale economies, and competitors obtaining critical mass and building the dominant brands. For example, such were the fates of Xerox in the copier market and the British motorcycle industry after they set short-run profit maximising prices. The right pricing decision is one that *maximises the net present value of long-run cash flow*, not short-run profits. This is the price that maximises value for shareholders. In the illustration this value-maximising price is £4.

It is important to note that maximising volume, revenue, profits and shareholder value lead to quite different prices. In particular, in growing markets the value-maximising price will often be lower than the price that maximises short-run profits or cash flow. One reason is that market share effects are often important, either because the distribution channels will only support the brand leaders, or because network effects mean that customers attach value to buying the leading brands. A second reason is that scale economies or experience-curve effects mean that brands that do not grow fast suffer increasing cost disadvantages. Pricing, like strategy generally, requires taking a longer-term view.

PRICING IN PRACTICE

The right price is the one that maximises value. In practice such an approach is more challenging to implement since it requires collecting information to estimate long-run demand relationships, competitive strategies, and the behaviour of costs over time. Instead, managers usually look to simpler mark-up formulas that add a standard margin to an estimate of the cost of the product or service. *Mark-up pricing* is a method widely practised on a day-to-day basis by, for example, accountants, solicitors and contractors.

For example, suppose a firm sells printers. It has a variable cost of £80 per unit, fixed costs of £2 million, and plans to sell 100 000 units annually. Then its unit cost is £100. If its standard cost mark-up is 33 per cent, then its price will be set at £133. Generally, the mark-up is expressed as a percentage of sales rather than costs. So if a firm had a target sales mark-up of 25 per cent, then its price is given by:

$$\text{Price} = \frac{\text{Unit cost}}{(1 - \text{target return on sales})} = \frac{£100}{(1 - 0.25)} = £133$$

A variation of this mark-up approach is *target-return pricing*. This method is popular among capital-intensive businesses such as public utilities and auto companies. Here the firm aims to price to achieve a target return on investment. For example, if the printer company had £13 million of invested capital and it aimed for a 25 per cent return, then the target price is given by:

$$\text{Price} = \text{Unit cost} + \frac{\text{target return} \times \text{invested capital}}{\text{Unit sales}}$$

$$= £100 + \frac{0.25 \times £13 \text{ million}}{100\,000} = £133$$

Managers like mark-up pricing because they find it easier to estimate costs than demand. It can also lead to more stability in prices if competitors are using the same methods. But mark-up pricing is not an effective way to price. It ignores demand and the perceived value of the product to the customer. For example, strong brands with added values should normally be much less price sensitive than weak brands. Mark-up pricing throws away the value created by effective marketing. It also ignores competition – standard mark-ups would be a disastrous policy if aggressive competitors were competing on price.

Mark-up pricing is also circular in its reasoning. For example, expected sales are a necessary input to determine the unit cost figure used in the formula to calculate the price. But unit sales themselves depend upon the price! Similarly, how is the percentage mark-up calculated? This must be dependent on demand and competition. In highly price-competitive markets the percentage must be lower than in those industries where competition is less fierce. Managers need to make pricing decisions on stronger foundations.

PRICING PRINCIPLES

There are four key principles that underlie effective pricing:

1. Pricing should be based on the value the product offers to customers, not on its cost of production.

2. Since customers attach different values to a product or service, prices should be customised so that these value differences can be capitalised upon.

3. Pricing decisions should anticipate the reactions of competitors and their long-run objectives in the market.

4. Pricing should be integrated with the firm's broad strategic positioning and goals.

PRICING FOR VALUE

The customer is not interested in what it costs the supplier to produce a product. The price a customer will pay for a product is determined by its value to him or her. If the customer believes competitors are offering similar products (or services), then he or she will compare prices and choose the cheapest. But the purpose of marketing is to differentiate the product and to create a competitive advantage by enhancing the satisfaction consumers receive. In addition, when customers choose a supplier there are often associated costs that can dwarf the price paid for the product. Putting these two points together means that a company can differentiate its offer by offering more satisfaction, or lowering the costs associated with purchase and use of the product.

The additional customer satisfaction can be in the form of functional benefits arising from differences in the features offered, or psychological benefits arising from confidence in the attributes, status or experience associated with the brand. In business-to-business markets, the primary differences are functional. *Economic value to the customer* (EVC) is a key concept for pricing in such markets. EVC measures the value of the functional benefits offered by the supplier.

Consider this example from the construction equipment market. The established market leader sells a bulldozer at a price of £100 000. Over the product's economic life averaging 12 000 operating hours, the customer spends £40 000 on diesel oil and lubricants, £80 000 on servicing and parts and £40 per hour on labour, making a total lifetime cost of £700 000. A new competitor with advanced technology enters the market and estimates the value of his features as a precursor to setting prices. He envisages launching two models. The basic model has new digital technology that has the effect of increasing bulldozer productivity by 10 per cent. The advanced model also has finishing technology that produces a higher quality result, which on average should enable the constructor to charge around £100 000 extra over 12 000 hours of work.

Figure 8.1 shows the economic value of the new machines. The basic machine 'saves' £60 000, implying that its EVC is £160 000. The advanced machine has an EVC of £260 000. At any price below the EVC, the customer makes

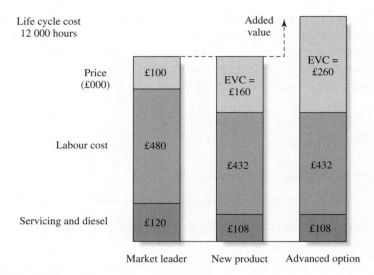

Figure 8.1 Pricing and Economic Value to the Customer

more profit with the new machine, 'other things being equal'. How far the new company can charge the price premium reflected in its EVC depends on the ability of its marketing and sales people to convince customers of its economic benefits. It also depends on persuading them that the support and service the company offers minimises the costs and risks in switching from the brand leader.

In consumer markets, emotional values can be as important as economic so that value-based pricing needs to estimate the worth of the emotional attributes. In the following section we look at some direct and indirect methods for obtaining information from consumers about how much a brand is worth to them.

Note that value-based pricing is based on quite different assumptions than mark-up pricing and that it will produce quite different recommendations. Value-based pricing makes much more sense because it is based on value to the customer, when the product is benchmarked against competitors' offers. It measures how much the consumer is likely to be willing to pay for the product, not how much it cost to produce it.

CUSTOMISED PRICING

Because of different attitudes and circumstances, customers differ in the value they attach to a product. Some people attach a very high value to owning a Porsche or having the latest mobile phone; others do not. If a company treats the market as homogeneous it will throw away opportunities to create value for both customers and shareholders.

Consider first an industrial example. An agrochemical firm invented a new breakthrough herbicide that raised agricultural productivity by 20 per cent. The variable cost of the product was £2 (1 unit was sufficient to spray 1 hectare) and fixed costs were estimated at £10 million. Statistics showed that there were 30 million cultivated hectares in the target market, yielding an average return to farmers of around £27 per hectare. The herbicide then had an average EVC of £5.40 per hectare. To incentivise use, the company decided to set the price so that half the EVC went to the farmer as increased profit. It believed it could then capture half the market, selling 15 million units. Unfortunately, despite a brilliant product, the budget suggested that the company would make virtually no profit. Its

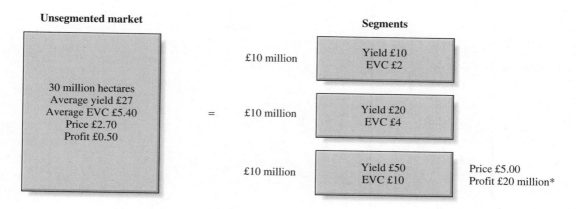

Unsegmented market		Segments

Figure 8.2   Customised Pricing, EVC and Profitability

revenue would be £40.5 million (15 million × £2.70) but its costs would amount to almost the same sum (variable costs 15 million × £2 plus £10 million fixed cost).

Before abandoning the product, the company commissioned some market research. Like most markets, this one proved to be highly segmented (Figure 8.2). The market could be divided into three segments of approximately equal size – around 10 million hectares each. The first was a low-value segment of rough grazing land in the north of the country, which yielded only £10 per hectare. A second segment of arable farming had a yield of £20, and the third was high-value fruit farming with a yield of £50 per hectare. The EVCs were then £2, £4 and £10, respectively. The research showed that at the original price of £2.70, the low-value segment would never buy because the price exceeded the EVC. In the middle segment the incentive to switch was also quite low. But if the company focused on the high-value segment, it could sell at £5, offering an attractive incentive to the farmers and making a profit of up to £20 million i.e. 10 million × (£5 – £2) – £10 million.

An important concept in pricing is the *consumer surplus*. The consumer surplus is the difference between the price the consumer would be willing to pay for a product and the price he or she actually pays. The existence of a consumer surplus means that the company is 'leaving money on the table' – missing out on profit that it could be making. Consider an obvious example – pricing seats on an aeroplane. Suppose the demand curve for a return flight to New York is like Figure 8.3. The price that just fills the 300-seater plane is £300, generating revenue of £90 000. The problem with this price is that the airline is passing up the consumer surplus represented by the triangle ABC – worth some £165 000 of revenue.[1] This is because many affluent customers who get the ticket for £300 would have been willing to pay substantially more. A more profitable ticket price for the airline would be £750, which generates revenue of £120 000. Here the consumer surplus shrinks to the triangle ADE, but because only 160 seats are sold, the airline misses out on the revenue from the 140 unfilled seats.

The obvious solution to this problem of minimising consumer surplus and maximising capacity is charging different prices to different customers. The airlines introduced First, Business Class and Economy to do this. In the example, the airline sells 50 first-class seats at £1200, 110 business-class seats at £750 and 140 economy-class seats at £300, generating total revenue of £184 500. Table 8.2, which estimates the variable and fixed costs associated with the flight, shows that the three-class solution more than doubles profits compared to the single-price solution.

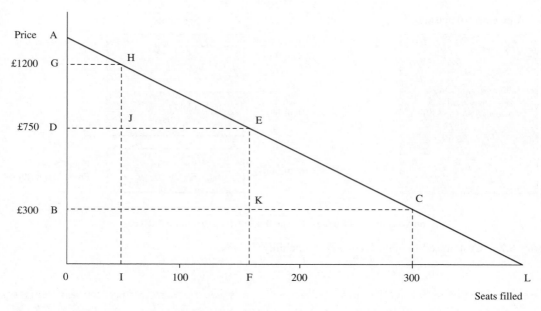

Figure 8.3   Pricing, Consumer Surplus and Demand for Airline Seats

Table 8.2   Illustrating the Profit Impact of Customised Pricing

Class	Passengers	Price £	Revenue £	Variable Cost £	Fixed cost £	Profit £
Single-price strategies						
Maximising seats	300	300	90 000	30	70 000	11 000
Maximising profit	160	750	120 000	30	70 000	45 200
Customised pricing						
First	50	1200	60 000	100		
Business	110	750	82 500	50		
Economy	140	300	42 000	25		
Total	300		184 500	14 250	70 000	100 250

Even with three prices profits are not maximised since there are still consumer surpluses represented by the triangles AGH, HJE and EKC. The best way of capturing these consumer surpluses is to negotiate a price with each customer. Individual customised prices would raise revenue by a further 38 per cent to £255 000 and profits by a further 70 per cent to over £171 000, if there were no additional costs involved. One of the important characteristics of the Internet is that it allows the possibility of low-cost, customised pricing on a much wider scale.

Customised pricing allied with product differentiation is, of course, very widely practised. Indeed, such tactics to capture consumer surplus are central to business-to-business strategy in virtually every industry.

ANTICIPATING COMPETITION

The company has to anticipate competitors responding strongly to a pricing strategy that aims at winning market share. Not only may competitors match a pricing move, but also a damaging downward spiral in prices can be triggered, leaving all the competitors worse off. In considering pricing decisions, managers therefore have to ask first: how will competitors react and what effect will these reactions have on profits? Second, is there a way of influencing competitors towards less damaging responses? As we shall see, competitor reactions and the ability to shape these responses depend on the nature of the industry.

COMPETITOR REACTION

The importance of considering competitive reactions can be illustrated through *game theory* and, in particular, the famous *Prisoner's Dilemma* game.[2] The game is as follows. Suppose companies A and B are the only producers of a certain product. There is only one client, who is willing to pay up to £50 per unit for a one-off contract of 10 000 units. The cost of producing the product, including an economic return on the capital employed, is £10 per unit. The company that offers the lower price wins the contract; if both charge the same prices the contract is shared equally between the two.

Figure 8.4 summarises the pay-offs of alternative pricing strategies. If both companies set their prices at £50 and divided the contract, each would make a profit of £200 000. However, this strategy, though attractive, is not individually optimal. If A undercut B and charged £49, then A would win the whole contract, making £390 000 profit, and B would be out of the market. Unfortunately, this strategy is also going to occur to B, which will also seek to maximise its individual profits by cutting price. When price wars like this break out, the price is likely to drop substantially below £49. In fact, at any price higher than £10, the two competitors can improve their individual situation by undercutting the other and obtaining the entire contract.

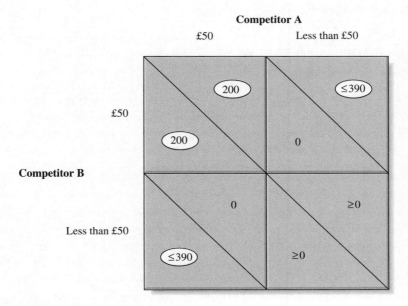

Figure 8.4 Pricing and the Prisoner's Dilemma

Only when both competitors are charging £10, and just making the minimum return necessary to stay in the market, is there no incentive for either to undercut the other. In the language of game theory, £10 is the only *Nash equilibrium* of this game – the only price at which neither competitor can individually improve its own situation by reducing prices. But if the two competitors are charging £10, they are both much worse off than they could have been if they had shared the contract at £50.

The Prisoner's Dilemma game is a simplified model of price competition but it does highlight a conclusion that holds generally. That is, the individual incentive to cut prices can lead to consequences that leave every competitor worse off. This result, however, does not always occur. The most important oversimplification of the model is that it is a one-off, static decision. In practice, competitors can usually react to each other's price decisions. If a competitor anticipates that a rival will respond, then it may not engage in price competition. Take a simple example of a town with two petrol stations next to each other and customers purely interested in getting the cheapest petrol. To begin with assume that both are charging the monopoly price – that price which maximises the joint profits of the two stations. What happens if competitor A lowers its price by 1p a litre? Competitor B, knowing that a price disadvantage will drive its market share to zero, is bound to immediately follow A's price down. Anticipating that this will happen, station A should not lower its price in the first place. The outcome of anticipating a competitive reaction is the exact opposite of the Prisoner's Dilemma – monopoly pricing, rather than competitive pricing.

Note that it is easy to predict a cooperative rather than a competitive price outcome in the petrol station example because of the assumptions that were made. These include: price starts at the monopoly level; both competitors implicitly agree what this level is; information about prices is available immediately and without cost to both competitors and consumers; there are only two competitors and no substitutes for the commodity. However, most markets have more complex features than the petrol station example, making predictions about prices more difficult (see box, 'Price Competition and the Internet'). The key to anticipating competitive pricing behaviour is to look at the characteristics of the industry.

Price Competition and the Internet

On first glance, economic theory might suggest the Internet would reduce price competition. Prices become more transparent, consumers and competitors have much fuller information at very low cost – all factors conducive to industry cooperation.

However, what makes price competition more rather than less likely is the lowering of barriers to entry. New entrants do not need to invest in expensive stores or spend on costly customer lists. This should increase the number of firms and the differences among them, making high prices much more difficult to sustain, except where firms have earned brand loyalty. New entrants with no brand name and unable to fund large advertising campaigns will find it necessary to compete on price to get a toehold in the market.

Further, the reduction in search costs and the ease with which customers can compare prices on the Internet encourage consumers to switch to lower price suppliers. Search and switching costs may be so low that negotiated prices become the norm. It may be much easier for customers to play suppliers off against each other, obtaining price quotes through email and making offers and counter offers among a large number of sellers. For example, Internet sites like uSwitch make it easy to play one power supplier off against another. Online auctions like eBay have become major growth businesses and online 'name your own price' businesses such as Priceline.com have further reduced the ability of suppliers to coordinate prices.

CONDITIONS AFFECTING PRICE COMPETITION

Cooperation usually leads to more profitable outcomes than competition. Cooperation can be explicit, as when companies get together to fix prices. However, explicit cooperation on prices, or collusion, is normally illegal. The other way of restricting price competition is by implicit cooperation. This occurs when competitors learn to trust each other not to cut prices. This is more difficult, but a combination of price signalling and tit-for-tat often produces this outcome. *Price signalling* involves tactics to make more transparent what the firm's objective is. A company might signal its intention of not reducing prices by public commitment to its published price list or advanced announcements of price increases. *Tit-for-tat* is a specific strategy that begins by cooperating with the competitor then matching the last price move by the competitor. This simple strategy has been found to give the most profitable outcomes for both competitors in repeated Prisoner's Dilemma games. What industry conditions favour price cooperation rather than competition?

1. **The number of competitors.** Such forms of implicit cooperation are more difficult to achieve where there are a large number of competitors.

2. **Differences among competitors.** Where companies have very different cost structures, market shares and product ranges it is more difficult to reach agreement on a cooperative pricing strategy.

3. **The short-run gain from price cutting.** Price competition is more likely to break out when there are potentially big short-run gains. These are greatest when firms have substantial excess capacity and when the products are relatively similar so that consumers can easily switch.

4. **Price transparency.** Transparent pricing encourages cooperation. If rivals immediately observe price cuts, aggressive pricing is deterred. On the other hand, if prices are the result of complex, private negotiations it is harder for implicit cooperation to develop because rivals cannot assess their opponent's actions.

CHANGING THE RULES OF THE GAME

Companies often seek to reduce price competition by changing the rules of the game. This involves shifting the above conditions to make them more favourable to cooperation. One way is to reduce the number of competitors through mergers and acquisitions. This may also reduce some of the differences between the surviving players, making cooperative behaviour more likely.

Another strategy is to reduce the gains to be had from price cutting. Building stronger brands, through such actions as advertising, market segmentation and product differentiation, reduces price sensitivity and the advantage rivals can expect from price cuts. Relationship marketing programmes are particularly effective. For example, a customer who is a member of the British Airways frequent flyer programme is less likely to respond to a low price offered by Virgin Atlantic on the same route. This reduces the incentive for competitors to cut prices. Higher ticket prices result.

Finally, there are a variety of methods that companies can use to make their pricing more transparent, to encourage competitors' trust. One way of avoiding price competition is for firms to follow a pattern of price leadership. Often this is preceded by announcements to build a consensus. The firm will test the water by press releases announcing 'unsatisfactory industry margins', 'the need to recoup increased costs' and 'a price increase being expected soon'.

ALIGNING PRICING TO STRATEGY

Prices are not determined in isolation but are influenced by the firm's strategy, the market positioning of the product, the other products it sells, and the various markets where it operates.[3]

VALUE NOT PROFITS

The firm's pricing should be geared to deliver value, not short-term profits. Value is measured by the net present value of the long-term cash flow that a pricing policy delivers. The value-maximising price can be higher or lower than the profit-maximising price. If prices fall over time, the price that maximises short-run profits may be below the value-maximising price. For example, some pharmaceutical markets are characterised by price elasticity and low variable costs, so that a lower price will increase profits. But in the Japanese market in the 1990s, the health authorities demanded 50 per cent price cuts every two years. In this situation, a higher initial price may mean lower short-term sales and profits but higher long-term returns.

More usually, however, the value-maximising price is lower than the short-run profit-maximising price. One reason is that price elasticity is higher in the long run than in the short run. Lack of information about alternatives and switching costs means that it takes time for customers dissatisfied with the firm's relatively high price to find new suppliers. Second, high short-term profits stimulate new competitors eager to capitalise on the opportunities offered by high prices. Finally, in growing markets high prices can prevent the firm gaining the critical mass in market share necessary to be attractive to customers and distributors and so to be viable in the longer term.

PRICE AND POSITIONING

Pricing is influenced by how the firm wants to position the product. All markets are segmented. Historically a three-tier segmentation of economy, mid-market and premium positioned brands has characterised many markets (Figure 8.5). Customers normally choose brands from within a specific segment. For example, in the car market the premium segment includes the higher-end Mercedes, BMW and Lexus brands; the mid-market includes the larger Ford, General Motors and VW ranges, and the economy has the lower-end Ford, Nissan and Fiat ranges. Brands within a segment are termed a *strategic group*.

Brands within a strategic group compete with each other to attract the same customers. The price elasticity within a strategic group is normally significantly higher than that between brands in different strategic groups. That is, a price cut by a mid-market brand will draw more sales from other mid-market brands than from other segments. Studies also suggest that where switching occurs between segments it is not symmetrical. Price cuts by a higher-quality tier are more powerful in pulling customers up from lower tiers, than lower tier price cuts are in pulling customers down from upper tiers. In other words, customers trade-up more readily than they trade-down.

A company that competes in only one group is called a *niche business*. As markets mature successful companies increasingly tend to seek to compete in all the groups to achieve economies of scale and scope. For example, American Express offers Blue, Green, Gold and Platinum cards. As the market matures niche businesses are often acquired. For example, in the car market Volvo was bought by Ford to penetrate the premium segment; VW bought Skoda to boost its share in the economy segment.

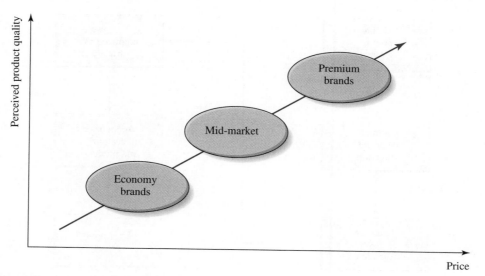

Figure 8.5 Three-Tier Value Positioning Map

Pricing then has to be designed to fit into a market positioning strategy. Prices that position a brand below the diagonal in Figure 8.5 will be perceived as poor value by consumers because their price is too high for the quality they are seen as offering. Pricing above the diagonal offers outstanding value with customers perceiving high quality brands at relatively low prices. A traditional approach to pricing follows the sequence:

$$\text{Design product} \rightarrow \text{Cost} \rightarrow \text{Price} \rightarrow \text{Market position}$$

But a strategic approach to pricing reverses the sequence. Management first defines its desired market position relative to its target customers and competing brands; this positioning defines the acceptable price, which in turn determines the acceptable level of costs. The product has then to be designed to meet the cost constraint. In summary, price determines cost – not the other way around.

One final point: while markets have traditionally been divided into three or four segments, the evidence is that the number is increasing. At the limit every customer can be an individual segment for which a separate product is designed and price set. This is referred to as one-to-one marketing. Several factors shape this trend. One is rising customer expectations for individually tailored solutions. These expectations are fed by greater affluence and more competition among suppliers. The second factor is information technology, which facilitates one-to-one communication between buyers and sellers. Finally, modern production methods, from flexible manufacturing to new networking relationships among supply chain participants, increasingly facilitate customised solutions.

SETTING THE PRICE

Managers set initial prices and these prices are changed, upwards or downwards, over time. We look first at how initial prices should be set. The firm has to set initial prices when it launches a new product or when it takes an existing product into a new market or distribution channel. The key steps in developing an initial pricing policy are shown in Figure 8.6.

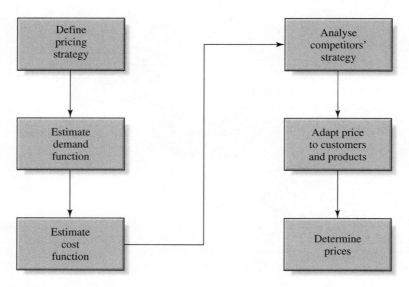

Figure 8.6   Determining Pricing Policy

DEFINING PRICING STRATEGY

The firm's pricing strategy is given by the answers to two questions: how does it want to position the brand in the market? What marketing objective will maximise shareholder value? Market positioning is defined by the choice of customers it wants to serve, i.e. economy, mid-market or premium quality-orientated customers, and by the brand's differential advantage. The choice of target customers will also imply a choice of target competitors. This market positioning choice will then determine the feasible range of prices that can be chosen. As emphasised in Chapter 6, strategy has to be dynamic: the right target customers and positioning today is likely to be wrong tomorrow. As a consequence pricing strategy will change over time.

The brand's differential advantage – the value target customers perceive it to offer – will determine the price that can be charged. If a customer believes a new product will enhance profits by £1000 then this is the maximum price he or she should be willing to pay to acquire it. A company can charge anywhere between 0 and £1000. For example, Skype decided to give its Internet telephony service away free, while Intel can charge £1000 to companies wanting to acquire its latest Pentium microchip. Charging a very low price – or even giving it away free – is usually termed market penetration pricing. Charging a high price, close to its value to the customer, is termed skimming pricing. In today's fast-moving, information-based economy, the choice between skimming and penetration pricing strategies has received renewed importance.

SKIMMING PRICING

With skimming pricing the firm sets the price high to achieve high unit margins. It recognises that this will limit its penetration of the market and is likely to encourage competitors to enter the market. Companies such as Hewlett Packard, GlaxoSmithKline and Du Pont have pursued this strategy in the past.

Skimming may be the best strategy for creating shareholder value under the following conditions:

○ High barriers to entry, e.g. *patents in the pharmaceutical industry make it hard for competitors to enter the market with lower prices.*

○ Demand is price inelastic, e.g. *in strategic consulting, customers perceive high value from obtaining the best advice. In some markets where product performance is difficult to judge, price may be taken as an indicator of quality.*

○ Clearly defined market segments, e.g. *in luxury goods, Rolex and Gucci can maintain premium prices because their customers are unwilling to trade-down.*

○ Short product life cycle, e.g. *Samsung, with its presence in the mobile phone and flat screen TV market, sees its highest profits being obtained in the first six months after launch, after which excessive competition commoditises the market.*

○ Few economies of scale or experience, e.g. *in some industries smaller companies do not suffer unit cost disadvantages.*

Where these conditions do not apply skimming pricing generally fails to optimise value.

PENETRATION PRICING

With penetration pricing the firm sets the price very low to maximise sales volume. It recognises that this will mean losses or low profits in the early years but believes this will create shareholder value through achieving higher long-run cash flow and a greater continuing value for the business. Penetration pricing may be the best strategy for creating shareholder value under the following conditions:

○ Low barriers to entry, e.g. *Internet businesses are cheap to start-up, making it very easy for competitors to enter the market with low prices.*

○ Demand is price elastic, e.g. *in commodity markets quality and standards are easy to assess and price becomes the dominant factor in obtaining market share.*

○ Network effects and critical mass. *In some markets customers see greater value and lower risk in buying the same brand as others, e.g. many people want Microsoft Office software because they perceive it is easier to swap files with colleagues, learn transferable skills and get the latest products. Small share brands are unattractive because they are not standard.*

○ Long product life cycle, e.g. *investors assigned high values to such e-companies as Google and Charles Schwab because they saw them creating new fundamental business models that should have long-term staying power.*

○ Economies of scale and experience. *In today's globalising marketplace, more and more industries offer cost economies to bigger companies. Many of the problems of smaller companies lie in the marketing and advertising investments required to build and sustain brands.*

Table 8.3 shows how penetration pricing is the superior alternative under the latter conditions. Under a skimming pricing strategy the company introduces a new product with a high price that captures a substantial proportion of the value it offers the customer. This leads to big cash flow in the early years but then this declines as new competitors enter the market with substantially lower prices. By contrast, under a penetration pricing policy cash flow is zero

Table 8.3 An Illustration of Skimming versus Penetration Pricing and Shareholder Value

| | Cash flow £ million | | | | | | | | | PV of continuing |
Year	1	2	3	4	5	6	7	Cumulative	value
Skimming pricing	10	11	12	8	6	3	0	50	
DCF ($r = 10\%$)	9.1	9.1	9.0	5.5	3.7	1.7	0.0	38.1	0
								Shareholder value	38.1
Penetration pricing	0	0	0	4	8	14	24	50	
DCF ($r = 10\%$)	0	0	0	2.7	5.0	7.9	12.3	27.9	63.2
								Shareholder value	91.1

in the early years because of the low prices and high capital requirements to support the faster volume growth. But then once a critical market share is achieved margins and cash flow improve rapidly. Note in the example that the cumulative cash flows over the 7-year planning period are identical. When the cash flows are discounted, the skimming pricing strategy value is £10.2 million greater. Nevertheless, the penetration pricing strategy delivers more than twice the shareholder value of the skimming strategy. The real difference lies in the continuing value of the two strategies: at the end of year 7 the skimmer has lost its market position and is economically worthless; the penetration strategy has a strong market position, resulting in a business with a continuing value of £63 million.

ESTIMATE DEMAND FUNCTION

Essential to a sensible price decision is an objective estimate of how demand will vary with price. Few companies make such estimates and instead rely on subjective judgements. Given the enormous impact price has on profitability and shareholder value, poor estimates are likely to be very costly. One problem is that different managers typically have sharply different views about the sensitivity of demand to price. Sales management invariably argue that customers are extremely price sensitive and push for low prices to maximise sales. Accountants, on the other hand, are more concerned with margins and push for higher prices. Another handicap to rational decision-making is that managers argue about what the 'the customer' is like. In fact, there is never an 'Identikit' customer: individual customers differ greatly in their sensitivity to price – some are highly price sensitive, others are much less so. It always pays to segment the market by grouping customers in terms of their price sensitivity. Generally, it then pays to develop segmented offers at different prices.

PRICE ELASTICITY

The sensitivity of demand in a market segment is called the *price elasticity* and is defined as:

$$\eta_p = \frac{\text{Percentage change in quantity}}{\text{Percentage change in price}}$$

For example, if the price is increased by 5 per cent and as a result the units bought falls by 10 per cent, the price elasticity is -2. Usually the minus sign is omitted, as the negative relationship is understood. If a change in price results in a more than proportionate change in quantity demanded, then demand is said to be *price elastic*; if a change in price produces a less than proportionate change in the quantity demanded, then demand is *price inelastic* (Figure 8.7).

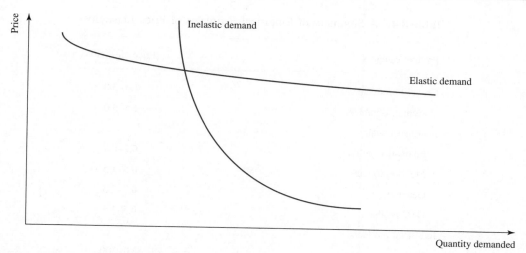

Figure 8.7   Elastic and Inelastic Demand Curves

Managers would like their products or services to be price inelastic so that they can obtain higher prices without substantial volume losses. Much of the expenditure on advertising, branding and loyalty programmes is aimed at reducing price elasticity and there is strong evidence that successful brands do have lower price elasticities. In general, price elasticity is reduced where:

○   *There are no good substitutes available*

○   *Customers in the target segment perceive the brand as having added values that strongly differentiate it from alternatives*

○   *Customers have poor information about the products and prices that are available*

○   *The product is only a small proportion of the customer's total expenditures*

○   *The risks consequent to buying the wrong product are perceived to be high*

○   *The decision-maker does not pay for the product (i.e. it is charged on to someone else)*

A challenge for many managers is that instant information and price comparisons over the Internet are increasing price elasticity, turning more and more products into commodities.

One has to distinguish between the industry demand curve and the firm demand curve. The firm or brand demand curve will normally be much more elastic than the industry curve. For example, a rise in the price of petrol will have little effect on total demand, but a rise in the price of one company's petrol price – if others do not follow – will have a huge effect on its sales. This is because it is easier to find substitutes for one firm's brand than for the commodity as a whole.

Studies have shown that the average price elasticity for products or brands is around 2. This means that a 1 per cent price increase reduces sales volume by 2 per cent. There are, however, huge differences across industries. Table 8.4 summarises the results of many different pricing studies. It is interesting to note that price elasticities tend to be much greater than advertising elasticities. The average advertising elasticity is around 0.2, meaning a 1 per cent increase in the advertising budget increases sales by 0.2 per cent.[4] This implies that price is about 20 times as powerful as advertising in affecting sales.

Table 8.4   A Summary of Empirical Estimates of Price Elasticity

Product category	Price elasticity
Grocery products	1.5–5.0
Consumer durables	1.5–3.0
Pharmaceuticals	
Innovative products	0.2–0.7
Me-too products	0.5–1.5
Generics	0.7–2.5
OTC products	0.5–1.5
Industrial products	
Standard products	2.0–100
Specialities	0.3–2.0
Cars	
Luxury	0.7–1.5
Normal	1.5–3.0
Services	
Airlines	1.0–5.0
Rail	0.7–1.0
Telecoms	
Air time	0.3–1.0
Subscriptions	2.0–1.5

Again, one has to remember that these advertising elasticities are averages and can disguise significant differences among segments. For example, Dolan and Simon found that overall demand for rail journeys was relatively price inelastic (less than 1.0), implying a price increase would increase revenue and profits.[5] But the overall demand is made up of two segments: commuters who are almost completely price inelastic – they have no alternative – and suburban off-peak users who are relatively price elastic. The obvious solution is to segment the market and introduce dual pricing to reflect the two different demand curves. Using the overall elasticity would be sub-optimal because it would lead to under-pricing of commuters and over-pricing and loss of revenue from off-peak users.

ESTIMATION METHODS

There are four main ways of estimating demand curves: expert judgements, customer surveys, price experiments and statistical analysis of past data.

○ **Expert judgements.** *Typically a number of industry experts are asked to predict volume at 'medium', 'low' and 'high' prices, and a consensus demand curve is developed. The advantages of this method are that it is simple and cheap and it is certainly preferable to traditional cost-plus pricing. Its major limitation is that experts' opinions can differ substantially from those of customers. This is particularly likely to happen where there are large numbers of customers with different price elasticities. The only way to get this important disaggregated information is through a consumer survey.*

○ **Consumer surveys.** *There are two approaches in common use. A direct price response survey asks consumers their probability of purchasing the product over a range of price levels. The demand curve is then plotted from those who say they would probably buy at each price. Again, this is simple and relatively cheap. The problems lie in its artificiality. In reality consumers compare products across a range of attributes, not just price.*

   Conjoint (or trade-off) analysis is popular as a more realistic method of collecting information from consumers. First, the key attributes in the purchase decision have to be identified. For example, for a car they may include the brand name, price, engine power, fuel consumption and size. Second, consumers are presented with descriptions of models with different combinations of these attributes and asked to rank the alternatives in order of preference. Then a computer program calculates the value to the consumer of different levels of these features. From the result one can construct a demand curve that predicts sales of any product at different price levels.[6]

○ **Price experiments.** *In price experiments, prices are varied and the effect on demand is observed. These experiments can take place in a laboratory with a simulated shopping environment or actually in the market using different shops or different geographical areas. The Internet and direct mail catalogues in particular facilitate price experiments. The advantage of experiments over surveys is that actual consumer behaviour is observed, although, unlike conjoint analysis, one does not get insights into which attributes could be altered to increase sales at a given price level.*

○

   Analysis of past data. In many markets prices have fluctuated over time and the effects of these changes on demand can be analysed by statistical methods, most usually by regression analysis. Statistical methods can provide direct estimates of price elasticity as well as the effects of other variables such as advertising and different economic conditions. A problem with historical analysis often lies in obtaining reliable data. It can also only be used on established products. In practice, while models can be constructed to impressively fit past data, it is rare that these estimators are nearly as effective in predicting future demand.

Whatever method is used it will need to be supplemented by managerial judgement. The previous estimation methods give an insight into the demand curve at a point in time. But to determine the strategy that creates the greatest value, management needs to augment this with long-term projections of the relationship between volume and price.

ESTIMATING COSTS AND INVESTMENT

Estimating the demand curve enables management to predict volume and revenue at different prices. But to estimate profits management also need to predict costs, and to estimate cash flow they also need to predict investment requirements. Since the objective is long-term value creation, they need to know not just how costs and investment vary with sales levels but also how they will change over time.

PREDICTING COSTS

Economies of scale mean that long-run unit costs usually decline with a higher volume. Companies have both variable and fixed costs; economies of scale apply to both. Greater purchasing power usually gives bigger firms an advantage in variable costs. Fixed costs include, of course, not just manufacturing, but also management, R&D, and particularly sales and marketing expenses. Unit costs for most of these tend to be lower with bigger volumes. The implication is that lowering prices to boost volume may not cut margins proportionately because unit costs will fall.

Experience-curve effects describe how costs vary with learning. After studying large numbers of products and services, the Boston Consulting Company famously observed a remarkable regularity in how unit costs declined. They concluded that unit costs decline by a constant percentage (typically between 20 and 30 per cent) each time cumulative output doubles (Figure 8.8).[7] These findings had a major influence on business strategy in the 1970s and 80s. In particular, they emphasised the importance of market share. If a company grows more quickly than its rivals, it will move down the experience curve faster than them and open up a widening cost advantage. For instance, if Boeing achieves 60 per cent of the world market for large jets and Airbus holds only 30 per cent, then Boeing's unit costs should be around 25 per cent lower than Airbus (other factors being equal). Market share is viewed as the primary determinant of relative costs.

The experience curve has an important implication for pricing policy. It suggests that the firm should price its products not on the basis of its current costs, but on anticipated costs. For example, Figure 8.8 shows a company producing 100 000 units with a price of £70 and a unit cost of £60. Based on an experience curve analysis, however, it realises that if it could double its output its costs would drop to £45 per unit. To drive for this volume it decides to drop its price from £70 to £55. The price is initially unprofitable but once the volume goal is achieved the firm restores the unit profit target, but now with a dominant market share.

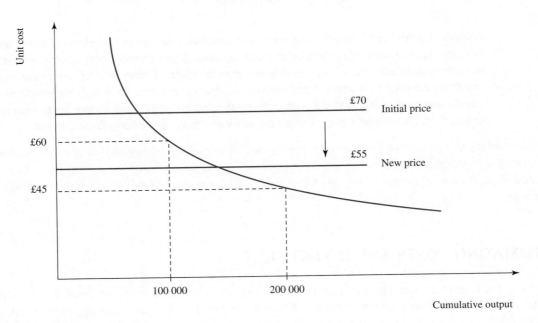

Figure 8.8 The Experience Curve

These dynamic cost relationships offer important insights into value-based pricing. In particular, they emphasise the dangers of cost-plus formulas and pricing aimed at maximising short-term profits. In growing markets especially, companies that do not maintain their market shares will often end up with non-viable cost structures, having missed opportunities to build scale and experience-curve economies. However, these relationships must be used with caution. If all the competitors are seeking to achieve scale and experience curve economies through ambitious strategies to build market share, then overcapacity will be the result and the anticipated superior profitability from market share will not emerge. A further problem is that focusing on optimising costs for existing products can open the firm to being leapfrogged by innovative products. TI, for example, used experience-curve pricing to capture market share in calculators when it invented them in the late 1960s, but missed out on profitable new markets such as PCs, hand-held computers and mobile phones.

PREDICTING INVESTMENTS

To calculate cash flow, incremental investment has to be deducted from after-tax operating profits. Incremental fixed investment is capital expenditures less the depreciation expense. A forecast of incremental fixed investment is usually obtainable from the long-term business plan. But this will have to be adapted to any revisions of the pricing strategy. The higher are predicted volume sales, the greater the fixed capital requirement. Incremental working capital investment represents net debtors, stocks and creditors that are required to support sales growth. Again, baseline forecasts are usually built from expressing the investment as a percentage of incremental sales.

Projections need to be adjusted for pricing policy. For example, lower prices will tend to raise the historic relationship between investment and incremental sales. On the other hand, advances in technology may lower it. There is also evidence that economies of scale mean that companies with a high market share have lower percentage investment requirements than smaller companies. Finally, any plans aimed at reducing investment (e.g. just-in-time stocking or manufacturing-to-order) have to be factored in.

ANTICIPATING COMPETITIVE STRATEGIES

Estimates of demand and pricing need to incorporate specific assumptions about competitors' current price-value combinations and their likely reactions to new product and pricing initiatives.

ASSESSING COMPETITORS' VALUES

Customers will choose products that offer the best perceived value. Value can be increased by improving perceived product quality or lowering the price. Competitive values can be compared using conjoint analysis or direct customer research. Here is an example of the direct research approach.[8] The method requires four steps:

1.   **Identify the dimensions of quality.** Use focus groups to find out what product and service attributes customers are looking for when they choose suppliers.

2.   **Weight quality dimensions.** Determine which attributes customers perceive as most important.

3.   **Measure competitors along attributes.** Conduct a survey to determine how customers rate competitors' offers along the attributes.

4.   **Discover value preferences.** Ask customers to rate which combinations of price and quality they prefer. Segment customers according to their preferences.

Table 8.5 Assessing Price and Value Competitiveness

Importance weights (%)	Quality attributes	Competitors			
		A	B	C	X
35	Precision	6	5	4	6
25	Reliability	6	6	3	4
15	Durability	5	3	2	5
20	Service	5	3	5	1
5	Delivery	2	5	5	5
	Weighted score	5.5	4.6	3.7	4.3
	Actual prices (£000)	29	21	15	22
	Market share (%)	27	45	20	8

For example, a manufacturer of industrial cutting equipment was concerned about its poor market share and wondered if price was the problem. It undertook a research study in which customers rated the competitors and its own product X, as shown in Table 8.5 The results were then mapped in Figure 8.9. The investigation showed that there were three segments in the market: a premium segment led by competitor A, an economy segment led by C, and the largest segment in the middle, dominated by B. Product X's problem was clear: it was competing directly against B, but customers saw X's reliability and service as significantly inferior. It was positioned below the value line, offering an uncompetitive combination of quality and price. The obvious requirement for the company was to reposition X by either enhancing its quality or lowering its price, to improve its relative value.

In using these techniques two caveats are needed. First, it is important to remember that all markets are segmented: not all customers desire the same value combinations. Pricing has to be geared to a specific segment. Second, the

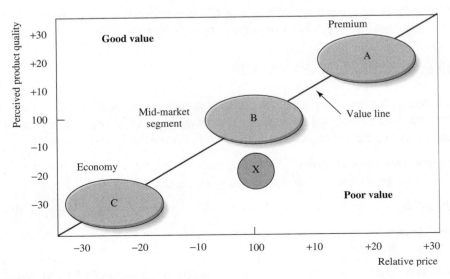

Figure 8.9 Value Map: Assessing Price Competitiveness

buying criteria generally vary among members of the decision-making unit. For example, in business-to-business markets, purchasing executives tend to be the most price sensitive; technical staff are more quality-orientated, and senior executives emphasise lifetime costs and whether the seller can offer a potential competitive advantage to the company. Consequently, by strategically tailoring selling and communications to specific members of the buying unit, the supplier can partly shape the importance attached to the different attributes.

ANTICIPATING COMPETITOR REACTIONS

If a competitor sets a price to offer customers an outstanding value combination, it should anticipate competitors reacting to defend their market share. The company will not want to trigger a mutually damaging price war – which, as the Prisoner's Dilemma game illustrates, can easily occur. Anticipating competitors' reactions requires first understanding their strategic objectives for the product. How important is it for the company's future? This will suggest how hard they might fight to retain market share. Second, management needs to estimate the company cost structure and financial strength. How much can they afford to cut prices and invest in defending the product?

ADAPTING PRICES TO CUSTOMERS AND PRODUCTS

The price of a product is rarely set in isolation. Its price has to be set in relation to the other products the firm is selling and to the various markets and types of customer who might buy it.

CUSTOMISED PRICING

In the early days of the industrial era, such companies as Ford with its Model T and Coca-Cola with its ubiquitous curved bottle practised undifferentiated marketing. The same product was offered to the whole market at the same price. But in the second half of the twentieth century, undifferentiated marketing gave way to segmentation and positioning. Companies differentiated their offers, tailoring products and prices to specific segments of the market. The information era has seen marketing strategies being customised even more precisely to customer needs with the emergence of one-to-one marketing. Airlines no longer just have three classes of ticket; any regular flight will contain people who have paid over a dozen different prices depending on when they booked, where they booked, who they booked with, how long they are away, their age, affiliation, past flights and so on. Internet-based-companies like Priceline.com even allow customers to name their own prices for a flight and invite airlines to compete. In consumer markets Internet auction sites such as eBay let customers bid at a price they are willing to pay and thereby customise prices. In business-to-business procurement Internet auctions are a pricing mechanism especially suitable to goods where a number of suppliers can meet a designated specification.

The importance of price on profits, cash flow and shareholder value has been constantly reiterated. A 5 per cent price increase can easily increase profits by 50 per cent or more. But in aiming to increase prices, it rarely makes sense to increase prices by 5 per cent to everyone. Consumers differ in price sensitivity. Some would switch to a competitor if faced with such an increase; others would not even notice. The same economic result is more likely to be achieved by raising the price by 10 per cent to half the customers, or by 20 per cent to a quarter of them. This principle of pricing is, as we have seen, based around capturing the consumer surplus – getting customers to pay the full amount that they are willing to pay.

CONSTRAINTS ON PRICE CUSTOMISATION

For price customisation, or what economists call price discrimination, to work certain conditions are required:

1.   The market must be segmentable and the segments must show different price elasticities.

2.   Customers in the lower price segment must not be able to resell the product to the higher price segment.

3.   Competitors must not be able to undercut the firm in the higher price segments.

4.   The cost of segmenting the market must not exceed the extra revenue derived from price discrimination.

5.   The practice should not breed resentment against the firm and its products.

6.   The form of price discrimination should be legal.

Customised pricing techniques seek to meet these constraints. Greater competition and deregulation have encouraged price discrimination in more and more markets. Information technology has facilitated price customisation. Scanners in stores and e-commerce companies can use software to monitor customer purchases and customise prices and promotions to each one. On the other hand, there is the increasing countervailing power with customers able to use the web to compare prices instantly and discriminate between suppliers.

TYPES OF CUSTOMISED PRICING

○   **Self-selection.** *By being offered different versions of a product at different prices consumers can self-select and segment themselves according to their price sensitivity. This is done extremely widely in both consumer and business-to-business markets. In consumer goods, car companies offer a range of versions of the same model. For example, a customer for a new Mercedes C class can pay anywhere between £20 000 for the basic version to over £50 000 for the top of the range. The Johnnie Walker Scotch whisky range is from £18 for a bottle of Red Label to £157 for the Blue Label. Microsoft offers its Office suite of programmes in Professional, Standard, Small Business and Home and Student versions. The examples are endless today. Prices can easily vary by a factor of 10 from the cheapest to the most expensive variant, with the cost differences between them being minor. The advantage of this form of pricing is that since all variants are available, no one can object to it being 'unfair'.*

○   **Controlled availability.** *Controlled availability pricing differs from self-selection in that the customer does not have a choice about the price. As one-to-one marketing becomes more prevalent it becomes possible to target different customers with different prices. E-businesses now offer individual customers special prices online, based on the information they have in their computer data banks of their past shopping patterns, and the price sensitivity these patterns imply. Supermarkets can do the same using the scanner data collected at the checkout. Sales promotions, coupons and direct mail catalogues can be similarly targeted. For example, General Motors sent a $1500 coupon incentive on a new car only to those who had expressed unhappiness with the previous model in a consumer survey. Victoria's Secret, the glamour underwear company, sent its catalogues with a $25-off coupon to male addressees but not to females.*

○   **Geographic pricing** *is another type of controlled availability. Companies like The Gap, Nike and Ralph Lauren routinely charge 30 per cent or more in the UK than they do in the more price competitive US market. Controlled purchase locations also facilitate taking advantage of different price elasticities. For example, the lower-price Eurail rail pass can only be purchased in the United States; the operators* *naturally do not want it to be available to regular European travellers. Negotiated prices, long a feature of business markets, look likely to become more significant in consumer markets with the development of e-commerce.*

○   Buyer characteristics. *Different types of buyers are given different prices. Ideally the criteria should be easy to apply and be effective in segmenting customers by price sensitivity. Common criteria are socio-economic variables such as sex, age, income, type of user and user status. In industrial markets, industry classification is often used. For example, some nightclubs allow women in free; children are allowed into many events at a lower price than adults; universities give scholarships to applicants from poor families; companies charge resellers less than they do end users; Microsoft sells new versions of its software to current users cheaper than to new users.*

   Simple socio-economic categories generally do not sort customers out very effectively according to price sensitivity.[9] A better method is researching price sensitivity directly. This involves interviews to determine what factors are most important in the purchasing process to individual customers and then grouping customers by responses. Generally the groupings do not correlate well with simple socio-economic or industry groupings. For example, studies by McKinsey and others have looked at industrial purchasing.[10] They found most markets, even mature commodity markets, could be segmented into three types of buying companies:

   ○   Price-sensitive buyers *who are primarily concerned with cost and less so with the quality and service provided. They exhibit little loyalty to suppliers.*

   ○   Service-sensitive buyers *who require the highest levels of quality and often have special service and delivery requirements.*

   ○   Relationship-orientated buyers *who want a close long-term commitment from their suppliers geared to developing superior customised products and processes.*

      Research needed to be done on a one-to-one basis because price sensitivity did not match obvious industry characteristics such as end-user industry, company size or value added. Armed with the right segmentation information, the supplier is in a much more effective position to apply customised pricing. The same is increasingly true in consumer markets where price-orientated shoppers, for a particular product, rarely fall neatly into a clear socio-economic group such as income or age.

○   Transaction characteristics. *Transaction characteristics often facilitate price discrimination. Timing is one criterion. In the airline industry, a ticket booked well in advance and including a Saturday night stay is a signal of a price-sensitive customer. Prices are varied by season, day and hour. For hotels and airlines 'yield pricing' – finely tuned pricing to mop-up anticipated vacancies – is a key to profitability. Quantity is another transaction characteristic widely used in pricing, the assumption being that customers who buy large quantities are more price sensitive and therefore receive discounts. Banks offer higher interest rates on larger deposits. Supermarkets offer 'buy six bottles and get one free'.*

In summary, customised pricing is very important to creating shareholder value. A single price policy, on the one hand, loses the consumer surplus because the price is too low for some customers, and at the same time it loses revenue because it is too high for others. The aim of segmentation is to group customers by price sensitivity so that different prices can be charged. Most schemes do this only approximately. For example, airlines offer cheaper tickets to customers who stay over a Saturday; cinemas give discounts for children, but many of these customers who obtain lower prices are not very price sensitive and the company loses the consumer surplus. Technology has offered scope for better segmentation schemes.

Care needs to be taken with price customisation plans. First, customisation usually entails extra costs and investment for modifying the product, service and communication channels to individual customers or segments. The company needs to assess that the plans are profitable. Second, discriminatory pricing can lead to customer disaffection; it can also be illegal. Airline or hotel customers can get upset to discover that the adjacent customer is paying half the price for an identical service. It also changes the relationship between the customer and the company's service staff. Customers sometimes feel they cannot trust the representative to give them a fair deal and the transaction focuses on price negotiation rather than solving the customer's problem.

PRODUCT MIX PRICING

Companies have increasingly broadened their product lines to meet the different needs of customers and to capitalise on their different price sensitivities. This means that managers do not price a product in isolation but rather have to consider in addition its impacts on the sales and prices of other products in the range. Products in a range can be complements or substitutes. *Complements* are where sales of one product stimulate sales of another. For example, if Nespresso sell more coffee machines, the company will also be able to sell more of its coffee capsules. For complementary products the optimal product line price is lower than the stand-alone price. *Substitutes* are where sales of one product reduce the sales of another. For example, sales of a faster model of a Dell PC may reduce the sales of its slower model. Several common situations can be identified.

PRODUCT LINE PRICING

There are several reasons why suppliers introduce multiple products. The most obvious is to meet the needs of different segments. For example, Nike offers separate shoes for runners, tennis players and so on. A second reason is that separate products permit the firm to charge different prices and capitalise on different price elasticities. For example, the Levi Strauss company offers a range of jeans from a standard priced Levis 501, to Engineered Jeans and a premium range of Vintage Jeans. A broad product line also allows the firm to encourage customers to trade-up over their life-cycle. So Vauxhall/Opel aims to capture younger buyers with its Corsa model and trade them up as they become older and more affluent to more expensive models. Finally, different products are sometimes tailored to adapt for differences among distribution channels. Discount channels operate on low gross margins; other distributors want exclusive products. A common solution to these conflicts is offering separate products. Sometimes these are under different brand names; sometimes the differences are in product quality or special features.

Without a line of targeted products firms would lose market share. The problem is that these products are at least partly substitutes for one another and low-margin products can easily cannibalise high-margin ones. Another danger is that downward extensions can threaten the exclusive image of the firm. It is important, therefore, to try to preserve the identities of the high-margin products and to set price points that take into account substitution effects.

PRICING FOLLOW-ON PRODUCTS

Some products require the use of ancillary products. These follow-on products are complements. For example, it will generally be more profitable for producers of razors or printers to price them lower than their optimal stand-alone prices to increase sales. The loss of margin is compensated by charging higher prices for the subsequent blades or print cartridges. The danger with the strategy is that the high prices of the follow-up products attract 'pirates', who capture much of the profits. Companies with follow-up products have to try to build unique designs, patents or guarantees that lock customers into the supply of 'original parts'.

BUNDLED AND OPTIONS PRICING

To reduce the perceived price, a product may be advertised at a low, stripped-down price. At the point of purchase, the salesperson then seeks to persuade the buyer to add high-margin features. A typical buyer of a £40 000 Mercedes will be persuaded to add another £10 000 on *options* and features that will contribute disproportionately to the company's margin. In contrast, Japanese auto companies have historically *bundled* a comprehensive range of features in the sticker price to offer customers a superior value proposition.

Options are complementary products. When they are bundled together the customer will normally obtain a significant discount to emphasise the value of the offer. For example, Microsoft Office, which bundles Word, Excel and PowerPoint, costs around 50 per cent less than buying the three programmes separately. Without detailed information about elasticities across the market, it cannot be predicted whether bundling or separate pricing is optimal. Bundling can be profitable when it allows the company to tap unexploited consumer surplus. Unbundling is better when there are opportunities to exploit new markets through selling the products individually.[11]

BLOCKING PRODUCTS

Often it makes sense for a firm to introduce a special product to block new low-price competitors from making inroads into the market. Cutting the price on the main product would be very expensive. Instead the company launches a blocking or 'fighter brand' aimed at those price-sensitive segments most at risk from the new competition. The company will make little or no profit from the blocker product but this is compensated for by its ability to preserve margins on its less price-sensitive customers and to limit penetration by competitors.

INTERNATIONAL PRICING

The globalisation of business has made international pricing a major issue. Currently big differences can exist in the prices the firm charges for its product in different countries. The barriers to trade that permit such divergences to persist allow the firm to significantly increase profits by capitalising on differences in price elasticities. However, declining trade barriers, notably in the trade areas such as the European Union and the North Atlantic Free Trade Area (NAFTA), are markedly reducing the scope of such divergences, with potentially damaging implications for profitability.

PRESSURES FOR PRICE HARMONISATION

Several factors are making it difficult to sustain major price differences between countries. These include:

1. Elimination of trade barriers between countries. This makes it easier to ship the product from a cheap country to a dear one.

2. Decreasing transportation costs. This makes it more profitable to undertake arbitrage transactions.

3.   Growth of arbitragers. Information agents and grey importers have been established to capitalise on opportunities from country price differences.

4.   Superior information availability. The information revolution has greatly enhanced the ability of companies to obtain up-to-the-minute data on international prices.

5.   Increased globalisation of brands. With brand names and packaging increasingly standardised, it becomes much easier for customers to accept grey imports.

6.   Growth of international sourcing. Corporate purchasing departments have increasingly focused on identifying the lowest regional and global prices and demanding them from suppliers.

INTERNATIONAL PRICE ALIGNMENT

Greater price harmonisation could be very damaging for many companies. Without careful planning, pressures for harmonisation can push prices to the lowest international price level with calamitous effects on margins (Figure 8.10). To prevent this, companies are recommended to plan for a 'price corridor' with a mean price in between the highest and lowest price countries. This entails sacrificing some market share in the low-price markets and some margin in the high-price ones. But some price differences will be retained, implying an acceptance of some level of grey imports. The exact structure of this 'least worst scenario' depends upon details of the market sizes and price elasticities in the individual countries, the expected growth of grey imports resulting from the price differentials in the corridor, and information on competition and distribution.[12]

Another important issue on international pricing concerns adjustments for exchange rate changes. A depreciation of the US dollar against sterling could wipe out the profits of a British exporter if it leaves its dollar price unchanged. On the other hand, if it raises prices to maintain its equivalent UK price, then its market share is going to collapse. As with the price corridor, the best solution is usually a compromise; in this case a 'moderate' price increase shares the burden of the change. As usual, strategic considerations have also to be taken into account. In particular, the longer-term repercussions on market position have to be considered. Adapting export prices to movements in exchange rates may be optimal in the short run but it may undermine the firm's long-run ambitions in the market.

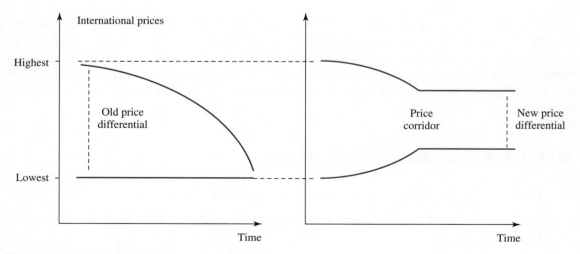

Figure 8.10   Planning for Price Harmonisation

PROMOTIONAL PRICING

Price cuts to stimulate purchase are widely and increasingly used by suppliers. Promotions are used with the objectives of accelerating purchases, getting new customers to try the product, encouraging customers to buy more, or gaining new sales from price-sensitive customers. The growth of promotional pricing reflects the increasing competitive pressures in many markets. It is a tempting competitive weapon because studies show that promotional price elasticities are often very high, up to four times normal price elasticities. A promotional price elasticity of around 8 means a 5 per cent temporary price cut typically yields a 40 per cent unit sales increase.

Promotional prices come in many forms. Some are *trade promotions* aimed at persuading retailers or distributors to carry the brand or more of the brand. They include various forms of discounts, allowances and contests. Others are *consumer promotions* aimed at getting consumers to buy more. They include coupons, price-off, cash rebates, low-interest financing and sales events.

Promotions have grown at the expense of advertising in their share of marketing budgets. However, they are a controversial tool among marketing professionals. One problem is that the powerful effects of price promotions almost guarantee that competitors will have to respond. The result then becomes a zero-sum game in which all the suppliers lose margin. If money is diverted from advertising and long-run brand-building investments to promotions this also threatens the manufacturer's long-run profitability. High short-run sales boosts are then outweighed by a decline in the brand's long-run competitiveness. Promotions also impose additional costs in the form of higher stocks and expenses in communicating and implementing the programme.

But the biggest concern with promotions is whether they cannibalise regular high-margin business. Studies clearly show that most of those who buy on promotion are the company's regular customers, who would have bought anyway.[13] If the promotions encourage customers to load up, then normal sales decline in proportion to the incremental business in the promotional period. The high promotional price elasticities may as a result be somewhat illusory. Profit then suffers a major hit because the disproportionate level of sales in the promotional period carry a very low margin. The long-run effects may be amplified in promotion-prone markets. Consumers come to see the sale price as the 'normal' price and become unwilling to buy at the regular price.

In attempts to break the vicious circle of promotions some companies, including such notable marketing heavyweights as Procter & Gamble and Wal-Mart, have sought to substantially reduce price promotions in favour of 'everyday low prices'. They believe this will reduce supply chain costs, enable them to develop consistent brand images and offer customers a better deal over the longer run.

Sales promotions are likely to be more effective for smaller brands. Price promotions can give customers an incentive to trial their new product. It is also more difficult to make advertising cost-effective for small brands. Companies are also becoming more conscious about ensuring promotions do not damage the brand's image. Hence the growth of 'cause-related marketing' whereby the seller associates the promotion with a good cause, usually a charity.[14] For example, Pizza Express ran a levy on sales of its Veneziana pizzas, with the Venice in Peril campaign as the beneficiary. Tesco ran a highly successful promotion whereby customers earned points that could be used by neighbourhood schools to buy computers.

CHANGING THE PRICE

From time to time management has to change prices. Naturally price increases are more difficult to implement than price decreases. However, achieving price increases is often essential.

PRICE REDUCTIONS

There are always pressures on management to reduce prices. When the industry is in recession and there is excess capacity these pressures are amplified. Sometimes price cuts are used proactively to increase the firm's dominance in the industry. This may be particularly appealing if the firm believes that there are major economies of scale or experience-curve advantages to be had from greater market share.

Price cuts offer more value to customers and a higher market share may be expected. But there are dangers. First, price cuts are easy for competitors to copy. If they do follow then all the players are worse off. Second, even if the company attracts new customers as a result of its price cut, these switchers are unlikely to be loyal and can switch again when a competitor takes an initiative. Third, price cuts can sometimes lead customers to question the quality or success of the brand, threatening its brand image. Finally, cuts can upset dealers or recent customers who see the value of their stocks depreciated.

Given the threat to profits that price cuts present, it is worth managers considering alternative ways to maintain or increase market share. These can include improving the perceived quality offered. After all, a 10 per cent cost increase is a lot less costly than a 10 per cent price cut. Another strategy may be to launch a fighter brand to serve those segments that have become most price sensitive.

PRICE INCREASES

As we have emphasised, price is one of the most vital determinants of shareholder value. In periods of high inflation, obtaining price increases is easier. With an inflation rate of 20 per cent a year, buyers do not see a 23 per cent price increase as remarkable, but with low inflation such real price increases are much harder to obtain.

Strategies to obtain high prices can be seen in terms of a trade-off between timing and feasibility (Figure 8.11). On the one hand, there are some techniques to improve prices that management can try immediately, but their feasibility is uncertain. On the other hand, there are some very straightforward ways of obtaining higher prices, but their deployment can take years. The only sure way of achieving higher prices is by finding ways to deliver greater value to customers. This may be via operational excellence, customisation, new marketing concepts or innovative products. For example, if a company can develop a new battery that will enable electric cars to operate with the flexibility of petrol-engine ones, or if a pharmaceutical company can develop a cure for cancer, then there will be no problem about attaining a price premium. Superior performance and innovation are the only sustainable means of obtaining better prices. The techniques for increasing prices are listed in order of their immediacy.

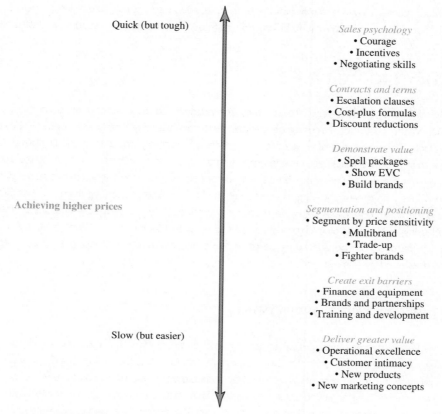

Quick (but tough)

Sales psychology
• Courage
• Incentives
• Negotiating skills

Contracts and terms
• Escalation clauses
• Cost-plus formulas
• Discount reductions

Demonstrate value
• Spell packages
• Show EVC
• Build brands

Achieving higher prices

Segmentation and positioning
• Segment by price sensitivity
• Multibrand
• Trade-up
• Fighter brands

Create exit barriers
• Finance and equipment
• Brands and partnerships
• Training and development

Slow (but easier)

Deliver greater value
• Operational excellence
• Customer intimacy
• New products
• New marketing concepts

Figure 8.11 How to Obtain Higher Prices

INFLUENCING SALES PSYCHOLOGY

Sales training and motivation can often produce higher realised prices relatively quickly. Generally salespeople are more orientated to volume rather than profits. They are often so concerned about not losing a customer that they cave in too easily on price. Management needs to encourage salespeople to be more *courageous* – to be willing to take more risks in pushing for price increases. After all, the objective is to maximise long-term profitability, not sales volume. Sales force *incentives* can also be changed to encourage a focus on price or gross margins. Some sales teams are still bonused on volume, which invariably undermines efforts to improve profitability. Third, training in professional *negotiating skills* is crucial for managers involved in price negotiations. Today, purchasing managers have become increasingly aggressive in their negotiating tactics.

CONTRACTS AND TERMS

With long-term contracts there can be a significant gestation period between order and delivery. Skilled managers can often negotiate *escalation clauses* that allow them to protect margins by having prices rise automatically with inflation. Over time, such clauses can have a marked impact on profitability and avoid the necessity of annual price negotiations. *Cost-plus formulas* are another contractual approach to margin protection. Suppliers can agree to meet new customer needs on the basis of protected margins. Finally, *discount reductions* act in the same way as price increases. Many companies allow satisfactory list prices to be eroded into unprofitable realised prices by giving away unnecessary discounts for on-time payment, buying minimum quantities, seasonal discounts and other allowances.

DEMONSTRATING VALUE

Most companies fail to optimise prices because they sell product features rather than demonstrating the value of their product to the customer. Focusing on product features invariably emphasises price as buyers compare competing products. There are several ways of focusing more productively on value to the customer. One is to *sell packages* rather than products. Packages include emphasising the services, technical support, terms and guarantees offered alongside the product. Even more effective is demonstrating directly the *economic value to the customer* (EVC) of the product. This means showing the customer the lifetime savings accruing from purchasing the product. Another value creator is *brand values* that give customers confidence in the product's qualities or the experience associated with using it. When a blue chip company signs up with McKinsey or a woman buys Armani they are willing to pay a price premium because they perceive the brand as unique, conveying an image, reputation and confidence not possessed by competitors.

SEGMENTATION AND POSITIONING

Basic to any marketing strategy, and critical to pricing, is the recognition that customers differ greatly in price sensitivity. For some customers, price is the most important criterion, but for others quality, service or image are much more significant. If a 5 per cent price increase can increase operating profits by 50 per cent, then this 5 per cent increase is invariably best achieved by *segmentation*. That means recognising that some customers will not accept any increase at all, while others will accept a 10 or even 20 per cent price increase. Implementation requires researching what factors are most important in shaping the buying decisions of individual customers, grouping customers according to similarity of need, and then *positioning* different offers at different prices to each group, or indeed customising it to each individual buyer.

A further step permitting even wider scope for price discrimination is the development of a *multibranding* or line extension strategy. Here differentially priced brands or lines are targeted to different segments of the market. So Distillers sells Johnnie Walker Red Label Scotch whisky at about £15, Black Label at about £22, Blue Label at £157, and so on. Such a policy also often facilitates a policy of *trading-up*, where customers start with an entry-level brand, e.g. the American Express green card, and are subsequently encouraged to move up to a more expensive option, e.g. the Amex gold or platinum card. A *fighter brand* is another tool for price segmentation and positioning. These are special brands introduced to defend against competitors in low-price market segments. A fighter brand allows a company to defend its market share without having to cut prices across its entire market.

CREATING EXIT BARRIERS

Skilful companies focus on creating exit barriers that make it difficult for customers to switch to cheaper suppliers. These include:

- ○   **Provision of finance or special equipment.** *Tetrapak, for example, leases sophisticated assembly line equipment to customers using its packaging. Switching suppliers would require customers to make major new capital investments.*

○   **Customer partnerships.** *Suppliers can integrate into the customer's research and development work, making divorce a major problem. Outstanding levels of service can also increase the customer's dependency.*

○   **Brand images.** *Customers who have developed associations and loyalty with a particular brand are reluctant to switch. Research shows that strong brands have relatively low price elasticities.*

○   **Training and development costs.** *For example, it is costly and difficult to switch from Microsoft products once staff are trained and expert on their use.*

○   **Electronic links.** *Where IT is integrating the two supply chains, changing suppliers entails increased risk and disruption.*

○   **Loyalty programmes.** *Where customers have built up privileges from loyalty programmes, e.g. frequent flyer schemes, they are reluctant to write off these assets.*

DELIVERING GREATER VALUE

In the long-run, offering customers added value is the only way to obtain consistently high prices. All the other routes are one-off or limited opportunities that eventually erode market share. Without bringing new value to customers, competitors and new formats inevitably commoditise a company's products and services. Added-value strategies that permit premium pricing can be grouped into four:

1.   **Operational excellence.** Customer value can be created by increasing the perceived efficiency of the current services offered to the customer. This effectively lowers the cost to the customer by cutting out hassle, inconvenience and the need to carry safety stocks. Service quality can be increased in five main ways:

    ○   **Reliability.** *Performing services more dependably and accurately.*

    ○   **Tangibles.** *Customers respond to the professional appearance of physical facilities, equipment, personnel and communications materials.*

    ○   **Responsiveness.** *Greater willingness to help customers and to provide prompt service.*

    ○   **Assurance.** *Improving knowledge and courtesy of employees and their ability to convey trust and confidence.*

    ○   **Empathy.** *Providing more care and attention to customers.*

2.   **Customer intimacy.** Customising solutions on a one-to-one basis can enhance pricing power. When customers perceive that they are getting a tailored solution, made and delivered to meet their individual needs, they believe that they are getting what they want rather than a compromised solution aimed at meeting the needs of a broader group with different needs. Today's information revolution is facilitating greater customer intimacy through (1) permitting flexible data banks of individual customer information to be constructed at very low cost, (2) allowing cheap one-to-one communication between the firm and individual customers and (3) the development of fast, flexible supply chains that permit customised manufacturing.[15]

3.   **New products.** The most obvious means of gaining a premium are to develop new products or services that offer customers superior economic, functional or psychological values. Customers value products that meet unmet needs or meet current needs in a superior way. Customers will pay more for pharmaceutical products that they perceive are more efficacious, batteries that last longer, computers that are faster, or equipment that is more productive.

4. **New marketing concepts.** New products require technological innovation; new marketing concepts add value by changing the way existing products are presented or distributed. They are more common than product innovations. New marketing concepts have included:

○ **Identifying new markets.** *For example,* Lastminute.com *identified a new market for customers wanting to go on holiday, go to a restaurant, go to a show, or send a gift, immediately*

○ **New market segments.** *Coke identified a huge market for diet colas. Marks & Spencer identified a major segment for chilled foods.*

○ **New delivery systems.** *The Internet, in particular, has stimulated new delivery systems of existing products that offer superior convenience or service to customers.* Amazon.com's *revolution of the book market is just one example.*

○ **New business systems.** *Customer value can be created from offering customers services rather than products. Castrol launched Castrol Plus, which instead of selling lubricants to workshops offered a service that maintained the efficient running of customers' equipment.*

○ **New information.** *New information can create value for customers. Suppliers such as Procter & Gamble and Cadbury offer supermarkets a category management service that enables retailers to increase the productivity of their space.*

PRICE MANAGEMENT

Effective pricing requires good strategy and good implementation. So far we have focused on the strategic issues.

PRICE IMPLEMENTATION

Implementation concerns achieving the profitability that the pricing strategy is designed to obtain. There are two important issues: obtaining reliable cost data to measure customer and product profitability, and optimising realised prices as distinct from invoiced prices.

DIFFERENTIATED COSTING

To target the right customers and prioritise the right products it is important to have accurate measures of customer and product profitability. Typically there are big differences in the costs of serving different customers and across different products in the line. For example, some retail chains want daily delivery to individual stores; others will accept twice a week delivery to a central warehouse. Others want special packaging and customisation. Products differ in the amount of R&D and technical service they require.

Most companies have standard cost systems that do not identify and allocate such differences in overheads. Tracking true customer and product profitability requires *activity-based costing* (ABC) that allocates both variable costs and overheads to the products and customers that incur them. When this is done profit margins on high value added products can be lowered by up to 10 per cent. In general, standard costing systems overstate the profitability of high-end products and customer segments, allowing simple products to subsidise complex ones and low-end customers to subsidise high-end ones.

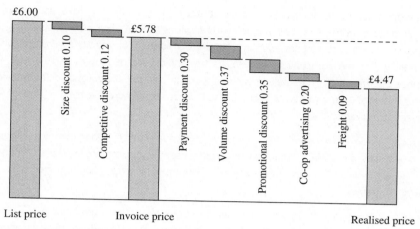

Figure 8.12   Realised Prices versus Invoiced Prices

ACHIEVING REALISED PRICES

There is often a significant difference between invoiced prices and realised prices, which can seriously impact on profits. Figure 8.12 illustrates this for a textile manufacturer selling to retailers.[16] The starting point in implementing a pricing policy is the *list price*. From this are normally deducted discounts for such things as larger orders and competitively negotiated terms to arrive at the *invoice price*. But in most firms the invoice price is not the actual *realised price*. From the invoiced price are deducted a whole new range of discounts for such things as prompt payment, volume bonuses, cooperative advertising and promotions. It is this realised price, not the invoice price, that determines the profitability of a customer or a product. Here the difference is big, amounting to almost 23 per cent off the invoice price per unit.

The problem is that management attention focuses on the invoiced price rather than the money the company actually realises. In fact, most accounting systems do not even measure realised prices. Many of these discounts get lumped into overheads and not allocated to individual products and customers. Again, with discounts varying enormously across transactions the profitability of individual products and customers can be seriously misunderstood.

SUMMARY

1. Effective pricing is of fundamental importance to strategies aimed at maximising shareholder value. On average, a 5 per cent price increase can raise economic profits by over 50 per cent. However, in the long-run, premium prices can only be sustained by offering customers superior value. Charging premium prices without offering higher value will undermine the company's market position.

2. The pricing strategy that maximises shareholder value is different from one that maximises market share or profits. Pricing to maximise market share or revenue leads to prices that are too low. But the price that maximises short-term profits is generally too high because it ignores the implications of economies of scale, competition and market share on long-term cash flows. The value-maximising price is the one that maximises the present value of future cash flow.

3.	Customisation is central to an effective pricing strategy. Many managers make dangerous generalisations about what price customers in their market will be willing to pay. The error is assuming that there is a typical customer. In fact, customers, even in what are considered commodity markets, differ greatly in their price sensitivity. For the company to achieve its twin objectives of growth and healthy margins it must employ price discrimination – generally meaning providing different products at different prices to different customers. This way, it can both cover more of the market and capture the consumer surplus available from less price-sensitive clients.

4.	Price elasticity is normally relatively high. Certainly, it is usually much higher than advertising elasticity. This means competitors are likely to react to price cuts, especially in mature markets. When a price war is triggered, all competitors can end up worse off. Consequently, pricing strategy needs to carefully assess competitive strategies.

5.	Information technology and the Internet increase the price elasticity of most markets. The web lowers the barriers to entry for companies competing on price. It also makes up-to-date information about products and prices more readily available to customers. Finally, it enables customers to be more proactive in negotiating prices and encouraging suppliers to compete for their custom.

6.	Pricing strategy needs careful implementation. Most companies do not have accurate data on the costs of serving different customers and selling individual products. They also lack data on realised prices, which can be quite different from the recorded invoice prices. As a result of inadequate pricing and cost information, companies can be prioritising the wrong customers and wrong products.

REVIEW QUESTIONS

1.	Illustrate how pricing decisions normally have a major impact on shareholder value.
2.	Why is the price that maximises the firm's profits likely to be very different from the one that maximises shareholder value?
3.	Discuss the concept of economic value to the customer (EVC) and show how it can be used in pricing decisions.
4.	What should determine the choice between a penetration and a skimming pricing policy?
5.	Show how customised pricing usually creates shareholder value.
6.	Suggest some techniques that can be used by firms in highly competitive markets to increase achieved prices.

NOTES ON CHAPTER 8

[1] The revenue in the triangle is given by $1/2$ base $\times$ height, i.e. ABC $= 150 \times £1100 = £165\,000$.

[2] For a review of game theory applications to business see Howard Raiffa, *Decision Analysis*, New York: McGraw-Hill, 1997.

[3] For more on pricing and marketing strategy see John W. Mullins, Orville C. Walker, Harper W. Boyd, and Jean-Claude Larréché, *Marketing Management: A Strategic Decision-Making Approach*, New York: McGraw-Hill Irwin, 2005.

[4] Raj Sethuraman and Gerald E. Tellis, Analysis of the tradeoff between advertising and price discounting, *Journal of Marketing Research*, 28 May, 1991, 168–176.

[5] Robert J. Dolan and Herman Simon, *Power Pricing*, New York: Free Press, 1997.

[6] On conjoint analysis see Jonathan Weiner, Forecasting Demand: consumer electronics marketer uses conjoint approach to configure its new product and set the right price, *Market Research*, Summer 1994, 6–11; Dick R. Wittnick, Marco Vriens and Wim Burhenne, Commercial uses of Conjoint Analysis in Europe: Results and Critical Reflections, *International Journal of Research in Marketing*, January, 1994, 41–52.

[7] Carl W. Stern and George Stalk (eds), *Perspectives on Strategy from the Boston Consultancy Group*, New York: John Wiley & Sons, Inc., 1998, pp. 12–24.

[8] Adapted from Peter Doyle, *Marketing Management and Strategy*, 3rd edn, London: Prentice Hall, 2001, Chapter 8.

[9] John Forsyth, Sunil Gupta, Sudeep Halder, Anil Kaul and Keith Kettle, A segmentation you can act on, *McKinsey Quarterly*, no. 3, 1999, 6–15.

[10] Louis L. Schorch, You can market steel, *McKinsey Quarterly*, no. 1, 1994, 111–120; V. Kasturi Rangan, Rowland T. Moriarty and Gordon S. Schwartz, Segmenting customers in mature industrial markets, *Journal of Marketing*, October, 1992, 72–82.

[11] A good discussion of price bundling is: Tony Cram, *Smarter Pricing*, Harlow, UK: Prentice Hall, 2006, pp. 135–145; Michael V. Marn, Eric V. Roegner and Craig C. Zawada, *The Price Advantage*, Hoboken, NJ, John Wiley & Sons, Inc., 2004, pp. 116–122; Thomas T. Nagle and Reed K. Holden, *The Strategy and Tactics of Pricing*, Upper Saddle River, NJ: Prentice Hall, 2002, pp. 244–249; Robert J. Dolan and Hermann Simon, *Power Pricing*, New York: Free Press, 1996, pp. 222–247.

[12] Johny K. Johansson, *Global Marketing*, New York: McGraw Hill, 2003, Chapter 13 Global Pricing, pp. 466–475; Hermann Simon and Eckhard Kucher, The European pricing time bomb: and how to cope with it, *European Management Journal*, **10**(2), June, 1992, 136–145.

[13] A.S.C. Ehrenberg, K. Hammond and G.J. Goodhardt, The after-effects of price-related consumer promotions, *Journal of Advertising Research*, July/August 1994, 1–10. See also: Leonard M. Lodish, Carl F. Mela, If brands are built over years, why are they managed over quarters, *Harvard Business Review*, July 2007.

[14] Hamish Pringle and Marjorie Thompson, *Brand Spirit: How Cause Related Marketing Builds Brands*, Chichester: John Wiley & Sons, Ltd., 1999.

[15] See Adrian J. Slywotzky, The age of the choiceboard, *Harvard Business Review*, January/February, 2000, 40–41.

[16] Adapted from Michael Marn and Robert L. Rosiello, Managing price, gaining profit, *Harvard Business Review*, September/October 1992, 84–93. See also: Michael V. Marn, Eric V. Roegner and Craig C. Zawada, *The Price Advantage*, Hoboken, NJ, John Wiley & Sons, Inc., 2004 (Pricing Architecture and the Pocket Price Waterfall, pp. 193–206).

9 Value-Based Communications

'There is growing pressure from shareholders to make marketing more accountable. Investors are becoming more active in analysing and questioning marketing expenditures.'

Dominic Cadbury, Chairman of Cadbury-Schweppes

INTRODUCTION AND OBJECTIVES

It is not enough for a firm to produce a good product; it also has to communicate its values effectively to potential customers. Today the number of products competing for the customer's attention is so great that gaining share of mind is a major problem. The business has to invest in communications to make people aware of the product, to communicate the value of its functional and emotional attributes, to persuade them of its advantages over competitive products, and to reassure customers once they have bought it. For a new company, unless it invests in communications its offer will be slow to take off, it will be quickly copied by competitors, and it will fail to get the level of market share necessary to achieve critical mass. For an established company, inadequate communications risks its skills being under-appreciated by its customers and new competitors eroding its image for leadership and innovation.

The communications that companies engage in take many forms. These include advertising, sales promotion, public relations, sponsorship, personal selling and direct response, including the growing number of online techniques. These advances in information technology mean that communications is increasingly being seen as a two-way, interactive process. It is not just about the company broadcasting information about itself and its products, but also about finding ways to encourage customers to talk to the company about their needs and their degree of satisfaction with the company's current products and services. Figure 9.1 gives an indication of the size and composition of communications expenditure in 2000, when over £50 billion was spent in the UK on communications. Companies, new and old, big and small, spent a great deal of money. Figures 9.2 and 9.3 show that on advertising alone, companies like Unilever and Procter & Gamble were investing up to 15 per cent of their sales and as much as 100 per cent of their operating profits. By 2005, spend on advertising alone, including TV, press, cinema and Internet, had risen to over £19 billion.

In the previous chapter we looked at the effect of price promotions, which primarily have short-term effects on sales. This chapter focuses on how communications can create long-term value for shareholders. By the time you have completed this chapter, you will be able to:

○   *Understand how effective communications creates shareholder value*

○   *Show the dangers of treating communications as an accounting cost rather than an investment*

○   *Describe how communications work to influence the choices customers make*

○   *Know how to define the objectives of a communications plan*

○   *Develop a comprehensive communications strategy*

○   *Understand how to conduct a shareholder value analysis of alternative communications strategies*

We begin by showing how managers conventionally look at expenditures on advertising and other forms of communication. Typically both marketers and accountants have an incorrect understanding of how communications

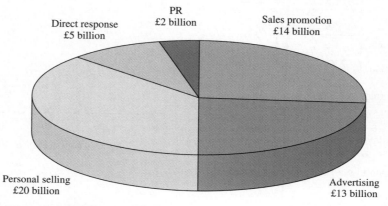

Figure 9.1   The UK Communication Mix, 2000

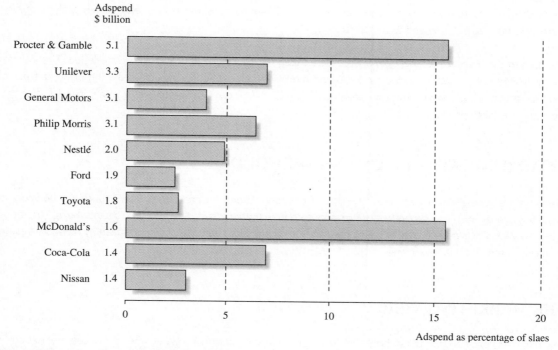

Figure 9.2   Adspend as a Percentage of Sales

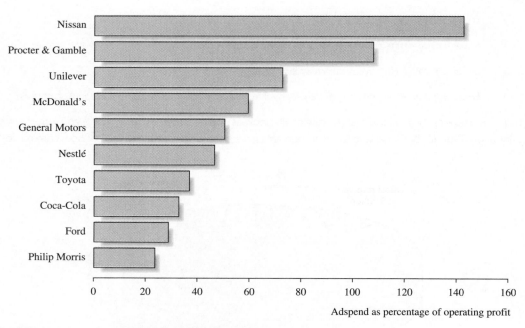

Figure 9.3   Adspend as a Percentage of Operating Profit

expenditures should be judged. Whether the money is spent on short-term promotions or image-building advertising, the campaign should be evaluated in terms of its effect on shareholder value. Generally, such a value-led approach will lead to quite different, and much superior, decisions on communications spending. The chapter then goes on to show how communications works in terms of influencing consumers. This leads to an analysis of how communications objectives need to be formulated.

The core of the chapter presents how a value-based communications strategy should be developed. This includes the analysis of the market, choosing messages and media, and allocating the budget across the different types of communications. Finally, we look at how shareholder value analysis can be used to estimate the financial value that the campaign might produce.

COMMUNICATIONS AND SHAREHOLDER VALUE

Managers are generally confused about the role of communications. Normally they take a functional perspective, marketing managers being generally positive about communications spending and accountants being suspicious. These two functional perspectives are evaluated and then contrasted with the approach taken by rational investors in judging communications spending.

THE MARKETING VIEW

Few marketing professionals think about their strategies in financial terms. They view the task of communications in terms of increasing sales, awareness or shaping the brand's image. For example, a study carried out in 2000 asked financial directors what criteria their marketing departments used to justify their marketing and communications budgets:[1]

Q. Which criteria are set by your marketing department?

	%
Sales volume	57
Market share	26
Awareness levels	35
Brand image	11

Source: IPA/KPMG

But such criteria do not make sense for budgeting decisions. If the objective is to maximise sales, market share or awareness, too much will be spent on communications. Spending more can always increase these levels, but beyond a point, increases in sales or awareness will cost more to gain than they bring in incremental economic profit. Another problem is that awareness and brand image have a weak correlation with sales and almost none to profit or value. Rolls Royce cars had a great image and universal awareness but these did little to halt declining sales and share price.

THE ACCOUNTANT'S VIEW

In contrast, conventional accounting takes a very short-term view of expenditures on marketing and communications. Only spending on tangible assets is treated by accountants as investment. This means spending on brand building and communications is treated as costs to be deducted immediately from revenue on the annual profit and loss account. Consequently marketing spending is only justified if it increases sales sufficiently to maintain profits. The accountant's model is:

$$\text{Communications spending} \longrightarrow \text{Incremental sales} \longrightarrow \text{Incremental profits}$$

For example, suppose a brand has the current profit structure shown in the first column of Table 9.1. How does the financial director respond to a marketing proposal to increase communications and marketing spending next year by say, £5 million? First he calculates the break-even – i.e. dividing the additional cost (£5 million) by the brand's profit contribution (50 per cent), to get a figure of £10 million. This is the incremental sales required if the additional spending is not to reduce profits (column 2). If he wants the spending to guarantee a target profit improvement, say to make another £5 million, then, as column 3 in the table shows, marketing needs to promise an additional £20 million sales – a growth of 20 per cent in one year.

This short-term view has several negative implications. First, it becomes very difficult to get marketing investments through a board of directors. It is rare to expect communications spending to produce enough short-term sales growth to meet the break-even figure. In general the elasticity of demand with respect to communications and the profit contribution margin are not high enough to achieve the short-term break-even sales level. For example, studies have suggested that the short-term advertising elasticity of demand is rarely above 0.2.[2] This means that an increase of £5 million in the marketing spending might expect to increase sales by only around 5 per cent.[3] As the final column of Table 9.1 illustrates, this result would be an expected drop in profits from £10 million to £7.5 million.

Not surprisingly, faced with pressure to increase profits, advertising and marketing expenditures have usually been the first things management looks to cut.[4] They see – generally correctly – that cutting such spending leads to little short-term sales loss and consequently a significant increase in the bottom-line.

Table 9.1 Communications Budgeting and Break-even, £million

	1	2	3	4
Sales	100	110	120	105
Variable costs	50	55	60	52.5
Contribution	50	55	60	52.5
Communications and marketing	10	15	15	15
Overheads	30	30	30	30
Operating profit	10	10	15	7.5

But such a policy has three weaknesses. It ignores the long-term effects of the marketing spending. The investment to develop a brand increases not just this year's sales but sales on into the future. The accountants' view highlights their different treatment of tangible and intangible assets. If accountants applied the same reasoning to tangible assets, companies would never invest, since plant and equipment rarely pays off in its first year. The accountant's approach leads to a dangerous bias against intangibles – those knowledge-based assets that are the key to competing in today's information age. The second weakness is that it assumes that if the company does not spend the money, sales and margins will continue at their current level. But as we shall see, in competitive markets this is not likely to be the case. If a brand receives inadequate support, both its sales and operating margins are likely to erode as it loses saliency to consumers and the trade. Finally, since investors take a long-term view of the value of assets they are not likely to react positively to the company pursuing short-term policies. Cuts in marketing budgets generally have a negative effect on the share price, even though they may increase profits in the short term.

THE VALUE-BASED VIEW

The approach of value-based marketing contrasts with both the marketing and accounting viewpoints. It evaluates marketing and communications spending not in terms of sales or immediate profits, but rather in terms of its projected impact on the net present value of all future cash flow. It employs the same criterion as outside investors use.

The value-based theory of communications is represented in Figure 9.4. Much of the organisation's communication spending is an investment to build intangible assets. These assets are the organisation's brands and its relationships with customers and other value chain partners such as retailers and suppliers. Developing a communications strategy also builds the organisation's knowledge and understanding of its markets. These assets enable the firm to enhance the effectiveness of its core business processes. For example, powerful brands, marketing expertise and strong relationships enable it to be more effective at launching new products, maintaining customer loyalty and running an efficient supply chain. In turn, these processes increase the firm's potential to increase shareholder value.

As we have seen in earlier chapters, the net present value of cash flow can be increased in four ways: (1) increasing the level of cash flow, (2) accelerating its timing, (3) increasing its duration and (4) reducing the risks attached to it (Figure 9.5). Marketing and communications expenditures, through the assets they create and the business processes they enhance, can influence all four levers.

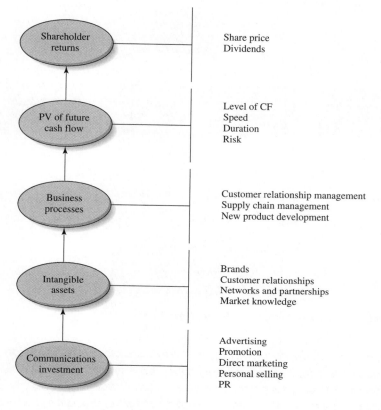

Figure 9.4 The Value-Based Communications Model

Many studies confirm that effective communications can increase the level of cash flow mainly by stimulating short- and long-run sales growth and by building a price premium for a brand. It can accelerate the timing of cash flow through a faster penetration of the market. The longevity of positive cash flows can be increased through the brand loyalty that communications contribute to creating. Finally, the risks attached to future cash flows, and hence the company's cost of capital, can be reduced through the effect of communications investments in building barriers to entry and reinforcing customer loyalty.[5]

Factoring in plausible assumptions about these effects, the dilemma of Table 9.1 can be reconsidered in value rather than short-term profit terms. Suppose if the additional communications spend of £5 million a year is not approved, marketing predicts that revenue will decline by 2 per cent a year. In contrast, with the additional spend, marketing predicts that they can maintain prices and grow volume by a conservative 1 per cent a year. The finance staff then estimates the cash flows and shareholder values resulting from the two strategies as follows:

Year	1	2	3	4	5	Present value of:		
						Cum.	Cont.	Total
Cash flow (no increase)	6.5	5.4	4.4	3.5	2.5	17.6	12.6	30.2
Cash flow (with increase)	3.4	3.7	4.1	4.4	4.8	15.1	32.8	47.9

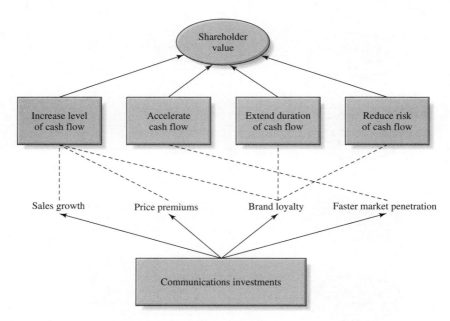

Figure 9.5   Communications and the NPV of Future Cash Flow

The results clearly demonstrate how short-term policies destroy shareholder value. If the additional spending is not made, cash flow is indeed higher for the first three years. But by year 4 investing in the brand begins to pay off as the cash flow benefits from increased sales and maintained gross margins. The table also shows the present value of the cumulative cash flows, the continuing value of the business at the end of year 5, and the total value of the business to shareholders. The investment strategy increases shareholder value by £17.7 million. This is because without the new level of communications spend, profits erode sharply over the period, undermining the continuing value of the brand.

BALANCING THE EVIDENCE

The above argument is not to suggest that all marketing spending is effective in increasing shareholder value. Money is certainly wasted if the communications strategy is poorly planned and executed, so that the sales targets are not achieved. It also destroys shareholder value if the growth is achieved but not at an adequate operating margin to cover the added investment required.

Management should not take marketing's sales forecasts on trust and they should hold them accountable for achieving the targets that are agreed and which form the basis for justifying the marketing spend. But the major point of the above analysis is to identify the dangers of a short-run accounting focus. As Figures 9.2 and 9.3 illustrate, companies like McDonald's, Unilever and Nestlé have spent heavily to defend their valuable current market shares and protect their price premiums.

COMMUNICATIONS AND CUSTOMERS

The main objective of communications is to positively influence customers and consumers towards buying the company's products. How communications work and its potential to influence people depends upon the type of decision the customer is making.

FACTORS INFLUENCING BUYING BEHAVIOUR

The firm's marketing communications are only one of many factors influencing the buyer's decision process. The various factors shaping choice can be grouped into four.

1.   **The buyer's role.** Organisational buyers make different decisions than people buying for themselves or their households. For example, senior managers will expect to fly business class when they represent their company, but on holiday they will fly economy. Organisational buyers often have different constraints, attitudes and objectives than personal consumers.

2.   **The buyer's background.** The cultural, social and personal background of the buyer influences decisions. For example, governments have been encouraging much wider access to the Internet across age, socio-economic group and gender to try and prevent a 'digital divide' among different groups of the population. Political, technological and economic forces also affect decisions. For example, firms increase their advertising budgets when the economy is growing and cut back in recessions.

3.   **The buyer's experience.** A person buying his or her first car approaches the decision quite differently from someone who changes their car every year. If the buyer has made the same decision many times before the choice will generally be a routine, low involvement one. If he or she is satisfied with the previous service they are likely to buy from the same source. For someone who has never bought before, the decision is a much more complex problem, requiring more information, an evaluation of the alternatives and often involving more people.

4.   **The buyer's information sources.** When buyers need to supplement their experience they have four sources of information:

     ○   Personal sources. *Information can be obtained from family, friends and neighbours. Organisational buyers can draw on the knowledge of other functional experts within the business.*

     ○   Public sources. *Television, newspapers, consumer-rating organisations and the Internet all provide information, comment and criticism about businesses.*

     ○   Experiential sources. *Buyers can often learn about the product before purchase by handling, examining and trialling it.*

     ○   Commercial sources. *The buyer receives information in two ways. First, from the company's presence in the market the buyer perceives the quality of its service, products, prices and positioning in the distribution channels. Second, the buyer can be influenced by the firm's marketing and communications – its advertising, promotions, web activities, PR, personal selling and direct marketing.*

This review suggests why most studies have found the direct effect of commercial communications spending on buying behaviour to be small. The firm's communications are only one of many factors shaping decisions. Most other forms of information are more credible than commercially sponsored communications. People recognise that advertising and marketing messages are biased. Finally, there are so many thousands of other commercial messages every day competing for the buyer's attention that it is difficult to have a strong impact.

HOW MARKETING COMMUNICATIONS WORK

The way advertising or other forms of marketing communication works depends upon the type of decision the buyer is making. It works differently when the buyer is choosing coffee than it does when he or she is choosing an airline flight. It works differently for an organisational buyer than it does for an individual consumer.

TYPES OF BUYING DECISION

Buying decisions can be categorised on two dimensions: involvement and rationality.

Involvement refers to the amount of investment in time and effort and the number of people contributing to the decision-making process. The investment is likely to be high when the decision is unique so that the buyer or buying team has little experience, when a large amount of money is involved, and when a mistake would pose major economic or social costs. In these circumstances buyers need to search for information to decide their needs, to identify and evaluate the alternatives, and to make an efficient choice. Conversely, the degree of involvement is likely to be low for routine decisions, low-cost decisions and when there are minimal risks. The two extremes are called *extensive problem-solving* and *routine problem-solving*. So most grocery shopping is an example of routine problem-solving, but the purchase of a house will be an example of extensive problem-solving.

A decision is *rational* if choice is based primarily on the perceived functionality or economics of the product. Most business buying is rational, as are most purchases of household essentials such as washing powder, petrol and life insurance. Decisions that are low on rationality are those that are made on the basis of subjective feelings or image. Perfumes, lagers, confectionery and sports cars normally fall into this category.

Figure 9.6 shows a simple categorisation of buying decisions on the basis of degree of rationality and involvement. Note that extensive problem-solving or high involvement decisions can be rational or subjective. Examples of category 1 decisions would be an organisation's choice of a new information system or a young manager's choice of an MBA programme. Category 2 decisions include choices of clothing, perfumes, whisky or sports cars. These are perceived as important, high-risk decisions by consumers, but image and associations play a more important role in the choice process than functionality and economics. Category 3 decisions are most consumables. Buyers are broadly rational, but because they are such frequent purchases, buyers do not need more information. Category 4 represents impulse items; choice is often random or a response to specific stimuli. Examples include purchases of soft drinks and confectionery.

TYPES OF COMMUNICATION MODEL

The way in which advertising and other forms of communication work depends upon the type of buying decision that they are seeking to influence. The task of communications in influencing routine decisions is quite different from

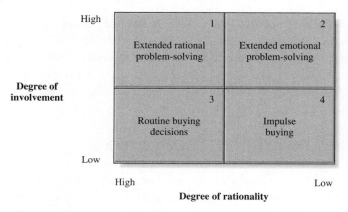

Figure 9.6   A Categorisation of Buying Decisions

that in high-involvement decision-making. There are two broad types of model describing how communications work; one describes its application to high-involvement decisions, the other to low-involvement decisions.

The high-involvement communications model. This model best describes the role of advertising and communications in high-involvement decisions. It is traditionally called the *hierarchy of effects* model and envisages the communications strategy assisting the buyer going through the learning process that precedes purchase. In the extended rational problem-solving situation (category 1 decisions) this is a cognitive ('rational thinking') process. First the task of communications is to make buyers aware of the product, then it has to get them to understand its features, then they have to be persuaded to desire it, which then hopefully culminates in purchases. Emotional or image-orientated extended problem-solving (category 2) follows a different hierarchy that is an affective (emotions and feeling) rather than a cognitive process. After creating awareness, the task of communications is to build positive feelings about the brand, rather than an understanding of its function. The rational model can be described as 'think, feel, do'; the image model is 'feel, think, do'.

Both types of the high-involvement model see communications as an aggressive activity geared to increasing sales. It is a reasonable way to describe the tasks of communications in situations when buyers have limited experience and information, and where the decision is important or high risk. It would also apply when a company is launching a new product or relying on direct-response marketing. Here the tasks are to create awareness, to create preference and to win new customers.

The low-involvement model. This model best describes the role of advertising and other forms of marketing and communications in low-involvement purchase situations. The main reason why consumers buying groceries or colas, or businesses buying consumables like oil or packaging, spend little time on the decisions is because they have made them many times before. Here the task of advertising is not to aggressively build awareness, comprehension, preference or purchase. This is already achieved. Virtually everyone in the target market is aware of Coca-Cola or Kellogg's Corn Flakes, they understand the products, have attitudes to them and have purchased them before. In the USA and Western Europe 99 per cent of people buying Coke or Kellogg's in the next month will have bought them before.

Here the task of communications is not aggressive but *defensive*. Its first role is not to win new customers, but to retain current ones. Given that some of these mature markets are huge this is an important role. Without continuing communications, the brand's market share would erode and with it the value of the brand to shareholders. The second role of communications is to defend the brand's price premium. Most successful brands have significant price premiums that contribute greatly to their value for investors.

Communications maintain the brand's value first by reminding customers of its continuing presence and relevance. Without being reminded some customers would eventually forget and drift to other brands. Second, advertising and communications act to reinforce buying decisions by confirming that customers have made the right choice, and that their brand is still good value. Finally, over time marketing communications will reposition the brand to keep it relevant as fashions, tastes and attitudes change.

Understanding the nature of the market and the appropriate communications model is critical for managers defining the objectives of communications and evaluating its results. The low-involvement model shows that in many situations it is not realistic to expect advertising or marketing communications to increase sales. The fact that advertising does not increase sales does not necessarily mean that it does not create value for shareholders. On the contrary, great value may be being created, by preserving the brand's market share and its operating margins, and sustaining its long-term cash flow.

DEVELOPING A COMMUNICATIONS STRATEGY

Figure 9.7 illustrates the steps management needs to develop a systematic communications strategy for a business unit or a brand.

UNDERSTANDING THE MARKET

As always, the process starts with understanding the market. There are three main issues to research. First, managers need to review the brand's performance and potential. This means looking at its marketing performance in terms of growth and market share and its financial performance in terms of economic profits and cash flow. The aim is to understand how well it is doing and to assess its potential to generate future cash. Managers need to understand the attractiveness of the market and whether the brand possesses a differential advantage.

Next, its communications profile has to be audited. This requires researching customers and others who influence the buying process to discover the level of awareness of the brand and its communications efforts, their understanding of the brand's key features and message, and finally their attitudes to the brand and the way it is communicated. The aim is to uncover what strengths can be built on and what weaknesses need to be overcome.

Third, managers need a detailed understanding of customers and the buying process so that they know who to aim at and what messages and media are going to be most effective. This includes researching what types of customers are buying the brand and why they are buying it, looking at how they use the product and where they buy it from, and finding who influences the decision process and how they influence it. The conclusion should be a clear definition of the most valuable customers to aim at, and an in-depth understanding of how to effectively communicate to them the brand proposition.

SETTING COMMUNICATIONS OBJECTIVES

It is important to set objectives for the communications strategy. The technical and specialised nature of communications means that much of the work will be done by outside agencies: advertising agencies, PR companies,

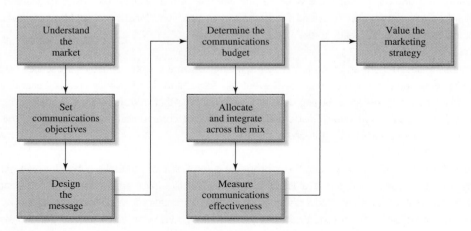

Figure 9.7   Developing the Communications Strategy

digital specialists, direct response businesses etc. Objectives align the different activities to common goals; they also provide standards to judge the effectiveness of the work.

Objectives should be specific, measurable and operational. Ultimately the primary objectives of a communications strategy are to increase, or at least maintain, long-term sales and operating margins. The problem is that it is difficult to make these operational as communications objectives. Generally it is impossible to disentangle the effects of advertising or other forms of marketing communication from the myriad of other factors influencing sales and margins. In addition, the purchase is often the end result of a long process of customer decision-making. Current communications investments, therefore, may not fully be reflected in sales until well into the future. Similarly, today's buyers of established brands like Coca-Cola or IBM are influenced not just by current communications expenditure but by that which took place in the years before.

As a result communications objectives are normally framed in terms of *intermediate goals* which better meet the criteria of being specific, measurable and operational. As noted in the discussion of communications models above, the buying process consists of three stages. The first is the *cognitive* stage – customers have to be aware of the product and understand its benefits. The next is the *affective* stage – positive attitudes, liking and preferences for it have to be induced. Finally comes the *behavioural* stage: purchase, repeat purchase or intermediate measures such as intention to buy or rebuy. Since these variables are easy to measure through surveys or customer panels, a standard way of setting objectives is to target improvements in these variables.

Judgement is required to determine which are the most important measures and what are reasonable targets. For rational high-involvement decisions, cognitive measures are generally the most important. Buyers have to understand the special features and benefits the product offers. For image or emotive decisions, affective criteria are more important. Targets also have to be appropriate to the market situation. For mature, established brands in low-involvement markets it is unreasonable to set ambitious targets for cognitive and affective measures or for big sales increases. Such targets are unlikely to be met, and setting them shows a misunderstanding of the role of communications in such situations. For established brands the main communications task is to maintain current performance levels or to produce marginal repositioning.

DESIGNING THE MESSAGE

Once the cognitive, affective and behavioural targets have been set, then communications messages have to be developed to achieve the objectives. Given the volume of products competing for the attention of buyers, messages have to have *impact*; to capture attention, they also have to suggest benefits that are *desirable, exclusive* and *believable*.

MESSAGE CONTENT

The message may be rational or emotional in appeal. *Rational appeals* make claims about the brand's uniquely superior attributes or economic value to the customer. In the past, brand managers at companies like Procter & Gamble were taught to write the message around a *unique selling proposition* (USP). Such messages make sense for attribute brands (see Chapter 7) and where decision-making is highly rational. They are still common in business-to-business markets. But increasingly, in today's highly competitive markets, the problem is that it is difficult to sustain real differences in functionality or cost.

Today, more messages are *emotional appeals*. They seek to present added values over and above functional or economic differences. Some offer aspirational messages, associating the brand with status and desired lifestyles. Others offer experiences or shared emotions. These can be based on negative or positive motivations. Negative appeals use fear, guilt or shame to influence people's behaviour (e.g. stop smoking, avoid drinking and driving). Evidence shows that overly negative campaigns are not usually effective. Positive appeals use humour, pride or affection to achieve their goals. The evidence suggests that communications that are liked tend to be more effective.

MESSAGE PRESENTATION

Effectiveness depends upon the presentation as well as the content of the message. The *style* of the message can be one-way or two-way. Personal selling and, perhaps more significantly, the Internet can be highly effective because they permit interaction between sender and recipient. Two-way communication permits the sender to tailor the message to the recipient's needs. Even for conventional advertising and direct response communications, getting consumer involvement increases the effectiveness of the message. This can be done by presenting the disadvantages as well as the advantages of the product, or leaving some ambiguity in the message to involve recipients, and encourage them to draw their own conclusions.

Many messages are delivered by *spokespersons* such as celebrities or opinion leaders to increase the impact and credibility of the message. Expertise, trustworthiness and likeability are the characteristics of sources who are most credible to audiences. The message's effectiveness is also a function of the creativity of the phrasing of the wording, the tone and the visual appeal of the message. Most communications messages are *pretested* against consumer groups to monitor impact and credibility. This has been enhanced with the emergence of social networking sites such as MySpace and Facebook, which enable people to share their thoughts with thousands of others about message presentation.

DECIDING THE COMMUNICATIONS BUDGET

With spending on communications routinely representing 15 per cent or more of sales, more effective budgeting potentially has a big impact on profits. But few managers in either marketing or finance know how to approach the decision of how much to spend. We explain how managers should decide on how much to spend on communications.

CONVENTIONAL APPROACHES TO BUDGETING

Deciding how much to spend on communications is difficult in practice because it is hard to judge the effectiveness of the expenditure. Many other factors such as the product's quality, its price, competition and economic conditions are affecting sales simultaneously. Effectiveness is also not just about how much is spent but how creatively it is spent. Some companies and their agencies get much more from a given budget than others. Many companies appear to give up any attempt to budget rationally.

Incremental budgeting is employed by many companies, whereby they increase last year's budget by a given percentage. The *percentage of sales* method is also common, where the communications budget is set at some percentage of current or anticipated sales. Other methods that research shows are widely used include *competitive parity* – spending the same percentage as competitors – and the *affordability method*, where the company spends what it feels it can afford from the budget.

None of these rules of thumb are rational because they do not consider the basic question of how different levels of communications spending might affect sales and cash flow. They lead to budgets that can easily be a hundred per cent too much or too little.

OBJECTIVE AND TASK METHOD

This method is regarded – incorrectly – as the superior method in many marketing circles. The idea is to define specific objectives, determine the tasks that must be performed to achieve these objectives, and then estimate the costs of performing them. For example, suppose Heineken wants to launch a new beer, Buzz.[6] The objective and task method proceeds as follows:

1. *Decide the market share objective.* The company estimates the potential number of drinkers in its region as 60 million and sets a target of a 5 per cent share, i.e. 3 million regular customers.

2. *Determine the percentage of the market that could be reached by the communications campaign.* Heineken aims to reach 75 per cent or 45 million prospects.

3. *Determine the percentage of aware prospects that should be persuaded to try the brand.* The company aims to get 27 per cent of aware prospects to try Buzz (12 million). Of these it expects 25 per cent to become loyal users, giving it its share goal of 3 million.

4. *Determine the number of communications exposures per 1 per cent trial rate.* The agency estimates that 30 exposures would be needed for every 1 per cent of the population to achieve the 27 per cent trial rate.

5. *Determine the number of gross rating points that would have to be purchased.* A gross rating point is one exposure to 1 per cent of the target population. Because the company wants to achieve 30 exposures to 75 per cent of the population it will need to buy 2250 gross rating points.

6. *Determine the budget based on the cost of buying a gross rating point.* The average cost per gross rating point is 3000 euros. Therefore to buy 2250 would cost 6.8 million euros.

The problem with the objective and task method is that much of the detail is spurious. There is no justification for the market share target or the objectives for awareness, trial or gross rating points. Different assumptions would give very different budgets and there is no criterion in the model for preferring one assumption to another.

VALUE-BASED BUDGETING

Since the objective of marketing is to maximise shareholder value, the right way to determine the communications budget is to spend that amount which maximises the net present value of the brand's future cash flow. This means considering the trade-off between communications spend and other investments to increase returns. It also means evaluating the implications of different levels of spending. The first step is to estimate how sales will vary with communications spend. This can be done directly or by separating out the components of revenue. For example, net revenue growth for a mobile phone operator is best estimated by predicting the number of subscribers it gains, the average spend per subscriber and the number of years an average subscriber is retained.[7]

There are three ways to estimate the sales response function. First, an *econometric approach* can be used, which correlates variations in spending with variations in sales. The data can be either historical or based on differences occurring cross-sectionally in different geographical areas. This method is most appropriate for mature products and where markets are relatively stable so that conditions in the future are not going to be too different from the past.[8] *Experimental estimates* can be used for new products. This involves varying the levels of spending in different regions and assessing the response function.[9] The third approach is *consensus estimates*. This requires members of the brand team to use their best judgements to make predictions about sales at 'low', 'medium' and 'high' levels of marketing spend; from these estimates a consensus response curve is developed.

The resulting levels of spend and sales forecasts are input into a shareholder value analysis to estimate the shareholder value added for the different budgets. Figure 9.8 illustrates this for the beer, Buzz, showing the shareholder value added with annual communications budgets of 5, 10 and 15 million euros. Note that market share is always maximised with the maximum communications budget, but the objective is to maximise value, not sales. Table 9.2 shows the calculation in detail for the optimum communications spend of 10 million euros. Here managers forecast sales reaching 35 million euros and the brand having a shareholder value of 27.8 million euros.

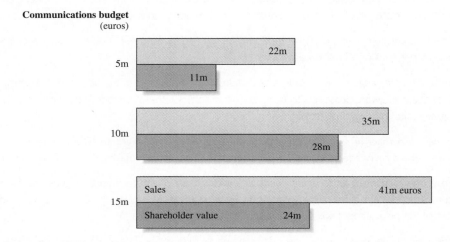

Figure 9.8   Value-Based Budgeting for Communications Investments

Table 9.2   Optimum Communications Budget for Buzz Beer

Year	1	2	3	4	5
Sales (euros m)	30.0	33.0	35.0	35.0	35.0
Communications budget	10.0	10.0	10.0	10.0	10.0
Operating profit	3.0	3.3	4.2	5.3	7.0
NOPAT	3.0	2.6	2.9	3.7	4.9
Net investment	15.0	1.2	0.8	0.0	0.0
Cash flow	−12.0	1.4	2.1	3.7	4.9
PV of CF	−10.9	1.2	1.6	2.5	3.0

Cumulative present value	−2.6
PV of continuing value	30.4
Shareholder value	27.8

ALLOCATING ACROSS COMMUNICATIONS CHANNELS

The budget has to be allocated and integrated across the various communications vehicles – advertising, sales promotion, public relations, direct response and the sales force. Companies even within the same market can employ very different strategies. Developing an appropriate set of channels will have a marked effect on the success of a campaign. Each of the channels has certain characteristics and advantages and disadvantages.

ADVERTISING

Companies can use advertising in a range of media including TV, radio, newspapers, magazines, billboards and web sites such as YouTube. The aims can be long-term brand development or quick sales response. The general features of advertising are:

- **Legitimises the brand.** *Exposure in major advertising vehicles expresses the company's commitment to the brand and conveys a measure of confidence among buyers.*

- **Creative expression.** *Advertising, through the use of pictures, colour and language, permits a more creative presentation of the brand's emotional and functional benefits.*

- **Image building.** *Advertising over a long period can be the most effective way of building a distinctive personality for the brand.*

- **Economical.** *Advertising can be a relatively low cost means of exposing the company's message to large populations. The downside is that it generally has smaller effects than personal selling or promotions.*

SALES PROMOTIONS

Sales promotion tools include money-off vouchers, samples, contests, trade-in allowances, gifts, exhibits and tie-ins. Their general features are:

- **Impact.** *By offering direct inducements to buyers they can have strong and quick effects on sales. Normally the elasticity of demand with respect to promotions is significantly higher than for advertising.*

- **Trial.** *Promotions can be an effective means of obtaining customer trial in low-involvement markets where other communications vehicles do not receive attention.*

- **Expensive.** *Promotions, particularly where they involve price reductions, can be expensive. They can also reduce margins by displacing sales from periods when promotions are not being offered.*

- **Image erosion.** *Excessive use of promotions can damage the quality image of a brand.*

PUBLIC RELATIONS

PR can include lobbying politicians and the media, publications, press handouts, speeches, charitable donations, word of mouth and sponsorships. Its main features are:

- **Credibility.** *News stories and features are more credible sources of information to buyers than ads and promotions that are obviously biased and paid for.*

○   *Imprecise. It is more difficult to control the message and target it to particular groups than with conventional commercial communications.*

○   *Low cost. Effective public relations can obtain substantial free media exposure.*

○   *Difficult. PR cannot depend upon gaining effective access to the most important media or community stakeholders. It depends upon the perceived importance and interest of the message.*

PERSONAL SELLING

Using the company's own sales representatives is a highly effective way of building up an understanding of the company's offer and creating preference. Its main features are:

○   *Two-way. Two-way communications are always more persuasive than one-way. The sales person is able to modify and tailor the information to the reactions and wants of the customer.*

○   *Closure. Personal selling allows the deal to be agreed. It also puts the buyer under psychological pressure to respond to the representative's visit.*

○   *Relationships. Personal selling facilitates the developments of friendships and lasting relationships that encourage continuing business.*

○   *Expensive. Personal selling is normally a much more expensive form of communication. With keeping a salesperson on the road costing up to £100 000, an individual sales call can easily cost £20 as against a few pence using ads or promotions.*

DIRECT MARKETING

Direct marketing includes digital communications, email, catalogues, mailings and telemarketing. (See box, 'The Impact of Digital Technology on Marketing'.)

○   *Personalised. The message can usually be addressed to a specific person and customised to their individual circumstances.*

○   *Responsive. Direct marketing usually invites a behavioural response from the buyer. Where effective, direct marketing can lead to a rapid increase in sales.*

○   *Interactive. Messages can be prepared quickly and can be changed depending on the customer's response.*

○   *Targeted. Direct marketing can be precisely targeted to specific market segments.*

What determines the right mix of communications for a brand? The allocation the manager should make depends upon the following factors:

1.   **The company's objectives and capabilities.** If the company's aim is to increase awareness in the mass market, then advertising is the obvious medium. On the other hand, if it wants to create trial, promotions are attractive. The resources available also influence the options. Television advertising is very expensive; PR can be cheap.

2.   **Characteristics of the target market.** If the target market consists of a relatively small number of customers, direct selling is likely to be effective. If the market consists of millions of customers, then mass media will be better.

3. **Type of product.** In general, personal selling is the most effective vehicle for products that are expensive, complex and high risk, and for markets with few, large buyers. Advertising and sales promotion are more efficient for products that are cheaper and routine, or where emotions play an important role in the choice process.

4. **Push versus pull strategy.** An important factor is whether the company is pursuing a push or a pull marketing strategy. A pull strategy uses advertising and consumer promotions targeted at end customers with the aim of getting them to induce the retailer or other channels to stock the product. Pull strategies create a demand from consumers. A push strategy directs selling and promotions to the trade with the aim of incentivising retailers and distributors to carry the product and in turn promote it to customers.

5. **Stage of market evolution.** The mix of communications instruments tends to shift as the product and market evolve. For a new product, advertising and public relations, including word of mouth, are usually the most appropriate vehicles to build awareness. In the mature phase, sales promotion and personal selling can become more important. In the decline stage, advertising, PR and direct selling are cut back as there is little new to say about the product and declining margins make it difficult to justify high investment. Sales promotion will often be necessary to stimulate the trade to continue to push the product.

The Impact of Digital Technology on Marketing

The Internet is radically affecting how the firm communicates with its customers and builds relationships with them.

Three factors have made the continued rapid growth of the Internet a certainty. One is the explosion of Internet access devices in addition to the personal computer, such as mobile phones, handheld devices, digital assistants, digital TV and games machines. The second is the rapid development of broadband communications, which enormously expands the speed and amount of information that can be accessed by customers. Third, and most important, is the sheer amount of customer-focused innovation being released by companies racing to capitalise on the opportunities presented by the new technology.

A survey of marketers around the world by McKinsey[10] in 2007 looked at what online tools are most important, how they are being used and on which ones companies plan to spend more. Along with established online tools such as email, information-rich web sites and display advertising, the respondents showed a lot of interest in more interactive and collaborative technologies known as 'Web 2.0' for advertising, product development and customer service.

These technologies include:

- **Blogs:** web log which are online journals hosted on a web site.

- **Podcasts:** audio or video recordings – a multi-media form of blog or other content, often distributed through 'aggregator' sites such as Apple's ITunes.

- **Social networks:** sites such as MySpace and Facebook enable members to learn about each other.

- **Virtual worlds:** sites like Second Life are highly social, three-dimensional online environments shaped by users who interact with each other and receive instant feedback through 'avatars'.

- **Wikis:** such as Wikipedia, which are systems for collaborative publishing.

INTEGRATED MARKETING COMMUNICATIONS

To make the communications investment effective it is important for management to integrate the various elements of the communications mix around a common set of objectives.[11] In recent years the major advertising agencies, such as Saatchi & Saatchi, J. Walter Thompson and Young & Rubicam, have bought agencies specialising in sales promotion, digital communications, direct marketing and public relations with the aim of making an integrated communications offer to clients. But this move has not been noticeably successful – most clients still prefer to choose their own set of specialist agencies and to develop strategies for individual elements of their communications mix.

Often these activities are poorly coordinated – each agency working in isolation, developing its own messages, themes and modes of presentation, and reporting to different specialist managers within the client company, jealously guarding their own areas. The results are communications efforts that fail to exploit the synergies between the company's advertising, digital, direct marketing and promotional initiatives, and that do not maximise the effectiveness of the large investment it may be making.

Integrated communications can be stimulated by a number of measures. First, management should have a single budget for marketing communications. One manager should have responsibility for the company's entire communications investment. The company's communications specialists should plan the communications strategy as a team and work out how it should be coordinated and implemented. Finally, senior managers should evaluate the results of the communications strategy as a whole in terms of overall, rather than specialist, goals. The world's biggest advertiser, Procter & Gamble, has adopted this approach to incentivise its managers and their specialist communications agencies to work as a team. It has moved away from the traditional approach of paying agencies a commission on the work they do, to paying them a performance fee based on the overall sales achieved by the business unit.

MEASURING COMMUNICATIONS EFFECTIVENESS

In spite of the huge sums being spent on communications, companies spend relatively little on judging whether their investments have paid off. More is spent on pretesting campaigns than on post-campaign results.

PRETESTS

Before the national or international launch of a major communications campaign, companies will sometimes test it in one region to assess its effects on sales. If the campaign fails, it can be dropped before more is spent. But because such real market tests take time, most companies rely on more flexible copy testing services. These involve showing proposed ads to audiences of potential consumers and having the messages rated for their ability to attract attention, achieve cognitive effects, and impact on customers' attitudes and intentions to buy. Most advertising agencies are sceptical about such pretesting, arguing that the methods overemphasise the rationality of consumers and ignore the ads' non-verbal effects on subsequent behaviour.

SALES EFFECTS RESEARCH

More companies, like Procter & Gamble, want to judge the success of marketing and communications spending through its effect on increasing sales. But caution is necessary in using short-term sales increases as a measure of value generation. Many factors affect sales besides communications investments. A longer period than a year has to be used to judge the effectiveness of an image-building campaign. Another factor, which we explore in the next section, is the benchline for judging sales effects. For many brands, especially in mature markets, the communications spend is necessary to prevent sales and margins declining. Looking at increased sales therefore may seriously underestimate the economic effect of the investment.

Managers can benchmark the effectiveness of their spend against competitors by comparing their share of voice to market share ratios. For example, the table below shows the three competitors in a market. Company A has a communications effectiveness score of 1.1 – its market share is 10 per cent higher than its relative communications spend. B, spending the same amount as A, is much less effective. Company C is the most efficient with a score of 1.3, suggesting it could profitably increase its market share by spending more on marketing communications.

	Communications expenditure	Share of voice (%)	Market share (%)	Communications effectiveness*
A	£10 000 000	40	44	1.10
B	£10 000 000	40	30	0.75
C	£5 000 000	20	26	1.30

*Market share divided by share of voice

Caution is required in such comparisons. For example, mature products benefiting from their past investments in the brand would expect to have higher scores than new ones. Differences can also be due to factors other than communications effectiveness. For example, C's high score could be the result of lower prices or superior quality.

INTERMEDIATE VARIABLES

Most evaluations of campaigns are still based on examining their communications effects. There are a variety of market research services that seek to answer such questions as how effective the campaign has been in creating awareness, building comprehension and achieving positive attitudes to the brand. Unfortunately, while these measures give useful diagnostics they are generally at best only weakly associated with sales and profits. As always, the only really satisfactory measure of the communications investment is whether it creates shareholder value, a subject we return to in a following section.

GENERALISATIONS ABOUT COMMUNICATIONS EFFECTS

There has been a vast amount of research on communications, especially on advertising. As always, when human behaviour is concerned there are no laws that can predict responses. There are big variations in the effectiveness of different communications campaigns depending on their creativity of execution, the competitive response, the nature of the market and the differential advantage of the product or service. Nevertheless, it is useful to summarise the general conclusions of the research as this provides some broad benchmarks on what can be expected from marketing and communications spending.

○ *The direct effect of communications on sales is usually small. Most studies find advertising elasticities around 0.2 or less, compared to elasticities of up to 2 for price promotions. This implies that a 10 per cent increase in advertising would increase sales by 2 per cent, while a 10 per cent price cut would increase sales by 20 per cent.*

○ *Communications are often critical for new brands. The advertising elasticity is higher for new brands. Communications create awareness and comprehension, and signals the brand's quality.*

○ *Once brands are established the role of communications is to reinforce existing buying behaviour. Communications add value by maintaining sales and prices rather than increasing them. While these may appear modest goals they can have a major effect on the value of the brand.*

○ *The effect of communications on maintaining price levels can be as important as its effects on volume. Brand advertising tends to reduce price sensitivity allowing the firm to obtain higher gross margins and be less sensitive to price competition.*

○ *Advertising has diminishing effects in terms of short-term sales results. The first exposure to an ad has the biggest effect on consumers' purchasing behaviour. After the third exposure, effects are usually very small. This means that reach soon becomes more important than frequency.*

○ *Communications are more effective when the brand has a differential advantage. Such an advantage can be based on functional or emotional attributes.*

○ *Because communications elasticities are normally low, the pay-off will vary with the brand's profit contribution. High communications budgets are unlikely to create value on low-margin products.*

These conclusions suggest that the power of communications, and particularly advertising, has often been exaggerated. The satisfactory experience of customers and habit tend to be more important than marketing and communications in maintaining sales. For new brands, companies have to employ additional and more powerful means to capture initial sales, including aggressive pricing, samples and word-of-mouth endorsements. At the same time, shareholder value is a long-term phenomenon. This means that small advantages in communications effectiveness will compound over time into surprisingly large value differences. This is illustrated next.

VALUING COMMUNICATIONS STRATEGIES

The basic principle of value-based marketing is that managers should develop and choose the marketing strategy that is most likely to maximise the return for shareholders. As we have seen, this is the strategy that maximises the net present value of all future cash flow. This is the principle that should be used in valuing and selecting communications strategies.

We have shown that there are two broad types of communications problems: high-involvement and low involvement. In high involvement purchasing situations the buyer is searching for information about the attributes or emotional benefits offered by competing products. The function of communications here is to help buyers solve this problem by providing information to take them through the process of learning about the product and building attitudes favourable to purchase. The ultimate test of this type of communications is whether it succeeds in increasing the number of buyers and the value of sales. Low-involvement buying is different. Here buyers are familiar with the product and have bought it before. The function of communications is not persuading customers to try it, but to reinforce current purchasing habits.

To determine whether a given investment in advertising and marketing creates value in high-involvement situations is straightforward. Managers have to forecast the effects of the expenditure on the components of sales, estimate the resulting free cash flows, discount them and calculate the shareholder value added. This is similar to the case summarised in Table 9.2. The problem becomes more controversial, however, in the low-involvement situation when marketing and communication expenditures do not increase sales. Is it in the shareholders' interest to spend money on advertising and communications when there is no increase in sales or profits? This answer to this very common problem is presented next.

COMMUNICATIONS IN LOW-INVOLVEMENT MARKETS

The problem of valuing marketing spend in a mature, low-involvement market is illustrated in this fictitious case study.

Sigma, from Associated Biscuits, is a brand leader in the impulse biscuit market. It had succeeded in maintaining sales despite the growth of retailer own-label brands and competitive new product launches from Cadbury and Nestlé. Awareness is very high and consumer attitude and usage studies confirm the brand's strong profile and franchise. However, a newly appointed finance director is less impressed about the brand, pointing to its low operating margin, lack of growth in recent years, and heavy spending on advertising and marketing. He observed that spending on communications amounted to 10 per cent of sales and exceeded profits by 150 per cent.

The marketing manager had proposed a communications budget of £30 million, the same as in the previous year. But the finance director had calculated that the breakeven on this expenditure amounted to £7.5 million (£30 million divided by the contribution margin of 50 per cent) and was unwilling to endorse the budget unless marketing could promise such a sales increase. He stated that profits would be higher without the campaign, with a cost saving of up to £30 million. He demonstrated this on a spreadsheet to the marketing manager. Column A shows the budget; column B shows the profits with no communications support, and column C shows the budget with the communications budget halved. Column D shows profits if advertising is eliminated and sales decline as a result by 5 per cent.

The marketing manager was alarmed since this clearly showed – to his surprise – that profits were significantly higher without the advertising and communications support. He also knew that there was no way that sales next year would increase by the 25 per cent necessary to achieve the breakeven on the communications budget.

£ million

	A	B	C	D
Sales	30	30	30	28.5
Variable costs	18	18	18	17.1
Contribution	12	12	12	11.4
Communications and marketing	3	0	1.5	0
Overheads	7	7	7	7
Operating profits	2	5	3.5	4.4

The manager discussed the problem with a friend who was a City analyst. The analyst criticised the financial director's approach. She said the director was using an old-fashioned accountancy approach, which investors had jettisoned years ago. Investors, she said, were interested in long-run performance, not just next year's results. Also, she said, shareholders were interested in cash, which was a much more objective and relevant figure than accounting profit. Finally, she thought the financial director was taking a very naïve and short-term view of marketing and consumer behaviour. Surely, she pointed out, cutting marketing support would lead to long-term erosion of the brand. It would also hit margins because retailers would need to be offered more discounts to give shelf space to a declining brand.

Drawing a handheld computer from her handbag, she suggested they explore three valuations: the value of the brand to shareholders with the past strategy being continued; the value using the financial director's plan, and an alternative strategy to boost operating profits.

VALUE WITH THE CONTINUING STRATEGY

Under the continuing strategy, the marketing manager believed that Sigma could hold market share and profits would remain around the present level for the foreseeable future. This meant shareholder value could be estimated by the perpetuity method. Assuming a tax rate of 30 per cent and a cost of capital of 10 per cent, then the value of the business was now worth £14 million.[12]

VALUE UNDER THE FINANCIAL DIRECTOR'S PLAN

The marketing manager reconsidered the implications of the financial director's plan. He thought that the idea of losing 5 per cent of sales if advertising and brand support was abandoned was reasonable. But if there was no brand support in the future years he thought it obvious that sales would continue to decline. He estimated this decline as around 2.5 per cent a year. Having negotiated with the major retail chains, he knew that a declining brand would become unattractive to them and he would have to pay higher discounts to retain shelf space. He figured this would have the effect of eroding prices by 2 per cent a year. Table 9.3 shows the new scenario.

Table 9.3 Implications of Eliminating Discretionary Communications Spending, £million

Year	0	1	2	3	4	5
Cases (m. units)	20.00	19.00	18.53	18.06	17.61	17.17
Unit price (£)	1.50	1.47	1.44	1.41	1.38	1.36
Sales	30.00	27.93	26.69	25.50	24.36	23.28
Variable costs	15.00	14.25	13.89	13.55	13.21	12.88
Contribution	15.00	13.68	12.79	11.95	11.16	10.40
Communications and marketing	3.00	0.00	0.00	0.00	0.00	0.00
Overheads	10.00	10.00	10.00	10.00	10.00	10.00
Operating profit	2.00	3.68	2.79	1.95	1.16	0.40
NOPAT	1.40	2.58	1.96	1.37	0.81	0.28
Net investment		−0.83	−0.50	−0.48	−0.45	−0.43
Cash flow	1.40	3.40	2.45	1.84	1.26	0.72
DCF	1.40	3.09	2.03	1.38	0.86	0.44

Cumulative present value	7.81
PV of continuing value	1.75
Shareholder value	9.56

In the first year, the financial director was correct: profits and cash flow would be higher if the advertising and marketing budget were cut. But from the second year profits and cash flow would fall precipitously as market share and prices eroded. At £9.56 million, shareholder value is one-third less under this policy than under the current strategy.

VALUE UNDER AN ALTERNATIVE STRATEGY

The analyst suggested that if the financial director was determined to improve short-term profits, then a strategy that might do less permanent damage to the brand would be to raise the price by 5 per cent. She suggested that a leading brand like Sigma would be expected to have a lower than average price elasticity, say around −1, suggesting this might erode the number of cases sold by around 5 per cent. They were pleased with the numbers that were generated from these assumptions: operating profits jumped by nearly 40 per cent to £2.77 million and shareholder value increased to £19.38 million. The market share loss over the planning period was only 5 per cent as against nearly 15 per cent under the financial director's plan.[13]

In summary, the three options gave the following figures:

	Shareholder value (£)	Market share, year 5 (%)
Current policy	£14 000 000	34
Finance director	£9 560 000	29
Alternative policy	£19 380 000	32

SUMMARY

1. It is not enough to have a good product; its values have to be communicated to create awareness, to build an understanding of its benefits, and to develop positive attitudes towards it. Without a decisive communications strategy competitors can catch up and usurp the brand's position in the customer's share of mind.

2. Usually neither marketing nor accounting managers know how to evaluate spending on communications. Marketers usually look at awareness and sales, accountants focus on the impact on short-term profits. Neither set of measures correlates with shareholder value.

3. Investing in communications and marketing increases shareholder value by creating and developing intangible assets which enhance the effectiveness of the business's core processes: new product development, customer relationship management and management of the supply chain.

4. The firm's commercial communications activities are only one of many factors affecting the buying process. In general their effects are quite small. Nevertheless, small differences in communications effectiveness can compound over a long period to significant differences in the value of the business to investors.

5. There are two broad models of how communications work: the high-involvement and low-involvement models. The former sees the role of communications primarily as persuading new customers to buy; the latter sees its role as reinforcing current buying behaviour.

6. Much advertising and communications investment is primarily about reinforcement. Such spending can still create shareholder value even though its effects on increasing sales is minimal.

REVIEW QUESTIONS

1.   How do advertising and communications create shareholder value?
2.   Contrast how accountants and marketing managers conventionally judge the effectiveness of spending on marketing and communications.
3.   How do advertising and communications influence buying behaviour?
4.   Describe how communications objectives will differ for mature products and new ones.
5.   Describe the steps in developing a communications strategy.
6.   Show how to evaluate the potential effect on shareholder value of a communications plan.

NOTES ON CHAPTER 9

[1] *Finance Directors Survey 2000*, sponsored by the Institute of Practitioners in Advertising and KPMG, London: IPA, 2000.

[2] Demetrios Vakratsas and Tim Ambler, How advertising works: what do we really know, *Journal of Marketing*, **63**, January, 1999, 26–43.

[3] The increase in sales is given by the elasticity times the percentage increase in the spend: 0.2×25 per cent $=$ 5 per cent. Sales would be expected to grow from £50 million to £50 million.

[4] *Finance Directors Survey 2000*, sponsored by the Institute of Practitioners in Advertising and KPMG, London: IPA, 2000.

[5] A good summary of supporting studies is in Rajendra K. Strivastava, Tasadduq A. Shervani and Liam Fahey, Market-based assets and shareholder value: a framework for analysis, *Journal of Marketing*, **62**, January, 1998, 2–18. See also: Werner Reinartz and V. Kumar, The mismanagement of customer loyalty, *Harvard Business Review*, 2002.

[6] Adapted from Philip Kotler, *Marketing Management*, New Jersey: Prentice Hall, 2000, p. 563.

[7] For a good example see, The FTSE's bright, the FTSE's Orange: how advertising enhanced Orange PLC shareholder value, *The IPA Advertising Effectiveness Awards 1998*, London: IPA, 1999.

[8] For a full account see Dominique M. Hanssens, Leonard J. Parsons and Randall L. Schultz, *Market Response Models: Econometric and Time Series Analysis*, Boston, MA: Kluwer, 1990.

[9] Leonard M. Lodish, Magid Abraham *et al*. A summary of 55 in-market experimental estimates of the long-term effects of advertising, *Marketing Science*, **14**(3), 133–140.

[10] Jacques Bughin, Christoph Erbenich, Amy Shenkan, How companies are marketing online: A McKinsey Global Survey, *McKinsey Quarterly*, September 2007.

[11] For a compelling example of how a well-planned integrated communications campaign can create value, see 'It only works if it all works: how troubled BT Cellnet transformed into thriving O2', *The IPA Advertising Effectiveness Awards, 2004*, IPA/WARC.

[12] After tax profit or NOPAT is £1.4 million. Dividing by the cost of capital at 10 per cent gives £50 million.

[13] It should be straightforward to rework Table 9.3 on a spreadsheet to check this alternative strategy.

10 Value-Based Marketing in the Digital Age

'Every now and then, a technology comes along that is so profound, so powerful, so universal, that its impact will change everything. It will transform every institution in the world. It will create winners and losers, it will change the way we do business, the way we teach our children, communicate and interact as individuals.'

Lou Gerstner, Chairman of IBM

INTRODUCTION AND OBJECTIVES

The growth and speed of the impact of the Internet on business and society has had few precedents. 'The Internet changes everything' is a cry heard on every business platform. What accounts for the obsession with the Internet? The Internet has offered such enormous improvements in operating efficiency and market effectiveness that, in many markets, traditional ways of doing business look to be unviable. The Internet is fundamental for marketing, despite the bursting of the dot.com bubble in the early 2000s. Most companies' web sites are managed by their marketing departments. More importantly, the Internet radically affects how the firm communicates with its customers and builds relationships with them.

By the time you have completed this chapter, you will be able to:

○   *Understand the development of the Internet and its key features*

○   *Describe the drivers of the new e-markets*

○   *Assess how the Internet is reshaping marketing and competition*

○   *Show how it can create value for customers*

○   *Analyse how the Internet affects marketing strategy*

○   *Summarise how companies need to respond to the threats and opportunities from the Internet*

The chapter begins by describing the growth and development of the Internet and the key features for marketing. It explains the three fundamental drivers of e-business: digitisation, the network economy and one-to-one communication with customers. It then shows how the web creates value for customers and companies. We then look at the implications for marketing strategy and communications.

THE GROWTH AND DEVELOPMENT OF THE INTERNET

GROWTH OF THE NET

The Internet refers to the web of computer networks that is making possible today's cheap, instantaneous global communications. Public interest in the Internet first exploded in 1994. But its origins go back 30 years earlier. Research into the Internet started in the USA and Europe in the early 1960s. In the USA the objective was to create an emergency military communications network that would be invulnerable to nuclear attack. In Europe the aim was to develop a communications system that would allow academics to share research ideas. The first practical implementation of the Net occurred in 1969, when the University of California at Los Angeles was connected to the Stanford Research Institute. In the following years today's universal Internet standards were developed, including the @ symbol in addresses (1971), remote accessing of computers through telnet (1972), multiple-person chat sessions (1973), and the downloading of files through ftp (1973). After these developments the embryonic Internet spread quickly among academics. In particular, the research community soon adopted email as an effective means of communicating with colleagues.

In 1994 three breakthroughs brought the Internet out of academia and into a much broader community. First, the US National Science Foundation, which effectively regulated the Internet, ended its ban on the commercial use of the Net. Second, low-cost computers and new software made it much easier and cheaper to access the Net. Third, the development of web browsers and web servers made it possible for people to navigate the Net more easily and for organisations to put richer content on to their web sites.

These breakthroughs created a communications and marketing revolution that is still ongoing. Now, anyone connected to the Net can communicate with anyone else through open, universal standards, instantaneously and at almost zero cost. Companies can communicate with other companies, individuals with other individuals and companies with individuals. Firms suddenly found themselves able to create marketing material that had global reach for very low cost. Small businesses could compete on a much more even footing with the largest firms in the world. Customers found that they could quickly find product and company information at the click of a mouse. Even more fundamental, companies and customers could engage in a dialogue and learn from each other.

Since 1994 the number of people connected to the Net has grown exponentially every year. By the end of 2007, there were over 1.3 billion users worldwide. Almost 70 per cent of the population were connected to the Internet in the USA in 2006. In Britain the equivalent figure was over 55 per cent, while in Germany, France and Italy it was around 1 in 2. Moreover, the amount of material on the web is increasing even faster than the number of users. As of 2008, there were at least 45 billion pages on the web and over 100 million web sites.

Three factors have made the continued rapid growth of the Internet a certainty. One is the explosion of new Internet access devices in addition to the personal computer: common methods of home access include dial-up, landline broadband (over coaxial cable, fiber optic or copper wires), personal digital assistants, digital TV and games machines, Wi-Fi, satellite and 3G technology cell phones. The second has been the rapid development of broadband communications, which enormously expands the speed and amount of information that can be accessed by customers. Third, and most important, is the sheer amount of customer-focused innovation being released by companies racing to capitalise on the opportunities presented by the new technology.

DRIVERS OF CHANGE IN THE NEW ECONOMY

Three forces are driving the growth of the Internet and e-commerce: digitisation, networks and customisation. These in turn are reshaping the role and tools of marketing and the ways companies create value for shareholders.

GOING DIGITAL: MOORE'S LAW

The digital concept is very simple. Something is digital when all its properties and information are stored as a string of zeros and ones. The smallest piece of this digital information is called a bit. All the text, pictures, music and videos seen on a computer screen or sent over the Internet are simply strings of bits. Digital devices that process bits are now all around us in the car, in the home, in digital cameras, digital TVs and digital telephones. Everything on the Internet is digital. The essence of the information revolution is this transformation of information into digital form where it can be manipulated by computers and transmitted by networks. Computers and digital devices are all built on semiconductors (or chips). The remarkable phenomenon about semiconductor production is the striking productivity gains that occur. Chips are becoming cheaper, smaller and more powerful at an amazing rate. The significance of this is that computing power has apparently boundless possibilities because of its power, cheapness and applicability.

This feature was first codified by Gordon Moore, founder of Intel, into what is now accepted as an equation of enormous power.

Moore's Law states that every 18 months, computer processing power doubles while cost stays constant.

Every 18 months, you get twice as much power for the same price, or the same power for half the cost. Moore's Law has proved to be remarkably accurate for the past 30 years, and most scientists expect it to hold for the next 30 years too. It means computing power is becoming almost free. It also means that storing, processing and communicating information becomes incredibly cheap. This provides new ways for marketing to create value for customers and shareholders. Let us look at some of the implications of Moore's Law.

RESOURCE SUBSTITUTION – 'ATOMS TO BITS'

In the new digital world bits replace atoms. To create shareholder value it means managers must seek to substitute cheap digital resources for those that are expensive – labour, raw materials and capital. So to stay cost competitive banks are replacing branches with the Internet; companies replace paper with online documents; letters and telephone calls are replaced by email; service staff by online customer support. Digital substitution also allows firms to become more effective as well as to reduce costs. Firms can offer benefits to customers that were virtually impossible before, such as '24/7' (twenty-four hours a day, seven days a week availability and service). Web sites can offer information in multiple languages, or even instantaneous translation.

THE DEVELOPING DIGITAL ENVIRONMENT

Currently many customers find the digital interface a poor substitute for the richness of shopping in the real world. But broadband access, faster connection speeds and advances in software have made cyberspace increasingly realistic, stimulating and user friendly. Web sites can now create a virtual space to simulate or enhance the real world, whether it is a shop, classroom or office. Customers can get feedback and interaction, and shopping agents can give advice or compare different products. Two- or three-dimensional images allow customers to 'walk around' products and even try them out under simulated conditions. Finally, the product assortment and information available on a well-designed web site can far exceed any 'bricks and mortar' site.

DIGITISING MARKETING PROCESSES

Moore's Law and the developing digital environment create major opportunities to increase the efficiency and effectiveness of marketing. To exploit these, the first step is to map out in detail the firm's marketing processes.[1] At the aggregate level these processes consist of first understanding customer needs, then involving customers in the design of products and services. Next, the products have to be communicated, sold and delivered. Finally, customer service has to be provided and customer relationships built. The second stage looks for opportunities to substitute digital material. Market research materials can be converted to online formats; the firm's intranet can be a vehicle for cross-functional new product development; web sites can augment the selling efforts; online customer support can be used to build an interface with customers. The third stage is to fundamentally redesign marketing processes to capitalise on digital capabilities. For example, the airlines are redesigning their marketing processes to cut costs and deal directly with the customer, eliminating the travel agent. The whole process, from enquiring about schedules and availability, making reservations, to obtaining an 'e-ticket', has now been digitised.

NETWORKS AND METCALF'S LAW

Moore's Law puts cheap computing power into the hands of millions. The Internet permits all these users to be linked together into a universal communications network. Once people are networked, new sources of consumer and shareholder value are created that go beyond the acceleration of computing power predicted by Moore. Digitisation is a technological phenomenon; networks that allow millions of people to communicate with organisations and with one another are social phenomena.

What explained why the Internet was so valuable was a law, proposed by Robert Metcalf, founder of 3Com Corporation.

Metcalf's Law states that the value of any network is proportional to the square of the number of users.

For example, a telephone service is not very valuable if only a handful of people is connected. Its value rises rapidly the more users are connected. When the Internet was only used by a handful of academics, it was not very valuable. Now that hundreds of millions of people and organisations are connected, it becomes essential. The explosion of connectivity that the Internet created has implications that promise to fundamentally change how businesses create value for their customers and shareholders.

UNBUNDLING PRODUCTS AND INFORMATION

Companies have traditionally provided customers jointly with both information and products. For example, shoppers go to a car showroom to collect information about features, credit terms, prices and availability. They visit a bookshop to see what is available and suitable for reading on holiday. This joint supply leads to compromises since the economics of information are very different from the economics of goods. Traditional bookshops and car showrooms are ideal neither for purchasing nor for obtaining information. For example, the information provided by a car dealer is biased and shoppers cannot see the range of competitors' cars that they might also want to consider. As a place to purchase cars, showrooms are too small to be efficient, nor can they carry a full inventory, even of their own brand. The Net is breaking these compromises across a range of industries, offering better solutions for customers. Book businesses like Amazon and car sites like Autobytel now separate the economics of information from the economics of products. Information is most effectively provided on the Internet, where it can be complete and unbiased. Products can be most effectively delivered from a single site, where economies of scale can be reaped and an encyclopaedic assortment held.

UNBUNDLING VALUE CHAINS AND RESHAPING INDUSTRIES

The separation of the supply of products and information is only one form of unbundling. Businesses typically undertake multiple processes. They undertook these processes internally rather than purchasing them in the market because transaction costs made it more economical to do it that way.[2] Cheap information networks have changed all this, making it more efficient and effective to specialise and focus on core competencies. Bundled companies are ceasing to work as customers use information networks to find cheaper or better specialists. Figure 10.1 illustrates this for a large assurance company.[3] In 1990 it was a fully integrated business undertaking its own administration, investment management and selling in-house products through its own large direct sales force of 15 000 representatives. During the 1990s it was attacked by new competitors with specialist innovative products and undermined by new channels of distribution like the Internet and independent financial advisors. Like many companies, it survived by unbundling. Ten years later virtually all its processes and most of its products had been outsourced, putting the company at the hub of a network of specialists, virtually rather than vertically integrated.

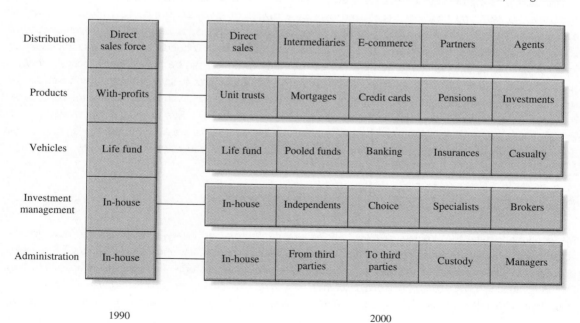

Figure 10.1   The Unbundling of Life Assurance Companies, 1990–2000

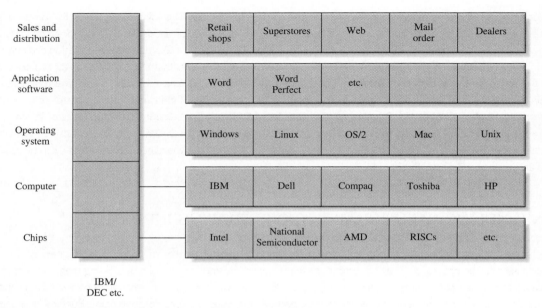

Sales and distribution		Retail shops	Superstores	Web	Mail order	Dealers
Application software		Word	Word Perfect	etc.		
Operating system		Windows	Linux	OS/2	Mac	Unix
Computer		IBM	Dell	Compaq	Toshiba	HP
Chips		Intel	National Semiconductor	AMD	RISCs	etc.

IBM/ DEC etc.

Figure 10.2   The Growth of Specialists in the Computer Industry

THE GROWTH OF SPECIALISTS

A company is vulnerable if any of its processes or products can be undertaken more effectively by a specialist. The advantage of integrated generalists disappears when customers can do their own integration. Figure 10.2 illustrates how specialists have grown in the computer industry. An industry that was once dominated by vertically integrated companies like IBM and DEC has been taken over by a myriad of specialists competing with one another at each stage of the value chain. Customers can use cheap information networks to put together any combination of components. Newspapers are another example of an industry threatened by unbundling and specialists. Newspapers jointly supply news, features and advertising. But each of these products can be done more effectively now by specialists. Classified ads for jobs or homes can be accessed more easily through specialist searches on web sites. If such ads migrate to the Net, the whole economics of the newspaper industry, with ads subsidising the cover price, is deconstructed. Worse, Net specialists like Google and Yahoo! are providing free 'newspapers' over the Internet, actually configured to the special interests of individual readers. Networks break down industry entry barriers, ushering in new competitors and exposing the weakness of the traditional leaders.

DISINTERMEDIATION AND REINTERMEDIATION

Networks undermine the business of many wholesalers, distributors and retailers. Producers can now achieve faster, cheaper communication and interaction themselves with customers, and then supply directly. This enables producers to take out distribution costs and recapture control over the customer relationship. Companies such as Dell in computing, Direct Line in personal insurance, First Direct in banking and Charles Schwab in stockbroking leapfrogged into industry leadership by such disintermediation. It is a change occurring today in market after market.

At the same time new types of intermediaries have emerged.[4] With the exploding volume of information on the Net, customers can find it difficult to identify and evaluate the myriad of alternatives offered by an expanding number of specialist web competitors. Infomediaries help customers through the maze by comprehensively searching for what is available, tailoring their recommendations to the individual customer's requirements, and providing unbiased advice. These infomediaries can be portals (e.g. Google), social networks/virtual communities (e.g. YouTube, MySpace, Facebook), net companies (e.g. Amazon) or shopping agents (e.g. ValueStar).

INDIVIDUAL CUSTOMISATION

The third driver of the phenomenal growth of the Internet and e-commerce is the opportunity it offers for one-to-one marketing. The essence of successful marketing is meeting the needs of the customer. When the company precisely meets the needs of the customer, the customer is satisfied and a basis for long-term loyalty is established. Until recently, at least in markets with large numbers of customers, this was hardly possible. Companies lacked the ability to interact and learn about customers on an individual basis. In the sales era, companies used broadcast media, advertising the same message to everyone. In the brand management period, markets were segmented and differentiated messages were sent, but it remained one-way communication (Figure 10.3). Even if companies had learned individual requirements, it was generally too costly to customise products. Businesses were built around the economics of mass production of standardised products.

Moore's Law and networks break the need for these compromises between economies of scale and customisation. The increasing numbers of customers connected to the Internet permits the company to identify its important clients and to have a one-to-one dialogue. The shift to the networked organisation enables the firm to use its extranet to tailor customised products, to make to order.

The benefits to the customer of individual customisation are a more precise matching to his or her specific requirements – greater value. In the past, customised products and personalised service have been the privilege of the elite. Only the rich could afford to have their clothes, homes or cars customised and made to order. Digitisation and networks democratise consumption, making customisation affordable to the many rather than the few. Personalisation becomes cheap because it is automated, made virtual, and leverages existing digital assets. So Internet pioneers such as Dell, Yahoo! and Amazon flourished by offering customers what they want, how they want it, when they want it.

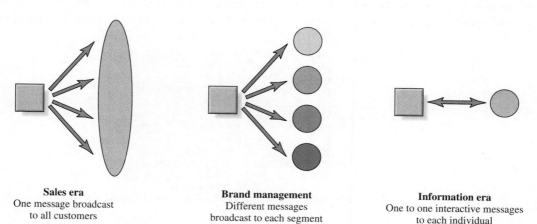

Sales era
One message broadcast
to all customers

Brand management
Different messages
broadcast to each segment

Information era
One to one interactive messages
to each individual

Figure 10.3　From Broad Messages to Interaction

These changes also help individuals make more rational decisions in purchasing situations where they lack experience. Online services like California-based ValueStar rate difficult-to-evaluate, non-standardised services such as local garages, hospitals and house repairers. Amazon helps customers choose books by recommending titles bought by other customers who have similar tastes. New opportunities are appearing everywhere for marketers that can develop personalisation techniques that help customers match products to tastes and eliminate unpleasant purchasing experiences.

For companies that succeed at individually customising their communications and products and service, the benefits are stronger customer relationships. This in turn increases the lifetime value of their customers and feeds directly into the shareholder value equation.

CREATING VALUE THROUGH THE WEB

We need to look at how the web offers enormous opportunities for managers to create shareholder value, and why failing to take advantage of these opportunities can destroy shareholder value. Since shareholder value is based primarily on offering customer value, we start by summarising what benefits customers can obtain from web-based businesses.

HOW THE WEB CREATES VALUE FOR CUSTOMERS

The web offers customers seven benefits that together account for the growth of online buying.

CUSTOMISATION

The Internet enables customers to have products and services personalised to their requirements, offering them higher delivered value. Customisation can be either in terms of how the offer is communicated to the customer or in terms of whether product attributes are personalised. Four forms can be distinguished (Figure 10.4).[5] *Cosmetic* customisers present a standard product differently to different customers. For example, many web sites give a

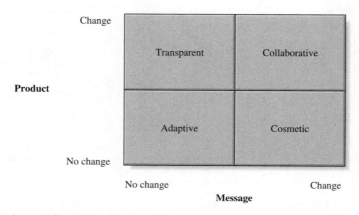

Figure 10.4   Dimensions of Customisation

personalised greeting to regular visitors, but the content of the site is unchanged. *Transparent* customisers provide individually customised products, but do not explicitly communicate this personalisation. For example, some sites make 'smart offers' – personalised presentations of goods, based on the visitor's history. The idea is to work out the visitor's needs and preferences without asking. *Adaptive* customisation uses the same product and message but the product has multiple settings, allowing the buyer to customise it. *Collaborative* customisation is the ultimate one-to-one marketing. It involves the company conducting a dialogue with individual customers to help them define their needs, to identify the precise offering that fulfils those needs, and to make customised products for them. Business-to-business extranets are examples of this form of customisation where purchasers provide the supplier with ongoing feedback through the new product development process.

GREATER ASSORTMENT

Web-based businesses can provide consumers with a much greater product assortment than bricks and mortar companies. Constraints on space and the need to achieve an economic asset turnover mean that conventional retailers and intermediaries can only stock popular items. The economics are completely different for online sellers: there are no space constraints in the virtual world, and centralised inventory holdings and networked contractors make it effective to stock a much larger numbers of items.[6] So Amazon.com or CDNow carry one hundred times the number of titles of a normal shop (the so-called 'long tail').

LOWER PRICES

A major reason why customers switch to the Net is that prices are usually substantially lower. A car buyer can easily save several thousand pounds; books can be 50 per cent cheaper. The basic reason is that a Net business has lower operating costs and a higher utilisation of assets than a conventional business. A second reason is that Net businesses often face greater price competition, as Internet buyers will typically visit several sites to make comparisons. A third reason is that most US online merchants do not have to charge sales tax. An offsetting factor is shipping costs that have to be added to the product. For digital information goods such as software, airline tickets and research reports that can be delivered over the Net, shipping costs are near zero. For bulky or perishable products shipping costs can eliminate any price savings.

GREATER CONVENIENCE

Internet shopping offers great convenience. Customers can shop when it is convenient for them, from their offices or home. Most sites offer 24/7 access and service. There is no hassle about parking the car or being disappointed that the wanted item is unavailable. Customers can do extensive comparison shopping without rising from their chair. Shopping agents will even do the comparison shopping for the customer. For example, comparison-shopping agents, also called shopbots, are web software applications that can help online shoppers find lower prices for products or services.

MORE INFORMATION

The Net offers customers almost unlimited information about products and companies, at virtually zero cost. Before ordering, customers can consult consumer guides for comparative ratings, visit specialist web sites for opinions and enter online communities to discover the views of other users. They can check prices, availability, specifications, service and features.

GREATER ASSURANCE

Web-based companies can often give customers greater confidence that their requirements will be satisfied. They retain information about previous visits and requirements forming the basis of a continuing relationship. Automated processes can remove the inconsistencies that occur with people-based service providers. They can also introduce services that specifically reassure customers that their business is on track. Federal Express customers, for example, can check online the exact location of their parcels and get up-to-the-minute details on delivery times.

ENTERTAINMENT

As companies shift to more sophisticated sites, shopping on the Internet becomes increasingly entertaining and challenging. Companies are amplifying the entertainment quotient through aligning chat rooms, instant messages and discussion groups alongside their direct e-commerce function. Auction sites like eBay owe much to the excitement customers get from being in active bidding competition with others. Further advances in the technology – such as Web 2.0 – encourage creativity, information sharing, and, most notably, collaboration among users. These concepts have led to the development and evolution of web-based communities and hosted services, such as social-networking sites, wikis and blogs.

HOW THE WEB CREATES VALUE FOR COMPANIES

Hanson distinguishes between improvement-based business models and revenue-based models.[7] We can also add a third type – mixed business models, which incorporate both benefits. Two other important benefits of Internet-based business are the acquisition of valuable customer information and the opportunity to make more effective investment decisions as a result of better measurement tools.

IMPROVEMENT-BASED BUSINESS MODELS

Improvement-based benefits from the web create shareholder value in three ways: cost savings, enhancing the brand image, and greater marketing effectiveness. These benefits are available to any firm, not just information or technology specialists.

O   **Cost savings.** *Cost savings have been a major reason for using the web, especially in B2B. Some firms have made savings of hundreds of millions of pounds a year. Posting manuals and customer support documents online can produce big savings. Online customer support also works out much cheaper than any other form of interaction. In banking, it has been calculated that the cost of a customer receiving personal service at a branch amounts to £1 per transaction, as against 40p by telephone, 20p using an ATM, 10p using a proprietary PC banking service and only 2p by Internet banking. At heart, customer* *self-service lies behind many of these savings. Customers do more of their own searching and problem-solving rather than relying on the company's staff.*

○ Enhancing the brand. *Traditional organisations such as the BBC, the Financial Times and Cadbury are using the web to enhance their brands. Creative, high quality web sites can give customers fresh insights into the capabilities and reach of the company and build stronger relationships with them. The Internet has also created powerful new brands such as portals like Google, and new Internet retailers such as Amazon and Travelocity.*

○ Greater business effectiveness. *The Internet revolutionises the firm's value chain, allowing it to do new things and to do old things better. It greatly enhances marketing effectiveness by allowing a closer dialogue with customers. It spread information about customers throughout the organisation. It is used to support outside sales people, dealers, retailers and suppliers. For example, GlaxoSmithKline's sales representatives can obtain immediate details of stock conditions, order status and delivery times over handheld computers.*

REVENUE-BASED BUSINESS MODELS

Improvement-based business models create indirect benefits because they do not immediately lead to a sale. Revenue-based business models, in contrast, generate direct benefits in the form of revenue from customers. There are two types of revenue-based models: one obtains revenues from purchasers, the other from providers paying fees to reach web site users.

○ Purchase-based revenue models. *Companies create revenues in three main ways. Sales of the company's products are the biggest and most obvious way firms such as Dell, Cisco and Federal Express have grown. A second way is pay-per-use whereby customers pay for information. Many online job search businesses charge this way. A third way is charging annual subscription fees, as do the Financial Times and Reuters business services.*

○ Provider-based business models. *Here the company obtains revenues not from users, but from other companies wanting to gain access to the web site users. These include sales commissions from providing links to other companies' sites, banner advertising, sponsorship and sharing access charges with telecoms operators. Provider-based business models generate the revenues for some of the most famous web brands, such as Google and Yahoo!.*

MIXED MODELS

Many companies create both improvement-based benefits and revenue-based benefits. Companies such as Dell and Cisco have streamlined their value chains to optimise their costs and asset utilisation, developed effective supply chain networks and built powerful brands. At the same time, they have achieved fabulous growth by moving sales online and using their web sites to attract income from customers, advertisers, sales commissions and sponsorship.

INFORMATION FOR RELATIONSHIP MANAGEMENT

Digitisation and networks allow companies to collect and hold detailed information about their customers. Before, the interaction often took place between the customer and an intermediary. This enabled the retailer or intermediary to build the brand and own the customer relationship. When this happens the supplier can be commoditised and the value in the supply chain appropriated by the intermediary or the customer. Only by holding consumer information and achieving direct interaction can a real relationship management programme to build loyalty and enhance the lifetime value of customers be created.

SUPERIOR INVESTMENT ALLOCATION

Unlike broadcast communications such as television or newspaper advertising, online marketing investments can often be directly evaluated in terms of their financial payoff. Marketing can then be held accountable for their spending because management can tell with considerable accuracy whether the spending created value. This greater ability to track online investments also allows managers to determine which types of investments – banner ads, prospect fees, sponsorship – work best to increase long-term profits. The effectiveness of online marketing is evaluated through the analysis of web chains stored in the servers. These are the sequence of steps a visitor clicks through to arrive at the company's web site. From web chains it can be determined whether, say, an ad bought on Google or Yahoo! is generating visitors and creating profitable sales. Web chain analysis can show the effectiveness of alternative strategies in achieving impressions and impact, and the expected value of prospects and customers that are stimulated.

IMPLICATIONS FOR MARKETING STRATEGY

The Internet is rapidly changing the nature of markets and marketing.

FROM CAVEAT EMPTOR TO CAVEAT VENDITOR

From buyer beware to seller beware. In the past high information costs protected the profit margins of many businesses. In the physical world, buyers face all kinds of obstacles to getting the best deal – far-flung suppliers, limited time to do research, intermediaries who hide the information. For consumers, it was generally just too tiresome to drive to three different places to save £1. The web changes the nature of markets and marketing. Internet commerce shifts the balance of commercial power to the buyer. Four factors strengthen the hands of buyers and intensify competition between suppliers.

- ○   **Instant choice.** *On the Net, competition is just a click away. If people are not satisfied with the price at Amazon.com, they can go to barnesandnoble.com.*

- ○   **Comparison shopping.** *There is a wealth of information on the Net to compare prices. CompareNet, for instance, offers detailed information on hundreds of thousands of consumer products.*

- ○   **Purchasing power.** *The Net allows consumers and corporate buyers from all over the world to band together, pool their purchasing power, and get volume discounts. For example, GE divisions pool purchases to get big price reductions on goods bought online.*

- ○   **Global reach.** *The Net eliminates the geographical protections of local and national businesses. Car dealers selling online, for example, have even drawn buyers from different countries.*

NEW MARKET OPPORTUNITIES

Electronic commerce has created entirely new high-growth markets and new sources of competitive advantage. The main sources of opportunities arise from the following:

- ○ Declining market entry barriers. *In the physical world new competitors were deterred from entry to many markets by the scale economies possessed by the incumbents, an inability to obtain distribution or good locations, established brand names and a lack of information among buyers. In the virtual world most of these barriers erode. In industry after industry – computers, travel, books, distribution, financial services – established leaders are being overtaken by new online entrants.*

- ○ Deconstructing value chains. *The increasing weaknesses of vertically integrated companies – high in costs and assets, inflexible and insufficiently specialist – are forcing companies to unbundle their value chains and outsource more and more of their products and processes. Such unbundling and the growth of virtual companies create an array of opportunities for specialist firms able to contribute products and processes to these networked organisations.*

- ○ Convergence of industries. *Common digital technologies and the Internet are leading many industries to converge. This is most obvious in the computer, communications and content industries. The results are new market opportunities and a rush of mergers, acquisitions, alliances and partnerships as firms try to capitalise on the new synergies.*

- ○ Superior customer value. *Online marketing can offer customers superior value through lower prices, greater choice, more convenience and one-to-one communication. These benefits enable companies that can quickly capitalise on them to possess differential advantages to outflank established competitors.*

NEW MARKETING STRATEGIES

The core of marketing strategy is segmentation and positioning. Segmentation refers to the choice of customers the firm is targeting for its product or service. Positioning refers to the differential advantage or choice of value proposition that the firm hopes will attract customers in the chosen market segment to its offer. In the information environment both these dimensions have to change subtly but significantly.

FROM SEGMENTATION TO PERSONALISATION

Only relatively recently has it become possible for companies in mass markets, such as Unilever and Tesco, to obtain and process information on individual consumers. Traditionally, information about consumers has been obtained through sampling. A few hundred or thousand consumers would be interviewed about their attitudes, wants and buying processes and the results would be partitioned and averaged by profilers such as age, sex, income or, sometimes, lifestyle characteristics. The aim of the market research would be to group customers into a handful of market segments with similar wants and characteristics. Then products and communications would be aimed at each of these segment averages. The result would be a compromise – products and messages that met the needs of some consumers better than others. How good or bad the fits were was often not clear since companies did not obtain direct feedback from individual consumers.

Digitisation and networks has made such compromises less necessary. Companies can now enter a dialogue with individual customers.[8] Of course, for companies with thousands or even millions of customers, investing in detailed interaction with all of them is not cost effective, so segmentation is still necessary. But the objective of segmentation is different; the aim is to segment not by similarity of needs but rather by the potential lifetime value of the customer to the organisation.

FROM BRAND PROPOSITIONS TO CUSTOMISATION

Traditionally marketing has focused on seeking to develop a unique selling proposition that would give the firm a differential advantage to a market or market segment. In the networked world competitive advantage is gained not from selling an unbeatable proposition to as many people as possible, but from matching the needs of the individual customer more precisely. It is about making *to* order rather than making *for* orders. The traditional marketing model has been based upon maximising the sales of a single product or brand by selling it to as many people as possible. The new model is based upon selling as many products as possible to each individual customer. In the language of economics, economies of scope become more important than economies of scale.[9]

What makes the transformation possible are the new capabilities that today's information technology provides. Digitally stored databases allow companies to tell customers apart and remember their individual requirements and purchasing behaviour. Interactive networks allow individual customers to talk to the company and update their learning. Mass customisation technology and networked organisations mean companies can increasingly customise their products and services at low cost.

What is forcing companies to adapt is that the old business model cannot any longer meet the increasing expectations of consumers. In attempts to meet the growing variety of consumer needs, suppliers such as Procter & Gamble or Du Pont and retailers and intermediaries such as supermarkets and distributors are being forced to carry inventories of ever increasing product ranges. A typical supermarket will carry 30 000 stock keeping units, and a supplier might have 100 varieties of steel or shoes. No single customer will want more than a minute fraction of such variety. The modern competitor is unbundling information from supply. The information about the available variety is put on the web site, the individual's requirement is then customised after the order is received, and finally it is delivered to the home or business.

THE CHANGING MARKETING MIX

Implementing marketing strategies in the information age requires companies to adapt their marketing mix.

PRODUCT POLICY

As discussed in Chapter 6, the demand for more customised products and communications has risen among customers as the technology enables companies to tailor what they offer. Customisation also allows companies to augment their products and differentiate them. Many products and services such as banking or insurance have become commodities. But what can differentiate them and create customer loyalty are personalised additions that enable them to meet requirements more effectively. These might be 24/7 access, helpful web sites, customised portfolio planning services or emails on special opportunities.

More generally, customisation shifts the company from competing in products to competing in services. Services are increasingly a more attractive area in which to compete. In the modern economy the service sector is twice the size of the goods sector and growing more rapidly. Services too tend to be more profitable. This is because products are standard and much easier for customers to compare. Also customers do not really believe there is much difference in quality between products such as computers, cars or detergents. Because services are hard to standardise they are more difficult to compare. Buying services is more risky. Customers often use price as an indicator of quality – high price means good service. The car industry is typical. Excess capacity and fierce price competition mean that few car companies make consistent economic profits. In contrast, margins on servicing cars, insuring and renting them are very attractive.

PRICING POLICY

Pricing is certainly even more critical in online markets. Customers have more information about prices than ever before, which is certain to increase price sensitivity in most markets. Companies seeking to dominate new markets are using low prices more often. But profits are so sensitive to price that ill-considered aggression can easily destroy the chances of new companies ever creating value for shareholders. (See Chapter 8 for more on pricing.)

COMMUNICATIONS AND PROMOTION

The communications mix companies have employed reflected the traditional trade-off companies have been forced to make between what Evans and Wurster call 'richness and reach'.[10] Reach refers to the number of people receiving information. Richness refers to the detail of the information and whether it can be customised through a dialogue between buyer and seller. Some communications media, such as TV advertising, allow high reach but sacrifice richness. Others, such as a sales force, allow richness but are too expensive to achieve high reach. With a given communications budget, managers choose a communications mix to achieve the best combination on the budget line (Figure 10.5). The significance of the Net is that it promises to enable much higher levels of reach without sacrificing richness. As such it is leading to significant changes in the communications mix.

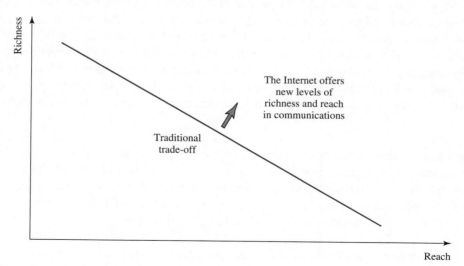

Figure 10.5   The Change in the Richness/Reach Trade-Off

Traditional advertising is a high-reach, low-richness medium since it employs a one-to-many communications model that allows only limited forms of feedback from the customer. The Internet operationalises a model that facilitates interactive multimedia one-to-one communication – a rich form of communication. Online communications differ in another important way. With conventional advertising the message is sent by the seller to customers, but with online communications the customer has to seek out the supplier's message. Online communications are self-selecting; the customer must be motivated to want to read the supplier's communication.

Online advertising possesses a number of advantages. One is that the advertiser can target the most valuable customers and not waste money on unproductive reach. This is achieved by having the ad appear only to customers with particular socio-demographic profiles, or who key in relevant words when using search engines. Increasingly advertisers can target promotions and ads on a one-to-one basis and thus build rich interactive relationships with users, one at a time. This is achieved through the personal information the user supplies when registering with a site or through 'cookies' – small data files stored on the user's hard disk, which reveal to the supplier the user's search patterns. Another strength of web communications is its ability to provide extensive product information, unlike traditional media. Finally, online advertising creates the opportunity for immediate interaction with customers, either by providing more information or completing an online order.

DISTRIBUTION

Digitisation and networks have major implications for how companies organise their distribution. The two primary functions of retailers and distributors are providing information (about availability, prices, the suitability of alternative products etc.) and supplying goods. The traditional logic of using intermediaries is that since the supplier has only a limited number of products, while customers desire a vast number of different products and services, it would be hopelessly inefficient for each producer to go to each customer, and vice versa. This is illustrated in Figure 10.6, which shows three producers, a farmer, a food processor and a beverage manufacturer, marketing to ten consumers. If there are no intermediaries, as in scenario A, then the costs of thirty separate contacts have to be paid. But with an intermediary, only thirteen contacts are required.

The Net changes this logic by permitting the separation of the economics of information from that of products. Over the Net companies and customers can interact at almost zero cost, so the model of scenario A is viable. What makes the direct model attractive to consumers is the potential of lower prices, greater assortment, more convenience and customised service. What makes it attractive to suppliers is lower costs, competitive advantage and the value-enhancing opportunities that accrue from a direct relationship with the customer. Many online marketers still need to handle the physical distribution of their goods. But when this is separated from the information function it can normally be handled from one or a small number of central distribution points, often by third parties like DHL or UPS.

This change offers disintermediation opportunities and with it big cost savings. For example, if airlines do direct booking and ticketing on the Internet they save agency commissions of at least 10 per cent. For an airline issuing a million tickets a year this amounts to a saving of around £40 million. A computer company selling direct can save around £200 per machine by eliminating the retailer. The network world is also creating opportunities for intermediaries to help buyers steer their way through the deluge of information.

The most exciting distribution breakthroughs are for digital products such as software that can be downloaded from the Internet as more products become digitised, such as music and films. More troublesome are physical products

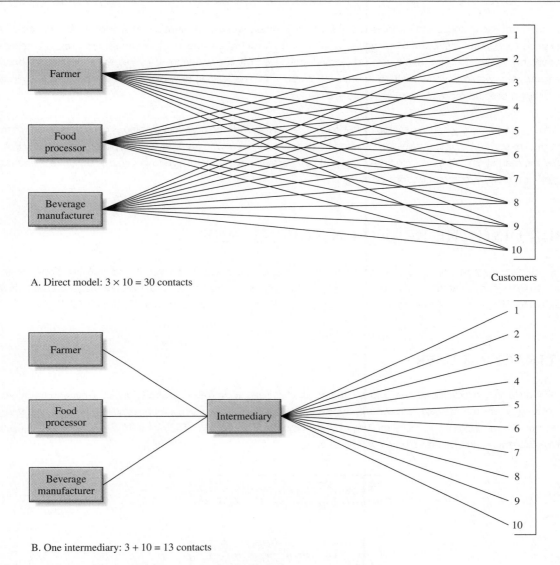

A. Direct model: $3 \times 10 = 30$ contacts

Customers

B. One intermediary: $3 + 10 = 13$ contacts

Figure 10.6 The Traditional Logic of Intermediaries

that have to be delivered by conventional logistics and which incur significant shipping costs that can negate the advantages of e-commerce. Some of the earlier pioneers invested in sophisticated web sites but failed to invest sufficiently in logistics and distribution. The result has been easy ordering but late and erratic delivery. Such hiccups can quickly erode customer loyalty.

SPEED TO MARKET

Marketers have always recognised that speed to market can offer important strategic advantages. Being first or at least early, to the market makes it easier to establish the brand's differential advantage. It can give it the opportunity to obtain the best locations and the best distribution deals. Pioneers also become magnets for companies wanting to form strategic alliances and partnerships. But the networked world adds another dimension to the importance of speed to market. This is the so-called 'network effect'. Metcalf's Law explains this – the more users a company obtains on its network, the more value customers perceive in it. If one web site carries the most holiday-break bargains, why would anyone want to consult the number 2? The leading network can develop a virtuous circle, attracting more and more customers from the also-rans.

Marketing plays the key role in developing fast-to-market strategies. It requires very ambitious objectives to dominate the market sector. Clear strategies are required to identify customers who are likely to be opinion leaders, anticipate how the market is likely to develop, take a global perspective, since the net has no geographical frontiers, and put together a creative communications campaign.

BUILDING THE BRAND ON THE INTERNET

The interactive, one-to-one character of the Internet creates new pressures for Net brand building. Yet it retains the marketing fundamentals: the need to understand the customer, environmental analysis and building competitive advantage. The process of Net brand building can be described in a five-stage process (Figure 10.7).[11]

ATTRACTING USERS

Traffic building is critical for success and it is the major challenge facing web marketers. Unlike direct and traditional marketing where the message is essentially imposed on customers, Internet marketing requires them to voluntarily seek out a web site. With so many millions of sites competing for users, generating traffic is expensive and difficult. Ways to attract users fall into the following categories:

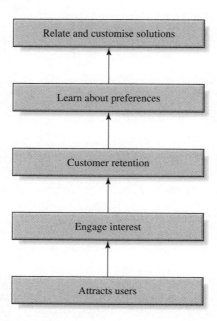

Figure 10.7   Marketing to the Digital Consumer

○ **Domain names.** *A good domain name can be an important traffic builder. The domain name is the address that customers use to find a web site. Like a brand name, a successful domain name should be easy to recall and be related to the positioning of the brand. Examples include Cocacola.com, Hyatt.com and Lastminute.com. Well-chosen names make it easy for users to remember and find the site without having to rely on search engines.*

○ **Portals.** *If a potential customer does not know the domain name, a search engine or directory such as Google or Yahoo! is the usual next step. The problem, and one which is frustrating to the user, is that a search will often list thousands of entries. If the desired site does not appear in the first dozen entries many users will give up. Such factors mean that ambitious online marketers are actively engaged in search engine optimisation, a process of improving the volume and quality of traffic to a web site from search engines.*

○ **Publicity and word-of-mouth.** *Publicity and word-of-mouth are highly effective in generating users. The Net amplifies the speed of feedback from users to potential adopters: emails, online forums and discussion groups can quickly spread good or bad news about a site (see box, 'Intel Finds Bad News Travels Fast'). Word-of-mouth follows the same dynamics as Metcalf's Law, diffusing through the network of individuals who communicate with one another. A well-designed marketing strategy targeting opinion leaders can be highly productive for diffusing information about a new site.*

Intel Finds Bad News Travels Fast

In 1994 a newly released Intel Pentium chip contained a bug that made certain complex calculations come out wrong. An early adopter – a US maths professor – noticed the flaw during his research. After emails documenting the problems were rebuffed by Intel, the professor posted the email correspondence on a CompuServe bulletin board. There they started a forest fire of comment, discussion, further examples and publicity. By the time Intel had worked out a proper response, the story had become front-page news internationally, a target of late-night jokes and a serious blow to Intel's reputation. Mishandling of the early problem eventually led to a very expensive product recall with compensation that cost Intel millions. Ironically, this eventually proved beneficial to the company. The extensive media coverage turned what was a technology brand into one recognised by millions of consumers and encouraged the company to change some of its business practices to be more end-user focused. The 'Intel Inside' campaign also helped transform perception of the Intel brand.

○ **Banners and buttons.** *These are ads which encourage users to click through to the advertiser's site. They include pay-per-click, pop-up ads and live banners which change content in real time. Banner ads have the advantage that their effectiveness can be measured, which facilitates trial and experimentation. But there is still scepticism about the effectiveness of this form of advertising because of what can be low click-through rates.*

○ **Traditional advertising media.** *Even new online companies can be heavy users of traditional advertising media. This can be more effective because target users are still not heavy users of the Internet. TV and radio are highly effective for creatively developing new brands, and newspaper ads allow the presentation of a high level of content. Particularly with B2C brands, it is difficult to create quick awareness without using traditional media. In addition, with web addresses increasingly integrated into them, traditional ads have direct traffic building effects.*

ENGAGING INTEREST

Once users have been attracted to a site it is essential to capture their interest and attention, otherwise they click out without looking at more than a couple of pages. The objective is to increase the visit duration. The longer the duration, the more time there is to communicate the messages of the site, the more chance to build commitment and loyalty, and the more opportunity to expose the user to advertising or alliance partners.

Interest is a function of the creativity of the site and the quality of its content. Creative site programming is increasingly essential to engage users. Simple sites that transfer content from conventional brochures or advertising do not work because they fail to create interaction. Successful sites are interactive, easy to use and entertaining. Simple guidance through the site is important. Users have limited tolerance for inappropriate material before abandoning their visit.

Content, or the substance of the site, is even more important. A web site must have a perceived differential advantage to engage users' interest. This may be a reputation for offering more bargains than competitive sites, greater variety or superior customisation. Being fast to market, and creating the largest network, can be key ways to create and sustain such a differential advantage.

Another technique for creating user interest is the development of online communities.[12] These bring together users of the firm's products or services to share ideas and applications. For example, GM has an online community for Saturn car owners to find and communicate with one another, while Nike has channelled investment away from traditional advertising and into non-traditional activities such as online communities, workout advice and sports competition in order to be able to interact with customers when they are online by enhancing the experience and services it offers.

CUSTOMER RETENTION

Because winning new customers is so difficult and expensive, retaining them becomes even more valuable. The enormous value of high retention to the cost of building a web site and the chance it has of becoming successful is easy to demonstrate.

Suppose a new web site has 50 000 active users and aims to grow to 100 000. It decides to run a banner advertising campaign costing £20 per thousand impressions and the click-through rate is estimated at 2 per cent. The cost for acquiring each new visitor is then £1. It decides to buy 1 million banner impressions each month until its objective is reached. Table 10.1 shows how the cost and time to build a successful site increase if retention rates are low. If retention were 100 per cent, so that all new visitors became loyal users, it would cost £70 000 and take 2.5 months to reach the 100 000-user target. With a 90 per cent retention rate it costs £100 000 and takes 4 months. The lower the retention rate the higher the cost and the longer the time needed to reach the goal. With retention rates below 80 per cent the objective can never be reached with this strategy.

Achieving high retention is about maintaining ongoing contact with users. Engaging a visitor's initial interest and maintaining loyalty are subtly different problems. Customers can visit a site initially out of curiosity but they will not return without a reason. To achieve high retention, the first requirement is for the content to be strong and kept continually up-to-date. Developing an effective online site is not a one-off project, but requires continued resource commitments over time. Many companies have seriously underestimated the costs of maintaining fresh ongoing content. One way companies seek to manage costs is by outsourcing web site maintenance to specialist third

Table 10.1 Effect of Customer Retention on Marketing Costs and Speed of Growth

Monthly retention rate (%)	Advertising costs (£)	Time needed to reach 100 000 regular users (months)
100	70 000	2.5
95	80 000	3
90	100 000	4
85	140 000	6
80	380 000	19
75	–	Not possible

From *Principles of Internet Marketing, 1st Edition*, by W. Hanson ©2000. Reprinted with permission of South-Western College Publishing, a division of Thompson Learning.

parties. Another approach is to involve users in maintaining interest levels. For example, a sports shoe company could allow its site to be used by athletic associations to publicise events and results. The site then begins to embody characteristics of an online community.

Another way of enhancing retention is to build switching costs that make it costly for users to shift to competitive sites. This occurs with shopping agents and financial sites such as Quicken. To exploit the advantages of these technologies customers have to invest time and energy providing personal information and details of their requirements. The more consumers have to invest in a site the less they wish to repeat the process elsewhere.

LEARNING ABOUT PREFERENCES

The unique feature of digitisation and the Net is the facility they offer the company to learn about customers, and exploit this learning to create value for them and for its shareholders. Online marketers need to design their web sites to make this learning possible. The more managers know about the importance, preferences, attitudes and behaviour of customers, the better it can meet their needs. Learning can be gained from registration processes, questionnaires, surveys, email communications, cookies and web chain analyses. Rapid software advances are providing more and more power to mine and utilise these information banks for creative marketing.

CUSTOMISED RELATIONSHIPS

The end result of the model is a series of profitable transactions with customers. Knowledge about customers enables the firm to target high-value prospects. The particular advantage of the Net model is that it allows personalisation. It means that the company can add value by developing customised communications and products, cross-selling more products to individual customers, and developing individualised pricing and promotional strategies to optimise differences in response rates.

FUTURE PERSPECTIVES

The Internet represents such a paradigm shift for every business that it is worth summarising how management, and particularly marketing, needs to respond. Nine recommendations are presented under four areas: the new context of business, the new strategic priorities, the implications for value-based marketing and the implications for business organisation.

RECOGNISE THE NEW CONTEXT OF BUSINESS

1. THE INTERNET CHANGES EVERYTHING

The Internet, by creating instantaneous, universal and almost free communications, changes the whole nature of business. It destroys the traditional model of business that links information to products. It unbundles industries, triggers new, better adapted competition and creates new distribution structures. The first industries to be transformed have been the 'low touch' industries such as computers, books, CDs, travel and financial services. But even 'high touch' businesses such as clothing, shoes and groceries are now feeling the impact. Here the effects are most immediate on the way the Internet is reengineering supply chains, cutting costs and accelerating asset turnover. It needs to be remembered that while online business-to-consumer commerce causes the most excitement, it is in business-to-business trade where the effects of the Internet are greatest.

2. REENGINEER THE BUSINESS MODEL

The Internet is not an innovation that can be adapted to simply by improving the efficiency of the traditional business model or by adding a web site. It is what is termed a 'disruptive technology' that destroys previously successful business models.[13] Many businesses need to change radically because what were once assets have become liabilities. Today, survival often means having to compete with, and cannibalise, one's traditional business model.

3. CUSTOMISE MARKETING

The Internet is most of all a marketing phenomenon, shifting power to customers, giving them much more access to competitors, to lower prices and better products and services. Indeed, it is spawning a whole new class of infomediaries and exchanges whose sole function is giving buyers more information and helping them get the best deals. The web is a threat because it is the customer – not the marketer – who decides whether to interact and who to interact with. The web is an opportunity, however, for companies that grasp the new possibilities to customise their products to the needs of individual consumers and so form enduring relationships.

CHANGING THE STRATEGY

4. THINK OUTSIDE THE BOX

Changing strategy is not just about selling through the web; it is about thinking creatively about the industry's whole value chain and the company's entire business processes. It means reappraising customer service and support and looking at how the Internet might offer radically new ways of communicating with customers, enhancing service levels and ensuring a better experience. Operations processes will have to be reengineered to permit the introduction of customised made-to-order products, to lower inventories and cut costs. New product development needs to be reviewed to expedite processes and consider new, unrelated products that could be cross-marketed to the customer base.

5. MOVE FAST

Competitors move fast in Internet time. When Amazon moved into selling CDs online it took just 45 days to become market leader; it took only nine days to seize leadership in video sales. Slow movers can find their market positions destroyed before they have even put together a plan. To move fast companies have to outsource much more radically. There are now hosts of Internet specialists and contract manufacturers that can develop and host the site, make-to-order and handle distribution. Tomorrow's businesses are network organisations.

6. TAKE AN OFFENSIVE POSTURE

It is not enough to be first into the market; strategies have to be developed and resources obtained to exploit the first-mover advantage and critical mass. In the networked world, customers often attach the greatest value to the sites that have most users.

RESTRUCTURING THE ORGANISATION

7. BUILD NETWORKS

New economy firms are built around networks. The information revolution has made vertical integration unnecessary and the speed of change has made it uneconomic. Creating virtual businesses with suppliers and partners offers speed, pooled expertise, lower costs and lower asset requirements. Using digital technology to form networks with customers creates relationships that build lifetime value out of expensively obtained assets.

8. INVEST IN HUMAN CAPITAL

The Internet revolutionises communications inside organisations, making bureaucratic structures obsolete and releasing human capital. It also makes employees with exceptional skills more marketable. If organisations are going to hold on to these people they will need to rethink payment systems and tie rewards more closely to the value employees create, and also make their work environments more rewarding.

9. MAKE MANAGERS RESPONSIBLE

Top management has to take responsibility for building a culture that recognises that creating value depends upon innovation, marketing and growth rather than cost-cutting and downsizing. They have to build planning processes that stimulate the development of such strategies. Finally, they need to introduce evaluation and reward systems that help implement such strategies and reinforce the behaviour of managers.

SUMMARY

1.   The Internet is a 'discontinuous change' that is leading to a fundamental restructuring in all industries. The three sources of this shift are the increasing power and declining costs of digital technology, the explosion of connectedness brought about by the Internet, and the new opportunities to customise communications and products.

2.   The web creates benefits for customers by facilitating companies to offer individualised solutions to their needs, lower prices, greater convenience, more information, assurance and entertainment. The most immediate impact has been on 'low touch' markets such as computers and business-to-business purchases, but in the longer run few markets will remain unaffected.

3.   The web creates direct benefits for companies by creating new opportunities to gain market share and earn revenues. It also produces major indirect benefits in lowering costs, reducing investment requirements and enhancing business effectiveness.

4.   The information revolution has major implications for marketing strategy. It changes the context of markets by increasing the power of customers over suppliers. It creates new marketing opportunities and leads to ways of thinking about segmentation and positioning. By breaking the trade-off between richness and reach it also leads to a reformulation of the marketing mix, emphasising direct one-to-one communications.

REVIEW QUESTIONS

1.   What are the drivers of the Internet revolution and how might the Internet be characterised?
2.   How does the Internet create value for consumers?
3.   How can the Internet create value for companies?
4.   How does the Internet affect marketing strategy?
5.   Develop the outline of a presentation to the board of directors of a large consumer goods company suggesting how they need to respond to the Internet.

NOTES ON CHAPTER 10

[1] Robert Hiebeler, Thomas Kelly and Charles Ketteman, *Best Practices: Building your Business with Customer-Focussed Solutions*, New York: Simon & Schuster, 1998.

[2] For more on how transactions costs shape businesses see Larry Downes and Chunka Mui, *Unleashing the Killer App: Digital Strategies for Market Dominance*, Boston, MA: Harvard Business School Press, 1998, pp. 35–56.

[3] Figures 10.2 and 10.3 are adapted from a presentation by Keith Beddell-Pearce, executive director of Prudential plc, at the Warwick Business School, March 2000.

[4] John Hagel III and Marc Singer, *Net Worth*, New York: McKinsey & Co, 1999.

[5] James H. Gilmore and B. Joseph Pine II, *Every Business a Stage: Why Customers Now Want Experiences*, Boston, MA: Harvard Business School Press, 1999, p. 95.

[6] For a good discussion of this, see Chris Anderson, *The Long Tail: Why the Future of Business is Selling Less of More*, Hyperion, 2006.

[7] Ward Hanson, *Principles of Internet Marketing*, Cincinnati, OH: South Western, 2000, pp. 126–127.

[8] For convenience, the words 'consumer' and 'customer' are being used virtually synonymously. It should be remembered, as emphasised in Chapter 3, that purchasing is generally a networked activity involving several members of the household or organisation. Marketers need to understand the whole buying process and experience. See Robin Wensley, The MSI priorities: a critical view of researching firm performance, customer experience and marketing, *Journal of Marketing Management*, **16**, April, 2000, 11–27.

[9] The earliest and most complete exposition of this change is Don Peppers and Martha Rogers, *Enterprise One-to-One: Tools for Building Unbreakable Customer Relationships in the Interactive Age*, London: Piatkus, 1997; see also Fred Wiersema, *Customer Intimacy*, London: HarperCollins, 1998. See also: Cliff Allen, Deborah Kania, Beth Yaechel, *One-to-One Web Marketing: Build a Relationship Marketing Strategy One Customer at a Time*, John Wiley & Sons, Inc, 2001 (2nd edition).

[10] Philip Evans and Thomas S. Wurster, *Blown to Bits: How the New Economics of Information Transforms Strategy*, Boston, MA: Harvard Business School Press, 2000.

[11] This model is adapted from Alexa Kierzkowski, Shayne McQuade, Robert Waitman and Michael Zeisser, Marketing to the digital consumer, *McKinsey Quarterly*, no. 3, 1996, 5–21.

[12] John Hagel III and Arthur Armstrong, *Net Gain: Expanding Markets through Virtual Communities*, Boston, MA: Harvard Business School Press, 1997.

[13] Clayton M. Christensen and Michael Overdorf, Meeting the challenge of disruptive change, *Harvard Business Review*, **78**(2), March/April 2000, 66–77.

Glossary

Book equity. The value of shareholders' funds as recorded in the published accounts of the business. It contrasts with the 'market value' of equity, which is its actual value as reflected in the market price of the business.

Cost of capital. This is the opportunity cost, or expected return, that investors forgo by investing in the company rather than in other comparable shares.

Discounted cash flow (DCF). Future cash flows multiplied by the discount factor to obtain the present value of the cash flows.

Discount factor. Present value of £1 received at a stated future date. It is calculated as $1/(1 + r)^t$ where r is the discount rate and t is the year.

Discount rate. Rate used to calculate the present value of future cash flows.

Intangible asset. Non-material asset such as technical expertise, brand or patent.

Market-to-book ratio. The market value of the business divided by the book equity value.

Net present value. The net contribution of a strategy to the wealth of shareholders: present value of cash flows minus initial investment.

Option. Option to buy an asset at a specified exercise price on or before a specified date.

Perpetuity. Investment offering a level stream of cash flow in perpetuity.

Present value method. The technique for comparing alternative strategies in terms of the present value of their cash flows discounted by the cost of capital.

Price/earnings ratio (P/E). Market price of the share divided by earnings per share.

Return on investment (ROI). Generally, book profits as a proportion of net book value.

Return on equity (ROE). Generally, equity earnings as a proportion of the book value of equity.

Risk premium. Expected additional return for making a risky investment rather than a safe one.

Tangible asset. Physical asset such as plant, machinery and offices.

Working capital. Net current assets, i.e. current assets less current liabilities.

Yield. The percentage which earnings per share bears to the share price.

The Advisory Board

TIM AMBLER

Tim Ambler joined London Business School in 1991 and is a Senior Fellow. His research includes brands and brand equity, neuro marketing, measuring marketing performance, advertising and promotions, measuring government regulation and deregulation.

His publications include *Marketing and the Bottom Line: Health Drives Wealth* (FT/Prentice Hall, 2nd ed., 2003); *Doing Business in China* (with Morgen Witzel, Routledge, 2nd edn, 2003); *The SILK Road to International Marketing* (with Chris Styles, FT/Prentice Hall, 2000); *Marketing from Advertising to Zen* (Financial Times Guide, FT/Pitman, 1996); and articles on advertising effectiveness. He was previously Joint Managing Director of International Distillers and Vintners (IDV – now part of Diageo), responsible for strategy, acquisitions and marketing. He holds a Master's degree in mathematics from Oxford and in business from the Sloan School at MIT. He is a qualified chartered accountant.

MICHAEL J. BAKER

Professor Emeritus Michael J. Baker of University of Strathclyde Business School was Founding Professor of Marketing and Head of the Department from its inception in 1971 to 1988. After serving as Dean of the School of Business Administration/Strathclyde Business School, 1978–84, he was appointed as Deputy Principal in 1984, Deputy Principal (Management) in 1988 and Senior Adviser to the Principal in 1991, Emeritus 1999. He is Former Chairman of Scottish Business Education Council (SCOTBEC), past Chairman of the Institute of Marketing and Governor of the CAM Foundation.

He has been President of the Academy of Marketing and Founding Dean, Senate of the Chartered Institute of Marketing, among a number of other professorial appointments. He is author/editor of over 40 books, including *Marketing* (7th edn, 2006), *Marketing: Theory and Practice* (3rd edn, 1996), *Dictionary of Advertising and Marketing* (3rd edn, 1998) and *Marketing Strategy and Management* (4th edn, 2008). He is the winner of the Institute of Marketing's Gold Medal and designated Author of the Year 1978 for a paper entitled Export Myopia and author of over 150 articles and papers.

TONY CRAM

Tony Cram joined Ashridge Business School in 1992. As a Programme Director, he designs and delivers programmes on business strategy and market innovation. His particular interests are understanding customer value, developing brands and the dynamics of long-term business relationships. He works internationally with experience in Europe, Asia and the Americas.

Before joining Ashridge, Tony held a general management position with Manpower. Previously, as Director of Marketing Services at TSB Bank, he controlled £20 million marketing expenditure. Earlier, he spent eight years with Grand Metropolitan at Board level. As a Marketing Director he played a key part in the launch of Foster's Draught Lager into the UK. For two years he had executive responsibility for 500 licensed retail outlets. He gained his MBA from Cranfield/University of Washington in 1980. Tony has taught at Vlerick Leuven Gent Management School, the Swedish Institute of Management, Stockholm School of Economics, PEF University Vienna and the University of Michigan, USA. His publications include *Smarter Pricing* (2006) and *Customers that Count* (2001), available in a number of languages published by Financial Times Prentice Hall. He speaks internationally at public conferences and company conventions on the themes of customer value, competitive marketing and innovation.

SUSAN HART

Professor Susan Hart is Dean of Strathclyde Business School. Previous posts held were Professor of Marketing and Head of Department at the Universities of Strathclyde and Stirling from 1995–98, and Professor of Marketing at Heriot-Watt University from 1993–95. In addition, Susan Hart has worked for a variety of private sector companies, ranging from multinational to small manufacturers in consumer and industrial enterprises.

Recent publications have appeared in the *Journal of Product Innovation Management* and *Industrial Marketing Management*. A member of the Executive Committee of the Academy of Marketing and the Senate of the Chartered Institute of Marketing, she is also a Fellow of the Marketing Society. She edits the *Journal of Marketing Management*.

Her books include *Product Strategy and Management* (with Michael Baker), (2nd edn, Pearson, 2007), *The Marketing Book* (with Michael Baker) (6th edn, Butterworth-Heineman, 2007) and *Marketing Changes* (ITBP, 2003).

JEAN-CLAUDE LARRÉCHÉ

Professor Jean-Claude Larréché is the holder of the Alfred H. Heineken Chair at INSEAD, where he is a specialist in strategic marketing and directs a number of activities aimed at achieving excellence in customer-based strategies. He is also a renowned consultant with leading global corporations and the author or co-author of many books. His latest is *The Momentum Effect: How to Ignite Exceptional Growth* (Wharton School Publishing, 2008). He has been a member of the INSEAD Board for 14 years and a member of the board of Reckitt Benckiser plc from 1983 to 2001. In addition, he is chairman of StratX SA, a company specialising in strategic marketing training and services.

His teaching, research and consultancy all focus on the secrets of sustaining exceptional, profitable growth. He has won many awards, including Marketing Educator of the Year and Business Week's European Case of the Year Award. Professor Larréché received a PhD in Business from Stanford University and an MBA from INSEAD. Before his business studies, he obtained an MSc in Computer Sciences from the University of London.

MALCOLM McDONALD

Professor Malcolm McDonald MA (Oxon) MSc, PhD, D.Litt, FCIM, FRSA was until recently Professor of Marketing and Deputy Director, Cranfield University School of Management, with special responsibility for e-business, and is now an Emeritus Professor at the University as well as being an Honorary Professor at Warwick Business School. He is also a Professor at Aston, Bradford and Henley Business Schools.

Malcolm is a graduate in English Language and Literature from Oxford University, in Business Studies from Bradford University Management Centre, and has a PhD from Cranfield University. He has written over 40 books, including the best seller *Marketing Plans: How to Prepare Them, How to Use Them*, and more than one hundred articles and papers.

Coming from a background in business which included a number of years as Marketing Director of Canada Dry, Malcolm has successfully maintained a close link between academic rigour and commercial application. He has consulted to many major companies from the UK, Europe, USA, Far East, South-East Asia, Australasia and Africa, in the areas of strategic marketing and marketing planning, market segmentation, key account management, international marketing and marketing accountability.

Malcolm is currently chairman of six companies and works with the operating boards of a number of the world's leading multinationals on all continents.

JOHN SAUNDERS

John Saunders is Professor of Marketing at Aston Business School. Until 2007 he was head of Aston Business School and, before that, head and director of research of Loughborough University Business School. His research is centred on strategy and product management and includes evolutionary marketing, sustainable marketing and business incompetence.

In his academic career he has held the posts of editor of the *International Journal of Research in Marketing*, President of the European Marketing Academy and Dean of the Chartered Institute of Marketing. He is a Fellow of the European Marketing Academy (EMAC), Chartered Institute of Marketing (CIM), the Royal Society of Arts and the British Academy of Management (BAM). He is currently serving on the business school research evaluation exercises of the United Kingdom and The Netherlands.

His research has appeared in the *Journal of Marketing Research*, *Journal of Marketing*, *Journal of Advertising Research*, *Marketing Science*, the *International Journal of Research in Marketing*, the *Journal of Product Innovation Management*, the *Journal of International Business Studies* and many other learned journals. Along with marketing gurus Philip Kotler, Gary Armstrong and Veronica Wong, Professor Saunders authors Europe's top selling marketing text, *Principles of Marketing*, the European edition of which now appears in seven languages.

VERONICA WONG

Veronica Wong is Professor of Marketing and Director of the Diversity, Knowledge and Innovation Research Programme at Aston Business School. She is an Academician (Academy of Social Sciences), a Freeman of the Worshipful Company of Marketors, and a Fellow of the Royal Society for the encouragement of Arts, Manufactures & Commerce (RSA) and the Chartered Institute of Marketing. She is a Member of the ESRC Postdoctoral Fellowship College and a Committee Member of the Product Development and Management (PDMA) UK & Ireland Chapter.

She is also Distinguished Professor at Audencia Nantes Ecole De Management, France and a Visiting Professor at University Technology Malaysia, Malaysia. Other external positions recently held include being a Member of the

ESRC Virtual Research College, the Chartered Institute of Marketing (CIM) Academic Senate and Vice-President (Conferences) of the European Marketing Academy Executive (EMAC).

In addition, Veronica reviews for several academic journals, professional associations and research councils. She is currently a consulting editor for the *International Journal of Management Reviews* and an editorial board member of the *Journal of Marketing Management and 21st Century Society* and the *Journal of the Academy of Social Sciences*.

THE EDITOR

LAURA MAZUR

Laura Mazur is a business journalist and partner in Writers 4 Management, a professional writing firm. She has contributed to a range of publications on topics such as strategy, leadership HR and marketing since leaving *Marketing* magazine, where she was editor. She has also acted as a ghost writer/editor on a number of books. She is co-author with Louella Miles of *Conversations with Marketing Masters* (John Wiley & Sons, Ltd, 2007).

Index